Conditions of work
digest

Volume 11   Number 2   1992

Preventing stress at work

International Labour Office   Geneva

ISBN 92-2-108265-2
ISSN 0257-3512

Annual subscription (1993) for two issues: 85 Swiss francs
Price for individual issues: 45 Swiss francs
Editor: Michele B. Jankanish

The International Programme for the Improvement of Working Conditions and Environment (PIACT) was launched by the International Labour Organisation in 1976 at the request of the International Labour Conference and after extensive consultations with member States.
PIACT is designed to promote or support action by member States to set and attain definite objectives aiming at "making work more human". The Programme is thus concerned with improving the quality of working life in all its aspects: for example, the prevention of occupational accidents and diseases, a wider application of the principles of ergonomics, the arrangement of working time, the improvement of the content and organisation of work and of conditions of work in general, a greater concern for the human element in the transfer of technology. To achieve these aims, PIACT makes use of and co-ordinates the traditional means of ILO action, including:

- the preparation and revision of international labour standards;

- operational activities, including the dispatch of multidisciplinary teams to assist member States on request;

- tripartite meetings between representatives of governments, employers and workers, including industrial committees to study the problems facing major industries, regional meetings and meetings of experts;

- action-oriented studies and research; and

- clearing-house activities, especially through the International Occupational Safety and Health Information Centre (CIS) and the Clearing-house for the Dissemination of Information on Conditions of Work.

ILO publications can be obtained through major booksellers or ILO local offices in many countries, or direct from ILO Publications, International Labour Office, CH-1211 Geneva 22, Switzerland. A catalogue or list of new publications will be sent free of charge from the above address.

Preventing stress at work

Table of contents

Pages

About this publication

The *Conditions of Work Digest* is published twice a year by the International Labour Office. Prepared by the Conditions of Work and Welfare Facilities Branch, Working Conditions and Environment Department, it is a reference source for all who are interested in working conditions and the quality of working life. Each issue is devoted to a subject of topical interest. The *Digest* includes information drawn from laws, regulations, collective agreements and other important texts. Additional features are included as appropriate, such as annotated bibliographies, relevant international standards, special sources of information and specialized glossaries.

Topics on conditions of work and quality of working life, such as the following, are covered:

- working time issues, including hours of work, shift work, part-time work and flexible hours;
- work organization and job content;
- the impact of new technologies on quality of working life;
- working conditions of specific groups, such as women workers, older workers, homeworkers and clandestine workers, and the subject of child labour;
- work-related welfare facilities and services.

Titles in the *Digest* series are as follows:

— Special issue on visual display units (Vol. 5, 1/1986);

— Flexibility in working time (Vol. 5, 2/1986);

— Alcohol and drugs: Programmes of assistance for workers (Vol. 6, 1/1987);

— Women workers: Protection or equality? (Vol. 6, 2/1987);

— The emerging response to child labour (Vol. 7, 1/1988) [out of print];

— Work and family: The child care challenge (Vol. 7, 2/1988);

— Part-time work (Vol. 8, 1/1989);

— Home work (Vol. 8, 2/1989);

— Telework (Vol. 9, 1/1990);

— The hours we work: New work schedules in policy and practice (Vol. 9, 2/1990);

— Child labour: Law and practice (Vol. 10, 1/1991);

— Workers' privacy, Part I: Protection of personal data (Vol. 10, 2/1991);

— Combating sexual harassment at work (Vol. 11, 1/1992).

Other ILO serial publications of interest to users of the *Digest* include:

— *Safety and health at work: ILO/CIS Bulletin.* References and abstracts covering books, articles, laws and regulations on all aspects of occupational safety and health (produced by the International Occupational Safety and Health Information Centre of the ILO);

— *International Labour Review.* Articles on economic and social topics affecting labour, research notes and book reviews.

— *Social and Labour Bulletin.* Notes on current significant events in the social and labour field, brief descriptions of major labour legislation, collective agreements, experiments in improving the work environment and so forth.

— *Labour Law Documents* (from 1919-1989 called *Legislative Series*). Reprints and translations of selected labour and social security legislation recently adopted in countries throughout the world.

Individual issues of the *Digest* and above ILO serial publications can be ordered from ILO Publications, International Labour Office, CH-1211 Geneva 22, Switzerland.

This publication may be cited as follows:

ILO: *Conditions of Work Digest* (Geneva), Volume 11, Number 2, 1992, on *Preventing stress at work.*

Acknowledgements

This issue of the *Conditions of Work Digest* was prepared by a team led by Vittorio Di Martino and including Begoña Casanueva, Tetsuya Ishii, Michele Jankanish, Ellen Rosskam, William Salter, Patricia Weinert and Linda Wirth. Special appreciation to Kristine Falciola for technical editing and the processing of the manuscript.

The Office would like to thank all individuals and institutions that contributed to this issue. Special thanks are due to Robert Karasek for writing the analysis of the case studies, and to Lennart Levi who, in addition to the preparation of case studies, greatly contributed to the conceptual framework and design of this ILO initiative. The contribution of Sylvia Hines on videos is gratefully acknowledged.

A special acknowledgement is due to the following experts who prepared the case studies on anti-stress prevention programmes which appear in Part III of the *Digest*:

Canada:	Nicolas Greco
Germany:	Karl Kuhn
India:	Ganesh Sastry
Italy:	Giovanni Costa
Japan:	Hiroyuki Asaba, Seishiro Chihara, Jun Koh, Makiko Okawa and Toshiaki Sakai
Mexico:	Miguel Matrajt
Sweden:	Torbjörn Åkerstedt, Bengt Arnetz, Carl Axling, Ingeborg Eriksson, Mats Frånberg, Sven Kvarnström, Lennart Levi, Vanja Moser, Kristina Orth-Gomér and Anna-Lena Undén
United Kingdom:	Tricia Allison, Cary Cooper, Peter Reynolds and Golnaz Sadri
United States:	Charles Barrett, Mark Braverman, Janet Cahill, James House, Margrit Hugentobler, Barbara Israel, Paul Landsbergis, Lisa May, Peter Schnall, Susan Schurman, Beth Silverman, Michael Smith and David Zehel

Part I

Preventing stress at work:
Overview and analysis

SECTION 1

Occupational stress: A preventive approach

Vittorio Di Martino[1]

Stress has become a major cause of concern for individuals, enterprises, social security operators and politicians. In the search for effective ways to deal with this devastating phenomenon of modern society, many strategies and intervention programmes are being designed and tested.

In Sweden, forward-looking legislation encourages employees to adjust their work environment to their abilities and needs, and calls for improvement in the "person-environment fit". Managers and supervisors are advised to allow or even promote such adjustments, the purpose being to reduce psychological and social strains as well as physical risks.

In the United States, the Office of Disease Prevention and Health Promotion reports that 60.8 per cent of work sites with more than 750 employees offer some form of programme to control stress. Over the past few years in the United States, no other preventive health measure has been as dominant in growth or size as stress control.[2]

In other countries, similar initiatives are under way yet, in most situations, little or nothing is being done to combat stress at work.

Where action has been undertaken to control stress, it has not always proved adequate. Self-appointed experts, pre-packaged programmes good for any occasion and situation, and remedial interventions focused on the effects rather than the causes of stress, have contributed to create a "stress industry" that is often over costly and scarcely effective.

A new generation of efforts is emerging which tackles problems related to stress at their roots, deals with them in a systematic and preventive way, and involves a long-term appreciation of the results of each intervention.

This issue of the *Conditions of Work Digest* analyses some of the most significant experiences with innovative approaches to preventing and combating stress at work.

What is stress?

Defining stress is a very complex matter which is the subject of different analyses and continuous debate among experts. Beyond the details of this debate, however, a general consensus can be reached about a definition of stress centred around the idea of a perceived imbalance in the interface between an individual and the environment and other individuals. When people are faced with demands from others or from the physical or psychosocial environment to which they feel unable to respond adequately, a response of the organism is activated to cope with the situation. The nature of this response will depend upon a combination of different elements,

---

[1] Conditions of Work and Welfare Facilities Branch, Working Conditions and Environment Department, International Labour Office.

[2] T. Barash: "'Blue-chips' forced to re-think stress strategies", in *Stress Management Advisor*, Vol. 1, No. 2, April 1991, p. 1.

including the extent of the demand, the personal characteristics and coping resources of the person, the constraints on the person in trying to cope and the support received from others.[3]

Under normal circumstances persons should be able, by activating their reaction mechanisms, to find new balances and responses to new situations. Stress is therefore not necessarily a negative phenomenon. It would be a mistake to concentrate only on the pathological aspect of stress without emphasizing its importance in the search for dynamic adaptation to a given situation. If health is considered as a dynamic equilibrium, stress is part of it for there is no health without interaction with other people and with the environment. Only excesses are pathological.

Some stress, then, is normal and necessary. But if stress is intense, continuous or repeated, if the person is unable to cope or if support is lacking, then stress becomes a negative phenomenon leading to physical illness and psychological disorders. From early disorders to real illness, the harmful consequences of stress cover a broad range from chronic fatigue to depression, by way of insomnia, anxiety, migraines, emotional upsets, stomach ulcers, allergies, skin disorders, lumbago and rheumatic attacks, and tobacco and alcohol abuse, and can culminate in the most serious consequences of all: heart attacks, accidents and even suicides.

Negative stress has many causes. Some of these are to be found in an unsatisfactory fit between the individual and the physical environment. Stressors of this type relate to noise, odours, illumination, temperature, humidity, vibrations, crowding, dangerous substances, machines and tools. Other stresses are generated primarily by the relation between individuals and their psychosocial environment. These can depend on the level of autonomy and responsibility, the load of activities, the organization of different activities, the arrangement of working time, the relationship with other individuals and communities, and so on. Reference is often made to physical stress, on the one hand, and psychosocial stress, on the other, although they are so interlinked that a real separation is almost impossible.

The notion of stress thus challenges traditional categorizations because it bridges physical, mental and social well-being. An attack on one means an attack on the others. A cut on the hand is a physical wound but at the same time affects the mind, provoking distress or anxiety, and can cause functional disability and incapacity to work. Similarly, the loss of a job has an impact on the mind and on the physical health of the individual. These considerations also apply to the distinction which is made between occupational stress and stress in families and in society. Certainly a number of stress factors are specifically related to work, such as the work environment, job content, work organization, working-time schedules and workload. Other stressors relate to the family situation, particularly the care of children. Still others relate to gender or to the particular conditions of certain categories of people within society, including the young, the elderly, migrants and the disabled. At the same time, all these factors are closely linked to each other. Occupational stress, for instance, can be aggravated by an entire host of extra-occupational problems. A worker might belong to a vulnerable category of people, have family or health problems, have difficulties with commuting or be faced with financial worries.

With this in mind, **the *Digest* will focus primarily, but not exclusively, on the negative consequences of occupational psychosocial stress and on preventive ways to combat this type of stress at the level of the workplace.**

The globalization of stress

Stress is becoming an increasingly global phenomenon affecting all countries, all professions and all categories of workers, families and society in general.

---

[3] T. Cox: "Stress, coping and problem solving", in *Work and Stress*, Vol. 1, No. 1, 1987, p. 6.

Stress affects both industrialized and developing countries

While stress at work most often has been considered to be a phenomenon affecting industrialized countries only, evidence is emerging, though scattered and incomplete, that it is affecting more and more people in developing countries. In India, a major coalmining company with over 80,000 employees has introduced extensive anti-stress programmes for senior and middle-level managers, operators and loaders, supervisors and maintenance staff.[4] In the Sudan, research showed high levels of stress in permanent night bakery workers, which was exacerbated by the strain resulting from an extremely hot working environment.[5]

In Brazil, a recent study carried out among 138 nursing staff at a hospital in the São Paulo area indicated that 60 per cent of the staff complained of stress or of related symptoms, such as tension, fatigue and exhaustion.[6]

Stress affects all categories of workers

Evidence indicates that a wide and growing range of occupations are prone to stress. The following table lists those occupations which equal or exceed the rate of 6 on a stress rating scale of 0 to 10 elaborated by the University of Manchester Institute of Science and Technology.

Occupation	Rating scale	Occupation	Rating scale
Miner	8.3	Broadcasting personnel	6.8
Police officer	7.7	Nurse	6.5
Prison officer	7.5	Film production crew	6.5
Construction worker	7.5	Ambulance personnel	6.3
Airline pilot	7.5	Musician	6.3
Journalist	7.5	Firefighter	6.3
Advertising executive	7.3	Teacher	6.2
Dentist	7.3	Social worker	6.0
Actor	7.2	Personnel manager	6.0
Doctor	6.8		

Source: University of Manchester Institute of Science and Technology: *Understanding stress: Part II* (HMSO, London, 1987).

---

[4] G. Sastry: "Using training to prevent or reduce stress in a coalmining company in India", in Part III of this *Digest*.

[5] M. Attia, Y. Abdallah and H.I. Giudeel: "Combined effects of shiftwork and health stress", in P. Lang (editor): *Shiftwork: Health, sleep and performance* (Peter Lang, Frankfurt, 1989).

[6] M.A. Villar Luis: *Working environment at an emergency assistance hospital*, paper presented to the International Symposium on Work-related Diseases: Prevention and Health Promotion, Linz, Austria, 27-30 October 1992.

In addition, numerous occupations have received special attention in research and the literature on occupational stress. These are mentioned below, with references to some of the studies that have been carried out on these jobs and occupations. The bibliography in Section 3 of Part II of this volume provides further references to occupationally focused studies on stress.

Managers. Occupational stress is often associated with managerial responsibilities. A 1988 study of 700 top executives in France[7] indicated that 46 per cent of them are at risk of serious mental health disorders and that they suffer largely from anxiety, depression and psychosomatic troubles (32 per cent suffer from cardiovascular symptoms, 63 per cent from asthenia and 24 per cent from sleep troubles). Despite this negative reporting, over 90 per cent of these executives declared themselves to be very satisfied with their jobs.

Blue-collar workers. Evidence, particularly from the United Kingdom, indicates that frequencies of deaths in the working population due to major causes increase as one moves from professional and white-collar jobs to the unskilled. This applies both to stress-related illnesses, such as ischaemic heart disease, and to other illnesses, such as pneumonia and prostate cancer. These data are very similar to mortality data from the United States and other developed countries. In terms of almost all the major and many of the minor causes of death among people in the working population, blue-collar and unskilled workers are at greater risk than white-collar workers and professionals. This extends not only to mortality statistics but also to morbidity data. Blue-collar workers show a greater number of activity days lost because of acute sickness and consultations with medical practitioners than do white-collar workers in the United Kingdom.[8] Attempts to identify features of shop-floor work that cause strain among blue-collar workers most frequently have focused on factors such as repetition of tasks, machine pacing, control over work, use of skills, hours of work, environmental conditions and social relationships.[9]

Air traffic controllers. The work of air traffic controllers is generally considered as demanding since it requires a high degree of skill, alertness and the ability to handle several problems simultaneously. Yet a number of studies have indicated that the level of stress experienced by these workers does not appear to be excessive compared to the population as a whole. It appears that the findings pertaining to stress-related health problems of air traffic controllers are conflicting, particularly as far as hypertension and peptic ulcers are concerned. Some of the air traffic controllers studied have a higher incidence of hypertension and/or peptic ulcers than the rest of the population, while others do not.[10]

Bus and truck drivers. Several studies in the United States have reported that bus drivers have higher rates of mortality, morbidity and absence due to illness than employees from a wide range of other occupational groups, which can be due to work stress.[11]

In studies from the Netherlands[12] and the United Kingdom,[13] it has been found that driving city buses is

---

[7] B. Stora and C.L. Cooper: "Stress at the top: The price of success among French corporate presidents", in *Employee Relations*, Vol. 10, No. 1, 1988, pp. 13-16.

[8] C. Cooper and M.J. Smith: *Job stress and blue collar work* (John Wiley, Chichester, 1985).

[9] R. Martin and T.D. Wall: "Attentional demand and cost responsibility as stressors in shopfloor jobs", in *Academy of Management Journal*, Vol. 32, No. 1, March 1989, pp. 69-86.

[10] K. Rodahl: *The physiology of work* (Taylor and Francis, London, 1989). See also G. Costa: "A seven-point programme to reduce stress in air traffic controllers in Italy", in Part III of this *Digest*.

[11] M.A. Winkelby, D.R. Ragland and J.M. Fischer: "Excess risk of sickness and disease in bus drivers: A review and synthesis of epidemiological studies", in *International Journal of Epidemiology*, Vol. 17, No. 2, 1988.

[12] M. Kompier et al.: "Absence behaviour, turnover and disability: A study among city bus drivers in the Netherlands", in *Work and Stress*, Vol. 4, No. 1, 1990, pp. 83-89.

an occupation with high risks for health and well-being, and that bus drivers demonstrate low levels of job satisfaction and unfavourable scores on mental health indices when compared with normative samples.

Studies from Germany indicate that the activity of full-time professional drivers both in commercial freight transport and works transport can be classified as very high-strain work. The level of strain for drivers is about the same as for occupational groups such as building labourers or metal workers. Thus, the working strains are to be regarded as a central factor in explaining health disorders and illnesses among drivers. [14]

Civil servants. In the United Kingdom, a survey of more than 1,000 senior civil servants indicated that, compared to their private-sector counterparts, they suffer from higher levels of stress, and have lower job satisfaction and poorer health. Of an average of seven days a year taken off sick, four were said to be attributable to stress. Factors contributing to stress levels of civil servants included the following: conflict between loyalty to the Government and providing service to the public; poor financial and promotional rewards compared with the private sector; using a photocopier as part of daily work; lack of consultation from above; and lack of support staff, which led to frustration because managers were having to spend time doing jobs below their level of competence. Female civil servants experienced the highest levels of stress and had more health problems than their male colleagues. [15]

Firefighters. Post-traumatic stress affects an increasing number of firefighters. Stress is a natural reaction to the traumatic events that members of the emergency services experience in their work. Victims experience sleep disturbance and loss of concentration, and become hyper-alert with vivid recall of traumatic events. If sufferers do not get help they can become a threat to themselves, locked in a circle of anxiety and depression. Their work will suffer, they will go absent from work and eventually their families will suffer. The worst outcome is major psychological breakdown. [16]

Health-care professionals. Various studies of the health-care professions have been conducted, which show that the particular characteristics of these professions cause stress. A study on stress and burnout among Finnish physicians, carried out by the Finnish Institute of Occupational Health in 1988, showed that stress appeared to be most common among physicians without a permanent job and those doing the majority of emergency duty. The strain associated with emergency duty was dominant in central hospitals, whereas burnout symptoms were most common among health-care centre physicians working with out-patients. The most stressful specialties include child psychiatry, general psychiatry and specialties which bring the physician into close contact with cancer patients or other seriously ill patients. [17]

Dentists also appear to suffer from high levels of stress. Causes of stress include coping with difficult patients, trying to keep to a schedule, attempting to sustain or build a practice, overwork, administrative duties, poor working conditions due to confined space and physical position, routine and dull work, and low patient appreciation. [18]

---

[13] C.A. Duffy and A.E. McGoldrick: "Stress and the bus driver in the UK transport industry", in *Work and Stress*, Vol. 4, No. 1, 1990.

[14] T. Schäfer and S. Steininger: *Health hazards and occupational turnover among professional truck drivers* (Federal Institute for Occupational Safety and Health, Dortmund, 1990).

[15] C.L. Cooper and J. Williams: *Report to the Association on Occupational Stress among First Division Civil Servants* (London, January 1991) (unpublished).

[16] "News and information", in *Work and Stress*, Vol. 3, No. 4, 1989, p. 373.

[17] "Annual report 1988 of the Finnish Institute of Occupational Health", in *Work and Stress*, Vol. 4, No. 1, 1990, p. 97.

[18] C.L. Cooper and J. Marshall: *White collar and professional stress* (John Wiley, Chichester, 1980).

Of all health professions, nursing is considered to be among the most stressful. It is reported to have one of the highest rates of suicide, and nurses are first on the list of psychiatric out-patient referrals.[19] Pressures are different for different kinds of nurses and depend on the extent of experience, the level in the organization and the degree of specialization. The exposure of nurses to death and dying leads to various problems presented by the care of dying patients, reactions to the deaths of patients and the nurses' concern for their own mortality. Nursing in intensive care units (ICUs), where critically ill patients are kept alive and continually monitored with the aid of highly sophisticated machines, and where emergencies and death are commonplace, carries a high potential for stress.[20]

Miners. Although miners are thought to be among those suffering from the highest levels of stress, little research has been carried out on them. The following are among the stress factors which have been identified in mining: (a) the work environment in coal mines; (b) the physiological demands of this kind of work, including work postures; and (c) the generally demanding nature of the job, in terms of production targets, deadlines, shift schedules and the impact on the family.[21]

Police. Numerous studies have verified that the job of policing is an extremely stressful occupation. The risks of police work can be compared to those of other types of emergency response work, such as firefighting and ambulance service. A significant stress factor specific to this occupation is the constant necessity to be ready to act in unexpected, emergency situations.

However, it is recognized that the types of stressors experienced by particular officers vary according to the type of job duty and rank, among other variables. From a mental or cognitive standpoint, the longer one is on the job, the more changes take place in one's thinking processes. Psychological changes can lead to police officers becoming unfeeling and unemotional, thus putting up barriers between themselves and their work.[22]

Postal workers. In the United Kingdom, stress has been identified as an organizational problem in postal work, where stress factors have been found to be one of the highest reasons for medical retirement. Furthermore, it has been reported that mail-handlers suffer excessively from job stress and related problems, and can be categorized as having jobs subject to high amounts of strain.[23]

Particularly stressful factors have been identified in manual sorting in post offices. These include the pace of work, regulations on working hours, the office climate, noise and dust, insufficient space, ergonomically poor design of equipment, long periods of standing, control by supervisors and inappropriate break times.[24]

---

[19] J.G. Jones: "Stress in psychiatric nursing", in R. Payne and J. Firth-Cizens (editors): *Stress in health professionals* (John Wiley, Chichester, 1987).

[20] Cooper and Marshall, op. cit.

[21] Sastry, op. cit.

[22] R. Loo: "Policies and programs for mental health in law enforcement organizations", in *Canada's Mental Health*, Vol. 35, No. 3, September 1987, pp. 18-22.

[23] C.L. Cooper, G. Sadu and T. Allison: "A Post Office initiative to stamp out stress", in *Personnel Management*, Vol. 21, No. 8, August 1989.

[24] European Foundation for the Improvement of Living and Working Conditions: *Stress and new technology: Postal and telecommunications sectors* (Dublin, 1985).

According to a 1990 American study, mail handlers, who sort mail and parcels and often move heavy carts and packages, are working harder, have less control and get less support than most other workers -- a combination repeatedly proved to be not only stressful but counterproductive.[25]

Teachers. A psychological test conducted in 1983 among Japanese teachers indicated that about 40 per cent suffered from mental or health problems, such as frequent headaches, depression and constant feelings of anxiety. The test also showed that younger teachers and female teachers had more serious problems.[26]

In the United Kingdom, there is mounting evidence that teachers are increasingly at risk from stress-related illnesses. A large British study on stress among teachers has found that at least 20 per cent of 1,800 teachers interviewed were suffering from levels of anxiety, depression and stress equivalent to or above that of mental health out-patients. Of the teachers questioned, 66 per cent had considered leaving the profession in the past five years, 28 per cent were actively looking for alternative employment and 13 per cent were seeking early retirement. Levels of drinking and smoking well above the national average were also discovered, with a significant number of teachers taking anti-depressant drugs. Low pay and a heavy workload were among the main causes of job dissatisfaction. Other reasons were the lack of opportunity to use their abilities, hours of work, physical working conditions, industrial relations, lack of recognition for good work, management of schools, and the lack of chances for promotion.[27]

Stress goes beyond the workplace

Beyond the workplace, stress factors are linked to the worker's home life, family and civil responsibilities, transport arrangements, leisure, and training or educational activities. Such factors may interact positively or negatively with stressful elements of the work environment and thereby affect overall job quality, satisfaction and productivity.

Among these sources of stress, family and gender conditions play an essential role.

With the increased participation of women in paid employment and the rise in the number of dual working parents as well as of single-parent families, more harmonious **interaction between work and family life** is becoming increasingly recognized as an issue for both employers and workers.

A survey in Canada found that 56 per cent of respondents felt "some" or "a great deal of" interference between their jobs and home lives. Of particular concern was the "amount of time that the job demanded" and the "irregularity of working hours" (including shift work). The interference affected family routines and events, child-rearing and household responsibilities, made workers moody and difficult at home, and conflicted with leisure activities and social life. The respondents felt that compatibility between job and home life required changes in the quantity and structure of the time demands of employment.[28]

---

[25] J. Cahill: *Postal workers on the edge: A study of mail handler job stress*, working paper prepared for the Mail Handlers Union (Glassboro, New Jersey, 1990).

[26] *The Japan Times*, 28 August 1983.

[27] C.L. Cooper: *Report to the National Association of Schoolmasters and Union of Women Teachers on mental health, job satisfaction and occupational stress among British teachers* (London, 1990), forthcoming in 1993 as a special issue of *Work and Stress*.

[28] Canadian Mental Health Association: *Work and well-being: The changing realities of employment* (Toronto, 1984), pp. 53 and 106.

A study of employees in a Swedish insurance company[29] found that the faster the pace of work, the greater the involvement in the work and the higher paid the work, the greater was the perception of a conflict between professional and family roles. The findings indicated that overstimulation at work causes fatigue after work, thus affecting the way people associate with their families.

Abrupt changes in work schedules, time-pressured work, unsympathetic treatment by management and co-workers, lack of control over the content and organization of work, and lack of flexibility in working time and possibilities to take leave for family reasons can be sources of stress reducing the capacity of workers to cope with either everyday family care or family emergencies. In particular, the more difficult, unsatisfactory or costly are child-care arrangements, the more likely are workers to experience stress on and off the job.

The ILO Workers with Family Responsibilities Convention, 1981 (No. 156), calls for measures to take account of the needs of workers with family responsibilities in terms and conditions of employment and in social security. Supplementing the Convention is another ILO instrument, the Workers with Family Responsibilities Recommendation, 1981 (No. 165), which recommends that particular attention be given to measures that aim at the progressive reduction of daily hours of work, the reduction of overtime and more flexible arrangements as regards working schedules, rest periods and holidays. Special needs of workers, including those with family responsibilities, should be taken into account in shift work arrangements and assignment to night work. With a view to protecting part-time workers, temporary workers and homeworkers, many of whom have family responsibilities, the Recommendation states that the terms and conditions under which these types of employment are performed should be adequately regulated and supervised. The Recommendation also provides that either parent should have the possibility, within a period immediately following maternity leave, to take leave of absence, commonly referred to as parental leave, without loss of job and employment rights. Leave of absence to care for a sick child or family member should also be available.

The Recommendation also addresses the issue of child care, which is a significant source of stress for many working parents. The competent authorities are called upon to take steps, in cooperation with the public and private organizations concerned, to organize or encourage and facilitate the provision of adequate and appropriate child-care and family services and facilities, free of charge or at a reasonable charge in accordance with the worker's ability to pay.

The **relation between gender, work and stress** is complex and varied. Several factors seem to magnify the impact of stress on women.

In a random sample of private sector American companies, a 1992 survey[30] of 1,299 full-time employees undertaken by Northwestern National Life Insurance found that gender, among other factors (the level of the employee in the organization, income, occupation and family situation), accounted for differences in job stress at the workplace. The survey found that stress affects women employees more than men, and that they are significantly more likely to report burnout, stress-related illnesses or a desire to resign from their jobs. The researchers suggested several reasons for this. For one, women are often paid less than men for their work, even if they hold college degrees. Further, many organizations lack policies that respond to family issues. Single women with children, along with low-paid college graduates, are at highest risk of burnout: 50 per cent of them, compared to 31 per cent of married women with children, reported burnout.

---

[29] G. Bradley: *Computers and the psychosocial work environment* (Taylor and Francis, London, 1989).

[30] Northwestern National Life Insurance: "Part 1: Employee stress levels", in *Employee burnout: Causes and cures* (Minneapolis, 1992), as reported in *Work in America*, Vol. 17, No. 6, June 1992, pp. 4-5.

In a 1987 survey by the Labour Ministry in Japan, 52.4 per cent of the women interviewed said they had suffered from anxieties, worries and stress, the main cause (60.6 per cent) being unsatisfactory human relations in the workplace.[31]

Another survey[32], published in 1987 in the United States, of relevant research on the effect of high job demands and low worker control over the job on the health of employed women, suggests that the types of occupation performed by women may have characteristics which account for stress at work. The survey reported on a study which examined the effect of employment, occupation, family responsibilities and behaviour on the incidence rates of cardiovascular heart disease (CHD) in women. In general, no significant differences were observed between the total group of working women and housewives. However, while white-collar women had the lowest incidence of stress, the CHD rates were twice as high among women holding clerical jobs. Both the work environment and the family environment contributed to excessive coronary rates among clerical workers.

The relevance of the type of occupation as a key generator of stress for women is confirmed by several studies. A study of visual display unit (VDU) telephone office workers in North Carolina,[33] mostly women, found that VDU exposure among telephone office workers is associated with a higher prevalence of eye strain, headaches, fatigue, tension and angina. Work on visual display units by women is often monotonous and characterized by higher job demands, including working fast, paying close attention to detail, meeting deadlines, experiencing excessive pressure with no decision-making authority, and dealing with the public -- factors which produce stress.

In the United Kingdom, a study on stress and woman managers[34] concluded that "women in management are experiencing higher pressure levels stemming from stressors in the work, home/social and individual arena, and more manifestations of psychosomatic symptoms and poorer work performance than are men managers". Women in junior and middle management experience the highest overall "occupational stress" levels, followed by male supervisors, senior women managers, male junior managers, female supervisors and male middle managers, and finally senior male managers, who report the lowest "occupational stress". Moreover, the total female management sample reported 50 per cent more combined high-stress factors and their outcomes than those reported by the total male management sample. The evidence was overwhelming that the majority of additional pressures experienced by female managers at work are stress factors beyond their control and are based largely on prejudice and discrimination from both organizational/corporate policy and other people at work.

Occupational stress factors arising from gender-related considerations particularly affect women physicians. Numerous sources of stress have been identified, as women physicians often work in a prejudiced, non-supportive environment with those who do not accept women's place in the profession. They experience feelings of fragmentation resulting from conflicts between occupational and traditional gender roles, both in terms of time management and in responding to emotional demands. Other problems might stem from a woman doctor's internal value conflicts. Guilt and worry, as well as identity crisis, can be emotional consequences of not feeling successful at both roles.[35]

---

[31] Ministry of Labour: *Survey on state of employees health*, Table 131, p. 250; "Working women suffer stress-related illnesses", in *Asahi Evening News* (Tokyo), 1 September 1992.

[32] Haynes and Feinleib: *The Framingham heart study* (1980), as discussed in S.G. Haynes, A.Z. La Croix and T. Lippin: "The effect of high job demands and low control on the health of employed women", in J.C. Quick et al. (editors): *Work stress: Health care systems in the workplace* (Praeger, New York, 1987), pp. 93-110.

[33] ibid., p. 106.

[34] M. Davidson and C.L. Cooper: *Stress and the woman manager* (Martin Robertson, Oxford, 1983).

[35] L. Kaufman Cartwright: "Occupational stress in women physicians", in R. Payne and J. Firth-Cozens (editors): *Stress in health professionals* (John Wiley, Chichester, 1987), pp. 71-87.

A study of night workers in 39 public hospitals in Paris[36] noted that although night shift conditions in hospitals are theoretically the same, the situations of men and women differed in terms of the sex composition and qualification levels. While the majority of the night workers had been working night shifts for less than four years, there were significantly more female auxiliary staff (less qualified) who were older than their counterparts and had worked for more than ten years on night shifts. The study found that, all other things being equal, women hospital night workers were twice as likely as their male counterparts to be particularly tired and frequently irritable. When the factors of gender and children in the home were considered together in the analysis, it appeared that women were significantly more likely to be affected negatively in their physical condition. However, no significant sex-related differences in health were found.

Another special cause of stress for women workers is their total workload in a day. It is commonly higher than that of men, given the time devoted to family responsibilities.

Figure 1: Total workload of women and men as related
to the number of children living at home

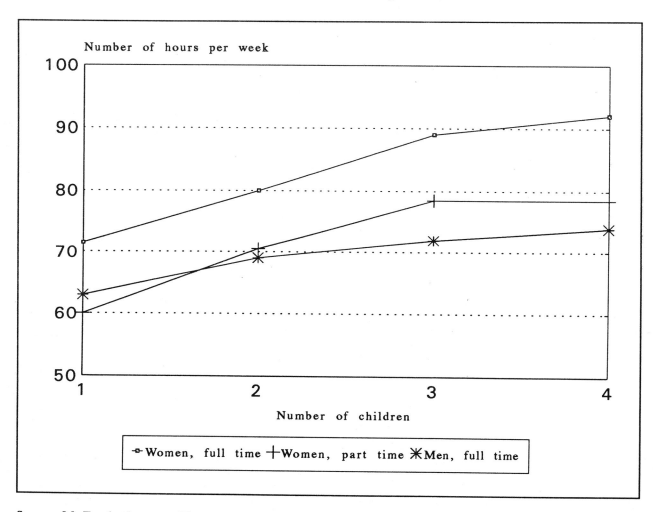

Source: M. Frankenhaeuser: *The measurement of the total workload of men and women* (Stockholm, 1991).

---

[36] M. Estryn-Behar et al.: *Impact of nightshifts on male and female hospital staff* (Paris, 1990).

Research carried out in Sweden,[37] found that the total workload of women employed full time is much higher than that of men employed full time, and the total workload for women employed part time is as much as men employed full time (see Figure 1). This is in a country where 86 per cent of women are in the workforce, but the division of labour between spouses at home has remained much the same.

Another research study carried out in Sweden[38] suggests that "work control" is a crucial factor in the stress and gender relationship. In nearly all 244 occupations examined, men reported higher levels of control than women. Even within female-segregated occupations, women had less work control than did men. In only one occupation did women have more control than men: cleaning. The same study also indicates that women and men were largely confined to working in jobs that were highly segregated, and that women had fewer occupations, of a less diverse character, from which to choose than did men.

The cost of stress

Costs for individuals

Stress may contribute to the development of heart and cerebrovascular disease, hypertension, peptic ulcers, inflammatory bowel diseases and musculo-skeletal problems. Evidence suggests that stress alters immune functions, possibly facilitating the development of cancer. Anxiety, depression, neuroses, and alcohol and drug problems are clearly associated with stress. These latter conditions contribute to the incidence of accidents, homicides and suicides. Considered together, these disorders are reported as responsible for the great majority of disease, death, disability and medical care use in the United States.[39]

Costs for industry and society

The cost of sickness absences for stress and mental disorders has been estimated in the United Kingdom at more than £5 billion a year.[40]

Statistics also indicate that psychoneurosis in the United Kingdom results in the loss of 30 million working days a year. This figure takes no account of time lost through "psychosomatic" complaints, that is physical illnesses which either originated in, or have been exacerbated by, psychological and stress-related problems. It also excludes the less measurable "costs" of human suffering to the people affected, their families and friends, and the cost of lost productivity and decreased efficiency due to low motivation, increases in alcohol and drug consumption, and

---

[37] M. Frankenhaeuser: *The measurement of the total workload of men and women*, paper presented at the Conference on a Healthier Work Environment, Stockholm, May 1991.

[38] E.M. Hall: "Gender, work control and stress: A theoretical discussion and an empirical test", in J.V. Johnson and G. Johansson (editors): *The psychosocial work environment: Work organization, democratization and health*, Policy, Politics, Health and Medicine Series (Baywood Publishing, New York, 1991), pp. 89-108.

[39] D.B. Baker: "Occupational stress", in B.S. Levy (editor): *Occupational health: Recognizing and preventing work-related disease* (Little, Brown and Company, Boston, 1983), pp. 297-315.

[40] Department of Health and the Confederation of British Industry: *Promoting mental health at work* (London, 1991).

time lost through what is sometimes called "presenteeism" -- being physically present at work, but mentally absent.[41]

In the Netherlands, psychological dysfunctioning is a main cause of disability in the working population: 116 people each day (one person every four minutes in the working day) receive a diagnosis of this type.[42]

Stress claims in Australian government employment currently comprise 4 per cent of all workers' compensation claims. Their cost, however, is 16 per cent of all claims. Stress claims are on average the most expensive of all categories of claims. The average total liability for stress claims is currently at A\$30,000, while the next most expensive claim category on average is A\$13,500.[43]

Companies in the United States are increasingly facing -- and losing -- compensation claims from employees suffering from job-related stress. Such claims accounted for about 15 per cent of all claims in 1988, up from less than 5 per cent in 1980, and the average settlement was twice that for an injury claim. Employees who have not traditionally filed such claims, such as white-collar workers, women and younger employees, are expected to do so in greater numbers. Other factors that figure in the rise include an increase in mergers, plant closures and relocations; job growth in the highly stressful service industries; and more workers turning to litigation to settle their claims.[44]

A 1990 study by the California Workers' Compensation Institute (CWCI) cites data from the State of California showing a 700 per cent increase in workers' compensation claims for mental stress between 1979 and 1988. It also identified serious shortcomings in the State's data on mental stress cases. Based on its own survey and extrapolations of the data, CWCI estimated the number of mental-mental (when psychological symptoms result from stress at work) claims in 1985 and 1987 to be 20,000 and 29,000 respectively. Using a conservatively derived estimate of the indemnity and medical benefits of \$13,200, the benefit costs of workers' compensation for mental-mental cases was \$263 million and \$383 million for those two years respectively.[45]

Even in countries such as Canada, where the stakes for many workers are not as high as those in the United States because of the extent of social security coverage, stress-related compensation claims are becoming more and more frequent and the object of growing discussion and concern.[46]

Finally, loss in productivity -- both in quantitative and qualitative terms -- is increasingly associated with stress. At a symposium held in the Philippines in 1988, it was pointed out that "increased productivity and social stability depend not only on the means of production available, but more so on working and living conditions and the health and well-being of workers and their families. Included among the stressful psychosocial factors are the physical environment, some aspects of the organization and the system of work, especially the quality of human

---

[41] "Handling stress at work", in *Industrial Relations Review and Report: Health and Safety Information Bulletin*, No. 125, 6 May 1986.

[42] Information received from the TNO Institute of Preventive Health Care, Leiden, Netherlands, May 1992.

[43] J. Neary, K.V. Elliott and J. Toohey: *The causes of workplace stress and strategies for management*, paper presented at the International Symposium on Work-related Diseases: Prevention and Health Promotion, Linz, Austria, 27-30 October 1992.

[44] H. LaVan, M. Katz and W. Hochwarter: "Employee stress swamps workers' comp", in *Personnel*, Vol. 67, No. 5, May 1990, pp. 61-64.

[45] P.S. Barth: "Workers' compensation for mental stress cases", in *Behavioral Sciences and the Law*, Vol. 8, 1990, p. 358.

[46] K. Lippe: "Compensation for mental-mental claims under Canadian law", in *Behavioral Sciences and the Law*, Vol. 8, 1990, pp. 398-399.

relations within the organization. Interacting with one another, these factors affect the psychological climate in the enterprise as well as the physical and mental health of the workers".[47]

In short, the data and studies mentioned above clearly show why occupational stress is an important concern for workers, enterprises and society. It has detrimental effects on workers' health (cardiovascular, gastro-intestinal, allergy, respiratory reactions; increased accident risks; emotional distress) and on the performance of enterprises (absenteeism, demotivation, turnover, low productivity, interpersonal tensions). The economic impact of stress on society is also large and growing.

A multiple response

Prevention

In the past, stress has sometimes been considered merely a personal problem to be tackled with remedial, occasional and often palliative interventions. The emerging approach, however, focuses on a pro-active response to stress, with emphasis on preventive measures and elimination of the causes of stress, rather than on the treatment of its effects.

This preventive approach is shared by a growing number of experts and organizations operating in the field. As Professor Lennart Levi points out, "an ounce of prevention is worth a pound of cure".[48]

> Unfortunately, however, occupational health services today are mainly concerned with interventions against precursors of disease or disease itself, usually at a stage where functional disturbances or structural injuries have already occurred. If, for example, a very monotonous but attention-demanding work situation has provoked a gastritis or a peptic ulcer, a physician may intervene with acid neutralizers and with drugs that inhibit the increased flow of impulses from the brain to the stomach and the duodenum. If a threat of job loss provokes palpitations of the heart, the physician may block the flow of impulses from the brain to the heart by means of other medications, or else intervene in the cerebral processes by administering tranquilizers to counteract anxiety. These methods are of course not readily dispensed with and should definitely not be underrated, especially when a disease or disability has already developed. It is important, however, to apply measures of prevention as well as of therapy, not only at the mechanism level but also with regard to possible *causes* in the work situation.

Source: L. Levi: *Preventing work stress* (Addison-Wesley, Reading, Massachusetts, 1981), p. 81.

Similarly, Professor Robert Karasek indicates that "the extraordinary breadth of the existing literature on psychosomatic causes of illness argues for integration of our understanding of environmental causes at work with the research on psychological and physiological mechanisms of individual response to the environment. Our

---

[47] E.A. Abueg and D.P. Estella: "Productivity implications of psychological problems", in *Proceedings of a Symposium on Psychological Factors and Problems at the Workplace*, Quezon City, 26-27 May 1988.

[48] L. Levi: *Preventing work stress* (Addison-Wesley, Reading, Massachusetts, 1981), p. 81.

approach is to link causes based in the environment and causes based in the individual, but with environmental causes as the starting point".[49]

The idea that prevention can be the winning weapon to combat stress has been strongly emphasized by the National Institute for Occupational Safety and Health (NIOSH) in the United States.

> A prevention strategy for health disorders must take account of both causal mechanisms and factors that perpetuate the disorders. Generic approaches tend to focus on the interplay of host, agent, and contextual factors.
>
> .....
>
> This concept of the health process is consistent with formulations in contemporary theory on stress and with empirical observations. The basic concept in most current approaches to job stress theory embodies an unfavorable interaction between worker attributes and job conditions that leads to psychological disturbances and unhealthy behaviors and ultimately to physiological ill health.
>
> Research findings confirm this view on a general level. Both physical and psychosocial job characteristics have been shown to play a role in the etiology of work-related psychological disturbances. These factors operate in concert with other factors -- such as stressful life events or familial demands and support -- and with physical and psychological traits, capacities, and needs of the workers (personality, age, gender, experience/ learning, etc.). The interplay among these variables is complex, however, and the relative influence of the different classes of variables is not thoroughly understood.
>
> The current understanding of psychological health processes, as described here, suggests key elements in a prevention strategy for work-related psychological disorders. These include abatement of known job (environmental) risk factors, research to improve understanding of these risk factors, surveillance to detect and track risk factors and to identify occupational groups at risk, and education to improve the recognition of risk factors and their control. At the same time, efforts are needed to improve mental health services for workers.

Source: NIOSH: *Proposed national strategies for the prevention of leading work-related diseases and injuries: Psychological disorders* (Cincinnati, 1988), pp. 6-7.

The same idea has been expressed in the resolutions of the 22nd World Congress of the International Federation of Commercial, Clerical, Professional and Technical Employees (FIET):

---

[49] R. Karasek and T. Theorell: *Healthy work: Stress, productivity, and the reconstruction of working time* (Basic Books, New York, 1990), pp. 8-9.

**Limitation of the work-related stress and
pressure affecting salaried employees**

The following specific policy-shaping elements must be included:

a) Preventive health protection starts with the way work is organised.

b) Trade union representatives must be involved in a comprehensive and timely fashion in deciding how work is organised and carried out.

c) This involvement also includes staffing requirements (personnel planning), as well as the introduction or modification of personnel information and performance evaluation systems.

d) Work schedules which cause great strain (e.g. night and shift work) are to be eliminated or reduced.

e) Work is to be organised in such a way that the individual worker can have independence and responsibility.

f) Measures to prevent, alleviate or compensate work-related pressures must not be subordinate to purely economic considerations.

g) Initial and further training opportunities must be offered which take the current and future qualification requirements of employees into consideration. This also includes a role for the trade unions in determining the contents of training courses in order to ensure that preventive health protection is included.

h) Individuals' rights to more self and co-determination at and about work must be revised.

i) Legislators are called on to take into account the increase of stress-related illnesses by further developing social legislation (recognition of stress-related illnesses as occupational illnesses).

j) As an accompaniment to the above-named measures, environmental measures at the workplace must be further developed in collective and company agreements.

Source: FIET: *Resolutions adopted by the 22nd FIET World Congress (San Francisco, 19-23 August 1991)* (Geneva, 1992), pp. 38-39.

Preventive approaches to stress are thus becoming increasingly relevant in terms of research and policy orientation, and are opening new paths for intervention in the fight against occupational stress.

Regulation

Action to combat stress also includes legislative and regulatory responses.

Legislators in a number of countries have adopted statutory provisions which take account of psychosocial risk factors in the workplace. Some of these provisions are of a general type, such as those in the 1970 Occupational Safety and Health Act in the United States,[50] which includes a requirement for investigations to be

---

[50] Occupational Safety and Health Act, dated 29 December 1970, Public Law 91-596, 91st Congress S.2193, page 21, Sec. 20(a)(1) [ILO: *Legislative Series* (LS) 1970-USA1].

carried out into psychological factors at work, and the 1974 Health and Safety at Work Act[51] in the United Kingdom, which is concerned with both mental and physical well-being. The definition of "personal injury" in this Act includes "any decrease and any impairment of a person's physical or mental conditions".

In a more significant and effective way, rules and regulations related to the work environment have been designed in a number of countries to facilitate the identification of stress-related problems and the types of preventive remedies to be applied. In 1977, the Norwegian Working Environment Act[52] paved the way towards fundamental changes in working life, which bear directly on occupational stress. This Act includes the following provisions:

- The work environment in the enterprise is to be fully satisfactory for individuals and in relation to all factors that may have an influence on the health and on the physical and mental well-being of workers.

- Technology, work organization, working time (e.g. shift plans) and payment systems are to be designed so as to avoid negative physiological or psychological effects on employees, as well as negative influences on alertness to safety. Employees are to be given possibilities for personal development and for the maintenance and development of skills.

- In the planning of work and design of jobs, possibilities for employee self-determination and maintenance of skills are to be considered. Monotonous repetitive work and work that is bound by machine or assembly line, in such a way that no room is left for variation in work rhythm, should be avoided. Jobs should be designed so as to give possibilities for variation, for contact with others, for understanding of the interdependence between elements that constitute a job, and for information and feedback to employees concerning production requirements and results.

- Workers or their elected representatives are to be kept informed about systems used for planning and control and any changes in such systems. They are to be given the training necessary to understand the systems and to influence their design.

This innovative approach to work environment is further developed in the Swedish Work Environment Act,[53] the most recent version of which states the following:

- Working conditions are to conform to people's differing physical and psychological circumstances.

- Employees are to be given opportunities to participate in the arrangement of their specific job situation, as well as in changes and developments that affect their jobs.

- Technology, work organization and job content are to be designed in such a way that employees are not exposed to physical or mental loads that may cause ill health or accidents.

- The matters to be considered in this context are to include forms of remuneration and the scheduling of working hours.

- Closely controlled or constrained work is to be avoided or restricted.

---

[51] Health and Safety at Work Act 1974, dated 31 July 1974, Chapter I, Article 53 [LS 1974-UK.2].

[52] Act No. 4 respecting workers' protection and the working environment, dated 4 February 1977 (*Norsk Lovtidend*, Part I, No. 4, 14 February 1977, page 77), as amended up to Act No. 25, dated 5 June 1987 (*Norsk Lovtidend*, Part I, No. 12, 1987) [LS 1977-Nor.1].

[53] Work Environment Act, Act No. 1160, dated 19 December 1977 (*Svensk författningssamling*, No. 1160, 1977), as amended up to Act No. 677, dated 21 March 1991 (*Svensk författningssamling*, No. 677, 1991) [LS 1977-Swe.4].

• An effort is to be made to ensure that work provides opportunities for variety, social contacts and cooperation, as well as continuity among individual work tasks.

• Furthermore, an effort is to be made to attain working conditions that provide opportunities for personal and occupational development, as well as for self-determination and occupational responsibility.

In Germany, the *Sozialgesetzbuch*[54] (Code of Social Laws) establishes that the *Krankenkassen* (Sickness Funds) must investigate the causes of health hazards and of damages to health and remove them. These funds also contribute to the prevention of occupational health hazards. These provisions have been the basis for several in-plant stress prevention programmes supported by the Sickness Funds.

Also relevant to a preventive strategy against occupational stress are legislative provisions in several countries which require information to be given to workers and their representatives, as well as provisions on consultation, negotiation, and co-determination rights concerning health and the environment at the workplace.

The importance of workers' involvement in these matters is strongly confirmed by several international instruments. A Directive of the Council of the European Community[55] on the introduction of measures to encourage improvements in the safety and health of workers at work stresses the central role of prevention, the provision of information and training. It includes the following obligations on employers:

— adapting the work to the individual, especially as regards the design of workplaces, the choice of work equipment, and the choice of working and production methods, with a view, in particular, to alleviating monotonous work and work at a predetermined work rate and to reducing their effect on health;

— developing a coherent overall prevention policy which covers technology, organization of work, working conditions, social relationships and the influence of factors related to the working environment;

— receiving all the necessary information concerning the safety and health risks and protective and preventive measures and activities in respect of both the establishment in general and each type of workstation and/or job.

The ILO Occupational Safety and Health Convention, 1981 (No. 155) expressly states that cooperation between management and workers and/or their representatives within undertakings is an essential element of organization and other measures to promote safety and health at the workplace. In this respect, the accompanying Occupational Safety and Health Recommendation, 1981 (No. 164) contains a number of provisions which have a significant bearing on stress prevention and control. In particular, workers' safety delegates, workers' safety and health committees, and joint safety and health committees or, as appropriate, other workers' representatives should:

• be given adequate information on safety and health matters, enabled to examine factors affecting safety and health, and encouraged to propose measures on the subject;

• be consulted when major new safety and health measures are envisaged and before they are carried out, and seek to obtain the support of the workers for such measures;

• be consulted in planning alterations of work processes, work content or organization of work, which may have safety or health implications for the workers.

National regulations also apply to specific types of work. For example, a considerable number of regulations on visual display units (VDUs), a major cause of stress, have evolved. Regulations, particularly the provision of

---

[54] Sozialgesetzbuch (Code of Social Laws) (SGB), Book V: Gesetzliche Krankenversicherung (Statutory Sickness Insurance), Chapter 1, Paragraph 20.

[55] "Directive of 12 June 1989 on the introduction of measures to encourage improvements in the safety and health of workers at work", in *Official Journal*, Vol. 32, No. L.183, 29 June 1989, Articles 6 and 10.

rest pauses, are in force in a growing number of countries. In Germany, VDU regulations were introduced in 1981 by the *Zentralstelle für Unfallverhütung und Arbeitsmedizin des Hauptverbandes der Gewerblichen Berufsgenossenschaften* (Confederation of Trade and Professional Associations, Headquarters for Accident Prevention and Occupational Medicine).[56] The regulations, although not legally binding in a strict sense, are recognized as having a quasi-legal status from the point of view of safety inspection and insurance matters. They also influence collective bargaining agreements on VDUs, hundreds of which have been signed, primarily at company level, along the lines of these regulations. A survey carried out in 1986 by the WSI, the research institute of the major German trade union confederation (DGB), on VDU agreements[57] clearly shows that these agreements touch all the major areas of decision-making concerning the introduction of VDUs. Job design, working time, performance monitoring, job security and income guarantees, training and retraining, and health and safety are among the areas where substantial influence has been exerted by employee representatives. Rights of information, consultation and co-determination for the works councils have been established.

Enterprise programmes

Organizations may adopt a number of different approaches to stress. One approach is not to tackle the problem at all. In 1989, BIS Applied Systems published a survey of stress in the British manufacturing industry. It showed that while 86 per cent of managers felt they were suffering from stress, nearly three-quarters of their companies provided no help whatever.[58] A second approach, fortunately not very common, is to use stress as a means to force people to do more work and supposedly to be more productive. A third way of tackling stress is to intervene when it has already manifested its negative effects, thus operating on the consequences rather than on the causes.

Finally, enterprises may develop preventive programmes which attack stress at its origin and which may lead to more permanent and long-term positive results. In fact, an increasing number of stress prevention and control programmes are being introduced.

These types of programme usually have the advantage of fitting "naturally" into the managerial, economic and social strategies of the enterprise. Managers maintain the initiative with assistance, as required, from external experts. In this context, dialogue with workers' representatives is often facilitated because of common interests. The costs of these programmes can be relatively contained and can become an integral part of the necessary organizational development of a sound enterprise. When a proper cost-benefit cycle is activated, stress prevention can eventually pay for itself.

Programmes can ensure that attention is given to measures to eliminate or reduce stress by improving work organization. This may include the following: improved job design and job content; setting realistic goals, performance standards, targets and deadlines; better organization of working time; or better interfaces between workers and machines or new technologies.

Because the manager often plays an essential role in connection with occupational stress, programmes sometimes concentrate on improving systems of work planning, control and evaluation, introducing supportive management styles, training to deal with stress of both management and workers, and so on.

---

[56] Draft proposals for new instructions on accident prevention on work on VDU equipment have been presented in December 1992 by the Confederation, which emphasize the importance of mental stress for work at VDUs and indicate concrete ways for reducing or avoiding stress-related consequences on the health of VDU operators.

[57] WSI: *Sondertarifverträge und -tarifvertragsbestimmungen für Bildschirmarbeit* (Regulations concerning special collective agreements and collective agreements for work at VDUs) (Dortmund, 1986).

[58] T. Tiernan: "All stressed up and nowhere to go ...", in *Works Management*, Vol. 42, No. 11, November 1989, pp. 16-19.

In addition, there are anti-stress initiatives based on improving interpersonal relationships within the enterprise. These include the following: the establishment of better channels of information and communication; the creation of autonomous working groups; measures to eliminate or reduce role conflict and role ambiguity within the organization; and programmes to improve cohesion among co-workers.

Finally, measures to raise the capacity of individuals to cope with stress are sometimes included in programmes which, when of a preventive type and in combination with other preventive measures, can prove particularly successful (i.e. health support programmes, counselling at work, "training to cope" programmes).

The analysis of the cases included in this *Digest* (see Part III) confirms the positive impact of preventive anti-stress programmes, both in terms of health and productivity. Some examples follow.

- **Anti-stress intervention for air traffic controllers in Italy**. As a consequence of the improvements carried out in the traffic management and control systems, and better performance by operators due to improved working conditions, the annual incidence of air misses from 1983 to 1989 showed a progressive decrease (almost half) despite the continuous increase in air traffic (over 30 per cent).

- **Anti-stress programme for managers and assembly-line workers in a multinational manufacturing company in Mexico**. Based on extensive involvement of all parties concerned in analysing and shaping work organization and individual responsibilities, this programme resulted, after 12 months, in a decrease in psychosomatic illness of 15 per cent, in a decrease in absenteeism and in an increase in productivity. The general human and work environment in the company improved substantially.

- **Anti-stress programme for blue-collar workers at ASEA Brown Bovery in Sweden**. By introducing an anti-stress programme based on job enrichment and job rotation, turnover was reduced in the area of intervention from 39 per cent to 0. Absences for sickness, which totalled up to 35 per cent in 1989 (one day lost every three working days), were significantly reduced. This reduction affected primarily workers without chronic health problems, lowering their rate of absenteeism from 14 to 2 per cent. Productivity increased. "On-time" deliveries, for instance, increased by 10 per cent to 98 per cent.

- **Anti-stress programme for postal workers in the United Kingdom**. Among the workers who benefited from stress counselling, anxiety was reduced by 29 per cent, psychosomatic disturbances by 40 per cent and absence for sickness by 46 per cent in terms of the number of events, and 60 per cent in terms of the number of days.

- **Anti-stress programme for officials of the Ministère de la Main-d'oeuvre, de la Sécurité du Revenu et de la Formation professionnelle in Quebec**. As a consequence of the programme, the rate of absenteeism of the officials involved in the initiative was reduced by 10 per cent in the period November 1989 to November 1991. During the same period, the rate increased by 4 per cent for officials who did not take part in the programme.

- **Anti-stress programme for managers, supervisors, operators, loaders, foremen and maintenance staff at Western Coalfields Limited in India**. As a result of to this programme, more than 50 per cent of operators and loaders (to limit it to two categories) indicated a reduction of monotony and boredom and improvements in their working schedules. Between 25 and 50 per cent indicated improved responses to the stressors in the physical environment, significant relief from somatic complaints and reduction in their smoking habits.

Beyond these examples, preventive anti-stress action can be carried out -- and is carried out -- in many more enterprises within their organizational development and in the day-to-day process of adapting to changing circumstances and needs. Discovering this reality and sharing the positive results of "ongoing" anti-stress action within these enterprises is a challenge which could not be fully met by this *Digest*, but is one where future projects and initiatives in this area will certainly take over.

SECTION 2

Stress prevention through work reorganization: A summary of 19 international case studies[1]

Professor Robert Karasek[2]

Introduction

There are many indications that the level of work-related stress is becoming a health problem of major proportions in societies all over the world. While the magnitude of this problem goes still largely unmeasured in formal statistical documentation, stress-related topics are now appearing with increasing frequency in discussions in many countries: increased job pressure, increased job insecurity, increased feelings of powerlessness at work. If the suspicion is correct that our modern mechanisms of production and international trade are now contributing to increased risks of stress all over the world, it is only natural that the ILO as a world organization should address the problem. In 1991, the ILO commissioned 19 case studies of stress prevention programmes in the worksite from nine industrialized and developing countries (see Part III of this *Digest*). This collection of studies, which covers a broad range of anti-stress programmes, is unique in so far as it attempts to address stress problems at their source by modifying the work situation rather than by attending to stress symptoms after the fact.

We can understand the significance of this unusual collection of case studies by placing them in an overall context in terms of occupations, industries, types of prevention methods and factors associated with success. The first section of this paper attempts to locate the cases in terms of the characteristics of the occupations selected for the prevention programmes. Secondly, we review the types of stress problems that were identified for the programmes to resolve. Thirdly, we highlight the importance of this group of case studies in terms of the broad range of prevention methodologies spanned -- with a concentration on the important, but less often practiced, environmentally focused workplace changes at several levels.

Finally, we attempt to review the factors for success, by establishing success criteria and associating these with programme characteristics in each of the case studies. This last goal is limited by our data: 19 case studies covering many countries, many occupations, many methods and with many different kinds of results, inevitably mean that the validity of any conclusions about what leads to programme success can be questioned. Nevertheless, some basic trends emerge which allow us, in the concluding section, to sketch a new picture based on stress prevention and the use of employee participation to reduce the negative burden of work stress, and raise the possibility of significant productivity improvements.

The coverage of the case studies

Types of occupation and industry

The broad range of occupational groups covered by the case studies is shown in Table 1.

---

[1] See Part III of this *Digest*.

[2] Co-Director, Lorin Kerr Ergonomics Institute, Department of Work Environment, University of Massachusetts Lowell, Lowell, Massachusetts 01854, United States.

Table 1: Case list and case characteristics

Case No.	Occupation	Country	Author
1	Full national workforce	Sweden	Levi
2	Clerical and service workers	United States	Landsbergis et al.
3	Auto machinists and operatives	United States	Israel et al.
4	Chemical production workers	United States	May
5	Air traffic controllers	Italy	Costa
6	Police (a) and steelworkers (b)	Sweden	Levi and Åkerstedt
7	Manufacturing managers (a) and assemblers (b)	Mexico	Matrajt
8	Clerical workers in social service	United States	Cahill
9	Meat cutters (a) and meat processors (b)	United States	Smith et al.
10	Clerical workers in public administration	Sweden	Eriksson et al.
11	Foremen (auto repair)	Germany	Kuhn
12	Crane operators	Germany	Kuhn
13	Electrical assemblers	Sweden	Kvarnström
14	Software designers	Sweden	Arnetz et al.
15	Psychiatric nurses	Japan	Chihara et al.
16	Postal workers	United Kingdom	Cooper et al.
17	Diverse workers trauma stress	United States	Braverman
18	Employees (a) and managers (b) in public administration	Canada	Greco
19	Coalmine managers (a), supervisors (b) and operators (c)	India	Sastry

In order to develop an overall understanding of these case studies, we use a model that describes workers' task characteristics that are associated with psychosocial stress. The **demand/control** model was developed by the author to predict job-related psychosocial stress and, alternatively, motivating behaviour.[3] According to this model it is not only the psychological demands of work that lead to stress and related illnesses, but the condition of high demands combined with low worker control over the work process that create risk. Stress results when workers are constrained from responding to the stressor on the basis of their own optimal psychological and physiological response pattern, because of external factors over which they have no control. (Alternatively, motivating behaviour can result when the task demands are performed according to a response pattern that is decided by the worker.)

---

[3] R. Karasek: "Job decision latitude, job demands and mental strain: Implications for job redesign", in *Administrative Science Quarterly*, Vol. 24, 1979, pp. 285-308; R. Karasek and T. Theorell: *Healthy work: Stress, productivity and the reconstruction of working life* (Basic Books, New York, 1990).

The model seems to capture some important stressful job circumstances: the low-control, high-demand tasks, particularly in combination with low social support.

In Figure 1, the vertical dimension of decision latitude (increasing toward the top) and the horizontal dimension of psychological job demands (increasing to the right) create four quadrants. If we quickly read the map in terms of health consequences of work, we would find the following: stress is strongest in the lower right quadrant (high demands, low decision latitude); the upper right quadrant (high demands, high decision latitude) is called active work; the diagonally opposite situation is called passive work (low demands and low decision latitude); and low strain work is in the upper left quadrant.

Since we do not have sufficient data on actual job characteristics for the case studies, we have used the occupational titles listed by the case researchers and then plotted the position **for average American workers** in such jobs. In the United States, large surveys have enabled us to determine the average job characteristics score for each detailed occupation and industry groups.[4] Cross-cultural comparisons, involving Sweden and the United States, have indeed shown rather good international comparability in terms of relative rankings of different occupations on job control and job demands.

Figure 1 shows that the vast majority of cases are, as might be predicted, from the high strain job categories with low decision latitude and high psychological job demands. Of the occupational groups that are significantly mentioned in the case studies, we can identify 23 occupational groups. Of these, 14 are in the high-strain quadrant of Figure 1, seven are in the active quadrant, one is in the passive jobs category, and possibly one is in the low-strain job quadrant. In these latter two cases, the jobs are close to the average in job demands. Thus, there are almost no jobs with low psychological demands included in the 19 case studies.

---

[4] See Karasek and Theorell, ibid., for a description.

Figure 1: Distribution of cases by occupational task characteristics

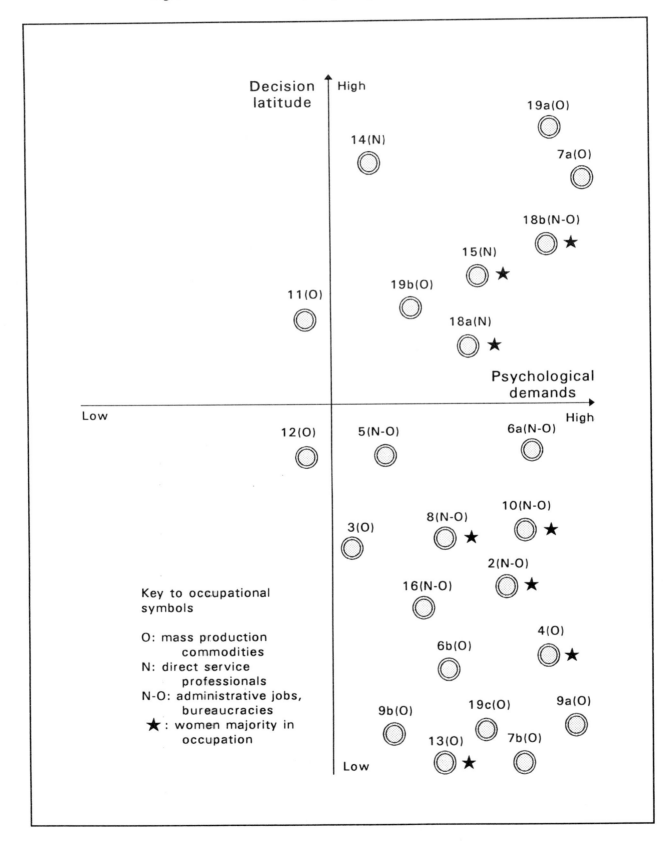

Another important conclusion from Figure 1 is that the cases, in a higher than expected frequency, involve mass production or commodity production (or commodity-like service production) exposed to international competition (nine of the 19 cases, noted "O" in Figure 1). This bolsters the concern expressed above that development of the globally integrated economy and expansion of multinational enterprises are increasing the stress burden of workers around the world (of course, the fact that these industries are included in the ILO programme means that such companies are also deciding to do something about the problem). By contrast, manufacturing jobs allowing skill development or decentralized, direct-contact service jobs which allow workers to use their judgement about skill use ("conducive" or "new value" jobs) represent a "healthy" type of production,[5] but are rarely the focus of the stress prevention cases (three cases noted "N"). A second category of common industries and occupations are administrative jobs often in large-scale public bureaucracies (seven cases noted "N-O"), particularly those which are short of resources owing to public sector budget cuts.

A final important characteristic of the 19 case studies relates to sex. In general, women are more often in high strain jobs than men. The programmes overall, however, do not reflect this possible higher exposure to job stress: only eight of the 23 occupations noted have women as a majority of workers treated.

Missing case areas: The implications

Several occupational groups that may be increasingly at risk for work stress are not included in the ILO study. One such group is temporary workers, often in office assistance, fast-food outlets and, increasingly, low-skill manufacturing jobs. These jobs can be highly stressful, and employees, often young, move from job to job. However, the chronic burden of such high-task stress and high job insecurity exposures is unknown. Personnel management strategies in many American companies during the 1980s, now seen increasingly in Europe, switched jobs away from employees with long-term benefits toward such temporary workers to handle fluctuations in demand, without incurring entitlement to long-term employee benefits. Moreover, recently many employees involved in distinctly non-cyclical activity have become included in the category of temporary workers: 30 per cent of the American workforce may have non-permanent employment status.[6] High turnover groups are usually precisely the groups excluded from scientific studies of job stress consequences because their job conditions are so irregular and they are not likely to be the focus of expensive prevention programmes in the company. Other missing occupational groups include waiters and check-out personnel in supermarkets, who could also be easily affected by the same "replaceable worker" philosophy.

Readers of the cases will note that only two of the 19 cases relate to developing countries. The small number of developing country studies, however, probably does not indicate that there are no stress problems there, but that these still are low in a scale of priorities often centred on survival and harsh competition.

Initiating stress-prevention programmes

Labour and management problem definitions

The reasons that workers/unions initiate stress prevention programmes are quite straightforward, and compared to management diversity (see below), there is little variety of approach. In the majority of cases with a union or worker initiator, the focal problem noted is simply worker stress or illness that must be reduced. The following major sources of stress were cited by **employees or unions**:

(a)   Occupation-specific stressors are noted in four cases.

---

[5] ibid.

[6] R. Belous: *Cutting jobs* (National Planning Association, Washington, 1992), as cited in *Los Angeles Times-Washington Post News Service*, 11-12 October 1992.

(b)   General stress is noted in two cases.

(c)   Physical hazards (ergonomics and injury) are noted in two cases.

(d)   Family-work interface is the major reason in one case.

Primary reasons of **management** for initiating stress prevention programmes differ substantially from programme to programme.

(a)   In two cases, the company's primary reason for initiating a worker stress reduction programme was to reduce the risk to employees' health. In five other cases, where a researcher (as initiative taker) has advocated a strong worker stress reduction approach that includes the union, management has also been very supportive of this goal.

(b)   The hope of improving the personal resources of workers to cope with stress is significant in three cases.

(c)   The hope of avoiding company liability for workers' illnesses appears to be an unmentioned major motivator in three cases.

(d)   Turnover is the major reason in two cases.

(e)   Absenteeism is the major reason in one case.

(f)   Disability costs is the major reason in one case.

(g)   The need to comply with national health and safety regulations is the reason in one case.

Initiator, problem definition and type of intervention

An interesting question is whether the type of problem or the initiator for the case has any impact on the type of intervention chosen. Here we find several rather clear conclusions. In management-initiated programmes, the majority of problems were seen to be with the person rather than the work environment. When unions or worker-linked researchers initiated the programmes, the "cause" of the stress problem was seen to lie in the environment in all nine cases. The interventions usually included both an environmental and a person-based component in these cases.

A second conclusion is that where management initiated the programme, the intervention utilized outside experts who analysed the problem and posed solutions in all cases. In the union- or researcher-initiated programmes, the intervention process usually involved worker participation, where discussion groups were formed to develop the workers' own problem analysis and solution.

Problematic and unstated goals for the stress programmes

One disturbing trend seen in several management-initiated programmes was the goal of increasing the capacity of workers to cope with stress. In one case study, coping strength is linked to a programme where demands on workers are expected or designed to increase. Here, coping strength is used to increase stresses on workers instead of improving health (of course, if the programme fails and demands are merely increased, it is the worker who pays the cost).

Another disturbing trend is observed in some case studies, where the impact of the multinational economy can lead to intense output pressure for workers (including work patterns and attitudes in strong contradiction to local culture). The commodity nature of production aggravates the problem. In the case study of Mexican manufacturing, simple percentage targets for manufactured output imposed a rigid constraint on organizational activity that seemed to contribute to stress problems. The case of meat cutters' jobs in the United States also discusses the adverse stress effects of international competition in commodity-like production due to deskilling of tasks and higher output quotas.

In some of the case studies, workers' health is stated as the concern, but details of the cases seem to argue for hidden management priorities. In one case, management is willing to accept the cost of treating employees' stress, but almost as an alternative to changing the work environment that could be quite stressful. This case also institutes a successful and broadly utilized employee assistance programme, but notes the built-in difficulty of stigmatization and fear of reprisal felt by employees who use it. Another case involves huge disability costs for a public service job, but since the job demands are assumed to be invariant, an added burden is placed on workers to reduce public expenditures on their illnesses by "learning to cope" better.

Different approaches to the prevention process

A model of the intervention process

To describe the effects of the stress intervention process we will use a variation on the model of the stress development process originally refined at the University of Michigan in the 1970s shown in Figure 2,[7] with several modifications added by the author. The objective of the modified Michigan model is to describe the process of stress evolution. This allows us to understand the different types of intervention that might be taken at each stage to stop the process of stress development.

The final, most undesirable, step in the development of the negative impacts of work stress is chronic illness, represented by the rightmost of the five categories in Figure 2. Chronically ill patients have rehabilitation as an intervention strategy, but these patient care solutions are beyond the scope of this paper, and imply a failure of more "preventive" approaches. The causal process leading (from left to right) to the illness state is represented by four different categories of causal factors. The first of these (category 2 from the right) is the individual's own response to environmental stressors: the response of "stress" as well as other emotions and behavioural reactions. Person-based stress prevention programmes intervene at this level by changing the individual's emotional responses and coping strategies to prevent further development of illness. Because the individual is already "stressed" at this point, such programmes are not strictly preventive since they treat symptoms rather than eliminate causes.

Further to the left come three categories of work environment effects that are considered to be the primary causes of the individual's stress reactions. At the micro-environmental level come task structure, and communication patterns at the person-environment intersection. Both of these are common points of environment-based intervention (black arrows in Figure 2). Larger-scale organizational issues, such as management strategy and production technology, in turn affect how the task is organized for individual workers. These issues are also common points of work environment intervention (two black arrows in Figure 2). Further to the left are macro-scale social and economic factors which affect the company's work organization policies, such as market conditions (global economic competition, etc.), cultural backgrounds of workers, and national labour relations programmes, which are largely beyond the change capabilities of company-based stress prevention programmes. It is interesting to note that one of the case studies in Sweden[8] discusses intervention at this level as well.

In summary, this five-level model gives us four distinctly different modes of work environment intervention and one person-based mode, spaced from right to left in Figure 2, which we discuss in greater detail below. The furthest left represents the most "preventive" approach since the changes are presumably closer to the origin of the problem, but also a more difficult approach because of its environmental breadth. An additional important issue is that the generality of stress responses means that several causes may evoke the same stress response (one cause

---

[7] J.R.P. French and R.L. Kahn: "A programmatic approach to studying the industrial environment and mental health", in *Journal of Social Issues*, Vol. 18, 1962, pp. 1-47; D. Katz and R. Kahn: *The social psychology of organizations* (Wiley, New York, 1978).

[8] L. Levi: "Managing stress in work settings at the national level in Sweden", in Part III of this *Digest*.

may also have several responses). This means that programmes should have multiple levels of intervention if they want to be certain to deal fully with the problem, and simultaneously have a broad range of viewpoints about what the problem is in the workplace that should be investigated.

Figure 2: A model of the work stress development process

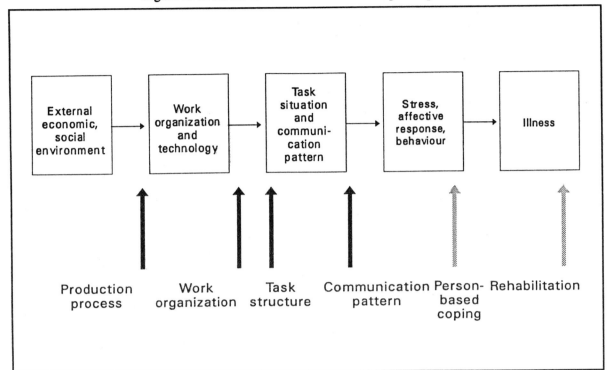

Person-based interventions

The most common method is after-the-fact individual counselling or treatment of troubled employees, sometimes in relation to the employment (employee assistance programmes), or outside. This strategy is not preventive of environmental stress problems, except in the sense of preventing even more acute response patterns. Person-based stress intervention methods include individual strategies to assist "relaxation" even in the presence of stress.[9] A major new direction involves cognitive reinterpretation of stressful events to make them seem less threatening.[10] Another direction emphasizes learning self-confidence for personal change via successful personal learning experiences.[11] All of these strategies are designed to increase the stress tolerance or coping capacity of individuals. The long-term consequences of these strategies have not yet been investigated from an occupational health perspective.

---

[9] H. Benson: *The relaxation response* (Morrow, New York, 1975); R.S. Lazarus and S. Folkman: *Stress, appraisal and coping* (Springer, New York, 1984).

[10] C. Patel, M.G. Marmot and D. Terry: "Controlled trial of biofeedback-aided behavioural methods in reducing mild hypertension", in *British Journal of Medicine*, Vol. 282, 1981, pp. 2005-2010.

[11] A. Bandura: "Self-efficacy mechanism in human agency", in *American Psychologist*, Vol. 27, No. 2, 1982, pp. 122-147.

```
┌─────────────────────────────────────────────┐
│                                             │
│            Person-based interventions        │
│                                             │
│        1.  Individual problem counselling    │
│                                             │
│        2.  Relaxation techniques             │
│                                             │
│        3.  Cognitive reappraisal             │
│                                             │
└─────────────────────────────────────────────┘
```

Communication pattern interventions (a person/social environment interaction)

This category spans boundaries: it focuses on changing the interactions individuals have with their social environment. We have included stress education programmes which explain the physiological origin of stress reaction and validate "feelings" arising from environmentally induced stress.[12] Many methods focus on eliminating conflict-inducing communication, building interpersonal trust and gaining a mutual understanding of issues via role playing. Some new methods for linking task structure and language development in an interpersonal communication context are discussed below.

```
┌─────────────────────────────────────────────┐
│                                             │
│        Communication pattern interventions   │
│                                             │
│     1.   Stress education programmes         │
│                                             │
│     2.   Elimination of conflict-inducing    │
│          communication                       │
│                                             │
│     3.   Building interpersonal trust        │
│                                             │
└─────────────────────────────────────────────┘
```

Micro-environment: Task structure interventions

This is perhaps the best-known category of preventive activities which could improve the psychosocial, stress-inducing aspects of work environments. These methods include increasing workers' skills and decision-making authority (job enrichment, job enlargement,[13] collective coping and decision-making capabilities, and autonomous groups[14]). Management-initiated motivation and quality enhancement strategies often incorporate similar elements of these "de-Taylorizing" processes to change the content of the worker's tasks. There have been large reviews showing the effectiveness of these methods, particularly in the United States and northern Europe since the late 1960s. A common problem of these micro-methods is the difficulty in changing the task structure when the embedding macro structure remains inconsistent.

---

[12] L. Schore and J. Aktin: "Stress in the workplace: Delivering individual and group stress services through union membership assistance programs (MAP)", in S. Akabas and P. Kurzman (editors): *Occupational social work* (National Association of Social Workers, Harrisburg, Pennsylvania, 1992).

[13] L.E. Davis and J.C. Taylor (editors): *Design of jobs* (Penguin Books, Harmondsworth, 1972).

[14] B. Gardell: "Worker participation and autonomy: A multilevel approach to democracy at the workplace", in *International Journal of Health Services*, Vol. 12, 1982, pp. 527-558.

Task structure interventions

1. Job enrichment

2. Team workers

3. Autonomous groups

Macro-environment: Work organization and production process interventions

There are a variety of approaches that focus on changing the organizational, political and technical context of workers' tasks. These methods focus on understanding the management (and union) policies that comprise "work organization" and on trying to embed task-changing activities within a supportive (or at least neutral) labour-management context at the firm level or even national programme level. New management styles which share authority and open up communications can be included here. Socio-technical design experiments emphasize that production process technologies can be embedded in non-hierarchical organizational structures, and via field experiments try to show good examples of such results.[15] The industrial democracy movement, originating in the same field experiments of the 1960s, began to prioritize democratic values of broad worker participation in the change process and embed support for these in a national labour relations organization.[16] Worker participatory interventions focus on the importance of a process which includes broad ranges of workers as well as managers and staff personnel, and which is ultimately taken over by local worker/manager groups. Here the process goals of active worker engagement, group solution formulation and programme self-direction are as important as finding the right solution. A new tradition in Scandinavia, where work organization change strategies have evolved the furthest, has built upon this democratic tradition, retaining the emphasis on process and the large-scale focus, but adds understanding that new structure requires new language and new communication processes emerging between all active parties.

Work organization and production process interventions

1. Labour-management dialogue

2. Socio-technical design alternative

3. New management styles

4. Participatory interaction methods

---

[15] F. van Eijnatten: *Classical socio-technical systems design: The socio-technical design paradigm of organizations*, Monograph BDK/T&A 001 (Eindhoven University of Technology, Eindhoven, 1990).

[16] B. Gustavsen and G. Hunnius: *New patterns of work reform: The case of Norway* (University Press, Oslo, 1981).

Classification of cases by type of intervention approach

To give a quick impression of the types of study presented, we describe most of them in one sentence below. While the descriptions are consistent with the analytic framework of this review, the great diversity of materials presented in the cases means that other short characterizations of the projects might well be made by the authors themselves, as the texts of the case studies reveal.

a. Large-scale work environment focus: Strategic

1. The development of exemplary legislation in Sweden based on prevention and on an integrated human/environment approach.

b. Large-scale work environment focus: Worker participatory processes

2. A union-initiated programme of education committees in the United States around stress topics raises consciousness and begins job change processes.

3. A participatory job reorganization project for American auto workers in a painfully difficult environment develops problem-solving skills at ever expanding levels.

4. A multiple location project for American chemical workers builds engagement around family/work conflicts and opens the door to discussions on job changes.

c. Large-scale work reorganization: Expert guided

5. A very comprehensive reorganization of work for air traffic controllers in Italy includes organizational level and engineering changes.

6. A shift work change programme for Swedish police officers reduces stress levels and improves work, but collides with leisure schedules.

7. A large problem analysis and work reorganization involves multiple groups, company wide, in a Mexican manufacturing facility for managers and assemblers.

8. A large clerical pool project in the United States builds a good discussion platform first and then accomplishes humane technological changes.

9. An ergonomic and work organizational redesign programme of meat-processing workers in the United States is prevented from making production process changes in a very constraining production process.

d. Task and work organization restructuring: Worker participatory processes

10. A multiple group project including clerical workers in Sweden begins with stress training and moves toward self-initiated work reorganization.

11. A multiple group project for foremen in Germany shows how to open communication channels in stress-loaded roles.

12. A multiple group project of locally developed job redesign in "health circles" for crane operators in Germany accomplishes many changes.

e. Task and work organization restructuring: Expert guided

13. A job enrichment programme for assembly workers in Sweden succeeds by a carefully designed learning-by-doing programme to undo Tayloristic job limitations.

14. A programme to reduce computer "hypersensitivity" for well-paid Swedish software designers succeeds via management "caring" but requires major investments in equipment.

15. A project in Japan opens up very limited discussions on the jobs of nurses feeling hopeless and caught in bureaucratic rigidities.

f. Person-based coping enhancement programmes: Expert guided

16. A counselling service programme for postal workers in the United Kingdom diminishes stress response and absenteeism, but has no effect on positive work attitudes.

17. An American trauma treatment programme temporarily augments coping resources, but appears mainly to protect the company against liability claims.

18. A person-based stress reinterpretation programme in Canada for unemployment assistance managers adds job redesign discussion groups for employees as a second step.

19. A person-based stress reinterpretation programme in India for coalmine managers and operatives adds job redesign discussion groups for workers as a second step.

Programme results

The general success of the stress programmes described in this volume is clearly demonstrated by results. Ninety per cent were successful in terms of either reducing stress symptoms, instituting positive work reorganization or making significant improvements in the problems identified. Of the nine cases with stress response information, eight report an improvement in stress response. Ten cases note a significant reduction in the problems identified at the initiation of the programmes. When organizational changes that are likely to lead to stress reduction are used as the success indicator, then 13 cases show significant improvement. Work reorganization processes which significantly involved multiple work organization levels occurred in six cases. In addition, other procedures, shown to diminish stress symptoms in other research, were also undertaken. Sixty per cent of the cases undertook a stress education programme which illuminated the environmental sources of stress. Seventy-five per cent of the cases started group discussions in natural workplace groups which identified sources of stress.

However, the figures above measuring programme success must be carefully interpreted. A truly accurate analysis of the results of the anti-stress programmes would require strict adherence to the primary goal of the stress reduction programmes: to reduce risks of workers' illness due to work stress. Obviously, worker-reported measures of stress or stress-related illness before and after the programme, or stress reports compared with a control group, would be the most straightforward measure. Unfortunately, we cannot use such measures to understand the results from our 19 case studies, except in a fragmentary manner, because the reporting of such outcomes is quite incomplete.

To compare all the cases, an alternative is to utilize data on positive changes in the work environment as the programme success criterion variable. All but one of the case studies allows assessment of the extent of change in the work environment. Work environment variables are the next most proximate dependent variable to stress in the causal chain leading to illness in Figure 2. Using the work environment change criterion places the appropriate emphasis on prevention of stress sources, but could undervalue the importance of individual coping approaches.

We can identify four kinds of changes reported in the case studies that reflect objective changes in the work environment: the dark vertical arrows in Figure 2. The first includes changes in **task structure**, such as psychosocial changes in skill, control, demand levels and support, or changes in physical interfaces and ergonomic and human factor considerations, or changes in other micro-elements of the work process affecting the worker. The second area of change in the work environment is the social context of the work process. This can include **communicative structural changes**: new communication linkages, interpersonal coping styles, new solutions to promote open communication and interpersonal trust. **Macro-organizational level changes** represent a third category which may include major changes in power relations or occupational categories in the companies, technological transformations, labour relations changes, management style changes, major policy changes, and changes in products and markets. Finally, as a fourth measure we have included **production process changes** (we also include productivity changes as an indirect indicator here, since productivity changes would be the combined result of person, technology and organizational factors).

In Table 2 below the measure of success is the combined scale of **total work environment change** per type of programme. This quasi-correlation analysis is not rigorous and, of course, the scale scores are the author's very rough estimates.

Table 2: Intervention type and success in work environment change
[Effectiveness = average work environment score (number of cases)]

Person-based coping enhancement programmes: Expert guided (4)	Ineffective
Task and work organization restructuring: Expert guided (3)	Moderate
Task and work organization restructuring: Worker participation process (3)	Effective
Large-scale work reorganization: Expert guided (5)	Effective
Large-scale work environment focus: Worker participation process (3)	Moderate/effective

"Ineffective" means no significant changes in any of four work environment change categories. "Effective" means significant change in at least two of the four categories, and some change in another category. "Moderate" means one to two categories with significant change, and "Moderate/effective" means greater than two categories with significant changes.

Factors associated with success and failure of programmes

Level of effort and programme success. The cases show that programme success is generally proportional to programme effort, as measured by the number of intervention steps taken. The exceptions are the "person-based" programmes which undertook some very comprehensive efforts, but which made little or no attempt to change the work environment using this platform of worker engagement. In five other cases, however, rather significant results were achieved, with limited efforts, by operating in the environmental change area. This can be important for readers who feel that starting programmes with environmentally oriented interventions is too difficult. Significantly, all but one of these programmes utilized participatory methods: worker discussions in work groups and stress awareness programmes. These programmes appeared to liberate energy to build a more extensive institutional support base.

Management's willingness to take the "risks" to relinquish some of its control over work organization is undoubtedly an important factor in programme success, but is hard to document with our data. Alternatively, the cases show that a management which was seemingly afraid to open up for such discussions and which opted for "person-only" intervention solutions ended up with programmes which had no positive impact in terms of increased employee engagement. The message seems simple: no risk, no reward.

Management/labour support and programme success. The degree of union participation toward the goal of creating a joint labour-management committee is associated clearly with programme success. The national labour relations context is important here. In the six cases from Germany and Sweden, the unions were considered a co-participant because of a legal mandate to have a participatory role. The three American joint programmes show that unions are willing to take an active role when they are given an opportunity to be involved. When programmes are initiated by management without strong union participation, programme success seems to suffer. When unions initiate programmes or when management and union both give strong support, programmes seem to have a much greater chance of success. One conclusion out of the case studies is that both unions and management have strong reasons to be supportive. Union membership benefits significantly in terms of improved health and more rewarding jobs, and probably increases when unions take an active programme role. Management gains in many ways through productivity increases which were reported in the case studies almost as often as reduced stress symptoms were reported. Of course, management also receives long-term gains through better utilization of the workforce and better employee relations.

Worker participation/expert guidance and programme success. Table 2 shows that active involvement by workers in planning or significant worker participation in group discussions on environmental changes were generally strongly associated with programme success. Expert-guided (often engineering intensive) programmes had a limited success in most cases, the only exception being programmes involving large-scale work reorganization changes, which proved successful.

Type of occupation and programme success. There appear to be four different occupational groups with different results.

1. The largest success occurs in a cluster of jobs that might be called skilled craft or operators' jobs. In these cases, significant changes have been made by combining substantial technical change with social processes that bring organizational change.

2. Another group consisting of manager and professional workers appears to report few significant changes. However, it should be noted that many of the programmes were person based for these jobs, perhaps reflecting the fact that the job conditions are already relatively good.

3. A third group with success represents lower-level service and clerical workers. Here substantial changes have been made, sometimes involving technical changes in the work process.

4. A fourth group has the highest potential stress because of its low decision latitude and high demands, including physical demands. Sometimes significant changes have been made here; however, person-based programmes show little effect on working conditions.

Team composition and programme success. Lack of complete data makes it difficult to assess the impact of project team composition. However, some potentially important skill areas appear to be present only to a limited extent. While all teams appeared to have some psychological and sociological awareness, there were seven that illustrated limited understanding by the team of social change processes. Only six of the cases appear to have had a medical professional involved; greater involvement here might have increased the quality of stress and health data, making it easier to assess the effectiveness of the programmes. Only six of the programmes appear to have had an engineer or technical team member, leading to a reduced likelihood of major work organization process changes. None of the project teams appeared to include an economist. Of course, employing team members with all these skills could make projects too expensive; thus, the solution would appear to be training in multiple skills.

Some productivity issues

An unexpected lack of productivity awareness. Pressures for increased productivity are clearly a component in many of the case studies, but there are curious omissions. Surprisingly, work reorganizations that might improve both direct labour productivity **and** health are rarely requested. Management's stated concerns for stress reduction programmes deal mainly with losses due to **indirect production costs** related to stress: health costs, turnover and absenteeism. However, reduction of **direct productivity losses** related to job stress (i.e. losses when workers are on the job, but working ineffectively because of stress) are noted as the main reason for the programme in only two of the cases. Direct productivity gains that could accrue to a company are, first, elimination of productivity losses that occur because of low worker motivation and poor work quality, and, second, reduction of losses in **potential** productivity that come from the diminished possibility of new learning, innovation and flexibility that are found together with stress.[17] This apparent "oversight" may only reflect researchers' reporting biases for a programme with stress reduction goals. However, the low priority may also indicate that managements still do not understand that worker stress can be behind many of the "otherwise invisible" productivity losses. We suspect that there is so much functional specialization in many firms that employee health issues are in one department, while productivity and production planning are in another.

Productivity improvements in the case studies. These cases provide fairly good evidence, albeit fragmentarily documented, that the stress prevention programmes can also lead to positive productivity improvements. This dual health **and** productivity result occurs particularly if significant work organization changes are also made. In six of the 12 cases in which the researchers have discussed productivity, results show significant gains in productivity. Significant future possibilities for productivity gains are noted in two other cases. We would tend to classify eight of the cases which report no productivity improvements as "missing data", unlikely to have even tabulated such information because they focused so specifically on personal stress coping (five cases), or they involved no significant work redesign, or the researchers had a strong health focus.

Lack of experts on productivity. Management's willingness to devote resources to a process which reorganizes the workplace, however important the stress reduction goals, will obviously be increased if productivity improvements could also be expected. This needed leverage for change was utilized in too few of the case studies. Case success shows that programmes which included personnel and resources to address the technical and economic issues involved in work reorganization were more successful in bringing about significant change. This reflects the need for more technical/economic breadth in the interdisciplinary focus of the programmes. This omission probably has disciplinary roots: medical professionals, psychologists and sociologists with interests in stress tend to focus on employee well-being, while engineers and economists often focus on productivity goals, closer to the direct interests of management. It should be noted that attention should be devoted to **humane** productivity issues. The humanistic sides of productivity de-emphasize quantity of output and emphasize, instead, skill-based aspects of productivity such as quality, innovation and customer adaptability which can be conducive to more humane, less stressful work organizations.[18]

Interpreting the results: Toward a model of the participatory stress prevention/work reorganization process

The above results clearly indicate that the success of anti-stress programmes is often related to workers' participation. However, for a participatory process to occur, broad institutional support is necessary, perhaps in the form of a joint labour-management programme, in order to create the trust necessary for open communication. Particularly important is the need to create the feeling, especially among low-status employees, that information workers share openly about their feelings of job stress, and their ideas for changes in the work environment, are protected from reprisals by management. Only within this atmosphere can shared new awarenesses, new vocabularies and joint new action necessary for a participatory programme be created. The union-initiated programmes confirm the possibility that the beginnings of a stress prevention programme could occur without management's support. However, for significant modification of environmental stress sources, a joint programme would have to be put into operation.

One important criterion of programme success from the perspective of worker involvement is whether the process of change becomes self-sustaining. The elements that are most associated with programmes that appear to be self-sustaining include the following:

(a)   employee feelings of self-worth are enhanced and validated by understanding stress reactions as normal and legitimate;

---

[17] Karasek and Theorell, op. cit.

[18] ibid.

(b)   worker groups are developed for discussion of work organization problems and development of action plans for solutions;

(c)   management places the needed economic and technical resources for change at the disposal of the process.

The most inhibiting aspects of programmes are the following:

(a)   programmes which direct attention far away from difficult working conditions, by treating symptoms only, orienting workers passively rather than actively to a job change process;

(b)   totally technical solutions which are imposed from the top. This probably robs the process of its self-sustaining benefits (of course, the programme could be positive in general);

(c)   management which retains constant control of the dialogue, either with awareness-limiting programme goals (development of coping strength) or management inhibition to discuss in work groups.

Using this understanding of the factors which either stimulate or impede a self-sustaining process, we can develop a model of participatory job change (Figure 3) out of our earlier stress development model (Figure 2).

We can first observe that many of the intervention steps in Figure 2 were observed within the same case, thus combining multiple intervention approaches, often in an ordered sequence. We see, for example, that stress education was often a first step, followed by group discussions of the problems and action planning sessions. In the few cases where technical and economic resources were addressed, they came at a later stage (except in expert-planned processes). The causal sequence also has some power. Even when the original programme design had nothing to do with job change, personal awareness of environmental issues was raised in the stress education seminars which seemed to lead to group discussions of work process problems as an almost inevitable consequence, particularly if the group members were from the same work situation.

Generalizing, we can say that the basic process we observe involves expanding workers' awareness and then providing workers with tools for active problem-solving in the new areas. This gives workers new understanding of linkages between persons and environments, which is an activating understanding. We can observe three types of activities at each stage in Figure 3: (a) workers gaining new awareness in areas such as stress, task organization and work system issues; (b) workers evolving for themselves new vocabularies of explanations to build action plans; and (c) workers evolving ever expanding understanding of work systems and possible solutions and limits, moving them to the next stage of awareness. In Figure 3 this process is represented by a process arrow which starts at the stress response discussions generating new awareness of the personal meaning of stress -- and moves leftward, in three stages, to the task situation and to work organization. Kuhn's crane operator study evolves the "health circle" concept to describe a similar process model. The Israel et al. automotive worker case study also presents a similar overview of their action research project: a series of overlapping phases in which movement from one phase to the next was triggered by the consolidation of accumulated learning into revised understandings of problems, problem contexts and intervention possibilities.

Figure 3: A model of the participatory stress prevention process

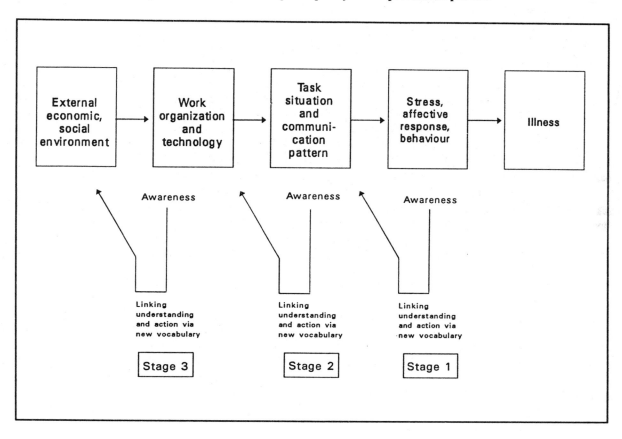

Stage 1: Awareness. Why do work humanization programmes dealing with stress begin with employee discussions of their health and its causes, when other work humanization programmes do not start this way? Simply because stress is not well understood in terms of its causes. Expanded awareness of stress's origins is a needed first step toward solution. This makes the stress-oriented work redesign different. Often negative feelings which may be caused by job stressors are not understood to have environmental causes by employees. Such anxieties are instead attributed by employees themselves or by management to personal weakness, family difficulties, and so on. A first step of awareness that employees' feelings may be caused by work validates the importance of such feelings and their naturalness.[19] In our own experience, when employees first clearly understand that the anxieties they are feeling are shared by other workers and can be clearly linked to the environment, and not to their own personal weaknesses, they are very relieved, feeling stronger and better about themselves. But workers are also angry at this point and ready to discuss energetically changes in the causes --often for the first time. The damaging stress feelings associated with depression about personal insufficiency are partially reduced by this awareness step alone. However, the energy liberated by this awareness must be dealt with by providing a forum for collective worker discussions about what to do, which lays a platform for the next step of activity.

Stage 2: Action vocabulary. A second step involves new vocabulary building. This activity occurs at each level of intervention, but is particularly important when workers review the task situation to develop new work organization ideas. In several of the case studies, group discussion about task-based stress led almost automatically to the next logical step of action planning to modify the work environment. But a new set of tools may be needed at this stage to clarify how aspects of stress are linked to different aspects of the job situation, since social organizational concepts can be too abstract for direct initial discussions. If workers, who otherwise have had little chance in their predominately rigid hierarchies to express themselves, can develop a new vocabulary, they can often dispel the feelings of impossibility of change and diminish the associated stress of depressive reactions. Once this

---

[19] Schore and Aktin, op. cit.

vocabulary is developed, workers can weigh and judge alternative solutions in verbal discussions. In the case studies, both Swedish public service workers and the German crane operators developed solutions via group discussions in this manner. It must be noted that this kind of communication involves truly free and creative interchanges among workers (and managers) that can occur only within an atmosphere of trust, often the result of a good joint labour-management agreement, a process initiated by the union, or aid from trusted outside experts.

Stage 3: System solutions. This process must now be extended a further step to the work organization change level. The crane operators in the German case succeeded in enacting their plans, not just in participating in drafting them, because they had the final ingredient of technical and economic support resources made available by management to effectuate the plans. In the Swedish public service worker case, in spite of the participatory planning, some of the groups did not enact changes because they had a restrictive organization context which, presumably, offered no such economic/technical support. After initial plans are discussed, the workers must be given practical support and resources for the process.

Workers must also be given information relating to larger-scale work organization issues, such as overall production flows and technology that affect their area, new product directions and competition. The impact of the economic and social environment, global economic competition, cutbacks, and so on, is directly felt and understood by all workers; thus workers can understand if data are given to them.[20] This context will quickly illuminate both the real constraints and the real possibilities the work situation offers.

New actors also are added to the process at this point. We observed above that the research teams almost always omitted an expert familiar with the economic and technical factors. Since these factors generally play a determining role in work organization, omitting them can limit the vitality of the intervention process. Presumably, such experts are omitted because they are assumed not to favour health-focused job redesign activity, but they should be included in the discussions. While opposition is certainly possible if the focus of the change is **health only**, once the psychosocial and work organizational issues needed for stress prevention are included, the picture automatically expands to include the productivity outcomes that are consequences as well. It is always possible in environment-focused stress prevention programmes to discuss **both health and productivity**. At this point, technical and economic experts and management representatives can also support the programme for its productivity advantages -- advantages that come from workers more willing to contribute when their well-being is improved by a stress reduction programme. This broadened focus may be inappropriately complex for the early stages of the process, but for final change making it is almost unavoidable to expand the range of participants in this manner.

Conclusion

The information in the case studies shows the importance of stress issues in workers' lives around the globe. One of the most striking illustrations of the health consequences of psychosocial stressors comes in workers' comparative statements about well-known physical work hazards. In one of the potentially most physically demanding jobs, coalmining, 28 per cent of Indian coal mine operatives report being disturbed about the physical demands of their jobs, while almost three times as many (72 per cent) are concerned about some of its psychological stressors. An analogous set of priorities was reflected by meat cutters in very physically debilitating jobs. When they could set their own agendas for discussing solutions, they switched from physical ergonomic hazards to the psychological stresses of their jobs.

When the new prevention strategies that these cases illustrate are combined with growing understanding of the magnitude of occupational stress problems around the world, they show that the time has clearly come for a shift in attention in occupational health prevention activities away from a "physical hazards only" perspective to a focus which includes full attention to psychosocial hazards. There is an accompanying need for new approaches to labour relations which move beyond wages and working conditions to encompass work organization.

---

[20] R.A. Karasek: *The 'conductivity game': Developing worker re-coordination vocabularies*, working paper prepared for the Center for Work Life Development, Halmstad University, Sweden (Halmstad, 1992).

Both of these challenges to our modern political institutional frameworks have been met in Sweden. The case study by Professor Lennart Levi describes "the case of Sweden", the nation. Sweden has created a strong platform for humane work environment change at the national scale with the revisions to the Work Environment Act of 1991 to include work organizational issues, combined with the participatory programmes of the Co-participation Act of 1978, the Joint Development Agreement of 1982, and the strong work research funding framework under the Swedish Work Environment Fund since the 1970s. The final element of this institutional and legislative programme was the work life programme of 1989 which recycled funds from companies into programmes for good work environment change programmes. These institutional solutions to the stress problem do not represent an alternative to the actions of participants in company-based case studies. Rather, the large number of Swedish cases included in this volume show that local action strategies and national institutional frameworks are complementary. The Swedish national framework has also served as a positive contribution to industrial productivity in Sweden, as is witnessed by the support the programme enjoyed from Swedish industry in the 1980s. Many workers and managers have already seen the benefits that such a comprehensive set of programmes can bring to both labour and management.

Resources on preventing stress at work

SECTION 1

Manuals and guidelines on combating stress

Begoña Casanueva[1]

Introduction

This section of the *Digest* analyses the most important features of a selected number of publications which provide guidance on how to combat stress at work. This analysis has the objective of introducing what is currently available for those who want to approach stress in a practical way.

The publications therefore have been selected for their common characteristic of giving practical advice. Yet they do so in many different ways, covering a wide range of contents, target groups and styles of presentation. Thus, for instance, some publications are very comprehensive and discuss in detail various methods to deal with stress at different levels, while others focus on some specific aspects, such as a strategy for stress reduction. Some are directed to a particular category of workers and others to workers in general, while some specifically address trainers. Some documents are written in an academic or scholarly style, while others are more practically oriented and use more concrete and plain language.

Despite all these differences, manuals on stress usually tackle the subject in the following sequence. First of all, the definition of stress is considered, with the objective of clarifying what is being faced. Secondly, the signs and symptoms of stress are analysed, with a view to helping readers to recognize the existence of stress and the need for action. Thirdly, the causes of stress or stressors are reviewed, in order to facilitate their identification, and the consequences of stress are assessed. Finally, after some understanding about stress has been grasped, action to eliminate or relieve stress is discussed.

This analysis follows the same sequence of presentation as manuals usually do. Because of the diversity of publications, on the one hand, and the overlap of items, on the other, only representative parts of a reduced number of publications are considered for each point under discussion.

A list of the publications reviewed, each one preceded by a number, is given at the end of this section of the *Digest* in alphabetical order by author. The number in front of the title will be given in brackets in the text when reference is made to a specific publication.

Defining stress

The concept of stress, taking into account the abstraction this term implies, has been extensively discussed in the literature. There is general agreement on the difficulty of defining stress in concrete terms. Regardless of this difficulty, it is agreed that one of the first steps to start combating stress is to define what it is.

The comprehensive guide *Understanding stress* (23) serves to illustrate this point. This guide has been prepared by the Office of the Minister for the Civil Service of the United Kingdom as a resource and working tool to assist all those who have an interest in stress.

When discussing what stress is, this guide, as well as many others, focuses on the response made by people to the demands made upon them, pointing out that these demands can be perceived as both positive and negative.

---

[1] International Occupational Safety and Health Information Centre, Working Conditions and Environment Department, International Labour Office.

Some degree of stress is necessary for people to function effectively. It is only when too much or too little stress occurs that performance deteriorates. The fact that stress results not only from major demands but also from an accumulation of minor demands is also indicated.

This physiological response to stress is presented as a process occurring in three stages:

— **primary stress response ("fight or flight") or alarm reaction**: it is the automatic reaction of the body to a perceived stressor, through which the individual prepares for action;

— **secondary stress response or stage of resistance**: when exposure to stressors continues, the body has no time to recover and, as a result of these demands from which the individual cannot escape, resistance occurs;

— **stage of exhaustion**: after long-continued exposure to stressors, adaptation energy eventually becomes exhausted and the individual falls into the third stage of the stress response, which may result in serious illness.

People have a capacity to withstand stress up to a certain limit, but they collapse or break down if that limit is exceeded. It is also pointed out that everyone has a different level of tolerance to stress and that the perception of stress-evoking demands varies from one individual to another. Consequently, each individual responds to stress in a different way.

The particularity of the guide *Understanding stress* (23) is that it has been designed to be read and used from several viewpoints: by the individual who wants to learn more about stress, its effects and how to manage it, as well as by the line manager, the trainer, and the welfare officer interested in the stress they experience and that of their staff, trainees and clients respectively. Hence, the guide consists of four parts.

Part 1, which is directed to the individual in general, begins by examining the concept of stress, its symptoms and the way to recognize stress responses. Factors which may cause stress are analysed, differentiating between personal and organizational stressors and measuring the cost of stress in general. Certain methods to manage and cope with stress are also presented. These include improving the general level of health through diet and exercise, relaxation techniques, counselling, job design, and participation and communication.

Part 2 is directed to line managers with the objective of helping them to recognize the existence of stress in the workplace and to reduce it. Unrealistic pace of work, lack of involvement, underload as well as overload, job isolation and lack of job security are some examples of job-related factors which increase stress at work. The following suggestions to reduce workplace stress are given: matching the individual to the job; listening and counselling; planning deadlines and objectives; and managing time and change.

Part 3 examines the role trainers can play in informing people about stress and helping them to control and manage it. A three-level approach (individual, occupational and organization) is suggested in order to look at individual problems in an appropriate context and to identify the most adequate solutions. It also contains a number of models of training programmes and certain resource training material to help to design training sessions.

Part 4 is designed to help welfare officers to recognize the preventive, pro-active role they can play in stress management and the way they can work with line managers and trainers to reduce individual stress and to manage occupational stress.

Manuals like this are very complete and provide detailed information not only on the conceptualization of stress but also on practical ways to deal with stress. On the other hand, there are publications that, while referring only succinctly on how to deal with stress, give complementary information to understand what stress is and how it is produced.

The documents *Stress och hälsa* (Stress and health) (15) by Lennart Levi and *Desgaste psíquico en el trabajo* (Psychic wear and tear at work) (3) may serve as examples. This latter publication, written by the Comisiones Obreras (CCOO), a major Spanish trade union, includes a questionnaire aimed at identifying physical and mental signs of workers' stress. Information on the nature of stress and the different responses to stress in female and male white-collar workers is contained in the booklet *Stress, health, job satisfaction* (7), which has been prepared by the Swedish Work Environment Fund as a summary of a series of research projects on stress and the psychosocial work environment. Looking at the negative consequences of stress for workers, the report *Stress, anxiety and depression in the workplace* (24) has been developed by the New York Business Group on Health in the United States. This report is intended to sensitize employers, managers and occupational health professionals to the prevalence of stress, anxiety and depression in the workplace and their impact on both employees and the work organization, and to promote their early identification and referral for appropriate intervention.

General information on stress and its effects can also be found in publications which cover different aspects of physical and psychic health such as, for instance, the booklet *Health and employment* (1) of the Advisory, Conciliation and Arbitration Service of the United Kingdom, which provides an introduction to measures employers may take to promote employees' good health. Stress is among the workplace health issues discussed in this guide. *The heart at work* (22) is another booklet of this type, developed by the Swedish Work Environment Fund, which looks at the stress caused by the social component of the working environment as an important factor provoking cardiovascular disease.

Recognizing stress

The importance of an early recognition of the signs and symptoms of stress is broadly emphasized in the literature. Manuals, in more or less detail, discuss signs and symptoms in the individual and in the workplace which indicate that stress is taking place and that it is necessary to act. Even though each of the signs and symptoms of stress may be due to other factors, the occurrence of various of these signs and symptoms at once may evidence the need to take anti-stress action.

The practical guide *Stress and the workplace* (2) has been developed by the Canadian Institute of Stress for the Industrial Accident Prevention Association of Ontario, with the objective of helping individuals and workforces to recognize the signs which indicate that stress is becoming a health and safety hazard in personal life or at work. This guide presents practical steps for controlling stress, pointing out that stress is better controlled when its signs and symptoms have been recognized.

The first part of the guide concerns personal stress control and presents a checklist aimed at helping individuals to recognize their first signs of stress. Physical, behavioural, mental and emotional signs and symptoms appear in this checklist, including respectively:

— dry throat and mouth, muscle tension, headaches, indigestion, tics, insomnia, high blood pressure, etc.;

— irritability, impulsive behaviour, difficulty making decisions, sudden increase in smoking or alcohol use, etc.;

— excessive worrying, feeling of worthlessness, brooding, forgetfulness, easily startled, day-dreaming, etc.

The importance of recognizing the occurrence of stress and the need for action is again pointed out in one of the basic suggestions given by this guide for achieving better control of personal stress: learning to pace yourself. Four steps for pacing yourself in situations which repeatedly cause too much stress are presented: recognizing the need for action; learning to relax and to reduce the tension build-up in your body; taking a second look at the situation causing your stress; listening to your own good advice about how you are going to deal with the situation. In dealing with any stressful situation these steps should be done in sequence, although in some cases one step might be omitted. However, recognizing the need for action is the first step towards controlling stress and must happen if the other steps are to work. Even the simple step of recognizing that the stress level is up, and deciding to stand back and take things a little slower, can be of help.

The second part of the guide deals with stress control in the workplace and includes a checklist for a first evaluation of stress. Low willingness to take responsibility or to make decisions, many complaints but few suggestions for solutions, little involvement with fellow employees, struggling to do normal tasks, arriving late and leaving early, frequent headaches and upset stomachs are some of the signs to be considered when evaluating stress levels within the enterprise.

Assessing stress

Given that the goal of any stress control programme is to manage specific causes of stress and their effects, related to both the work situation and the personal characteristics of the individual, an effective programme requires proper identification of the stressors causing high-stress situations and assessment of the work performance and personal problems derived from stress.

With a view to proper assessment of stress in the workplace, the guide *Stress and the workplace* (2) proposes involving workers in identifying those stressors which they feel cause unnecessary stress in their jobs, and in rating them to establish priorities for intervention. The assessment should be done in a systematic way and employees should be asked to express their concern about any situation that may be causing stress at work. Action planning for dealing with the selected stress targets should be subsequently established.

The *Occupational stress indicator* (5), developed by Cary Cooper, Stephen Sloan and Stephen Williams to gather information on groups of individuals, consists of six different questionnaires aimed at measuring both the sources and effects of stress in the workplace. The questionnaires are concerned with the following personal topics: feelings of satisfaction or dissatisfaction about work; assessment of current state of health, involving feelings and behaviour affected by the pressure at work and frequency of occurrence of manifestly physical problems; general behaviour; interpretation of events occurring around the subject and feelings about the ability to influence these events; sources of pressure at work; and experience of coping with stress. The final objective of this stress indicator is to allow organizations to measure the indicative aspects of stress and to quantify hidden factors provoking stress, in order to be in a position to take appropriate action.

Organization Design and Development, Inc. of the United States has published the *Burnout assessment inventory* (10) with the objective of evaluating signs and symptoms of burnout in the workplace. This document, developed by John Jones and William Bearley, looks at "burnout" as a generalized state of the organism that is characterized by a depletion of energy and significantly lessened personal effectiveness. The authors indicate that burnout is a result of four forces (system stress, habits, self-concept and quality of relationships) and has three dimensions (behaviour, attitudes, feelings). There are many different ways of experiencing burnout, which means that there is no one particular pattern of symptoms. However, it is also indicated that burnout signs and symptoms tend to group themselves into four main clusters: negative feelings about oneself, antagonistic feelings towards others, feelings of alienation, and feelings of withdrawal from one's immediate environment. This inventory is directed to detect signs and symptoms related to these four categories.

Blaming oneself, feeling guilty, sense of failure and impatience with oneself are examples of negative self-concept symptoms. Antagonism includes symptoms such as general negative attitude, feeling sarcastic and bitter, feeling defensive. Symptoms of alienation involve feeling bored, resisting going to work each day, experiencing rigidity in thinking, feeling immobilized. Withdrawal takes in such symptoms as feeling depressed, avoiding discussions, lacking energy, feeling indifferent, being absent from work frequently.

An action plan to identify sources of burnout and counteracting measures is described, as well as a so-called model of personal effectiveness, based on general strategies related to taking responsibility for oneself and managing personal energy.

Along the same lines as the previous questionnaires, the *Personal stress assessment inventory* (11) has been developed by Herbert Kindler from the Center for Management Effectiveness of the United States to help people recognize areas of their lives, at work and outside work, that may be contributing to excessive stress and evaluate their effects. This inventory consists of clusters of symptoms and causes of stress grouped into various scales. These scales are directed to assess the following: predisposition to stress; resilience caused by stress; both personal and work-related occasional sources of stress; both personal and work-related ongoing sources of stress; overall stress factor; physical and psychological symptoms; and personal reactions, which serves as a form of honesty check on the responses to the inventory but also may reflect sources of stress. Guidance in interpreting scores and some general advice are given in the last page of the document.

Combating stress

Once the existence of stress has been recognized and the stressors identified, action to deal with stress should be taken. Assuming that stress is a misfit between the demands of the environment and the individual's abilities, the imbalance may be corrected, according to the situation, either by adjusting external demands to fit the individual or by strengthening the individual's ability to cope, or both. At this point, it should be kept in mind that since stress is a multifaceted phenomenon, no simple solution is available. Furthermore, it is impossible to provide a unique solution to manage stress because of the particular circumstances of each case.

Practical guidance on the management of stress is found in the literature in a wide range of forms and approaches. In general and regardless of their differences, publications conclude that the ideal solution to combat stress would be to prevent its occurrence. This might be achieved by tackling the core of the problem -- the cause. However, there is no single cause of stress and the elimination of all stressors is an utopian task. Therefore, action should be aimed at eliminating as many causes as possible, so that the action taken reduces stress and prevents future stress. As this cannot always be achieved in the short term, it is generally agreed that improving the ability to cope with stress is a valuable strategy in the process of combating stress.

Preventive strategies

Despite the great interest in preventive anti-stress strategies, only a few manuals clearly focus on this type of approach. The Institute of Preventive Health Care of the Netherlands has prepared the manual *Handboek werkstress: Systematische aanpak voor de bedrijfspraktijk* (Handbook of stress at work: Systematic approach for enterprise practice) (12). This manual, intended for researchers, professional staff in organizations and workers' representatives, presents a systematic step-by-step procedure to tackling the stress problem at its source, with a view to preventing stress. Based on the handbook, the authors have produced another manual, *Stress door werk? Doe er wat aan!* (Stress at work: Do something about it!) (13), aimed at informing more specifically employees and trade unions on the possibilities they have to identify and handle stress at work.

Both manuals emphasize that effective prevention of stress at work should include a coherent set of steps.

Step 1 concentrates on the detection of the problem and preliminary activities, such as project team, budget, facilities and commitment of the parties involved.

Step 2 deals with the measurement of the causes and consequences of stress at work. Several instruments are mentioned: work and health questionnaires; checklists to help to determine well-being, job content and social relations at work; psycho-physiological tests; and administrative registration systems that serve to assess, for instance, absenteeism and disability.

Step 3 discusses the criteria to be taken into account when selecting which measures will be implemented to deal with stress problems. These criteria refer to the source of the problem, the objective to be tackled, the risk involved, the number of people at risk, the chance of success with the specific measure, and the potential for linking up with other measures.

Step 4 covers the anti-stress measures to be implemented which may be directed to the work situation, with a view to decreasing demands and increasing control, or to the individual, in order to increase the individual's capacity to cope.

According to the different aspects of the work situation which are to be looked at, measures can be addressed to:

— **the job content and job control**: adaptive measures (e.g. elimination of control problems) or reformative measures (e.g. job rotation, job enlargement, job enrichment);

— **the working conditions**: improving ergonomics in the workplace;

— **the terms of employment:** optimization of working schedules, adjustments in pay, increasing job security; and

— **the social relations at work:** changing management style, establishing consultation meetings at work.

With respect to the individual, the following measures are discussed: recruitment policy, vocational guidance, training, human resources management, vocational rehabilitation and health promotion activities.

It is argued that the implementation of the measures requires commitment of all parties, appropriate information and good preparation.

Step 5 deals with the evaluation of the results of these measures.

The book *Organizational stress and preventive management* (18), by J.C. Quick and J.D. Quick, points out that the destructive effects of stress in the workplace may be reduced through proper application of diagnostic methods and preventive management interventions. Thus, after discussing potential stressors and their consequences at the workplace, as well as methods of organizational stress diagnosis, practical advice on prevention is given. Effective action to deal with organizational stressors should consider both organizational and individual levels.

Methods of preventive management at the organizational level involve the modification of work demands, on the one hand, and the improvement of relationships at work, on the other. Methods directed specifically to one or another category of demands of the organization to which the individual is subject at work are task redesign, participative management, flexible work schedules, career development and design of physical settings. These methods are primarily concerned with modifying the formal organization in order to alter the demands that it places upon individuals. Organizational methods for improving the individual's working relationships deal with role analysis, goal setting, social support and team building, and aim at preventing the stress caused by role and interpersonal demands placed on individuals in organizations.

Prevention of stress at the individual level can consist of primary prevention, directed to the stressor with the objective of changing the individual's perception of potential stressors (e.g. constructive self-talk, planning and time management), secondary prevention, directed to the response in order to alter the individual's response patterns to stressors (e.g. relaxation and meditation, physical exercise), and tertiary prevention or treatment of specific stress-induced problems, directed to the symptom (e.g. counselling, medical care).

Coping strategies

Looking at various strategies which may help people to cope with stress in the workplace, the teaching pack *Living skills* (26) has been produced by the South East Thames Regional Health Authority in the United Kingdom. This handy publication has been designed for the use of health educators and aims at teaching people the skills they need to get the most out of their lives, in order to deal effectively with challenges and difficulties, and to cope with stress. The emphasis of this volume is on practical exercises in a group setting, as this practice provides opportunities to experience the elements of each skill presented in the pack and to obtain feedback from others.

The pack contains six practical units, each one dealing with a particular category of skills. Complex skills can be broken down into smaller units, which can be practiced separately before being put together. The units are presented as follows:

— the **Caring for yourself unit** discusses ways in which we look after other people, and uses this information to begin considering ways in which we can look after ourselves better;

— the **Assertion and fighting unit** looks at what assertion means and the different aspects of assertive behaviour, and describes some techniques which can improve assertiveness;

— the **Rational thinking unit** presents exercises to look at the relationship between thoughts and feelings, and suggests methods of counteracting thoughts in order to remove their unpleasant consequences;

— the **Relationships unit** examines skills which are important in keeping relationships working well, including those skills involved in listening and communicating, negotiating and caring for people;

— the **Stress management unit** focuses on practical ways of controlling the unpleasant effects produced by stress;

— the **Planning and organizing unit** analyses four groups of skills aimed at increasing our control over our lives, such as setting goals, managing time, keeping oneself motivated and making decisions.

A handbook with practical material for the groups is included in the pack. The different sections of this handbook cover aspects such as understanding stress, coping and advice on running groups.

The volume *Handbook of organizational stress coping strategies* (20), by A.S. Sethi and R.S. Schuler, is also concerned with stress in the workplace and the coping strategies that individuals and organizations need to develop. A process model of organizational-stress coping is described. This model offers a methodical approach to coping with stress that individuals as well as organizations may find useful. Several specific coping strategies are also presented. Those described in more detail are methods to enhance time management and ways to improve employee communication behaviours, the latter being aimed primarily at supervisors and managers. In addition, new practices for minimizing job burnout and the positive uses of social support groups, and the way these can be developed and promoted within the organization, are analysed. Finally, techniques that can be used at the individual level to cope with organizational and personal stress are explained in detail. These are meditation, yoga, biofeedback and physical activity.

There are publications that, when discussing methods to cope with stress, concentrate on specific strategies.

The second part of the book *Breaking the stress habit* (8), by A.G. Goliszek, illustrates various relaxation and meditative exercises as ways to help people to cope with stress. These practical exercises are discussed on the basis of conscious relaxation as a stress management technique which helps individuals to change their attitudes and behaviour, as well as to bring their bodies back into a state of rest and balance. The book highlights the need to develop people's ability to evoke a relaxation response -- instead of a stress response -- in a way that it becomes instantly and automatically available. In this respect, the following techniques are described in detail: progressive muscle relaxation, tension relaxation, meditation, and imagining and self-healing. Signs and symptoms of stress and job stress are also covered by this book, including various self-help tests and evaluations.

Many authors have emphasized the importance of counselling in order to help people through problematic periods which affect their satisfaction and performance on the job. An example of counselling as a stress-coping strategy is given in *The manager's guide to counselling at work* (19), by M. Reddy. This book examines the role of managers in the management of problems which affect performance at work. The skills of counselling are described in detail and structured into three phases: understanding (defining the problem), challenging (redefining the problem), and resourcing (managing the problem). The final part of the book looks at the ways the organization's goals may be in conflict with the individual's, and how this discrepancy will affect the way in which counselling can be translated into the context of the organization.

Practical guidelines

A considerable number of publications contain general practical advice on how organizations can assist in combating stress in ways that benefit both the employees involved and the organization itself. The book *Controlling work stress* (16), by M.T. Matteson and J.M. Ivancevich, provides practical guidance for the prevention and management of work-related stress. Attention is paid to the diagnosis of stress at work, as well as to stress management interventions at the organizational level and strategies to cope with stress for individual use. Specific programmes which may be useful to organizations, such as stress management training programmes, employee assistance programmes and health enhancement programmes, are also addressed.

Another publication which looks at how to control and minimize the amount of stress that employees are suffering is *Stress management techniques* (4), by V. Coleman. This book, useful for those who are interested in reducing the unnecessary exposure to stress of their employees, contains general suggestions on how to manage stress in terms of work organization and personal relationships.

General suggestions and basic guidelines for dealing more effectively with the stress individuals experience in organizational settings are contained in many other types of publications. The paper entitled *Stress management in the workplace* (9), by the Washington Business Group on Health, and the book *Stress management in work settings* (17), by L.R. Murphy and T.F. Schoenborn, describe, the latter in more detail, different aspects of worksite stress-management programmes. With regard to stress arising from processes of organizational change, the occasional paper *Managing stress in organizational change* (25), prepared by the Work Research Unit of the Advisory, Conciliation and Arbitration Service in the United Kingdom, describes some strategies for reducing pressures on individuals that may result in stress during these processes. Alteration of the production system, introduction of new equipment and establishment of new relationships are examples of changes which can take place within organizations. Aimed at trade union members, the publication *Stress at work: The trade union response* (14) has been proposed by the Labour Research Department of the United Kingdom, an independent, trade union-based research organization. This training guide looks at various aspects of stress, such as common symptoms, causes at work, women and people with disabilities, to finally discuss the trade union approach to stress and the action that may be taken to combat workplace stress.

Since everyone responds differently to stressors, each individual has to find his or her preferred methods of dealing with stress. In this respect, the author of *Managing stress* (6), D. Fontana, brings together the many insights offered by a psychological approach to stress and discusses the role of personality and the role of individuals' underlying belief systems in creating and fostering stress. It is argued that, when dealing with stress, individuals must look first at the environment to identify the demands made upon them and see whether these demands can be altered in any way, and secondly at themselves to see whether personal reactions to these demands can be similarly modified.

With respect to the demands made upon individuals, this book refers to three different ways to deal with stress:

— immediate action, covering those stressors about which something can be done at the moment (e.g. unclear role, poor communications, uncertainty);

— future action, covering those about which action can be taken, but the exact type and timing is not yet clear (e.g. overwork, too many meetings);

— ignorance or adaptation, covering those stressors which are beyond reach, at least for the foreseeable future, and which just have to be coped with as they are (e.g. powerlessness, poor back-up, poor pay).

With regard to the individual, this book emphasizes the aspect of "managing yourself" in terms of how to train people so that their cognitive appraisals do have a significant effect on the way they respond to stressors. Suggestions given in this respect are practicing meditation and relaxation techniques and physical exercise, letting go emotions, improving personal relationships and communication, and reappraising what is happening in your life in order to think about what is good and what could be improved.

Finally, in a very familiar style, the booklet *Sixty ways to make stress work for you* (21), by A.E. Slaby, presents simple ideas that each individual can put into practice to redirect the stressors of daily life. These ideas are grouped as follows: general suggestions to get people started in turning the stressors in their lives to their advantage; ways to learn to recognize physical signs of stress and to keep physical health in shape; ideas to develop self-awareness about stressors of daily life and to release emotions; general skills to improve social and interpersonal relationships; tips to help to reduce the pressure of workplace stressors; and ideas to learn to relax. The author concludes that turning the natural stresses of life to people's advantage involves combining awareness of physical health, nutrition, exercise, home or workplace environment, and interpersonal relationships into a personal plan for stress reduction.

List of manuals and publications
containing guidelines

1. Advisory, Conciliation and Arbitration Service: *Health and employment*, Advisory Booklet No. 15 (London, 1990).

2. Canadian Institute of Stress: *Stress and the workplace: A practical guide* (Industrial Accident Prevention Association, Toronto, 1984).

3. Comisiones Obreras: *Desgaste psíquico en el trabajo* (Psychic wear and tear at work), Cuadernos sindicales de salud laboral No. 1 (Valencia, 1991).

4. V. Coleman: *Stress management techniques: Managing people for healthy profits* (Mercury Books, London, 1988).

5. C.L. Cooper, S. Sloan and S. Williams: *Stress: Occupational stress indicator* (NFER-NELSON, Windsor, 1988).

6. D. Fontana: *Managing stress*, Problems in Practice Series (British Psychological Society, London, 1989).

7. M. Frankenhaeuser: *Stress, health, job satisfaction* (Swedish Work Environment Fund, Stockholm, 1989).

8. A.G. Goliszek: *Breaking the stress habit: A modern guide to one-minute stress management* (Carolina Press, Winston-Salem, 1988).

9. D.T. Jaffe, C.D. Scott and E.M. Orioli: *Stress management in the workplace*, WBGH Worksite Wellness Series (Washington Business Group on Health, Washington, March 1986).

10. J.E. Jones and W.L. Bearley: *Burnout assessment inventory* (Organization Design and Development, King of Prussia, Pennsylvania, 1984).

11. H.S. Kindler: *Personal stress assessment inventory* (Center for Management Effectiveness, Pacific Palisades, California, 1981, revised 1991).

12. M.A.J. Kompier and F.H.G. Marcelissen: *Handboek werkstress: Systematische aanpak voor de bedrijfspraktijk* (Handbook of stress at work) (Nederlands Instituut voor Arbeidsomstandigheden, Amsterdam, October 1991).

13. M.A.J. Kompier, S. Vaas and F.H.G. Marcelissen: *Stress door werk? Doe er wat aan!* (Stress at work? Do something about it!) (Nederlands Instituut voor Praeventieve Gezondheidszorg, Leiden, November 1990).

14. Labour Research Department: *Stress at work: The trade union response* (London, February 1988).

15. L. Levi: *Stress och hälsa* (Stress and health) (Skandia, Stockholm, 1990).

16. M.T. Matteson and J.M. Ivancevich: *Controlling work stress: Effective human resource and management strategies* (Jossey-Bass, San Francisco, 1989).

17. L.R. Murphy and T.F. Schoenborn: *Stress management in work settings* (Praeger, New York, 1989).

18. J.C. Quick and J.D. Quick: *Organizational stress and preventive management*, McGraw-Hill Series in Management (McGraw-Hill, New York, 1984).

19. M. Reddy: *The manager's guide to counselling at work* (British Psychological Society, London, 1987).

20. A.S. Sethi and R.S. Schuler: *Handbook of organizational stress coping strategies* (Balinger, Cambridge, Massachusetts, 1984).

21. A.F. Slaby: *Sixty ways to make stress work for you* (PIA Press, Summit, New Jersey, 1988).

22. T. Theorell et al.: *The heart at work* (Swedish Work Environment Fund, Stockholm, 1987).

23. United Kingdom. Cabinet Office: *Understanding stress* (HMSO, London, 1987).

24. L.J. Warshaw: *Stress, anxiety and depression in the workplace: Report of the NYBGH/Gallup survey* (New York Business Group on Health, New York, 1989).

25. G. White: *Managing stress in organizational change*, WRU Occasional Paper No. 31 (Work Research Unit, London, May 1984).

26. B. Wycherley: *Living skills pack* (South East Thames Regional Health Authority, Bexhill-on-Sea, East Sussex, September 1988).

Section 2

A selection of videos dealing with stress at work

Sylvia Hines[1]

About this selection of videos

This is a first selection of videos dealing with stress at work carried out by the Mental Health Media Council in London. In view of the predominantly English-speaking audience of this publication, practically all the videos reviewed are in English. Although a considerable effort has been made to extend the geographical coverage of this selection, it includes primarily British material. This may be reflected in the specific cultural background of some of the videos, as well as their availability in other countries.

However limited in number and scope, this selection has the advantage of focusing exclusively on videos about occupational stress, choosing from the enormous quantity of videos dealing with stress at large. Within videos on occupational stress, the selection has emphasized those which approach stress in a preventive way, dealing with aspects such as job design, interpersonal communication at the workplace, supportive management styles, and so on.

Only a few videos were found which met this selection criterion. The selection was therefore extended to include those videos -- a majority -- which concentrate on raising the capacity of the individual to cope with stress, dealing with aspects such as individual counselling at work, "training to cope", health support, and so on. Videos focusing exclusively on the alleviation of the effect of stress at the individual level were not considered. Further selection aimed at including only those videos which deliver an updated message and those which are of good technical quality.

Why use a video?

There is no doubt that including a video can make presentations or training sessions more effective and participative. They can provide a change of pace and can offer concrete illustrations of a particular situation that can then be considered by the whole group.

Alternatively, they can deaden a session and leave participants feeling cheated and frustrated. What makes the difference? Contrary to most people's expectations, the key element is often not the quality of the video, but the way the trainer has handled its presentation, how it has been integrated into the training course, and whether it has been planned with specific learning in mind.

Evaluating videos for training is therefore not easy, as so much depends on the group with which it is used, the setting, the overall relevance to the session and many other factors.

Of course, one of the problems for trainers is knowing exactly what a tape will cover. A complete description of each tape is therefore given below, together with brief evaluative comments and some suggestions as to how each tape may be used. These should help trainers to choose a video that is relevant for the session, but the success of the session will depend on how it is used. More detailed guidelines for trainers are given at the end of this section of the *Digest*.

---

[1] Director, Mental Health Media Council, 380-384 Harrow Road, London W9 2HW, United Kingdom.

Selected videos

☞ CAPTIVE LABOUR

Distributed by: Cinenova
Producer: Karen Ingham
Production details: VHS video; 35 mins.; 1988; UK

Summary

A look at the employment conditions of women outworkers.

Description

Focuses mainly on the hosiery industry in Leicester, which makes extensive use of women outworkers, often from minority ethnic groups. The tape includes interviews with women who work from home, who talk about why they need to do this, its advantages and disadvantages and the inherent stresses. The tape also covers in detail the underpayment of women outworkers and how they can also be expected to undertake dangerous work without proper health and safety supervision. Their situation makes it hard for the women to get together and organize.

Organizers of the Leicester Outwork Campaign talk about the difficulties the women face and how the campaign can help. The tape also includes an interview with a woman who is now working in a factory, who says how much better she finds it because of the companionship available.

Evaluation

A simply made tape, poorly edited in one section. However, it provides a useful perspective for organizations looking at increasing working from home, to prompt consideration of some of the difficulties, and is particularly relevant to workers from minority ethnic groups.

☞ COUNSELLING AT WORK: EXPLORING THE PROBLEM and FINDING NEW PERSPECTIVES

Distributed by: Creative Vision
Producer: National Association of Citizens Advice Bureaux (NACAB)
Production details: VHS video; 90 mins. and 60 mins. respectively; 1987; UK

Summary

This two-video pack provides information on counselling as a method to help employees release their anxiety derived from stress by allowing them to talk about their problems and to begin to manage those problems better. The two videos examine the counselling skills which need to be used in order to make an interview both effective and productive.

Description

The first of the two videos, *Exploring the problem*, examines the basic counselling skills that the supervisor needs to put into practice to help an employee in a caring and constructive way before a problem becomes unmanageable. Examples of ineffective and effective interviews are given and exercises aimed at discovering the negative and positive aspects of these interviews are presented. The video highlights the importance of allowing employees to talk about their problems and explore their anxieties.

The video presents basic counselling skills: setting the scene, giving full attention, showing confidentiality and empathy, and choosing the appropriate environment; listening carefully and actively; using body language, eye contact, silences and level and tone of voice; and giving space and permission to show feelings to help in coping with emotions.

In addition, this tape presents several general points for supervisors: finding time to talk; identifying a problem; handling interruptions; and dealing with unwillingness to talk.

The second video of the pack, *Finding new perspectives*, illustrates the further two stages of the counselling interview, where more sensitive and intuitive skills are demonstrated alongside the basic helping skills.

This video discusses once more the first stage of the counselling interview, exploring the problem, presenting again different examples of interviews between manager and employee, and analysing in depth these interviews. The importance of recognizing the need for discussion and looking for the right occasion to talk is pointed out.

A deeper level of the counselling interview is illustrated with a view to helping the individual look rather more objectively at the situation and bring a change in his or her perspective.

Evaluation

A practically-oriented pack, directed to users and to trainers, which examines in detail the role that counselling can play in combating stress at the workplace. Basic notions are constantly -- perhaps too often -- repeated throughout the two tapes.

☞ DANGEROUS LIVES: THE STRESS EPIDEMIC

Distributed by: Academy Television
Producer: Yorkshire Television
Production details: VHS video; 38 mins.; 1989; UK

Summary

Looks at the physiological effects of stress and at the types of jobs that are particularly stressful. Concentrates on increasing understanding of the incidence, underlying causes and symptoms of stress rather than giving positive examples of how working conditions could be improved.

Description

Opens with the claim that stress used to be thought of as affecting executives, not workers, but that it is now seen to be affecting people on the shop floor.

A worker on the futures market talks about how a health check helped him to realize the risks he was running because of his lifestyle and how he has now started to relax, take regular exercise and to watch his diet. An expert explains the link between health care and business: senior executives are expensive to replace and a good business needs its top people to perform effectively. A health and safety consultant talks about how stress used to be associated with mental stigma and was very difficult to talk about, but suggests that this is now changing.

The tape then presents a number of case studies. Ambulance officers are shown to be particularly vulnerable, as they have to deal with other people's distress, but are not helped to cope with the feelings it invokes in them. The stories of two ambulance officers are intercut; one who has suffered a stroke and can no longer work and one currently off work with a stomach disorder. The health and safety consultant then talks about the physiology of stress and two ambulance officers are monitored through 24 hours of work: this shows that their heart rates increase significantly when they are called out. Union officers and management are both shown to say that more resources are needed in order to improve the situation. Bus drivers talk about the symptoms of stress they experience. This is contrasted with the attitude of management; a transport personnel director claims that an element of stress is welcomed by the drivers as it stops the job being boring. A refuse collector talks about the major problems he experienced as a result of work underload and isolation when he was transferred to work as toilet attendant. For him, the problem was not the work itself, but the isolation.

Finally, the tape looks at examples of how new technology can create new demands. A variety of workers talk about the sense of being slave to a machine; about no longer feeling trusted because the machines are monitoring their performance; or, in the case of a factory worker, of not even being able to go to the toilet until someone can be found to take his place. One worker makes a plea for a value system that will take into account the human costs of systems.

Evaluation

The tape covers a great deal of information and many different types of jobs. Made for television, it has a good pace and variety. Could be useful for a session focusing on health risks, although some people may find the message rather heavy handed. However, the experiential information from different workers is excellent in drawing attention to poor job design and other stress factors -- not always those expected. In a session aimed at increasing awareness of job design faults and thinking about possible solutions, sections of this tape could be used as a prediction exercise. Participants would be given a range of jobs and asked to anticipate the most stressful elements. Their responses would then be compared with the information given on the tape. For managers, it raises the question of how well their systems work to enable them to hear the experiences of their workforce; for workers on how in touch their managers are and how their needs could be better communicated.

☞ ELECTRONIC SWEATSHOP (Quel numero? - what number?)

Distributed by: Cinenova
Producer: Sophie Bissonette
Production details: VHS video; 58 mins.; 1986; Canada

Summary

Women workers talking about how their work is controlled by the electronic machines they operate and how this makes them feel.

Description

Opens with footage of a supermarket checkout counter. A woman tells a long and amusing story about when the tills all crashed and how, after having tried to solve the problem, her position became intolerable and she had to leave. The women identify the main problem as being that they are expected to use systems and equipment they do not understand, with no back-up when things go wrong. Another woman talks about the humiliation of the way that the system checks on workers, creating the sense that they are not trusted. Workers are also asked to keep an eye on each other and thus team spirit is eroded.

The next section shows women doing extremely boring work at a post-sorting office. They describe how it has affected them at home as well as at work, saying that it is impossible to be unaffected by how you have to be all day. The final section looks at women telephone operators and the increased pressure that they face. Strict guidelines about how many calls they are meant to deal with in an hour mean that interaction with the customer has to be kept to a minimum.

The sections are a mixture of actuality footage and women talking to each other and acting out some of their experiences. It is warm and funny. The women predominantly speak French, with an English voice-over.

Evaluation

A long but enjoyable tape. There is extensive footage of work situations which could lend itself well to detailed analysis. The women's recreation of a stressful situation could be a good exercise to repeat with other workers to get rid of initial frustrations and then act as a prompt for role-play exercises about assertiveness.

☞ THE HIRED HANDS

Distributed by: Cinenova
Produced by: Broadside
Production details: VHS video; 30 mins.; UK

Summary

Looks at secretarial work: its stresses; the difficulty of moving up in the company; the dangers of sexual harassment and the implicit expectations of secretaries.

Description

Women talk about working as a secretary. Figures are presented to show that in the United Kingdom 98 per cent of secretaries are women, while 90 per cent of their bosses are men. A good secretary is felt to be too valuable to promote. One woman describes how she most resents making her boss's coffee: that if her time and skills were valued, she would not be asked to do that work. Several women say that the main problem is that it is seen as a manual job, with no intellectual challenge in the work. The next section looks at secretarial training colleges and the sexist assumptions that these make: that the women should be subservient, attractive and solicitous.

Many women also experience sexual harassment. The director of a temporary recruitment agency says that women often come to her having left their positions suddenly because they were being harassed, either by the boss or by others in the office. Finally, the tape looks at the changes that new technology will bring, but with little hope that any benefits for women will result.

Evaluation

Of average quality. The emphasis is on the difficulties; there is no attempt to address how secretaries' working situations could be improved. However, it is the only tape included here which explicitly mentions the problems of sexual harassment for women.

☛ HOW TO LAST A LIFETIME: WORKING FOR SURVIVAL

Distributed by: Academy Television
Producer: Yorkshire Television
Production details: VHS video; 26 mins.; 1985; UK

Summary

Looks at some of the different work situations that can cause stress; at the maladaptive behaviours that can result; and at how workplace counselling can help. Concludes by looking at the stresses of long-term unemployment.

Description

Part of a broadcast series, which looked at health issues for the nation. Studio-based with filmed inserts.

The video opens by comparing British attitudes to stress with those in Sweden or Norway, where employers have a legal obligation to protect employees from stressful situations. In Britain, it is claimed, there is a reluctance to talk about stress as it can imply that you are 'not up to the job'.

Two people with stressful jobs - a hospital sister in a cardiac care unit and a man working in a world money centre - talk about their work. It is clear that the pressures are high and the responsibility great, but both find it stimulating and challenging.

This is contrasted with the story of a woman -- now a successful investment manager -- who talks about a particularly difficult time she had when she joined an all-male management team and was constantly undermined and denied responsibility. She now handles an important portfolio and finds this far less stressful than that earlier undermining of her abilities.

In the studio, Professor Cary Cooper comments on the above footage, particularly drawing attention to how stressful jobs can lead to maladaptive behaviour -- such as smoking or drinking too much -- even when one is enjoying them.

The next filmed insert considers how under-utilization of skills can be equally stressful. Workers in manufacturing industries talk about the problems that arise from having to work at great speed, causing an unusually high incidence of people with weak hearts or ulcers, and occasional instances when a worker just loses control. A union representative claims that employers will often withhold evidence from the workforce and are unwilling to co-operate in looking at the real stresses on the workforce. In the studio, Professor Cooper asserts that employers who ignore the dangers of stress have not done their costings: that dealing with these problems at source actually does save money.

It shows example of workplace stress counselling at a bank, where the counsellor describes the service they offer. While this is an important first step, Professor Cooper suggests that one should also be looking much more broadly at issues such as mobility, regular medical screenings for all workers and autonomous work groups (none of these are shown). The final section looks at the stresses of long-term unemployment through interviews with two unemployed people. Both describe how they lapsed into depression and how their health suffered.

Evaluation

A well-made and useful tape, focusing on stress as it affects the wider workforce -- and the unemployed -- rather than managers alone, and covering most of the important issues.

☞ **HOW TO SURVIVE THE NINE TO FIVE: WORK IS A FOUR LETTER WORD**

Distributed by: Academy Television
Producer: Thames Television
Production details: VHS video; 41 mins.; 1985; UK

Summary

The first of a series, presented by Professor Cooper, this sets the general context of stress at work. What is it? How can we recognize it? What are the warning signs? It moves on to consider theories about why individuals react so differently to the same situations and concludes with one example of how people can deal with negative attitudes and habits.

Description

The tape opens with a montage of different workers -- ambulance driver, salesperson, tax officer, dentist, electronics assembly worker, company director, assembly worker -- talking about the stresses of their jobs. Professor Cooper talks about stress and how it affects our health as well as our self-esteem and confidence, and shows an on-screen self-diagnosis checklist.

Some people who enjoy their job then talk about their work. Two gardeners, who like the tranquility and seasonal rhythms of their employment, are contrasted with two reporters, both constantly active and busy, but who thrive on the stimulation. Why do individuals react so differently? A visit is made to a sports stadium, the setting for a detailed explanation of the physiology of stress reactions. Blood analysis of people competing on a race track is used to show that the chemistry of the entire body can be affected by the way an individual reacts to stress, and that "failing" in particular has a disastrous physical effect. A private clinic is then shown where personal profiles are used to assess whether people are in jobs which do not suit their personality and which therefore pose a threat rather than challenge. Different personality types are briefly described.

The final section looks at another, but very different, personal approach; one which starts by considering early childhood influences and how they affect attitudes to work, success, failure, and so on. It is suggested that you can effectively tackle other difficulties only when you have gained this type of insight.

An outward-bound programme for a group of women is shown as an example of how people can overcome their own negative attitudes. Working on the basic principle that conquering fear in these situations will help to conquer fear in other circumstances, these courses are also shown to offer many opportunities for problem-solving and team-building.

Evaluation

This tape is the most detailed of those reviewed on how different individuals will experience and react to stress. The first section, illustrating physiological responses and using the analogy of the race track, is common to many of the tapes reviewed here, but this is the only one to cover personal psychological histories. This could therefore be useful with a group thinking about definitions and causes of stress.

☞ HOW TO SURVIVE THE NINE TO FIVE: INVISIBLE CHAINS

Distributed by: Academy Television
Producer: Thames Television
Production details: VHS video; 41 mins.; 1985; UK

Summary

Focuses on the amount of control workers have, and suggests that stress will decrease, and productivity increase, the more control workers are given over their own time.

Description

This programme opens by showing how the different jobs within just one factory will offer very different levels of responsibility and satisfaction, through interviews with a marketing assistant, a process operator and a sales manager. It then moves on to a more detailed look at how people cope within different levels.

An ex-company director talks about the pressures of competition and his ambitious lifestyle. He is used to introduce the idea of Type A and B personalities. Friedman and Rosenman's study is described and followed by an explanation of the physiology behind this. The programme looks at how personality type is assessed and shows an example of talking groups as a way of changing Type A behaviour. Generally, it is suggested that telling people of the dangers to their health does not help them change behaviour; they will be more likely to do so if they can be convinced that they will work more effectively and efficiently in another way. This section concludes with a self-diagnosis chart identifying different behaviour types.

The programme next looks at the stresses in clerical and administrative jobs. A tax officer describes how the emphasis of his work used to be helping people to pay the right amount of tax, which felt productive and useful. Now he is under pressure simply to process cases as fast as possible and to collect as much tax as possible. This creates two major sources of pressure: that from the irate public, which they have to deal with, and that from management. Gareth Jones from the London Business School talks about how middle grades in particular are not consulted enough in the development of a business or service. They know a great deal about the way the work is actually organized and can contribute to restructuring or cutting back.

The final section of the programme looks at the shop floor, where lack of influence is even more of a problem, combined with an additional stressor -- boring and repetitive work. Three workers in the car industry talk about how it feels to be tied to the production line: not being able to go to the toilet without permission, the boredom and how this can lead people to violence. This is contrasted with another model of work where manufacturing is organized without charge hands or supervisors. The work is carried out by small groups of about ten people who decide themselves how to operate their equipment and organize their material. The workers talk about their various responsibilities, how they feel the stress is shared with their colleagues and how they prefer it to how things used to be organized. Two managers talk about it from their perspective. The work manager says that the aim was to create as flat a hierarchy as possible and to spread decision-making as widely as possible, paying everyone at the same grade. An under-manager says that is probably more stressful for the people at his level, but that he feels it is a structure which can work.

Professor Cooper concludes that the case for self-management is well-proven and that all industries should be looking to increase participation and be prepared to see this through to a share in the company profits.

Evaluation

The sections looking at middle management and the shop floor are particularly helpful and, as with the rest of this series, are very good at getting the perspectives of people actually doing the work. It could be a useful impetus for having managers consider what their workers would say and whether their workers' skills are being used properly.

☞ HOW TO SURVIVE THE NINE TO FIVE: ONE THANK YOU A WEEK

Distributed by: Academy Television
Producer: Thames Television
Production details: VHS video; 41 mins.; 1985; UK

Summary

Looks at the work of people who are providing a service; the stresses and strains that come from working with other people, the help that colleagues can give and how staff training or structural change can make pressures more manageable .

Description

Air staff (air traffic controller, cabin crew, etc.) talk about their work and how important they find it to have support from their colleagues when handling a difficult situation, or just to 'blow off steam' about awkward customers. A former secretary talks about the difficulties she experienced when working for a boss who never explained the context of her work and simply regarded her as an extension of her machine. She is very clear that the problem was not simply that he was difficult, but that she had no support. An example of training to help individuals to deal with these situations is then shown: in this instance assertiveness training through role play, as part of a gestalt-based stress management course. A self-diagnostic list is also shown.

The video goes on to look at the particular stresses of people who have to deal with the public. A one-man bus operator talks about the level of responsibility, made much harder to deal with because his job allows no real contact with the public. A social skills training session for police officers on how to defuse potentially confrontational situations is shown and a social worker talks about the particular pressures she found when working primarily by herself. Bureaucratic structures and hierarchies can cause another problem, illustrated by a hospital porter describing how he was rejected by the nurses with whom he trained.

The video concludes by looking at how a health authority in a rural area has adopted an integrated approach in dealing with these potential problems of isolation and lack of support. Community-based nurses can call on peers for support when in difficult situations and there is continuity of care and good communication. The authority considers that its investment in training is well-rewarded by the improved morale and reduced sickness absence.

Evaluation

Most of these segments could be useful discussion triggers. How is appreciation shown in your work situation? How are secretaries viewed? Are there workers in an isolated situation? Is team support encouraged, or are workers encouraged to compete against each other? What are the effects of formal and informal hierarchies in your organization? And so on ...

☞ HOW TO SURVIVE THE NINE TO FIVE: TAKING IT LIKE A MAN

Distributed by: Academy Television
Producer: Thames Television
Production details: VHS video; 41 mins.; 1985; UK

Summary

This final part of the series takes an overview of changing patterns of work; how having to find a new type of work can affect an individual's whole sense of identity; and how greater flexibility in working arrangements can benefit the female workforce.

Description

The tape opens with a Welsh farmer describing how his livelihood was destroyed by EEC legislation and the bitterness he now feels. From this introduction the tape moves on to a look at various trends in work and how they have affected people's sense of self.

Men who used to work in heavy industry talk about how deeply their identity has been challenged since their factory shut down. Examples are shown of men for whom it has offered an opportunity: they talk about their various responses: moving to a different industry, setting up a business, or taking early retirement and using existing management skills to help run a community centre. For others, however, the result of these changes is long-term unemployment. One man describes the social contact and support he gets from voluntary work as being similar to that at work and how for him it has been a positive development. Another man talks about how difficult he found it to lose the role of provider and how he took another, quite poorly paid job simply in order to be working again.

The programme looks at the challenges faced by women managers in traditionally male firms.

Two different models are shown of structures which allow women to combine their careers with a family. In one bank, women are able to take a break for as long as they like and, provided that they work two weeks every year, can then return to work at any mutually convenient time. An example is also shown of a service which allows women to work flexitime from a home base. Various women employees talk about the benefits of this arrangement and the manager talks about how she meets the extra demands which this places on building up social and business communication networks. Professor Cooper suggests that this could be extended into other industries and that it is by no means only appropriate for professional women.

The video describes employee assistance programmes (EAPs) and claims that they are well used by employees and are cost-effective for employers -- one American company is quoted as having saved US$10 million in one year in terms of improved productivity and decreased absence.

The tape, and the series, concludes by encouraging individuals to do something to help themselves: to identify the problem first and then to do something about it.

Evaluation

Another useful tape if thought of as a series of segments. The strongest section is that looking at how working structures could be adapted to suit women better. This could be used as a trigger for managers or workers considering the potential benefits of flexible working.

☞ JOB DESIGN/JOB PRESSURE - TEAM VIDEO

Distributed by: Team Video
Producer: Team Video
Production details: VHS video; 25 mins.; 1988; UK

Summary

Examines elements of poor job design in a number of service industries; and at the increased stress under which staff often have to work.

Description

Simply but neatly constructed video in six parts, looking primarily at work within the public sector.

1. **Job design: The importance of interesting work.** Shows a range of office jobs which have been broken down into very simple and repetitive tasks; workers talk about how these jobs make them feel.

2. **Job design: An alternative.** Looks at jobs where the employee has a wider range of tasks to do and is able to organize his or her own time systems. The employees interviewed say that this has made their work more interesting and a trade union representative outlines the benefits for workers and for management, while also drawing attention to possible dangers.

3. **Job design: Training.** A young computer operator talking about her work is used to illustrate how the skills of workers are not fully recognized or developed. Workers in this service are given no information about how their job fits into a larger picture. Training is almost entirely 'on the job', rather than a more structured system of staff development.

4. **Stress: When the pressure builds up.** Staff dealing with the public talk about the stress they feel. Most identify two main problems: the sheer volume of enquiries they have to deal with and the hostility they sometimes receive. A service manager draws attention to the fact that stress is greater for those who do not have the opportunity to manage their own time or workload.

5. **Stress: The hard sell.** Bank workers talk about how the expectations of their jobs have been changing and how they are now expected to sell products, rather than simply to serve the customer. A bank manager says that the philosophy has changed and that staff need to adapt to a new culture.

6. **Stress: Owning up to it.** A range of workers talk about stress and whether it is something that can be discussed at work. The common view is that one can identify problems, but that to admit how these problems are making you feel personally will be seen as a sign of weakness. A middle manager who had to take time off work because of the stress he was under says that he received a lot of support and it has made him a better manager.

Evaluation

A very simple but effective video, particularly for organizations wanting to look at job design. It covers a good range of jobs in the public sector and is very strong in its interviews with workers. It would be useful for workers and trainees, and especially for management training as the voice of people doing different jobs comes through so strongly. Each section could be shown as a stimulus to allow managers to consider the issue in their workplace. Questions could be asked, such as: Would your workers feel like this? How do you know what your workers feel? How could you look at job structures to consider whether they could be improved? How would you respond to someone who said they were suffering from stress?

☞ LIVING UNDER STRESS (PERSPECTIVE)

Distributed by: CFL Vision
Producer: London Television Service
Production details: VHS video; 26 mins.; 1990; UK

Summary

This video discusses the harmful effects of stress on the human body, showing the physical reactions which take place when an individual is under stress. Causes, signs and symptoms, and consequences of stress, as well as preventive measures and treatment, are indicated.

Description

Starting with images of busy women at work, causes of stress are analysed, not only at work but also in everyday life. The "fight or flight" theory is described. After simulating stress with video games and tests during a normal day of work of a young waiter, the stress response is measured through physical signs and symptoms. The process by which stress affects the brain, producing chemicals which have an effect on the body, is explained. It proposes that stress can be diagnosed physically and emotionally in terms of blood pressure, blood chemistry, cholesterol and level of satisfaction.

The tape then refers to the consequences of the stress derived from changes occurring in modern society. It describes Type A behaviour individuals as a category of people at risk. Teaching is seen as a very stressful profession.

It is indicated that when tolerance to stress reaches its limit, the individual becomes exhausted and his or her general performance decreases. Therefore, measures directed to prevent and treat the consequences of stress are presented, in particular learning how to relax, sleeping well, breathing properly, osteopathy, exercise, positive thoughts, and yoga and meditation.

Evaluation

Useful for individuals who want to know more about stress, especially its physiological mechanism. The video concludes that although people cannot escape from the pressure placed upon them, they can change the way they tackle this pressure. Some simple suggestions are given on how to change people's behaviour for a different approach to everyday life, such as setting priorities, practising positive thoughts and taking pleasure from simple things.

☞ MANAGING PRESSURE AT WORK

Distributed by: BBC Training Videos
Produced by: BBC Training Videos
Production details: VHS video; 20 mins.; 1991; UK

Summary

A concise overview of the definition and causes of stress in the workplace, its costs to business and the preventive measures that can be taken.

Description

The tape opens by offering a definition of stress as occurring when the amount of pressure exceeds an individual's ability to cope. Physiological parallels are drawn between how the body reacts to the excitement and risks of the racing track and a stressful day at the office. The cost to business of the working days lost due to stress-related illnesses is strongly emphasized. The video explains the difference between pressure and stress and shows the standard chart of a worker's efficiency, stressing that every individual's chart would be different, so that part of the task of managers is to find the right person for the job. It recalls that managers must be sensitive to the human needs of their workers, the pressures of home life, etc., and they should offer preventive maintenance, rather than simply remedial strategies. It goes on to describe the health problems that stress can cause and the physiological reasons, and shows some of the early warning signs, such as difficulty in making decisions, resistance to change and specific physical symptoms such as backache or stomach aches, as well as a high incidence of sick leave and turnover.

The second part looks at ways to reduce stress levels. It puts forward the idea of stress carriers, those who are not badly affected themselves, but create stress in others. It goes on to draw attention to the problem of 'rust-out' (the opposite of burnout), the sheer boredom that many workers experience, that is an important cause of stress.

The tape concludes with a set of recommendations: vary the job; give people more control, look at flexi-working, say thank you.

Evaluation

This is a pacy, well-produced overview and analysis of the issues of stress at work. It moves quickly over many topics, and so offers less depth than many of the others, but makes up for this with its speed and energy. It is also very directive, using several charts and checklists, rather than exploring issues. It comes with a clear and well thought-out training pack, but also lends itself very well to self-directed learning on the part of managers, rather than as part of a training session.

☞ MANAGING STRESS

Distributed by: Melrose Film Productions (UK); CRM Films (USA)
Producer: CRM Films
Production details: VHS video; 26 mins.; 1990; USA

Summary

Short, well-paced overview of causes and physiology of stress and ways of dealing with it. Produced as a training video, including trainers' notes.

Description

The video opens with some brief dramatized scenarios, to open a discussion about "what is stress?". The "threat, fight, flight" theory is illustrated through a cartoon; and then through an acted scenario which shows how the stress response can help us survive (a pedestrian avoiding an oncoming car). This theory is then put into the context of the office, where people are asked to meet mental rather than physical demands. A dramatic scenario is acted out where two people are asked to give a presentation at a very pressured meeting: for one it is a positive challenge; for the other it is too much. This video uses the terminology "stress" and "negative stress" to describe what many would identify as "pressure" and "stress". It likens negative stress to a virus, which affects both us and those around us (also illustrated by a dramatic scenario).

The second section considers job design, quoting a study of pilots during the Second World War which showed that it was the co-pilots, those not in charge, that were more likely to experience nervous problems. It describes how a survey of manual occupations shows that stress occurs most in assembly-line workers, who have little control over their work, are often isolated from co-workers and get little support from their supervisors.

The next section looks at personality types and how individuals can make pressures worse by their own self-imposed rules. A cartoon illustrates Friedmen and Rosenman's A and B type personalities and goes on to show how the vicious cycle can be broken, through steps such as learning to live with change, taking risks, or opening lines of communication.

The video concludes by briefly mentioning employee assistance programmes and other steps individuals can take to relieve their stress: physical exercise, good nutrition, mental relaxation, allowing themselves to feel bad or angry for a fixed amount of time and then to move on, letting off steam with others, establishing a support network, establishing priorities and taking each task in order, and delegating.

Evaluation

Well constructed and fast moving, making good use of varied visual material from cartoons to dramatized sequences. It was refreshing to see different illustrations of the physiology of stress than the over-used trip to the race track. It is also rare amongst the videos reviewed here in its portrayal of Black people, who are presented in strong and competent roles. Many of its issues are mentioned rather than fully explored, but this makes it a rich training tool which could work well with many different groups of people.

☞ STRESS AND YOU

Distributed by: Gower
Producer: Occupational Health Department of ICI Polymers and Chemicals
Production details: VHS video; 45 mins.; 1987; UK

Summary

This video examines signs and symptoms, possible causes and practical ways to deal with stress, with a view to helping individuals to manage their stress, both at work and in their personal life. It is supported by a handbook for participants as well as a guide for trainers.

Description

Illustrated with cartoons, the three parts of the video emphasize respectively the importance of recognizing the signs and symptoms of stress, of identifying its causes at work and outside work, and of developing a positive approach to stress management.

The first part defines what stress is and why it occurs. It is pointed out that some amount of stress is necessary for individuals in order to function properly. Attention is paid to individual differences and to the fact that even desirable events which involve change can create stress. The physiological mechanism through which stress occurs is analysed. Finally, three categories of symptoms of stress are explored: emotional (e.g. depression and anxiety in the long term); behavioural (e.g. drinking, smoking); and physical (e.g. tense and painful muscles, high blood pressure, diarrhoea or constipation).

The second section analyses some common causes of stress, presenting situations which most individuals find stressful: change, which is as inevitable as is stress; too many demands at work and outside, as well as the opposite situation of not enough stimulation; other people, such as colleagues, family and the society; oneself because of the unnecessary pressures people put on themselves; worries and fears that individuals suffer; and poor communication, not only at work and at home but also to oneself.

The third section of the tape presents different techniques to help individuals to manage stress. These include relaxation, which may include simple activities as well as more sophisticated techniques, such as hypnosis; talking things over, whether to specialists or to a partner, friend or colleague, and listening to others; self-talk in order to think rationally and positively, to control one's own reactions to an event; time management and identification or priorities; and making action plans, to identify what is and what is not under one's control, to change some of the causes of stress in one's life.

Evaluation

A well-structured and practical video, useful to both individuals and trainers. Subjects are clearly presented and a summary is given following the discussion of each one. The participant's handbook contains useful checklists in each section presented.

☞ STRESS AND YOU

Distributed by: Video Communication Services
Producer: Northampton Health Authority
Production details: VHS video; 16 mins.; 1985; UK

Summary

This video illustrates the causes of stress and its effects on the individual, discussing ways to recognize and manage stress. People in different occupations (school teacher, caretaker, secretary and housewife) refer to their own experience in relation to stress.

Description

The video firstly defines stress and explains how it is produced. The presenter indicates that to be able to tackle stress, one should first find out what stress is. He explains that the natural response to demands made upon individuals in the course of their daily life develops in three stages: alarm, action (which can take the form of fight or flight), and relaxation. Whenever the energy built up is not released in the third status, harmful effects can occur. The effects of too much stress are reviewed, ranging from minor illnesses, such as common colds, headaches and indigestion, to serious disorders such as heart disease. The effect of increased tension leading to an increase in blood pressure and cholesterol level and then causing heart problems is explained. Excessive stress can result in anxiety or depression. Signs which help to recognize anxiety include abnormal eating habits, nervousness, trembling, inability to slow down or relax, and trouble breathing. Depression can be manifested in terms of feelings of helplessness, worthlessness, sleeplessness, and loss of interest in food, sex and life in general.

The importance of identifying the causes of stress is also emphasized. Change, both negative and positive, such as loss of the job, personal loss (divorce, death of a close relative), retirement, starting a new job, being promoted, holidays, moving home, marriage or the birth of a baby, is an important cause. Individuality, referred to as trying to be one's own person while taking into account societal norms, is described as another cause.

Finally, the video presents some suggestions on how to cope with stress, including adopting a positive attitude, practical habits that make people feel in control and exercise, as well as practicing yoga, meditation and hobbies.

Evaluation

Varied and useful overview of different occupations suffering from stress, analysing in detail issues such as the negative consequences of stress, and giving practical advice on how to manage stress.

☞ STRESS MASTERCLASS

Distributed by: Melrose Film Productions (UK)
Produced by: Melrose Film Productions (UK), Video Learning Systems (USA)
Production details: VHS video; 20 mins.; 1991; UK

Summary

A round table studio discussion between Professor Cooper and managers in public service, a charity and business.

Description

The group begins by working towards a definition of stress and its symptoms. The stress process is then illustrated with a diagram showing how individual and environmental factors all contribute to a state of stress. The tape continues with members of the group talking personally about the situations they find stressful: all of them identify feeling undervalued as a major factor. This leads into discussion about how management style is a major factor in workers' stress. The group discusses coping and preventive strategies.

One of the women participants then talks about how she deals with the interface between work and home. She describes the conflicts of having two areas of responsibility and her methods for relaxing. This leads into a distinction between "adaptive behaviour", such as seeking support, talking to colleagues, and the like, and "maladaptive behaviour", seeking distractions, avoiding situations, smoking or drinking.

To conclude, the video invites its viewers to consider whether they are under stress, what the symptoms are and how to deal with it. It also talks about the value of employee assistance programmes, of holding company stress audits to find out how people are feeling, introducing more flexible working arrangements and finally, expressing appreciation of the work people do.

Evaluation

The tape benefits from Professor Cooper's energy and humour and covers its chosen ground well and thoroughly.

☞ STRESS SERIES

Distributed by: Concord Video and Film Council
Producer: Guardian Royal Exchange
Production details: VHS video; 4 x 15 mins.; 1991; UK;

Summary

This is a series of four case studies of individuals who have experienced extreme stress. Each tape has the same beginning and ending.

Description

Common features: each tape opens with the easily identifiable conventions of a horror film to make the point that stress cannot be easily recognized; if it could, it would not be such a problem. Stress is defined and the tape goes into a scripted interview with a particular individual. It concludes with comments on the case and a summary of general stress indicators and individual steps that can be taken to deal with it. The case studies are primarily talking heads with dramatized inserts.

Case studies

Peter Rogers. Following a promotion at work, he relocated and his wife gave up her job. Ostensibly everything was going well. However, his work started to encroach into his home time, causing him to miss important family occasions and creating conflict with his wife. He began to suffer severe headaches and finally just could not go to work one day. Looking back, he identifies his main mistake as being not to trust the people he was working with, taking more and more on himself rather than delegating.

Pauline Marshall. Pauline describes how she had been employed as a catering assistant, work that she had enjoyed, particularly for the good relationship with her colleagues. Her problems began when she was promoted to the position of supervisor. She no longer felt one of the group, could not cope with the paperwork, and was afraid to ask for help. The stress she was feeling at work began to affect her home life. As a result, she changed her job and became much happier.

Bob Fraser. Now retired, Bob describes how he found it very difficult to establish a new sense of identity when he left work. He had enjoyed the challenges, the fact that he was relied on and the social life it offered. Outside work, he had no social networks and was suddenly left with nothing to do. We see him at the point he is beginning to do some of the things he always wanted to.

Sandra Taylor. Sandra is a young and successful personnel manager. Her success at work caused her relationship with her husband to break down, as he felt quite competitive with her. This left her feeling vulnerable at the same time as she had a new manager who expected her to be more accountable. The difficulties came to a head when asked to make a speech at a conference, which she felt she could not cope with.

Evaluation

The tapes have been made on a low budget and are of poor technical quality. In addition, they are stylized and appear to be scripted and acted throughout. However, they allow a detailed consideration of particular situations and are useful in drawing attention to how home and work can both suffer. They could be used as a springboard for detailed work with a group identifying stressors, how home and work interrelate, and planning remedial measures.

☞ WORKING TERMS

Distributed by: Team Video
Producer: Team Video
Production details: VHS video; 20 mins.; 1984; UK

Summary

An early film taking a detailed look at the introduction of new technology into a public service setting in England.

Description

Includes interviews with workers, management and the union. The introduction of new technology into the service was poorly managed and caused a dispute with the union, as a result of which a new technology agreement was drawn up between management and the union. Women workers talk about the inadequate training and preparation they received; how this made them feel and how angered they were when their complaints were met by a 'hard-line' management threat of suspension. Management meanwhile place the blame on the union for blocking the change for too long. Workers in the typing pool worry about the staff reduction new technology will cause, even though redeployment has been offered.

A conflict is apparent between middle and senior management about management styles - middle management feeling that this type of agreement is limiting their right to manage; senior management feeling that they have to manage by consensus and that this is the way to move forward.

Evaluation

Simply constructed. The video is almost entirely 'talking heads', but aside from this and a slightly dated feel, it remains powerful because of the strength of the interviews. Potentially very useful as a case study of the difficulties which change can cause, especially as a result of poor communication. Viewers could be given the situation and asked to predict the responses of different groups and then compare these with how the groups did react. Alternatively, the tape could be viewed and viewers then asked to plan a different way of handling the situation.

Guidelines for trainers

Evaluating your practice

How many times have you used a video in training? And how many of these times did you ask the group to watch the entire programme and to discuss it afterwards? Did you give the group guidance, by asking them specific questions, or did you just ask them "what did you think"? There can be many reasons why we use a video in this way - it can save the time of preparing an input or presentation; it can fill an awkward gap in a session, or the video may seem so good that it deserves to be seen in its entirety; or you may just be stumped for other ideas.

Evidence from trainers suggests, however, that in the vast majority of cases this unguided use of video is a poor training tool. It can deaden a session, putting people into a "passive" mode. Asking people for immediate responses almost always draws out negative and critical responses first and this can then make it hard to focus the discussion on other aspects of the video. It is worth taking a few minutes to think about the ways you have used a video and the impact it had: when did it work best? what were the contributory reasons?

The suggestions below are intended as a repertoire of ideas that you can adapt for different occasions. Not all will always work: the key is to keep trying and keep on evaluating and reviewing your practice.

Choosing a tape

Don't let your ideas be governed by the tape. Trainers often look for the tape that will present all the information they want to cover, perhaps even more authoritatively than they feel they can -- by having the benefit of an "expert", for example, or of clear graphs and diagrams. You may feel that a definition of stress coming from an expert will have more authority than one you can give, or one that you elicit from course participants. This is not necessarily so: participants will usually remember a definition that they have worked towards far better than one they have simply been told or shown. There are other ways to engage people. Why not use the tape as "devil's advocate", showing something you disagree with, for example, and generating a lively discussion.

It is also tempting to choose a tape that covers working practices or industries most similar to yours. This is not necessarily the most effective approach. Sometimes relatively small differences can become a distraction and the discussion can too easily become focused on them. Showing a completely different industry can allow people to see things they no longer notice around them, and these insights can then be applied to their current situations.

Your repertoire of tapes

The above tapes are all made specifically about stress at work. However, there are many other resources you can use to think about the same issues. Many television programmes include footage or dramatized portrayals of work situations: these can be used to analyse the stress that the workers or characters may be under, even if it is not the purpose of the programme.

Showing extracts

When you are planning your session, watch the whole tape and keep a note of the information it presents. Then ask yourself the following questions:

- Is all this information relevant to the aims of this training session?
- Would some of it have more impact if covered in another way?
- Will you have already covered some of the information?
- Do you agree with all the messages (both overt and covert -- see later for more about this) of the tape?

- If there are messages that you do not agree with, are they none the less representative of dominant views about the subject?
- Might there be a value in looking at them and discussing why they are problematic?

Having answered these questions, draw up a plan of the tape in its different segments, marking which ones you will want to use. If you have enough time you may want to use the whole tape, but in different sections throughout the day, rather than showing it as a whole.

Working with extracts

Generating hypotheses. Show an extract of the tape and ask participants to make various hypotheses.

For example, a number of the tapes described above include footage of men or women who have extremely stressful jobs, but who enjoy their lifestyle and who have adopted various means of coping with it. This could be shown as a discrete extract, with the group then being asked to evaluate what they have seen in terms of their potential health risks/benefits; the impact on others in the individual's organization/family, and so on. They could then go on to look at their own behaviours and impacts.

Close analysis. Focusing on one extract can allow close analysis of what is actually going on. Turning the sound down can help with this even further.

For instance, many of the videos show footage of particular work situations. This could be shown and group participants asked to identify the particular stress factors in the work situation shown and, further, how these could be reduced. Their predictions could then be compared with what the workers themselves say.

Role-play. Lack of assertiveness or conflict at work can be major causes of stress and many of the tapes include people describing situations where they have felt 'put upon' or unappreciated.

Such an extract could be shown and participants then asked to role play how they would deal with such a situation.

Covert messages

Video is a dense and complex medium. While all the videos described above have their very clear overt messages, often spelt out by the guiding 'expert', many other messages can be conveyed implicitly through the choice of the information and views selected. For example, the video tapes are mostly very poor in representing Black or Asian employees among the workforce. None address the stress that can be caused by racism in the workforce and few address that caused by sexism. It will be important to bring this out when using any of the tapes. It is necessary to draw participants' attention to this and ask them to consider the situation in their own workplace. What *isn't* shown can be as important as what is.

In conclusion

Your video is a resource for you as a trainer to use, just as much as a flipchart. The flipchart would never run a training session -- neither should a video.

Distributors' addresses

Academy Television

104 Kirkstall Road
Leeds LS3 1JS
United Kingdom
Tel: (0532) 461528

BBC Training Videos

United Kingdom
BBC Training Videos
Woodlands
80 Wood Lane
London W12 0TT
Tel: (081) 576 2361

Australia
BBC Training Videos
Suite 101
80 William Street
East Sydney, NSW 2011
Tel: (02) 360 3111

United States
BBC Training Videos
630 Fifth Avenue
Suite 2220
New York, NY 10111
Tel: (212) 373-4100

Canada
BBC Training Videos
Cinevillage
65 Heward Avenue
Suite 111
Toronto, Ontario M4M 2T5
Tel: (416) 469 1505

CFL Vision

P.O. Box 35
Wetherby, West Yorkshire LS23 7EX
United Kingdom
Tel: (0937) 541010

Cinenova

113 Roman Road
London E2 0HU
United Kingdom
Tel: (081) 981 6828

Concord Video and Film Council

201 Felixstowe Road
Ispwich
Suffolk IP3 9BJ
United Kingdom
Tel: (0473) 726012

Creative Vision

Burton House
Burtonhole Lane
London NW7 1AL
United Kingdom
Tel: (081) 959-0275

CRM Films

2215 Faraday Avenue
Carlsbad, CA 92008-7295
United States
Tel: (619) 431-9800

Gower

Gower House
Croft Road
Aldershot, Hampshire GU11 3HR
United Kingdom
Tel: (0252) 331551

Melrose Film Productions

16 Bromells Road
London SW4 0BG
United Kingdom
Tel: (071) 627 8404

Team Video Productions

105 Canalot
222 Kensal Road
London W10 3BN
United Kingdom
Tel: (081) 960 5536

Video Communication Services

Eden Lodge
St. Crispin Hospital
Berrywood Road
Auston, Northampton NN5 6UN
United Kingdom
Tel: (0604) 580944

SECTION 3

Annotated bibliography on occupational stress

Introduction

This annotated bibliography covers a wide range of publications on stress at work, including scientific, organizational, managerial, psychological and physical aspects of the problem. Hence, the monographs, articles, reports and conference proceedings described in this bibliography are aimed at a wide variety of audiences. Special attention was given to including publications with a practical orientation and about preventive approaches. Although some of the publications refer to medical and occupational safety and health aspects of stress at work, technical publications which focus in-depth on those subjects are not generally included.

The bibliography is divided into two sub-sections. The first covers documents on stress in general, while the second describes documents on stress in different occupations or kinds of work. The publications referring to specific occupations have been selected in line with, and to complement, the occupations covered by the case studies on occupational stress appearing in this volume of the *Digest*.

Entries are generally restricted to publications issued after 1985, with emphasis on the most recent ones. The language covered is primarily English, although publications in other languages are also included.

Annotations for manuals and publications which contain guidelines on the prevention and management of occupational stress are presented separately in Section 2 of this part of this *Digest*. However, the titles and bibliographic information are listed in this section as well.

The publications included in this bibliography have been located through a variety of sources, particularly the ILO's International Occupational Safety and Health Centre (CIS), the ILO library's information system, LABORDOC, and with the assistance of several experts on the subject.

A. Documents on stress in general

1

ANESHENSEL, CS   RUTTER, CM   LACHENBRUCH, PA
> "SOCIAL STRUCTURE, STRESS, AND MENTAL HEALTH: COMPETING CONCEPTUAL AND ANALYTIC MODELS"
in AMERICAN SOCIOLOGICAL REVIEW (New York), 56, April 1991, 166-178.

The authors distinguish between sociological models that focus on the consequences for mental health of patterns of social organization, and sociomedical models that emphasize the social antecedents of mental disorders. They point out that both models incorporate social characteristics, stress and psychological dysfunction, but differ in their conceptualizations of the relationship between these constructs. It is argued that the sociomedical paradigm is well-suited to identifying the etiologic factors of particular disorders, but inherently inadequate for identifying the repercussions of social organization on mental health. Gender was chosen to illustrate many of the authors' points. The sample for the research was selected from two mental health catchment areas in metropolitan Los Angeles, one predominately Hispanic and one predominantly non-Hispanic white. The results demonstrated that gender differences in the impact of stress are disorder-specific and do not indicate general differences between women and men in susceptibility to stress. The authors conclude that stress research focusing on a single disorder does not accurately portray social variation in stress processes and mental health outcomes.

Language(s) of text: English
ISSN: 0003-1224

2

ARROBA, T   JAMES, K
> PRESSURE AT WORK: A SURVIVAL GUIDE
MAIDENHEAD, McGRAW-HILL, 1987, xvi, 192 p.

This book aims at enabling managers to develop strategies and skills for dealing with work pressure. It is divided into two parts. The first part emphasizes that managing work pressure is an essential skill for managers. The authors outline what stress is and how to recognize it. They then explain how to develop skills for dealing with pressure. The second part focuses on the need to recognize when inappropriate pressure exists in the organization and how a manager can design an organizational survival guide. The book indicates three approaches to survival: enhancing the helping skills necessary for dealing with people who are under stress; taking steps to prevent stress occurring in the organization; and making the organization more fit to deal with pressure.

Language(s) of text: English
ISBN: 0-07-084931-5

3

ARROBA, T   JAMES, K
> "REDUCING THE COST OF STRESS: AN ORGANISATIONAL MODEL"
in PERSONNEL REVIEW (Bradford), 19(1), 1990, 21-27.

This article develops a model for understanding the kinds of interventions which can be made to reduce organizational stress.   The model presents organizational stress management as a four-stage process to avoid a piecemeal and random approach.   First, get the organization to recognize stress and prepare the ground for further stages by raising awareness;   second, train individuals in the techniques of stress management;   third, provide a skilled support system within the formal organization;   and in the final stage, take steps to identify and counter the stress-producing factors within the organization.

Language(s) of text: English
ISSN: 0048-3486

4

ASHFORD, SJ
> "INDIVIDUAL STRATEGIES FOR COPING WITH STRESS DURING ORGANIZATIONAL TRANSITIONS"
in JOURNAL OF APPLIED BEHAVIORAL SCIENCE (Greenwich, Connecticut), 24(1), 1988, 19-36.

This article examines the coping mechanisms used by employees to adapt to a major organizational transition.   The research was conducted in the marketing department of a regional telephone company in the United States during restructuring.   It examined how individuals' stress levels are affected by the interaction of coping responses and resources for dealing with stress.   The data were collected through questionnaires completed by the employees one month before and six months after restructuring.   The results suggested that perceived uncertainty and fears about the impact of the transition were related to employee stress and that this relationship was only moderately affected by the coping mechanisms.   The results also gave some indication of the relative value of the various coping resources and responses in moderating the stressor-strain relationship.   Feelings of personal control and the ability to tolerate ambiguity were linked with improved stress levels, whereas active attempts to structure the situation by obtaining information and feedback either failed to affect stress levels or actually increased them.

Language(s) of text: English
ISSN: 0021-8863

5

BARKHAM, M   SHAPIRO, DA
> **"BRIEF PSYCHOTHERAPEUTIC INTERVENTIONS FOR JOB-RELATED DISTRESS: A PILOT STUDY OF PRESCRIPTIVE AND EXPLORATORY THERAPY"**
in COUNSELLING PSYCHOLOGY QUARTERLY (Oxfordshire), 3(2), 1990, 133-147.

This article reviews existing interventions for occupational stress problems. Three areas of concern are identified: (1) the current predominance of interventions aimed at understanding and addressing workers' behaviour in connection and in response to occupational stress (cognitive-behavioural types of intervention); (2) the effectiveness of stress-intervention programmes; and (3) the methodological procedures employed in intervention studies. The authors address the first issue by presenting the results of a study aimed at evaluating the effectiveness of both cognitive-behavioural ("prescriptive") and relationship-oriented ("exploratory") therapies. The view that personal distress expressed as work stress can be addressed therapeutically in different ways was supported by the findings. Concerning the effectiveness of intervention programmes, personal accounts of the respondents indicated that the issues of concern lay at both the intra- and interpersonal level. The authors point out, however, that changes at the organizational level do not necessarily take account of issues and concerns stemming from employees' personal histories.   Concerning methodological procedures, three major aspects are covered: (1) predominance of cognitive-behavioural techniques;   (2) modest cost-effectiveness of existing techniques;   and (3) sampling and measurement procedures.

Language(s) of text: English
ISSN: 0951-5070

Reprints of this article are available from Mr. Michael Barkham, Medical Research Council, Social and Applied Psychology Unit, Department of Psychology, University of Sheffield, Sheffield S10 2TN, United Kingdom.

6

BIBEAU, G   DUSSAULT, G   LAROUCHE, LM   LIPPEL, K   SAUCIER, JF   VEZINA, M   VIDAL, JM
CONFEDERATION DES SYNDICATS NATIONAUX
> **CERTAINS ASPECTS CULTURELS, DIAGNOSTIQUES ET JURIDIQUES DU BURNOUT: PISTES ET REPERES OPERATIONNELS**
(Certain cultural, diagnostic and legal aspects of burnout)
MONTREAL, 1989, ii, 54 p.   (Travail et Nouvelle Pathologie series)

What is burnout or professional fatigue? Which methods are most appropriate to obtaining a credible diagnosis of burnout? Is burnout an occupational disease, and how far is it covered by social security?   The Groupe interuniversitaire de recherche en anthropologie médicale et ethnopsychiatrie (GIRAME) [Inter-university Research Group in Anthropology, Medicine and Ethnopsychiatry] in Quebec looks into the various diagnostic and legal aspects of burnout with a view to providing answers to the above questions. The first part of the publication focuses on models and diagnostic instruments to determine burnout clinically as a disease. It points out the problems of applying a specific diagnostic model to ascertain the existence of burnout. The second part of the book deals with relevant legal aspects of burnout in Quebec. Since burnout is not considered as a disease per se, it is not covered by health-related legislation. Legislation on work accidents and occupational diseases was therefore evaluated. A review of court cases revealed the difficulties of obtaining legal compensation for occupation-induced burnout. The authors hold that, in most cases, there is inconsistency between prevailing legislation and court sentences. In conclusion, the authors call for a clear and coherent policy in Quebec.

Language(s) of text: French

This publication is available from the Centre de documentation, Confédération des syndicats nationaux (CSN), 1601 rue DeLorimier, Montreal, Quebec H2K 4M5, Canada.

7

BRIEF, AP   ATIEH, JM
> "STUDYING JOB STRESS: ARE WE MAKING MOUNTAINS OUT OF MOLEHILLS?"
in JOURNAL OF OCCUPATIONAL BEHAVIOUR (Chichester), 8(2), April 1987, 115-126.

This article examines the relationship between working conditions and job-related mental stress. It defines and discusses potentially harmful working conditions which may adversely affect the psychological well-being and quality of life of those exposed to them. Among the critical work events studied, defined as experiences which impair one's psychological well-being, are reduction in work-related income, the extreme of which is job loss, and pressure for higher income. Personal and environmental factors that may condition worker reactions are examined. The article concludes with a brief consideration of some methodological issues relevant to the study of the sort of working conditions discussed, as well as to the study of job stress in general.

Language(s) of text: English
ISSN: 0142-2774

8

CANADIAN INSTITUTE OF STRESS
> STRESS AND THE WORKPLACE: A PRACTICAL GUIDE
TORONTO, INDUSTRIAL ACCIDENT PREVENTION ASSOCIATION, 1984, 32 p.

See Section 1 on manuals and guidelines on combating stress.

Language(s) of text: English

This publication is available from the Industrial Accident Prevention Association (IAPA), 2 Bloor Street West, 31st floor, Toronto, Ontario M4W 3N8, Canada.

9

COLEMAN, V
> STRESS MANAGEMENT TECHNIQUES: MANAGING PEOPLE FOR HEALTHY PROFITS
LONDON, MERCURY BOOKS, 1988, 124 p.

See Section 1 on manuals and guidelines on combating stress.

Language(s) of text: English
ISBN: 1-85252-036-6

10

COMISIONES OBRERAS. GABINETE DE SALUD LABORAL
> DESGASTE PSIQUICO EN EL TRABAJO
(Psychic wear and tear at work)
VALENCIA, 1991, 51 p. (Cuadernos Sindicales de Salud Laboral No. 1)

See Section 1 on manuals and guidelines on combating stress.

Language(s) of text: Spanish

This publication is available from the Gabinete de Salud Laboral, CCOO, Pça. Nàpols i Sicilia 5, 3 piso, E-46003 Valencia, Spain.

11

COOPER, CL   PAYNE, R
> **CAUSES, COPING AND CONSEQUENCES OF STRESS AT WORK**
CHICHESTER, JOHN WILEY, 1988, xii, 418 p.   (Wiley Series on Studies in Occupational Stress)

This book brings together leading international experts in the field of occupational stress who focus on recent research findings, theories, methodological issues and action for coping with stress at work that are relevant to individuals and to organizations.   It explores the stress of repetitive manual work and managerial and professional stress in large organizations, as well as more recent issues such as the impact of new technology and the pressures resulting from difficulties in industrial relations.   Individual differences and coping strategies are analyzed, since the significance of coping, both as a determinant and consequence of stress, is central to the discussion of contemporary stress research.   The volume also looks at the person in the work environment.   It examines health promotion in the workplace and management interventions for stress reduction and prevention [employee assistance programmes (EAPs), stress management training, stress reduction strategies], while highlighting the increasingly numerous approaches and the research that has evaluated them.   Finally, the authors examine methodological issues, such as self-reporting measures, longitudinal designs and the validity of questionnaires, and the future of physiological assessments.

Language(s) of text: English
ISBN: 0-471-91879-2

12

COOPER, CL   SLOAN, S   WILLIAMS, S

> **STRESS: OCCUPATIONAL STRESS INDICATOR**
WINDSOR, NFER-NELSON, 1988, 12 p.

See Section 1 on manuals and guidelines on combating stress.

Language(s) of text: English

This publication is available from NFER-NELSON Publishing Company, Darville House, 2 Oxford Road East, Windsor, Berkshire SL4 1DF, United Kingdom.

13

CORLETT, EN   RICHARDSON, J
> **STRESS, WORK DESIGN AND PRODUCTIVITY**
CHICHESTER, JOHN WILEY, 1981, xvi, 271 p.   (Wiley Series on Studies in Occupational Stress No. 4)

This book presents a selection of papers on the methodology for the measurement of mental stress in the work environment and the remedial role of job design.   It aims to show workers the need for improved human work and how this can be done within the context of a profitable organization.   Physical effort as well as the physiological measures of mental effort are discussed.   Techniques used in industry to design tasks are then described, with emphasis on the importance of considering the requirements of human operators in system planning and building.

Language(s) of text: English
ISBN: 0-471-28044-5

14

COX, T
> **"STRESS, COPING AND PROBLEM SOLVING"**
in WORK AND STRESS (London), 1(1), 1987, 5-14.

This article outlines the growing consensus on the nature of stress, and defines occupational stress in terms of coping behaviour. It then examines the concept of coping and its role in stress theory. The classification of coping strategies and the investigation of the process of coping, as two different approaches to the study of coping, are reviewed. It is argued that coping from a process-oriented viewpoint -- coping as problem solving -- is a valid alternative to the classification of all possible strategies and resources. Two different processes are described: a person's appraisal of his or her ability to cope with the demands made of him or her, which underpins the stress state and initiates coping; and the way in which a person might rationally solve problems as a form of coping with stress. The author examines the nature of rational models of problem solving and appraises their usefulness and application to stress management. He concludes that the problem-solving model may provide a framework for training individuals in personal coping skills and for planning interventions at both the individual and organizational levels.

Language(s) of text: English
ISSN: 0267-8373

15

CRESPY, J
> **"STRESS ET PSYCHOPATHOLOGIE DU TRAVAIL"**
(Stress and psychopathology at work)
in CAHIERS DE NOTES DOCUMENTAIRES (Paris), (116), July-September 1984, 353-362.

This article clarifies the scope and definition of stress at work, and examines the factors and characteristics of stress and methods of evaluation. The interrelationship between stress, fatigue and psychopathology are discussed, and occupation-related stressors are specified. The author refers to many studies and surveys that measure occupation-related stress in specific work categories, mentioning briefly the stressors that affect women in particular. Methods to evaluate stress at work essentially apply two types of criteria: biochemical and physiological, and criteria related to performance, behaviour, absenteeism, and so on. However, the author questions the reliability of this latter group of criteria: they are too general to reflect real stress situations and are more likely to indicate poor working conditions or organizational dysfunction. He considers that better working conditions and equipment, a pleasant atmosphere and greater consideration of workers' needs and motivation can attenuate work stress.

Language(s) of text: French
Language(s) of summary: English
ISSN: 0007-9952

16

DeFRANK, RS COOPER, CL
> "WORKSITE STRESS MANAGEMENT INTERVENTIONS: THEIR EFFECTIVENESS AND CONCEPTUALISATION"
in JOURNAL OF MANAGERIAL PSYCHOLOGY (West Yorkshire), 2, 1987, 4-10.

The authors argue for stress management and reduction at the workplace. They recommend that intervention programmes be considered and designed at three levels, namely the individual, the individual in the organization, and the organization. A list of interventions is outlined for each level with possible outcomes described. At the individual level, proposed coping techniques include relaxation, meditation, exercise and time budgeting. The outcomes are assessed in terms of mood state, psychosomatic complaints, physiological condition (blood pressure, muscle tension) and sleep disturbances. Interventions for the individual in relation to the organization include relationships at work, issues related to roles, participation and work environment. Here, impacts of the programme could be measured by indices such as job stress, job satisfaction, burnout, absenteeism and turnover. Intervention at the organizational level focuses on the organizational structure, recruitment, training, environment and job rotation. The impact can be assessed by the level of productivity, turnover, absenteeism and success in retaining employees. Finally, as studies analysing management interventions are limited both in scope and content, the authors recommend more research to sharpen the understanding and effectiveness of stress management programmes.

Language(s) of text: English
ISSN: 0268-3946

17

DEJOURS, C
AREA DE ESTUDIO E INVESTIGACION EN CIENCIAS SOCIALES DEL TRABAJO, BUENOS AIRES; CENTRE DE RECHERCHE ET DOCUMENTATION SUR L'AMERIQUE LATINE, PARIS; FACULTAD DE PSICOLOGIA DE LA UNIVERSIDAD DE BUENOS AIRES, BUENOS AIRES
> TRABAJO Y DESGASTE MENTAL: UNA CONTRIBUCION A LA PSICOPATOLOGIA DEL TRABAJO
(Work and mental wear and tear)
BUENOS AIRES, HUMANITAS, 1990, v, 242 p. (Colección Ciencias Sociales del Trabajo No. 7)

This book deals with work psychopathology. The first part discusses the negative mental consequences of poor work organization, particularly in relation to repetitive work. Anxiety is discussed in detail. Direct and indirect signs of anxiety, its different forms and individual, as well as collective, defensive strategies are presented. Conditions of work, job satisfaction and dissatisfaction for various categories of workers, such as construction workers, telephone operators and pilots, are studied. The second part of the book considers new perspectives in work psychopathology, and presents steps to be followed when investigating in this field. In addition, psychopathological reactions to retirement, dismissal and illness are reviewed.

Language(s) of text: Spanish
ISBN: 950-582-283-5

This publication is available from CEIL-HUMANITAS, Carlos Calvo 644, Buenos Aires, Argentina.

18

DEWE, PJ
> "EXAMINING THE NATURE OF WORK STRESS: INDIVIDUAL EVALUATIONS OF STRESSFUL EXPERIENCES AND COPING"
in HUMAN RELATIONS (New York), 42(11), November 1989, 993-1013.

This article explores the validity of current occupational stress research practices by addressing a number of issues considered to be important by occupational stress researchers. Some of these are investigated by comparing the results obtained using alternative, or qualitative, methodologies with the results obtained through quantitative approaches. An investigation took place in a large British mail order company. Data were gathered from interviews and a questionnaire on the sources of work stress, the impact on individual health, work relationships, job satisfaction and life outside work, and the strategies individuals used to cope. The results demonstrated that important information can be gleaned from a qualitative or more open-ended exploratory approach. They also indicated new directions for future research such as giving more attention in measuring stress factors to aspects such as intensity, frequency and the way individuals interpret events. Future research should also explore the nature of direct action and palliative strategies and investigate more thoroughly the appraisal process and its role in shaping stressful events.

Language(s) of text: English
ISSN: 0018-7267

19

DOYLE GENTRY, W   BENSON, H   DE WOLFF, CJ
> BEHAVIORAL MEDICINE: WORK, STRESS AND HEALTH
DORDRECHT, MARTINUS NIJHOFF, 1985, xii, 323 p. (Series D: Behavioural and Social Sciences No. 19)

This volume contains the proceedings of a North Atlantic Treaty Organization (NATO) Advanced Study Institute held in 1981 in France. It includes an examination of the psychosocial susceptibility and resistance factors to work stress, which interact to determine the health status of individual workers. Concerning individual susceptibility, psychological as well as social variables are included. At the organizational level, the nature of employment, and the type and extent of demands placed on workers are discussed. "Resistance factors" directed to individuals include social support and relaxation, while interventions at the organizational level are less evident. The research papers emphasize the need for additional study of resistance factors, both at the individual and systems level, and a shift toward a "balance sheet approach" to effective stress management. Additionally, the relationship between workload and cardiovascular disease is examined, with reference to various occupations. Type A behaviour patterns and how to reduce coronary risk in individuals classified as Type A are also reviewed.

Language(s) of text: English
ISBN: 90-247-3264-6

20

EUROPEAN FOUNDATION FOR THE IMPROVEMENT OF LIVING AND WORKING CONDITIONS
> INTERACTION OF WORKERS AND MACHINERY: PHYSICAL AND PSYCHOLOGICAL STRESS
LUXEMBOURG, OFFICE FOR OFFICIAL PUBLICATIONS OF THE EUROPEAN COMMUNITIES, 1987, 120 p.

This report examines the extent to which the physical and mental requirements of workers are taken into account in the design of machinery and systems operations. It also investigates the relationship of previous research in this area to the introduction and use of new technology. The study covers different work areas that have been affected by the introduction of computer-based technology. The constraints of equipment design on worker-machinery interaction and the use made of ergonomics in equipment design are evaluated. It is argued that owing to technology, jobs are becoming increasingly cognitive in nature and involve handling information, and that particular attention must therefore be paid to the mental workload of tasks. The study analyses health and safety problems, both long and short term, associated with the use of new technology, and looks in particular at the effects of a persistent underload or overload of mental activity in certain jobs. The need to train workers adequately to interact effectively with equipment is discussed, as are qualification and training requirements. The report also examines the process of introducing new equipment into the workplace, and reviews the problems that may arise from a participatory approach. The volume also includes tripartite evaluation reports.

Language(s) of text: English
ISBN: 92-825-6485-1
This publication is available from the Office for Official Publications of the European Communities, 2 rue Mercier, L-2985 Luxembourg, Luxembourg, catalogue no. SY-47-86-624-EN-C.

21

EUROPEAN FOUNDATION FOR THE IMPROVEMENT OF LIVING AND WORKING CONDITIONS
> PHYSICAL AND PSYCHOLOGICAL STRESS AT WORK
DUBLIN, 1982, 1 v.

The objectives of this conference report on physical and mental stress hazards in the work environment include (a) collating the existing knowledge on stress, with particular reference to working conditions; (b) developing a conceptual framework for interpreting the studies on stress, which specifies its identifiable causes and effects; and (c) providing considerations for policy-makers, including legislative provisions. The study was evaluated by representatives of governments, employers' organizations and trade unions who, after weighing the findings, put forward proposals to improve the situation. The concept of stress and various indicators are discussed to understand the impact of industrial society on the health, well-being and psycho-biological adaptive capacity of the individual. The sources of stress for several occupations are reviewed, together with variables which influence how stress affects the individual. Health care professionals, industrial managers, shiftworkers and women workers are included. Concerning intervention strategies aimed at reducing stress in industry, the report refers to the improvement of the workplace and its environment, the development of occupational health services, and the need for long-term studies on the effects of stresses and strains on the working population.

Language(s) of text: English

This publication is available from the European Foundation, Loughlinstown House, Shankill, Co. Dublin, Ireland. It is also available in Danish, Dutch, French, German, Greek and Italian.

22

FONTANA, D
BRITISH PSYCHOLOGICAL SOCIETY
> MANAGING STRESS
LONDON, ROUTLEDGE, 1989, ix, 118 p. (Problems in Practice Series)

See Section 1 on manuals and guidelines on combating stress.

Language(s) of text: English
ISBN: 0-901715-98-0

This publication is available from the British Psychological Society, St. Andrews House, 48 Princess Road East, Leicester LE1 7DR, United Kingdom.

23

FRANKENHAEUSER, M
SWEDISH WORK ENVIRONMENT FUND
> STRESS, HEALTH, JOB SATISFACTION
STOCKHOLM, 1989, 20 p.

See Section 1 on manuals and guidelines on combating stress.

Language(s) of text: English

This publication is available from the Swedish Work Environment Fund, Box 1122, S-111 81 Stockholm, Sweden, Order No. 6019250.

24

FRASER, TM
ILO
> HUMAN STRESS, WORK AND JOB SATISFACTION: A CRITICAL APPROACH
GENEVA, 1982, 72 p. (Occupational Safety and Health Series No. 50)

The relationship between working conditions, mental stress and job satisfaction is examined. The study deals with the psycho-physiology of human stress, taking into consideration the person-machine-environment system, and points out that stress is caused by a disequilibrium in this system. The author distinguishes between physical and skilled work, and studies their relation with fatigue and stress. The extent to which stress is implicated in the generation of dissatisfaction, emotional disturbance and psychosomatic disorder is examined, together with the application of social psychology and ergonomics to occupational health and safety in the interests of quality of working life. Suggestions on how to make work more human and satisfactory are given.

Language(s) of text: English
ISBN: 92-2-103042-3
ISSN: 0078-3129

This publication is available from ILO Publications, International Labour Office, CH-1211 Geneva 22, Switzerland. It is also available in French and German.

25

GEARE, AJ
> "JOB STRESS: BOON AS WELL AS BANE"
in EMPLOYEE RELATIONS (Bradford), 11(1), 1989, 21-26.

The author sees two fundamental deficiencies in the social science literature on job stress. The first is the tendency to emphasize the harmful and undesirable effects of job stress, though it is equally important to emphasize that job stress can be both desired and desirable. However, the article does not deny that excessive stress may cause physiological and psychological strain and result in adverse behavioural changes, illness or even death. The second deficiency is the failure to use a reasonable and adequate definition of job stress. The author indicates that an acceptable definition of stress should fulfill a number of requirements: it should make clear the entire stress sequence; be reasonably close to the popular understanding of the term; and recognize that stress can have beneficial, as well as harmful, outcomes. The article concludes that stress must be recognized as a physical or psychological demand on a person which can result in either stimulation or strain, or both, and that before job stress can be understood, managed and controlled, there needs to be genuine acceptance that it can lead to stimulation, enjoyment, challenge and productivity, as well as anxiety, behavioural problems and breakdown.

Language(s) of text: English
ISSN: 0142-5455

26

GEBHARDT, DL   CRUMP, CE
> "EMPLOYEE FITNESS AND WELLNESS PROGRAMS IN THE WORKPLACE"
in AMERICAN PSYCHOLOGIST (Washington), 45(2), February 1990, 262-272.

In view of the exponential growth of worksite fitness and health promotion programmes in recent years, this article reviews the literature on these programmes to examine their impact. The study focuses essentially on fitness programmes, but includes some references to wellness programmes. The scientific basis and the need for fitness and wellness programmes are discussed. Two types of fitness programmes are described: general fitness programmes, aiming at overall improvement in fitness and health; and job-related fitness programmes, which focus on the specific physical capabilities and critical tasks required for successful job performance. The authors examine the relation between reduction in health-care costs, absenteeism, turnover, injury and the implementation of comprehensive health promotion programmes. Issues related to participation rates, programme implementation and evaluation are also addressed. The article analyses a number of factors that have been identified as contributing to successful employer-sponsored programmes; they relate to programme goals and objectives, staffing, evaluation and recruitment. Finally, the authors recommend a concerted effort to promote greater participation in fitness and wellness programmes, and a multidisciplinary approach to planning, implementing and evaluating the programmes.

Language(s) of text: English
ISSN: 0003-066X

27

GOH, CT   KOH, HC   LOW, CK
> "GENDER EFFECTS ON THE JOB SATISFACTION OF ACCOUNTANTS IN SINGAPORE"
in WORK AND STRESS (London), 5(4), October-December 1991, 341-348.

It has been argued that because of family responsibilities, biological factors, social expectations and work relations, female accountants experience stress that men do not and thus have lower job satisfaction. Various empirical studies have shown conflicting and inconclusive results. In this study of accountants in Singapore, the effects of gender on job satisfaction are examined as well as the effect of age and type of job and the relationship between gender and age, gender and type of job, and age and type of job. The study was conducted through questionnaires to 1,130 accountants, with 608 usable responses, 51.8 per cent female and 48.2 per cent male. Job satisfaction was measured in terms of the nature of the work, present pay rate, opportunities for promotion, degree of supervision and relations with co-workers. One of the main conclusions of the study is that gender does not directly affect job satisfaction. It is observed, however, that within certain age groups, gender can affect the degree of job satisfaction. Female accountants who are over 45 years old report less satisfaction, while for the group 25-45 years, no variation is detected in the level of job satisfaction.

Language(s) of text: English
ISSN: 0267-8373

28

GOLISZEK, AG
> BREAKING THE STRESS HABIT: A MODERN GUIDE TO ONE-MINUTE STRESS MANAGEMENT
WINSTON-SALEM, CAROLINA PRESS, 1987, 263 p.

See Section 1 on manuals and guidelines on combating stress.

Language(s) of text: English
ISBN: 0-9616475-2-3

29

HAINES, VA   HURLBERT, JS   ZIMMER, C
> "OCCUPATIONAL STRESS, SOCIAL SUPPORT, AND THE BUFFER HYPOTHESIS"
in WORK AND OCCUPATIONS (Beverly Hills), 18(2), May 1991, 212-235.

The authors discuss the stress-strain model of health, in which stress is an environmental change followed by an attempt to adapt by the individuals concerned, and strain is generated by faulty adaptive efforts. The effects of stress and social support are considered jointly in the "buffer hypothesis", which predicts that high levels of stress will produce strain in individuals experiencing low levels of social support but not in individuals with good social support. The article analyses the studies that back up this model, arguing that they have theoretical and methodological limitations. When these limitations are corrected, the findings suggest that stress caused by job constraint significantly increases strain, regardless of the level of social support, and that, by contrast, the effects of stress caused by workload and conflict are dependent on the level of social support at work.

Language(s) of text: English
ISSN: 0730-8884

30

HALL, EM
> WOMEN'S WORK: AN INQUIRY INTO THE HEALTH EFFECTS OF INVISIBLE AND VISIBLE LABOR
STOCKHOLM, KAROLINSKA INSTITUTET, 1990, 1 volume

This book is a dissertation on five studies that examined stress in the lives of women in a number of different contexts and settings, mainly in Sweden. Its aim is to evaluate the effects of paid employment and unpaid work in the home on the psychological and physical health of women by studying their social and working conditions across a variety of exposure alternatives and comparing these conditions with those of men. The studies indicate that for women and men the impact of working life on mental and physical health is comparable in magnitude. However, the findings demonstrate that for women the sources of stress are more diverse and diffuse than for men. The author concludes that a balance of demands and resources is important in both the work and home setting, and that the sources of stress and, consequently, stress-related illnesses may be different for men and women as they generally inhabit different social structures.

Language(s) of text: English
ISBN: 91-628-0000-0

This publication is available from the Karolinska Institutet, Statens Institut för Psykosocial Miljömedicin och Institutionen för Stressforskning, S-104 01 Stockholm, Sweden.

31

ILO
> AUTOMATION, WORK ORGANISATION AND OCCUPATIONAL STRESS
GENEVA, 1984, viii, 188 p.

This report contains the proceedings and working papers submitted to an international meeting of experts organized by the ILO in 1983. It provides a comparative study of the effect of automation on work organisation and mental stress in industrialized countries. The impact of technological change on different categories of workers and the diversity and complexity of problems which automation poses concerning conditions of work and work organisation are analysed. The report stresses the need for social partners to take these multiple factors into account in determining their policies and carrying out activities. The working papers review labour legislation and collective agreements, policies and practice, and the impact of new technologies on job content, skills and job satisfaction. The relationship between work organisation and occupational stress, and various strategies to cope with stress are also reviewed, pointing out the importance of a preventive approach to stress.

Language(s) of text: English
ISBN: 92-2-103866-1

This publication is available from ILO Publications, International Labour Office, CH-1211 Geneva 22, Switzerland. It is available in French, Spanish and Japanese. It is also held in microfiche.

32

ILO
> **PSYCHOSOCIAL FACTORS AT WORK: RECOGNITION AND CONTROL**
GENEVA, 1986, viii, 81 p. (Occupational Safety and Health Series No. 56)

This report analyses the impact of socio-psychological factors at work, such as workload, arrangement of working time, management and technological change, on health. A series of effects, including absenteeism, alcoholism, occupational diseases and accidents, are examined and related to individual vulnerability and social support. The report reviews the methodologies for measuring and monitoring the effects of psychosocial factors at work, particularly medical examinations and questionnaires. Several measures to be undertaken at enterprise level in the area of job design, work organisation and ergonomics are indicated, and various means of prevention are proposed, including education, workers' participation and practically-oriented research. The need for a multidisciplinary approach which takes into account the multi-causal nature of health problems and disturbances related to psychosocial factors is stressed. A bibliography after each chapter and several tables complete the report.

Language(s) of text: English
ISBN: 92-2-105411-X
ISSN: 0078-3129

This publication is available from ILO Publications, International Labour Office, CH-1211 Geneva 22, Switzerland. It is also available in French and Spanish.

33

IVANCEVICH, JM MATTESON, MT FREEDMAN, SM PHILLIPS, JS
> **"WORKSITE STRESS MANAGEMENT INTERVENTIONS"**
in AMERICAN PSYCHOLOGIST (Washington), 45(2), February 1990, 252-261.

This article provides a framework for examining organizational stress interventions, and reviews some of the stress management intervention literature in the context of this framework. It refers to three different points in the stress cycle to which stress management interventions can be targeted: (a) the degree of stress potential in a situation; (b) the employee's appraisal of a potentially stressful situation; and (c) the ways to cope with the consequences of stress. The need for cooperation between employees, employers and relevant persons from outside the organization is emphasized. The final part of the article identifies issues that could be appropriately addressed by organizational psychologists. The authors point out that the twin goals of answering practical organizational questions and conducting rigorous research should be pursued and that the theoretical assumptions about the nature of stress should play a major role in the choice of interventions. Finally, they indicate that research should be more organization-oriented and that the role of individual differences should be taken into account.

Language(s) of text: English
ISSN: 0003-066X

34

JAFFE, DT SCOTT, CD ORIOLI, EM
WASHINGTON BUSINESS GROUP ON HEALTH
> **STRESS MANAGEMENT IN THE WORKPLACE**
WASHINGTON, 1986, 32 p. (WBGH Worksite Wellness Series)

See Section 1 on manuals and guidelines on combating stress.

Language(s) of text: English

This publication is available from the Washington Business Group on Health (WBGH), 229 1/2 Pennsylvania Avenue, SE, Washington, DC 20003, United States.

35

JANSSEN, H
> **"ZUR FRAGE DER EFFEKTIVITÄT UND EFFIZIENZ BETRIEBLICHER GESUNDHEITS-FÖRDERUNG: ERGEBNISSE EINER LITERATURRECHERCHE"**
(About the efficacy and efficiency of workplace health promotion programmes: Results of a literature search)
in ZEITSCHRIFT FÜR PRÄVENTIVMEDIZIN UND GESUNDHEITSFÖRDERUNG (Zurich), 3(1), 1991, 1-7.

Based on a literature search, this article analyses experiences and results gained from workplace health promotion programmes. Approximately 50 studies, mainly from the United States, were examined. Most studies stress that illness-related costs have decreased where health promotion programmes have been introduced, which often is reflected in a lower rate of illness-related absences. However, a number of authors emphasize the limited value of such cost-benefit calculations. An overwhelming number of companies in the studies, particularly large-scale enterprises apply health programmes. Over a third of all programmes cover activities against smoking, while more than 25 per cent deal with strategies to cope with stress. A high rate of success was evidenced, particularly with programmes to control tobacco consumption, cholesterol, blood pressure and weight, and with fitness and nutrition programmes.

Language(s) of text: German
ISSN: 0044-3379

36

JAPAN. MINISTRY OF LABOUR
> KAITEKI SHOKUBA NO JITSUGEN NI MUKETE: KAITEKI SHOKUBA NO ARIKATA NI KANSURU
KONDANKAI KOUKOKUSHO
(Towards the realization of a pleasant workplace: A report regarding how pleasant workplaces ought to be
designed)
TOKYO, 1991, 1 v.

This is the report submitted by a roundtable committee composed of academics, trade union representatives,
employer representatives, and occupational safety and health consultants, set up by the Ministry of Labour to
consider the problem of the increasing number of workers affected by occupational stress in Japan. The report
recommends the following: work and the workplace should be pleasantly organized; lighting, air conditioning,
temperature and humidity should be maintained properly; work operations should be arranged so as to avoid
unnecessary heavy workloads, e.g. by introducing ergonomic arrangements; a "support system" for work should
be established; training should be provided for managers on human relations and leadership; and welfare facilities,
such as canteens and changing rooms, should be provided. Finally, the report recommends that the Ministry of
Labour set up guidelines for the improvement of working conditions to enable enterprises to establish their own
guidelines; promote the concept of a pleasant workplace; establish a model for small and medium-sized
enterprises; introduce low-interest loans and tax alleviation for workplace improvement measures within
enterprises.

Language(s) of text: Japanese

37

JOHNSON, JV   JOHANSSON, G
> PSYCHOSOCIAL WORK ENVIRONMENT: WORK ORGANIZATION, DEMOCRATIZATION AND
HEALTH
AMITYVILLE, BAYWOOD PUBLISHING, 1991, 335 p. (Policy, Politics, Health and Medicine Series)

This book, which is the result of a joint effort by international researchers, aims to contribute to the understanding
of the psychosocial work environment by examining aspects of work organization which are of particular importance
in terms of their impact on health, by suggesting strategies to improve the nature and content of the work process
and by recommending new approaches to research. One major consideration is that research should be geared
towards generalized knowledge, leading to the collective determination of changes in technology and work
organization. The concept of work control in relation to work organization is addressed from different analytical
standpoints: the psychological, the social, the organizational, the historical and the political-economic. The volume
also examines the application of a democratization strategy to transform work with the participation of rank-and-file
workers. Examples of "action research" strategies are given and the Scandinavian experience, also applied in other
countries, is described. Finally, the dissemination and development of psychosocial work environment research
and practice in Australia, Canada and the United States are discussed.

Language(s) of text: English
ISBN: 0-89503-078-0

38

JONES, JE   BEARLEY, WL
> **BURNOUT ASSESSMENT INVENTORY**
KING OF PRUSSIA, PENNSYLVANIA, ORGANIZATION DESIGN AND DEVELOPMENT, 1984, 14 p.

See Section 1 on manuals and guidelines on combating stress.

Language(s) of text: English

This publication is available from Organization Design and Development, Inc., 2002 Renaissance Boulevard, Suite 100, King of Prussia, Pennsylvania 19406, United States.

39

KARASEK, R   THEORELL, T
> **HEALTHY WORK: STRESS, PRODUCTIVITY, AND THE RECONSTRUCTION OF WORKING LIFE**
NEW YORK, BASIC BOOKS, 1990, xiii, 381 p.

The authors examine, from a multidisciplinary perspective, the importance of psychosocial job design and its impact on health and productivity. This volume analyses the relationship between working conditions and stress-related illness through a number of stress indicators, such as anxiety, depression and mental fatigue. The importance of extending the individual decision latitude component, together with the need to reorient existing production systems, are emphasized as ways to counteract occupational stress. A set of guidelines for the redesign of work examine the productivity implications of group processes, organizational change, impact of technology and interoccupational conflict. Finally, the authors urge companies to decentralize authority and involve workers in decision-making, since they believe the only real solution to stress is a participatory redesign of work.

Language(s) of text: English
ISBN: 0-465-02896-9

40

KARASEK, R
> **"LOWER HEALTH RISK WITH INCREASED JOB CONTROL AMONG WHITE COLLAR WORKERS"**
in JOURNAL OF ORGANIZATIONAL BEHAVIOR (Chichester), 11(3), May 1990, 171-185.

This article describes a questionnaire study carried out in Sweden to examine the associations between job control and health status, including psychological strain, in a sample of full-time workers from the national white-collar labour federation. One-fourth of the subjects had undergone a company-initiated job reorganization in the previous few years. Indicators of physical illness, psychological distress and health-related behaviour were developed, and the impact of the company-induced job reorganization was measured in terms of the employees' possibility of influencing the change in their work situations. The findings supported the author's primary hypothesis that illness symptom levels are substantially lower in workers who have obtained increased control and participation in the work process, although the process of job reorganization itself was associated with significantly higher psychological and physical symptoms. The author remarks that the ameliorative effects of increased job control are often more than sufficient to negate the impact of stressful change processes and result in health improvement.

Language(s) of text: English
ISSN: 0894-3796

41

KINDLER, HS
> PERSONAL STRESS ASSESSMENT INVENTORY
PACIFIC PALISADES, CENTER FOR MANAGEMENT EFFECTIVENESS, 1991, 12 p.

See Section 1 on manuals and guidelines on combating stress.

Language(s) of text: English

This publication is available from the Center for Management Effectiveness, P.O. Box 1202, Pacific Palisades, California 90272, United States.

42

KOLLMEIER, H
GERMANY. BUNDESANTALT FÜR ARBEITSSCHUTZ UND UNFALLFORSCHUNG
> STRESS AM ARBEITSPLATZ: VORTRÄGE DER INFORMATIONSTAGUNG AM 1/2 JUNI 1981 IN DORTMUND
(Stress at work: A collection of papers presented during the information conference held in Dortmund, 1-2 June 1981)
DORTMUND, 1981, 1 v. (Schriftenreihe Arbeitsschutz No. 31)

This book compiles a collection of papers presented by researchers from different disciplines to a conference on the epidemiology of stress, psychological instruments of stress research, biochemical methods of stress analysis, stress epidemiology of risk factors and specific stress illnesses. In particular, two articles focus on the development of an anti-stress therapy strategy, and on measures to prevent occupational stress. The first article discusses measures of prevention and therapy at three levels: (a) raising a subject's resistance to stress with the help of, for instance, relaxation exercises, therapeutic exercises or group discussions to modify the internalized behaviour which triggers emotional stress; (b) reducing occupational risk situations, such as noise, night work or constant time pressure; and (c) building up somatic and emotional protective factors to prevent stress. The second article identifies three strategies to prevent occupational stress; adapt a work situation to the individual; adapt an individual to a work situation; match individuals and work situations without having to modify one or the other, for instance exclusively recruiting particularly healthy workers for shift work.

Language(s) of text: German
ISBN: 3-88314-188-7

This publication is available from the Bundesanstalt für Arbeitsschultz und Unfallforschung, Postfach 170202, D-4600 Dortmund 17, Germany.

43

KOMPIER, MAJ   MARCELISSEN, FHG
NEDERLANDS INSTITUUT VOOR ARBEIDSOMSTANDIGHEDEN
> HANDBOEK WERKSTRESS: SYSTEMATISCHE AANPAK VOOR DE BEDRIJFSPRAKTIJK
(Handbook of stress at work: Systematic approach for enterprise practice)
AMSTERDAM, 1991, 197 p.

See Section 1 on manuals and guidelines on combating stress.

Language(s) of text: Dutch
ISBN: 90-6365-054-X

This publication is available from the Nederlands Instituut voor Arbeidsomstandigheden (NIA), Postbus 75665, NL-1070 AR Amsterdam, Netherlands.

44

KOMPIER, MAJ   VAAS, S   MARCELISSEN, FHG
NEDERLANDS INSTITUUT VOOR PRAEVENTIEVE GEZONDHEIDSZORG
> STRESS DOOR WERK? DOE ER WAT AAN!
(Stress at work? Do something about it!)
LEIDEN, 1990, 80 p.

See Section 1 on manuals and guidelines on combating stress.

Language(s) of text: Dutch
ISBN: 90-9003878-7

This publication is available from the Nederlands Instituut voor Praeventieve Gezondheidszorg (NIPG/TNO), Postbus 124, NL-2300 AC Leiden, Netherlands.

45

LA ROSE, M
> "STRESS E LAVORO: TEMI, PROBLEMI, IL CONTRIBUTO DELLA SOCIOLOGIA ED I RAPPORTI INTERDISCIPLINARI"
(Stress and work: Themes, problems, the contribution of sociology and interdisciplinary relationships)
in SOCIOLOGIA DEL LAVORO (Bologna), (44), 1991, 5-318.

This periodical includes a series of studies carried out by different groups of scientists (from medicine, psychiatry, psychology, ergonomics and sociology) within a national interdisciplinary research project of the Consiglio Nazionale delle Ricerche (CNR) [National Research Council] on stress and work. The first part of the monograph is devoted to the definition of a theoretical/interpretative model based on the study of the interrelationship between stress, work organization, occupational risk, mental fatigue and decision-making. The second, more empirical and problem-oriented part of the book, covers specific topics, such as the problem of pathogenous organizations and the associated risks of stress, and stress in particular professions, including pilots. This part also contains an analysis of stress connected to managerial activities in complex and high technological settings, and stress in social and health services. A last study deals with women's work and stress. An extensive bibliography on stress, work and management concludes the book.

Language(s) of text: Italian
Language(s) of summary: English
ISBN: 88-204-7486-7

This publication is available from the Centro Internazionale di Documentazione e Studi Sociologici sui Problemi del Lavoro (CIDOSPEL), Dipartimento di Sociologia, Università di Bologna, Casella postale 413, I-40100 Bologna, Italy.

46

LABOUR RESEARCH DEPARTMENT, LONDON
> STRESS AT WORK: THE TRADE UNION RESPONSE
LONDON, 1988, 24 p.

See Section 1 on manuals and guidelines on combating stress.

Language(s) of text: English
ISBN: 0-946-89835-9

This publication is available from the LRD Publications Ltd., 78 Blackfriars Road, London SE1 8HF, United Kingdom.

47

LAMBERT, SJ
> "COMBINED EFFECTS OF JOB AND FAMILY CHARACTERISTICS ON THE JOB SATISFACTION, JOB INVOLVEMENT, AND INTRINSIC MOTIVATION OF MEN AND WOMEN WORKERS"
in JOURNAL OF ORGANIZATIONAL BEHAVIOR (Chichester), 12(4), July 1991, 341-363.

This article explores the issue of gender differences and similarities in job involvement, intrinsic motivation and job satisfaction. The characteristics of workers' family lives are also studied in order to assess the extent to which they help explain men's and women's work responses. Two different hypotheses are analysed: (a) the expectation hypothesis, which states that women have lower expectations of the workplace and therefore have greater satisfaction than men under similar job conditions; and (b) the value hypothesis, which posits that job satisfaction depends on whether one receives what one expects and thus, on average, women appear as satisfied with their jobs as men. The investigation addresses these questions to a nationally representative sample of workers in the United States. An examination of the relationship between job characteristics and work responses provides little support for the expectation hypothesis, and moderate support for the value hypothesis. In general, the results of the study strongly support the importance of meaningful work in determining how both men and women experience their jobs. The article also concludes that the permeability of work responses to family responsibilities takes on a different form for men and women.

Language(s) of text: English
ISSN: 0894-3796

48

LATACK, JC
> "COPING WITH JOB STRESS: MEASURES AND FUTURE DIRECTIONS FOR SCALE DEVELOPMENT"
in JOURNAL OF APPLIED PSYCHOLOGY (Arlington), 71(3), August 1986, 377-385.

This article presents and evaluates three scales for the measurement of coping behaviour related to job stress, the development of coping measures being a major empirical concern for researchers. The three categories of coping were conceptualized as control, referring both to actions and cognitive reappraisals that are proactive; escape, consisting of actions and cognitive reappraisals that suggest an avoidance mode; and symptom management, alluding to strategies that manage symptoms related to job stress in general. Data were collected from managers and professionals in a medium-sized manufacturing firm and in an osteopathic hospital. The results show some evidence that it is possible to develop coping measures that can be applied both independently and generally. The overall pattern of correlations suggest that individuals adopting a control strategy are less likely to report job-related anxiety, job dissatisfaction or to leave the organization, and that individuals adopting an escape or symptom-management strategy are more likely to report psychosomatic complaints. The data also suggest that a control strategy is less likely to be adopted where role ambiguity is high. The final part of the article gives suggestions for future development of scales for measuring coping behaviour.

Language(s) of text: English
ISSN: 0021-9010

49

LEVI, L
> STRESS OCH HÄLSA
(Stress and health)
STOCKHOLM, SKANDIA, 1990, 56 p. (Skandias Series Vår Hälsa)

See Section 1 on manuals and guidelines on combating stress.

Language(s) of text: Swedish

This publication is available from the Karolinska institutets institution för stressforskning, Box 60205, S-104 01 Stockholm, Sweden.

50

LOGOS, PARIS
> ACTES DU 2e COLLOQUE INTERNATIONAL: STRESS, SANTE ET MANAGEMENT
(Report of the Second International Workshop on Stress, Health and Management)
PARIS, 1992, 90 p.

This workshop was held to discuss the links between stress, health and management by means of a multidisciplinary approach. Participants came from a variety of disciplines (psychology, psychiatry, management, sociology, etc.). Discussions focused on the following issues: (a) the cost to work performance of workplace stress. In this context, the initial results of an ILO study on stress prevention programmes and stress management programmes in a Japanese corporation are described and analysed; (b) the possibility of developing feasible methods either to improve workers' adaptation to the organization or to adapt organization management to workers; and (c) the degree to which health should be a matter of concern to management, the limits of health intervention at management level, and the difficulty of involving management in occupational health activities. It was concluded that more management involvement could be achieved by alerting management to the costs of ill health, for example by incorporating a health-work-management component in training programmes.

Language(s) of text: French

This publication is available from Logos, 56 rue Perronet, F-92200 Neuilly sur Seine, France.

51

MARSHALL, J COOPER, CL
> COPING WITH STRESS AT WORK: CASE STUDIES FROM INDUSTRY
ALDERSHOT, GOWER, 1981, xvi, 236 p.

The objective of these case studies of the occupational psychology of managerial mental stress is to persuade companies to take an interest in reducing stress. The monograph covers a range of approaches to stress management, including both preventive and remedial possibilities. The benefits of training and the role of industrial physicians in health education are covered. The promotion of physical and mental health as a means to coping with stress are also examined, with examples of physical fitness programmes and relaxation techniques. The case studies also describe remedial action to help individuals cope with stress and its symptoms. Examples include the setting up of an occupational health service in a company of approximately 1,000 employees, experiments with counselling services in different companies, and remedial action against alcoholism and drug addiction. The final part of the volume illustrates ways in which environments can be changed to reduce stress. Reference is made to legislation in Scandinavian countries.

Language(s) of text: English
ISBN: 0-566-02338-5

52

MATTESON, MT   IVANCEVICH, JM
> **CONTROLLING WORK STRESS: EFFECTIVE HUMAN RESOURCE AND MANAGEMENT STRATEGIES**
SAN FRANCISCO, JOSSEY-BASS, 1989, xvii, 378 p. (A joint publication in the Jossey-Bass Management Series, the Jossey-Bass Health Series, and the Jossey-Bass Social and Behavioral Science Series)

See Section 1 on manuals and guidelines on combating stress.

Language(s) of text: English
ISBN: 1-55542-062-1

53

MURPHY, LR   HURRELL, JJ
> **"STRESS MANAGEMENT IN THE PROCESS OF OCCUPATIONAL STRESS REDUCTION"**
in JOURNAL OF MANAGERIAL PSYCHOLOGY (West Yorkshire), 2, 1987, 18-23.

This article describes the early stages of a process-oriented approach to occupational stress reduction applied in a department of a federal agency in the United States. The authors aim to illustrate that stress management has a complementary role within a more comprehensive stress reduction programme. The first stage of the experimental programme, stress management training, aimed to improve conceptual understanding of stress and its consequences, equip workers with the ability to diagnose personal and environmental stressors, and foster the development of personalized action strategies for averting the negative effects of stress. In the second stage, a committee was set up to make recommendations to management on strategies for reducing employee stress. The final stage consisted of an employee questionnaire survey, through which perceptions of job characteristics and job satisfaction were assessed. For the purpose of the study, data-entry operators, machine-paced assembly and warehouse workers constituted high stress groups, while clerical workers represented a lower stress group. Several recommendations are made for reducing job stress and increasing job satisfaction.

Language(s) of text: English
ISSN: 0268-3946

54

MURPHY, LR   SCHOENBORN, TF
US. NATIONAL INSTITUTE FOR OCCUPATIONAL SAFETY AND HEALTH
> STRESS MANAGEMENT IN WORK SETTINGS
CINCINNATI, 1987, viii, 190 p.

This publication offers guidance on how stress management programmes can be developed, implemented, evaluated and maintained in work settings. The document is divided into three parts. Part I contains three chapters that deal with organizational stress and its assessment. Part II contains four chapters that describe aspects of stress management as applied in work settings. Part III is a collection of resources for training materials, products and equipment. Two leading themes are developed. First is that stress management, as currently defined, has a limited role in reducing organizational stress because no effort is made to remove or reduce sources of stress at work. Focusing on the individual as the prime target for organizational intervention creates a dilemma of "blaming the victim". A more appropriate application of stress management would be as a complement to job redesign or organizational change interventions. The second theme is that conceptual issues are as important as logistical ones in determining programme success. Considerable effort should be expended at the outset to define the purpose of the programme, delineate organizational and individual goals, acquire organizational support, and integrate the programme with existing occupational safety and health efforts. In this way, the foundation is laid for more stable and holistic programmes. The direction is away from brief stress workshops and towards more comprehensive action that targets both the organization and the individual.

Language(s) of text: English

This publication is available from the National Institute for Occupational Safety and Health (NIOSH), Robert A. Taft Laboratories, 4676 Columbia Parkway, Cincinnati, Ohio 45226, United States, DHHS(NIOSH) Publication No. 87-111.

55

MURPHY, LR   SCHOENBORN, TF
> STRESS MANAGEMENT IN WORK SETTINGS
NEW YORK, PRAEGER, 1989, viii, 174 p.

See Section 1 on manuals and guidelines on combating stress.

Language(s) of text: English
ISBN: 0-275-93271-0

56

NELSON, DL   SUTTON, C
> "CHRONIC WORK STRESS AND COPING: A LONGITUDINAL STUDY AND SUGGESTED NEW DIRECTIONS"
in ACADEMY OF MANAGEMENT JOURNAL (Mississippi), 33(4), 1990, 859-869.

The critical issue in work stress research is distinguishing between symptoms that reflect dispositional influences or personal life stress and symptoms attributable to an individual's work situation. This study sets out to examine the effects of coping strategies on distress symptoms and performance, and to analyse the relationship between distress symptoms experienced on a new job and those brought to the job. Different variables are studied: independent ones, such as work demands and the focus of coping, and dependent ones, including distress symptoms, self-reported mastery and supervisor-rated performance. Findings show that distress symptoms brought to the job by newcomers account for a significant proportion of the distress symptoms reported by employees nine months into their jobs. The article emphasizes the need to re-examine traditional measures of coping: the instruments currently used to measure strategies for coping with stressful life events may simply not be appropriate for studying coping in a work setting. It also suggests that employers should be cautious about pursuing stress reduction strategies aggressively. If personal characteristics predispose an individual to distress symptoms, environmental interventions, such as job redesign, may be of limited value in symptom reduction; symptom-specific interventions might be more appropriate.

Language(s) of text: English
ISSN: 0001-4273

57

NEWTON, RJ   KEENAN, A
> "COPING WITH WORK-RELATED STRESS"
in HUMAN RELATIONS (New York), 38(2), 1985, 107-126.

This study examines the coping behaviour of a group of individuals in response to stress incidents experienced at work over a limited period of time. The different types of coping behaviour are analysed and classified in five categories: talking to others, direct action, preparatory action, withdrawal and helplessness/resentment. Each category is then examined in relation to the characteristics of the person experiencing the stress, the situational differences and the individual's own appraisal of stress. Analysis indicates that all three predictor groups -- stress appraisal, individual characteristics and environmental characteristics -- had a bearing on the coping behaviour reported. It is also suggested that some types of coping response are behaviour correlates of particular individual characteristics, whereas others are more likely to be related to differences in the environmental context and to the way in which the stress incident is appraised. In conclusion, the authors stress the benefits of work redesign programmes which facilitate the control of stressful demands by changing the work environment and involving the individual.

Language(s) of text: English
ISSN: 0018-7267

58

NEWTON, TJ
> "OCCUPATIONAL STRESS AND COPING WITH STRESS: A CRITIQUE"
in HUMAN RELATIONS (New York), 42(5), May 1989, 441-461.

The author reviews past research on occupational stress, arguing that there has been a lack of conceptual and operational clarity in the areas of stress, strain, coping behaviour and coping style. Occupational stress research often overlooks one important factor: the appraisal of demands, i.e. the cognitive processes of the individual who appraises an event as stressful. Lack of attention to stress deriving from particularly stressful episodes or incidents at work is a limitation to defining stress, and emphasizes the need for further research into acute stress and its relationship with ongoing chronic stress. Concerning strain, the author considers that the semantic overlap between stress and strain appears still to be a problem, as does the rather narrow conceptualization of strain which focuses predominantly on anxiety and satisfaction and overlooks other affective responses. On coping, the study indicates the need to differentiate between the behaviour actually exhibited in dealing with a specific event, and any pattern which can be distinguished in an individual's coping over time and which is related to an ongoing demand. The paper concludes with recommendations for future research methodology to overcome or limit some of the problems of current definitions and measurement.

Language(s) of text: English
ISSN: 0018-7267

59

PERREWE, PL   GANSTER, DC
> "IMPACT OF JOB DEMANDS AND BEHAVIORAL CONTROL ON EXPERIENCED JOB STRESS"
in JOURNAL OF ORGANIZATIONAL BEHAVIOR (Chichester), 10, 1989, 213-229.

This article examines the impact of behavioural control on work strain experienced under conditions of work overload. The authors base their study on the hypothesis that control interacts with job demands, and that demands have less impact on strain when control is high. The hypothesis was tested in a laboratory experiment in which undergraduate students in an introductory management course were placed on a mail sorting task with either a high or moderate workload and either a high or low level of behavioural control. Strain responses were assessed by measuring job satisfaction, psychological anxiety and physiological arousal. The results suggested that jobs perceived as being highly demanding led to both dissatisfaction and psychological anxiety. In addition, jobs perceived as containing low levels of personal control led to psychological anxiety. According to the authors, this implies that strain experienced by workers could be reduced by increasing control rather than lowering job demand levels. Given the constraints on the manipulation of work overload inherent in the laboratory environment, the results of the study were considered to be a conservative estimate of the effects of quantitative job demands and personal control on satisfaction, psychological anxiety and physiological arousal.

Language(s) of text: English
ISSN: 0894-3796

60

PREVENIR, PERIDOCIAL
> "FATIGUE: VECUS, ENJEUX, ANALYSES"
(Fatigue: Experiences, issues and analysis)
in PREVENIR (Marseille), (8), December 1983, 3-141.

This periodical is a compilation of articles by researchers from different disciplines. It aims to contribute to a better understanding of fatigue and to the search for practical solutions. The concept and the different forms of fatigue and its causes, including the cumulative effects of work organization and social life, are some of the major issues addressed. Fatigue is an active process. Its role and function must be determined and the underlying processes identified before the process can be understood. Fatigue also reveals the presence of a psychological and social barrier. The authors therefore advocate both a clinical and a socio-psychological approach. Do particular work situations generate more fatigue than others? Can the intensity of fatigue be linked to particular job situations? To answer these questions, case studies are presented to identify the most frequent occupation-related symptoms of fatigue. The volume also looks at the role of the works physician in fatigue. Acupuncture is presented as one possible medical alternative. Finally, one article analyses the business aspect of fatigue in the context of the pharmaceutical market.

Language(s) of text: French
ISSN: 0247-2406

This publication is available from the Coopérative d'édition de la vie mutualiste (CVM), 5-7 rue d'Italie, F-13006 Marseille Cedex 6, France.

61

QUICK, JC   QUICK, JD
> ORGANIZATIONAL STRESS AND PREVENTIVE MANAGEMENT
NEW YORK, McGRAW-HILL, 1984, xviii, 346 p. (McGraw-Hill Series in Management)

See Section 1 on manuals and guidelines on combating stress.

Language(s) of text: English
ISBN: 0-07-051070-9

62

QUICK, JC   BHAGAT, RS   DALTON, JE   QUICK, JD
> WORK STRESS: HEALTH CARE SYSTEMS IN THE WORKPLACE
NEW YORK, PRAEGER, 1987, xvii, 329 p.

This book takes a first step in establishing an interdisciplinary dialogue in the area of work stress, and provides a basic framework for continuing research activities and action to prevent stress at work. The goal is to focus attention on work stress as a threat to health and effective functioning in the workplace and to promote a better utilization of research in preventive or therapeutic health programmes. It contains information about research, prevention and therapy in relation to work stress, addressing the issue of how to design and implement effective workplace interventions. Preventive actions, such as those to improve relationships in the organization and team-building interventions, as well as health and fitness programmes, are discussed. Several models of occupational health therapeutic activities are also described. Further research is needed to provide management, unions, individuals and society with a clearer understanding of what preventive interventions can accomplish.

Language(s) of text: English
ISBN: 0-275-92329-0

63

REDDY, M
BRITISH PSYCHOLOGICAL SOCIETY
> **MANAGER'S GUIDE TO COUNSELLING AT WORK**
LONDON, METHUEN, 1987, 145 p.

See Section 1 on manuals and guidelines on combating stress.

Language(s) of text: English
ISBN: 0-901715-70-0

This publication is available from the British Psychological Society, St. Andrews House, 48 Princess Road East, Leicester LE1 7DR, United Kingdom.

64

REYNOLDS, S   SHAPIRO, DA
> "STRESS REDUCTION IN TRANSITION: CONCEPTUAL PROBLEMS IN THE DESIGN, IMPLEMENTATION, AND EVALUATION OF WORKSITE STRESS MANAGEMENT INTERVENTIONS"
in HUMAN RELATIONS (New York), 44(7), July 1991, 717-733.

This article examines some of the conceptual assumptions of stress research. The authors consider that occupational and clinical psychologists could collaborate in developing methods to reduce occupational stress, focusing on the interaction of individuals with their working environment and the impact of this interaction on individual well-being and organizational efficiency. Stress management training and employee counselling are analysed. It is pointed out that, although there are differences between them (the first is primarily preventive and the second a treatment strategy), both can be seen as an attempt to increase employee tolerance of noxious or unacceptable job characteristics without reducing or removing stressors from the environment. The study highlights the advantages of interventions which target changes in organization and job characteristics, and mentions that researchers are more likely to opt for an interactional model of stress comprising both organizational and individual factors. The authors also discuss organizational development, i.e. recourse to behavioural science interventions in order to enhance organizational effectiveness and the well-being of employees, and consider that one advantage of organizational development is its compatibility with clinically oriented interventions.

Language(s) of text: English
ISSN: 0018-7267

65

RODAHL, K
> PHYSIOLOGY OF WORK
LONDON, TAYLOR AND FRANCIS, 1989, vi, 290 p.

This book focuses on the application of physiology to the assessment of the stress encountered in a wide variety of occupations, using original data and specific case studies. The biological basis of human work and the development of the discipline of work physiology are reviewed. The author states that many of the problems of present-day workers are a consequence of static work and stress with which they are unable to cope, and presents some of the factors affecting their ability to perform physical work. Methods are proposed for the evaluation of different parameters such as physical work capacity and workload, and of the working environment. Different occupations and activities are analysed from this physiological point of view. Illustrations include studies of managers, shiftworkers and air traffic controllers, who experience mental and emotional stress; studies of polar and sea-going workers; and the problems of workers in polluted atmospheres. The book deals with applied techniques which technical staff in industry can use to assess the work environment.

Language(s) of text: English
ISBN: 0-85066-478-0

66

SAUTER, SL   MURPHY, LR   HURRELL Jr., JJ
> "PREVENTION OF WORK-RELATED PSYCHOLOGICAL DISORDERS: A NATIONAL STRATEGY PROPOSED BY THE NATIONAL INSTITUTE FOR OCCUPATIONAL SAFETY AND HEALTH (NIOSH)"
in AMERICAN PSYCHOLOGIST (Washington), 45(10), October 1990, 1146-1158.

This paper is a first attempt to fashion a comprehensive national strategy to protect and promote the psychological health of workers. The strategy focuses on psychological disorders of general concern in the occupational health arena, especially those that bear a relation to working conditions, such as "job stress". Affective disturbances, such as anxiety, depression and job dissatisfaction, maladaptive behavioural and lifestyle patterns, and chemical dependencies and alcohol abuse are included. First, to give an idea of the magnitude of the problem, the authors present data, mainly from the United States, on the cost of stress and the proportion of workers affected. Secondly, the paper examines distinct categories of action for preventing work-related psychological disorders: (a) job design to improve working conditions, focused principally on the social environment at work, organizational aspects of the job, and the content and certain operational aspects of the tasks performed; (b) surveillance of disorders and risk factors, to detect and react to emerging problems and to evaluate interventions; (c) information dissemination, education and training to increase awareness and appreciation of psychological disorders as an occupational health problem; and (d) enhancement of psychological health services for workers. Several recommendations for identifying the specific actors and the necessary actions are included.

Language(s) of text: English
ISSN: 0003-066X

67

SETHI, AS   SCHULER, RS
> **HANDBOOK OF ORGANIZATIONAL STRESS COPING STRATEGIES**
CAMBRIDGE, BALLINGER PUBLISHING, 1984, xiv, 319 p.

This book collects the views of several experts on the subject of coping with stress in organizational settings, reflecting a concern about the negative and cumulative effects of stress in the workplace and highlighting the need for individuals and organizations to develop strategies to cope with stress.   The problems of ageing, adapting to retirement, communications, human relations, workload and time management as related to stress, are examined. Strategies for reducing and controlling occupational stress are presented, such as methods to enhance time management and improve employee communications;   new practices for minimizing job burnout, especially in human service professions;   the positive uses of social support groups and how they can be developed and promoted within the organisation;   and practical guidelines for coping with job stress for managers.   In addition, four techniques that can be used at the individual level to cope with organizational and personal stress are explained in detail: meditation, yoga, biofeedback and physical activity.   The authors also discuss research issues and future directions in order to prevent or minimize the negative effects of organizational stress.

Language(s) of text: English
ISBN: 0-88410-745-0

68

SLABY, AE
> **SIXTY WAYS TO MAKE STRESS WORK FOR YOU**
SUMMIT, NEW JERSEY, PIA PRESS, 1988, viii, 54 p.

See Section 1 on manuals and guidelines on combating stress.

Language(s) of text: English
ISBN: 0-929162-02-1

69

THEORELL, T ALFREDSSON, L KARASEK, RA KNOX, S PERSKI, A SVENSSON, J WALLER, D
SWEDISH WORK ENVIRONMENT FUND
> **HEART AT WORK**
STOCKHOLM, 1987, 16 p.

See Section 1 on manuals and guidelines on combating stress.

Language(s) of text: English

This publication is available from the Swedish Work Environment Fund, Box 1122, S-111 81 Stockholm, Sweden, Order No. 60-19-12.

70

UK. ADVISORY, CONCILIATION AND ARBITRATION SERVICE
> HEALTH AND EMPLOYMENT
LONDON, 1990, 55 p. (Advisory Booklet No. 15)

See Section 1 on manuals and guidelines on combating stress.

Language(s) of text: English
ISBN: 0-906073-45-6

This publication is available from the Advisory, Conciliation and Arbitration Service, 27 Wilton Street, London SW1X 7AZ, United Kingdom.

71

UK. OFFICE OF THE MINISTER FOR THE CIVIL SERVICE
> UNDERSTANDING STRESS: PART 1
LONDON, HER MAJESTY'S STATIONERY OFFICE, 1987, 110 p.

This is the first in a series of four books, which have been produced as resource and working tools to assist persons interested in stress. Part One examines the concept of stress. It states that stress can result from major demands but also from an accumulation of minor demands, and that the individual differences in responding to stress should be taken into account. It also examines the symptoms of stress and how to recognize stress responses. Factors which can cause stress are analysed, differentiating between personal and organizational stressors. A list of occupations in relation to stress rates is included, as well as a measure of the cost of stress in general. The book also deals with how to manage stress and describes methods of coping with stress, such as relaxation exercises, improving the general level of health through diet and exercise, complementary medicine, counselling, time management, job design, participation, and so on. A list of organizations and individuals and a bibliography are also included.

Language(s) of text: English
ISBN: 0-11-430019-4

72

UK. OFFICE OF THE MINISTER FOR THE CIVIL SERVICE
> UNDERSTANDING STRESS: PART 2; LINE MANAGER'S GUIDE
LONDON, HER MAJESTY'S STATIONERY OFFICE, 1987, 46 p.

Part Two of this series is written for line managers who wish to understand more about how stress affects them and their staff by helping them to recognize the existence of stress in the workplace. The book also helps to identify potential stressors in relation to the environment, individual and work, and symptoms of stress, paying attention to the role of the line manager in this respect. It analyses job-related factors which increase stress at work and includes some suggestions on how to reduce job-related stress, such as matching the individual to the job, listening and counselling, managing and directing work, controlling time and managing change.

Language(s) of text: English
ISBN: 0-11-430020-8

73

UK. OFFICE OF THE MINISTER FOR THE CIVIL SERVICE
> **UNDERSTANDING STRESS: PART 3; TRAINER'S GUIDE**
LONDON, HER MAJESTY'S STATIONERY OFFICE, 1987, 73 p.

The third book of the series examines the role the trainer can play in informing people about stress and helping them to control and manage it. A three-level approach (individual, occupational and organizational) is necessary to look at individual problems in an appropriate context and to identify the most appropriate solutions. A selection of training programmes is included which illustrate examples of training events (seminars and workshops) from a variety of civil service departments and outside organizations. The volume also contains certain basic materials (examples, sample handouts, questionnaires), developed by various organizations, that can be adapted and/or incorporated into training events.

Language(s) of text: English
ISBN: 0-11-430021-6

74

UK. OFFICE OF THE MINISTER FOR THE CIVIL SERVICE
> **UNDERSTANDING STRESS: PART 4; WELFARE OFFICER'S GUIDE**
LONDON, HER MAJESTY'S STATIONERY OFFICE, 1987, 27 p.

The fourth book of this series is designed to help welfare officers recognize the existence of stress in the workplace, and to identify stress symptoms and the preventive pro-active role welfare officers can take in stress management. It defines stress and reviews the causes, symptoms and signs of stress, including the physical, psychological, emotional and behavioural, and the social responses to stress. A list of coping strategies is provided. There is also reference to how welfare officers can work with line managers and trainers to reduce stress in individuals and to manage occupational stress.

Language(s) of text: English
ISBN: 0-11-430022-4

75

WARSHAW, LJ
NEW YORK BUSINESS GROUP ON HEALTH
> **STRESS, ANXIETY AND DEPRESSION IN THE WORKPLACE: REPORT OF THE NYBGH/GALLUP SURVEY**
NEW YORK, 1989, 21 p.

See Section 1 on manuals and guidelines on combating stress.

Language(s) of text: English

This publication is available from the New York Business Group on Health, Inc., 622 Third Avenue, 34th floor, New York, New York 10017-6763, United States.

76

WHEELER, S   LYON, D
> "EMPLOYEE BENEFITS FOR THE EMPLOYER'S BENEFIT: HOW COMPANIES RESPOND TO EMPLOYEE STRESS"
in PERSONNEL REVIEW (Bradford), 21(7), 1992, 47-65.

This article presents the results of research on stress-related problems in 30 British companies. Managers in these companies were interviewed using a semi-structured questionnaire. The interviews concentrated on concrete situations and the way stress was managed. The research showed that there is little commitment in these companies to dealing with stress per se in terms of a company-wide strategy. Where efforts are made to deal with stress-related problems, managers often lack understanding of stress-related symptoms and thus suggest ineffective solutions, such as "time off to sort things out", or attempt to deal with emotional problems with inadequate skills. Although there was some availability of training on interpersonal skills for managers in the larger companies, most were expected to grow into the job in this respect or were assumed to possess sophisticated interpersonal skills. The authors conclude that the companies involved in this study, and many other British companies, could benefit from considering the causes and effects of stress on their employees and reviewing their work practices, expectations, training programmes, welfare benefits and personnel policies with stress in mind.

Language(s) of text: English
ISSN: 0048-3486

77

WHITE, G
UK. ADVISORY, CONCILIATION AND ARBITRATION SERVICE. WORK RESEARCH UNIT
> MANAGING STRESS IN ORGANIZATIONAL CHANGE
LONDON, 1984, 5 p. (WRU Occasional Paper No. 31)

See Section 1 on manuals and guidelines on combating stress.

Language(s) of text: English

This working paper can be ordered from the Work Research Unit, Advisory, Conciliation and Arbitration Service, 27 Wilton Street, London SW1X 7AZ, United Kingdom.

78

WYCHERLEY, B
UK. SOUTH EAST THAMES REGIONAL HEALTH AUTHORITY
> LIVING SKILLS PACK
BEXHILL-ON-SEA, EAST SUSSEX, 1988, 1 v.

See Section 1 on manuals and guidelines on combating stress.

Language(s) of text: English
ISBN: 0-9503162-4-5

This publication is available from the Marketing and Public Relations Department, South East Thames Regional Health Authority, Thrift House, Collington Avenue, Bexhill-on-Sea, East Sussex TN39 3NQ, United Kingdom.

B. Documents on stress in specific occupations

79

ARSENAULT, A   DOLAN, SL   VAN AMERINGEN, MR
> **"STRESS AND MENTAL STRAIN IN HOSPITAL WORK: EXPLORING THE RELATIONSHIP BEYOND PERSONALITY"**
in JOURNAL OF ORGANIZATIONAL BEHAVIOR (Chichester), 12(6), November 1991, 483-493.

This article explores the relationship between job demands, personality traits and a variety of both individual and organizational outcomes in a hospital environment. It is postulated that the level of mental strain can be partially accounted for by certain personality traits, while other facets of personality correlate only marginally with symptoms of strain. Full-time employees were given a questionnaire containing scales related to job stressors, personality trait measures, and psychological strain self-assessment scales. After adjustment for differences in personality traits, difficulties with the role played on the job were the strongest factors contributing to mental strain. From this could be inferred inconsistencies on the ward in terms of patient management and difficulties in dealing with patients' families. The second job stressor found to be related to mental strain was the degree of professional latitude. Conflicting demands from staff, patients and families where there is restricted clinical discretion, decreased participation, and low professional recognition create an atmosphere conducive to mental strain. Workload problems also appeared to be associated with symptoms of strain independent of personality traits.

Language(s) of text: English
ISSN: 0894-3796

80

BECKER-CARUS, C   GUENTHNER, G   HANNICH, HJ
> **"STRESS AND SITUATION SPECIFIC COPING BEHAVIOUR IN INTENSIVE CARE UNIT NURSING STAFF"**
in WORK AND STRESS (London), 3(4), 1989, 353-359.

This article addresses the significance and effectiveness of different behavioural responses in intensive care staff. It points out that little research has been conducted in this field, despite the fact that intensive care wards appear to be unique in terms of the number of stress-producing demands, responsibility and permanent exposure to extreme physical distress and mental suffering. Each of the nurses taking part in the study underwent a partly standardized and focused interview relating to ten typical, frequently experienced stress situations. The authors established three criteria for describing and analysing coping behaviour: individual/no individual strategy, internal/external action, and active/passive action. An evaluation of the data revealed that most of the subjects resorted to individual, active, external actions. Situations involving occupational stress were connected with active coping behaviours, whereas passive strategies were primarily used in situations involving personal stress. It was also observed that discontentment with coping behaviours occurred mainly in passive behaviours. Active coping in situations considered as occupationally stressful was consistently experienced as satisfactory.

Language(s) of text: English
ISSN: 0267-8373

81

DOLAN, SL   VAN AMERINGEN, MR   ARSENAULT, A
> "PERSONALITY, SOCIAL SUPPORT AND WORKERS' STRESS"
in RELATIONS INDUSTRIELLES = INDUSTRIAL RELATIONS (Quebec), 47(1), 1992, 125-136.

The objective of the study is to examine the direct and indirect relationships between social support and workers' strain in the light of intrinsic and extrinsic job demands on four personality types. Social support is construed as the perceived support that can be obtained from superiors, colleagues and family. The three main forms of psychological strain (depression, anxiety and irritation) are considered. The four personality types are the competitive, the hyperactive and optimistic, the controllers and less competitive, and the quiet and faithful. The sample consists of 807 hospital personnel of whom about 80 per cent are women. The data source is a questionnaire that elicits information on perceived job demands, individual personality traits and sources of social support. A detailed statistical analysis of the variables reveals most importantly that social support has a moderating impact on strain; there is a significant correlation between intrinsic and extrinsic job demands, the three forms of psychological strain and the three sources of social support; in all four personality types only the extrinsic job demand factors are significantly correlated with the three types of strain, and there is a prominent negative correlation across all four personality types. The study also identifies and describes unique relationships between each personality group and the social support and psychological strain variables. In conclusion, the authors emphasize the need to examine multiple variables and their relationships in seeking effective coping strategies.

Language(s) of text: English
ISSN: 0034-379X

82

FITTER, M
EUROPEAN FOUNDATION FOR THE IMPROVEMENT OF LIVING AND WORKING CONDITIONS
> IMPACT OF NEW TECHNOLOGY ON WORKERS AND PATIENTS IN THE HEALTH SERVICES: PHYSICAL AND PSYCHOLOGICAL STRESS
LUXEMBOURG, OFFICE FOR OFFICIAL PUBLICATIONS OF THE EUROPEAN COMMUNITY, 1987, x, 116 p.

The study assesses the impact of new technology (health monitoring and health support equipment) particularly on nurses and patients in the hospital intensive care unit. It is based on reports and case studies from six countries: Denmark, the Federal Republic of Germany, Ireland, Italy, the Netherlands and the United Kingdom. A consolidated analysis of the case studies shows that the stress factors affecting nurses relate to heavy workload, responsibility, emotional reactions towards dying patients and their relatives, rapid technological and medical developments, and rapid workpace. Additional causes of stress in the intensive care unit are the risk of accidents, tense environment, increasing cognitive requirements, inadequate training, poor design and breakdown of equipment. On the other hand, high job quality and better opportunities for advancement and promotion act as counter stressors for nurses. Nurses in the intensive care unit are not found to experience more stress than their counterparts. The study also reveals that the nurses are generally appreciative of new technology and wish to be involved in its planning, design and development. Measures are recommended to make the introduction of new technology smoother and more effective.

Language(s) of text: English
ISBN: 92-825-6797-4

This publication is also available in French and German.

83

HANDY, J
> "STRESS AND CONTRADICTION IN PSYCHIATRIC NURSING"
in HUMAN RELATIONS (London), 44(1), January 1991, 39-52.

This article is based on an in-depth case study of two wards in a large psychiatric hospital and a community psychiatric nursing unit attached to the same hospital, using a variety of predominantly qualitative techniques. After analysing recent sociological theory on the contradictory role of the psychiatric system, the author presents data illustrating the ways in which the structural contradictions of the psychiatric sector affect the daily lives of all who participate in the system. It is suggested that many of the problems encountered by staff during their working lives are rooted in their use of maladaptive and collective social defence systems which have the unintended consequence of exacerbating the various structural contradictions of the psychiatric system. Feedback was provided through a series of workshops and through written reports circulated to both the nurses and the nursing management, to increase the nurses' awareness of the various ways in which their personal experiences were moulded by the structural contradictions of the psychiatric sector, and to explore ways in which the negative personal effects could be reduced. Finally, the article discusses the need for organizational-level interventions to relieve occupational stress in welfare institutions.

Language(s) of text: English
ISSN: 0018-7267

84

PAYNE, R   FIRTH-COZENS, J
> STRESS IN HEALTH PROFESSIONALS
CHICHESTER, JOHN WILEY, 1987, xxiv, 288 p. (Wiley Series on Studies in Occupational Stress)

Health professionals are widely recognized as one of the groups exposed to high degrees of stress. This book reviews the literature to identify the main causes of stress and the ways to cope with them for selected health occupations. Part I concentrates on medical doctors, and has chapters on stress experienced during medical training by physicians in the United States, by general practitioners in the United Kingdom, by surgeons and by psychiatrists. A chapter focuses on the pressures that a career in medicine creates for women. Part II deals with other health professions, including dentists, staff working with the mentally disabled, psychiatric nursing and social workers. The last two chapters are devoted to the stress generated by the introduction of new technology affecting nurses, medical technologists and laboratory technicians. Part III outlines the difficulties which hospitals face in dealing with the problems of budget cuts alongside the increasing sophistication of a technology which allows lives to be saved, but at such an economic cost that doctors and administrators face complex ethical decisions.

Language(s) of text: English
ISBN: 0-471-91254-9

85

COLE, M   WALKER, S
> **TEACHING AND STRESS**
MILTON KEYNES, OPEN UNIVERSITY PRESS, 1989, xii, 177 p.

This book contains a collection of articles and reports presented to a 1987 conference on teaching and stress. The articles are grouped into two categories. The first category deals in detail with the nature and negative implications of stress from teaching and burnout. More specific issues, such as mental health problems among teachers, are also treated. Most articles conclude that teaching is an inherently stressful occupation. The second category treats issues relating to coping with and controlling stress. One article identifies the major groups of stress factors, recommends strategies to minimize and prevent stress among teachers, and suggests what individual teachers might do for themselves. Another article evaluates coping strategies used by teachers, and concludes that stress can be minimized not only by organizational strategies, but also by strengthening personal and interpersonal mechanisms. A third article demonstrates that learning experiences (short-term training and workshops) in communication, counselling skills, assertiveness training and goal setting, can be an effective tool for mitigating and coping with stress. The last chapter points out that teachers' stress is also closely related to the education system and thus broader issues must also be taken into account.

Language(s) of text: English
ISBN: 0-335-09548-8

86

SCHONFELD, IS
> **"COPING WITH JOB-RELATED STRESS: THE CASE OF TEACHERS"**
in JOURNAL OF OCCUPATIONAL PSYCHOLOGY (London), 63, 1990, 141-149.

This article investigates the relation between coping measures and psychological distress and job-related morale in veteran teachers. Items for use in coping measures were developed from a review of stress literature and the suggestions of the respondents to a questionnaire. Five occupational coping scales were constructed: seeking advice, applying discipline, making positive comparisons, selectively ignoring the job's difficulties and taking direct positive action. The analysis of the results with controls for social-demographic factors and adversity in the job environment indicated that seeking advice and taking direct positive action were most consistently related to lower depressive and psycho-physiological symptom levels. In addition, making positive comparisons and taking direct positive action were significantly related to higher job satisfaction and motivation to continue in the profession. Selectively ignoring the job's difficulties appeared to buffer the impact of environmental adversity on symptoms. The findings of the study suggest that teachers who employ identifiable occupational coping behaviours are less likely to experience psychological symptoms and low morale. The author concludes that the school may be less impersonally organized than many other work settings, making for a work environment in which coping behaviours can alleviate distress and enhance job satisfaction.

Language(s) of text: English
ISSN: 0305-8107

87

SEIDMAN, SA   ZAGER, J
> "STUDY OF COPING BEHAVIOURS AND TEACHER BURNOUT"
in WORK AND STRESS (London), 5(3), 1991, 205-216.

The study described in this article explores the relationship between teacher burnout and adaptive personal coping strategies, as well as organizational support strategies. The sample consisted of classroom teachers from north Texas, predominantly those working on a regular basis. Significant correlations were found between teacher burnout factors and various external and internal responses to stress. The data suggested that teachers with higher burnout scores used certain maladaptive strategies to cope with stress. They also showed a greater frequency of marital and family difficulties. On the other hand, the use of several positive or adaptive coping approaches was found to be associated with lower burnout. It is further suggested that participation in workshops may be a useful strategy for dealing with teacher burnout, but that discussions with colleagues seems to be either counterproductive or of insignificant value. In addition, the analysis revealed the existence of a significant relationship between many physical and psychological problems, such as stomach ache and depression, and aspects of teacher burnout.

Language(s) of text: English
ISSN: 0267-8373

88

BROWN, JM   CAMBELL, EA
> "SOURCES OF OCCUPATIONAL STRESS IN THE POLICE"
in WORK AND STRESS (London), 4(4), 1990, 305-318.

This article describes a questionnaire study of occupational stress carried out within a large non-metropolitan police force in the United Kingdom. The aims of the study were to examine the frequency with which police officers were exposed to sources of stress, to establish the degree to which exposure was associated with self-perceived stress and to measure levels of psychological distress. The highest overall exposure rates were found to relate to organizational and management stressors rather than to routine operational duties. Different ranks of officers showed differential rates of exposure, perceived stress and distress. Sergeants were found to be exposed to the greatest number of stressors and probation constables the least. It was concluded that rank had an impact on the exposure of officers to stress and there was some indication that gender was also a key differentiating factor. The findings confirmed that the most frequently reported sources of stress for police, as noted in earlier studies, are work overload, long hours, lack of resources, shortage of staff, failure by the courts to prosecute offenders, increased bureaucratic procedures and management styles.

Language(s) of text: English
ISSN: 0267-8373

89

LOO, R
> "POLICIES AND PROGRAMS FOR MENTAL HEALTH IN LAW ENFORCEMENT ORGANIZA-
TIONS"
in CANADA'S MENTAL HEALTH (Ottawa), 35(3), September 1987, 18-22.

This article examines the development of organizational policies and programmes to prevent the negative impact of job stress on police forces. The sources of stress in law enforcement organizations and physical, psychological and behavioural reactions to stress are presented in table form. The author points out that resistance on the part of employees, cost and lack of professional staff may be obstacles to policy and programme development. Indications are given on how to introduce mental health programmes in law enforcement organizations, and a formal strategic planning model is proposed. Finally, a case study of the Royal Canadian Mounted Police is used to show how psychological services can be introduced and the types of prevention and treatment programmes and other activities for promoting and maintaining mental health.

Language(s) of text: English

90

CHAMBERLAIN, AG   JONES, DM
> "SATISFACTIONS AND STRESSES IN THE SORTING OF MAIL"
in WORK AND STRESS (London), 1(1), 1987, 25-34.

This article compares two types of mail sorting, manual sorting and code sorting, to investigate differences in stress and satisfaction. In psychological terms, both jobs seem to condense a number of factors which purportedly influence stress. Mechanized work was found to have little variety, autonomy and social interaction, and to require a rapid pace. Higher levels of satisfaction were found among manual sorters. In the code-sorting work, great dissatisfaction was usually accompanied by higher levels of stress, and the level of commitment was an important determinant of the degree of dissatisfaction. Among the manual sorters and supervisors, stress took the form of fatigue and tiredness, whereas the code sorters experienced anxiety or tension.

Language(s) of text: English
ISSN: 0267-8373

91

COOPER, CL   MARSHALL, J
> WHITE COLLAR AND PROFESSIONAL STRESS
CHICHESTER, JOHN WILEY, 1980, xiii, 257 p. (Wiley Series on Studies in Occupational Stress)

This book examines the situation of white-collar workers in the United Kingdom and the United States in an effort to identify problem areas and occupational sources of work stress. Health-care professionals are examined, particularly dentists and nursing staff in hospitals, including nurses in intensive care units. Suggestions for reducing stress are made. The problems of teachers and school administrators are also examined, as are various coping strategies available to them for dealing with stress. Both the British and American approaches are studied in relation to teachers: the former focuses on classroom sources of stress and personality characteristics associated with "teachers at risk", while the latter emphasizes the changing role of teachers in a changing society. Police and social workers are also discussed. It is noted that both groups are experiencing more job-related stress owing, in part, to their changing roles in society. Legislators and trade union officials are also included. Due to rapid technological developments in industry, a variety of new stressors are emerging. The sources of these are discussed.

Language(s) of text: English
ISBN: 0-471-27760-6

92

KOMPIER, M   MULDERS, H   MEIJMAN, T   BOERSMA, M   GROEN, G   BULLINGA, R
> "ABSENCE BEHAVIOUR, TURNOVER AND DISABILITY: A STUDY AMONG CITY BUS DRIVERS
IN THE NETHERLANDS"
in WORK AND STRESS (London), 4(1), 1990, 83-89.

The authors examine the issues of well-being, health complaints, absenteeism and turnover among city bus drivers as interrelated symptoms of a long-term process of work stress.   The study was carried out in the Netherlands where city bus drivers are public employees.   The percentage of absenteeism among the drivers was two to three times higher than the national average, and the most common form of absenteeism was long-term (more than 42 days).   Very few of the employees stopped working at the official retirement age of 60, whereas a large percentage had to leave their jobs owing to disability or for medical reasons at a younger age than public employees in other sectors.   The risk of disablement was more than twice as high as for male Dutch public employees in general. Mental disorders were one of the main precursors of disablement in bus drivers.   A considerable proportion of the absenteeism proved to be related to future disability, and it was also shown that long-term absenteeism was a strong precursor of future disability.   The research points to a work-related process of progressive deterioration of health and well-being over a reasonably long period.

Language(s) of text: English
ISSN: 0267-8373

93

SCHÄFER, T   STEININGER, S
GERMANY. FEDERAL INSTITUTE FOR OCCUPATIONAL SAFETY AND HEALTH
> HEALTH HAZARDS AND OCCUPATIONAL TURNOVER AMONG PROFESSIONAL TRUCK
DRIVERS: POSSIBILITIES FOR INTEGRATED DATA COLLECTION AND UTILISATION WITH A
VIEW TO PREVENTION
DORTMUND, 1990, ix, 226 p.   (Research No. 558)

This study, based on quantitative data from company case studies and interviews with experts, examines the extent of health hazards and occupational mobility among professional truck drivers, and suggests remedies.   The major strain "constellations" identified among truck drivers in local and long-distance freight transport include excessive and multiple tasks, heavy physical work, optimization pressure, time pressure, competitive pressure, inadequate training and qualifications, and exposure to special hazards.   The book elaborates on the consequences of such strain, and identifies poor health and high occupational turnover as the main ones.   Finally, measures are recommended for preventing and minimizing strain and stress among professional truck drivers, such as adjusting the organization of work, resetting task boundaries, preventive socio-medical care, improved road safety training, better working conditions (noise, vibration, gases, high temperatures, etc.) in truck cabins, and consideration of truck drivers' private living conditions.

Language(s) of text: English
ISBN: 3-89429-030-7
ISSN: 0932-3856

This publication is available from the Federal Institute for Occupational Safety and Health, P.O. Box 170202, D-4600 Dortmund 1, Germany.   This version is a translation of the original report in German: Krankheiten und Berufsverläufe von Kraftfahrzeugführern des Strassengüterverkehrs, ISBN 3-88314-833-4.

94

WINKLEBY, MA   RAGLAND, DR   FISHER, JM   SYME, SL
> "EXCESS RISK OF SICKNESS AND DISEASE IN BUS DRIVERS: A REVIEW AND SYNTHESIS OF EPIDEMIOLOGICAL STUDIES"
in INTERNATIONAL JOURNAL OF EPIDEMIOLOGY (Oxford), 17(2), 1988, 255-261.

This article reviews epidemiological studies of the relationship between bus driving and various diseases. Its purpose is to consider elements of the bus-driving environment that may contribute to heightening the risks associated with this occupation. The studies looked at cardiovascular disease, gastro-intestinal illnesses and muscular-skeletal problems as the main disease categories, and consistently reported that bus drivers had higher rates of mortality, morbidity and absence due to illness than employees from a wide range of other occupational groups. Increased disease rates were found across all the research methodologies, measurement techniques and comparison groups used. Several factors to which bus drivers are exposed and that may directly contribute to increased health risks are reviewed; they include elements of the physical environment, and conditions such as rigid time schedules, long working hours, shift work and multiple demands over which drivers have little control. The authors nonetheless point out that certain questions still need careful assessment before firm conclusions can be drawn as to the link between increased disease rates and bus driving.

Language(s) of text: English
ISSN: 0300-5771

95

MUNDAL, R   ERIKSSEN, J   BJORKLUND, R   RODAHL, K
> "ELEVATED BLOOD PRESSURE IN AIR TRAFFIC CONTROLLERS DURING A PERIOD OF OCCUPATIONAL CONFLICT"
in STRESS MEDICINE (Chichester), 6, 1990, 141-144.

This article reports the results of several studies on the stress experienced by air traffic controllers at three different times: when they were in the throes of a dispute over wages and working conditions, a year later when the conflict was resolved, and again six years later when working conditions were normal. Blood pressure, as a stress indicator, and resting heart rate were measured during the three periods using exactly the same standardized technique. The study showed a transitory elevation of blood pressure associated with involvement in a labour dispute, while resting heart rates remained essentially unaffected. However, the authors note that the question remains as to how long such a situation has to be maintained for the transient elevation of blood pressure to become permanent so that it may be classified clinically as a state of hypertension. They also suggest that the relationship between abnormal emotional or social situations, including labour relations conflicts, and hypertension should be kept in mind when considering blood pressure levels in occupational groups.

Language(s) of text: English
ISSN: 0748-8386

96

SLOAN, SJ   COOPER, CL
> **PILOTS UNDER STRESS**
LONDON, ROUTLEDGE & KEGAN PAUL, 1986, ix, 230 p.

This book contains the results of research which investigated the nature and effectiveness of coping strategies used by commercial aircraft pilots. The basic data of the study were drawn from a sample of 442 pilots, who provided information based on questionnaires. The study evaluates 33 variables that could have an impact on the ability of pilots to cope with stress. Four major factors are identified: (a) stability of relationships and home life; (b) interaction between working and domestic lives; (c) social support; and (d) involvement of spouses. Among the four factors, the most significant is the first. This indicates that pilots, who are generally thought to possess better coping skills, are as vulnerable to external factors as other workers in dealing with psychosomatic stresses. The authors conclude by stressing the importance of coping strategies that are external to the individual, even in situations where such individuals might be judged on an "a priori" basis as being amply equipped to cope with psychosocial stresses.

Language(s) of text: English
ISBN: 0-7102-0479-5

97

VAERNES, RJ   MYHRE, G   AAS, H   HOMNES, T   HANSEN, K   TONDER, O
> **"RELATIONSHIPS BETWEEN STRESS, PSYCHOLOGICAL FACTORS, HEALTH, AND IMMUNE LEVELS AMONG MILITARY AVIATORS"**
in WORK AND STRESS (London), 5(1), 1991, 5-16.

Sixty-four aviators of the Royal Norwegian Air Force participated in this study, which examines and confirms the hypothesis that there is a correlation between immunoglobulin levels and work stress and personality factors among air force aviators. Inventories of the psychological state, the work environment and health of the pilots were made. Immunological tests were also administered. Those who manage to cope with environmental stress factors are found to have acceptable immune resistance, while those who perceive experiencing stress tend to have a reduced immunoglobulin level and reduced immune resistance. It is also concluded that immunoglobulin is a good measure of stress at group level, but not for individual immunological susceptibility.

Language(s) of text: English
ISSN: 0267-8373

98

ELO, AL
> "HEALTH AND STRESS OF SEAFARERS"
in SCANDINAVIAN JOURNAL OF WORK, ENVIRONMENT AND HEALTH (Helsinki), 11(6), December 1985, 427-432.

This study examines the relationship between perceived health and stress of seafarers and personality characteristics and work-related stress factors. The sample involves 591 seafarers of the Finnish Merchant Fleet who work at different occupations and organizational positions and 194 variables known to have impact on the health and stress of seafarers. Major variables include occupational characteristics, social relations and personality, and perceived stress and health. The nature of problems causing stress and the extent of stress vary from one type of occupation to another. Analysis of the variables that relate to the work environment shows that rough seas is the most disturbing factor to all occupational groups. Engine officers and the engine crew experience the highest level of stress as they are subjected significantly to noise and heat. The deck crew experience stress from being exposed to cold, humidity and polluted air. A fast workpace is a major stress factor for the catering staff, while the slow pace of activities is the main reason for stress and depression among radio operators. Seafarers in all occupations generally consider their jobs to be monotonous. The study confirms that relations among shipmates, officers and crew are generally good and not a factor affecting health. Rather, personality and occupation-related factors are the most significant in explaining perceived stress and ill health among seafarers.

Language(s) of text: English
ISSN: 0355-3140

99

BARTON CUNNINGHAM, J
> "COMPRESSED SHIFT SCHEDULE: DEALING WITH SOME OF THE PROBLEMS OF SHIFT-WORK"
in JOURNAL OF ORGANIZATIONAL BEHAVIOR (Chichester), 10(3), July 1989, 231-245.

This article examines some of the psychological and behavioural effects of a particular form of compressed workday, a 12-hour compressed shift schedule, on coalminers in western Canada. The purpose of the experiment was to provide data to assist the Government in deciding whether to implement similar schedules, since labour codes prohibited their use in mining industries. Workers in two open-pit coalmines were studied; one coalmine experimented with the 12-hour compressed shift schedule, while the other served as a comparison group. The participants filled out questionnaires containing a number of indices of perceived work and non-work behaviour, and underwent several health-related tests. The results showed that the sleep problems frequently reported by shiftworkers were not ameliorated by the compressed shift schedule. Neither did the schedule seem to have any effect on job satisfaction and tensions. With regard to family relationships, married individuals spent less time with their families on workdays, and did not spend any more time with them on their days off. However, family satisfaction seems to have improved, perhaps because the new schedule reduced the amount of night and weekend work, which were highly unpopular among shiftworkers. There was no suggestion that the compressed shift schedule had any negative effects on the health of individuals.

Language(s) of text: English
ISSN: 0894-3796

100

FRESE, M   SEMMER, N
> "SHIFTWORK, STRESS, AND PSYCHOSOMATIC COMPLAINTS: A COMPARISON BETWEEN WORKERS IN DIFFERENT SHIFTWORK SCHEDULES, NON-SHIFTWORKERS, AND FORMER SHIFTWORKERS"
in ERGONOMICS (London), 29(1), January 1986, 99-114.

This article looks at the relationship between shift work, ill health and occupational stress in blue-collar male workers. The authors analyse a questionnaire study carried out in the chemical industry in the Federal Republic of Germany to compare shiftworkers with workers who had never worked shifts, workers who had previously worked shifts but stopped on medical advice, and workers who left shift work for reasons other than health. Variables to check on stress at work, age and level of training, and social context were used. The results showed that psychological and environmental stress were closely related to ill health, implying that stress may well add to the effects of shift work. It is pointed out, however, that stress at work is an important predictor of ill health, independently of shift work. The findings also suggested that, in terms of ill health, the introduction of the 12-hour shift system might be less advantageous than expected, though workers may prefer the fast-rotating schedule because of its added leisure time. The comparison between shiftworkers and workers never having worked shifts showed that serious psychosomatic complaints and irritation/strain symptoms were higher in the group of shiftworkers. Health differences also appeared between the groups of shiftworkers: shiftworkers and former shiftworkers who had left on medical advice showed a similar degree of reported ill health, which was higher than that of former shiftworkers who had left for other reasons.

Language(s) of text: English
ISSN: 0014-0139

101

OLSSON, K   KANDOLIN, I   KAUPPINEN-TOROPAINEN, K
> "STRESS AND COPING STRATEGIES OF THREE-SHIFT WORKERS"
in TRAVAIL HUMAIN (Paris), 53(2), 1990, 175-187.

The psychological study described in this article is based on the transactional theory of stress and coping, as well as clinical experience of occupational health care and mental health work. Stress is conceptualized as an imbalance between the person's resources and appraised demands of the environment. Coping strategies were divided into active and passive styles. Three groups of shiftworkers, men and women in the paper industry working in a fixed five-shift system, and nurses working in an irregular three-shift system, were compared in terms of their well-being and symptoms and how they coped with stress. Data were gathered from a comprehensive questionnaire and personal interviews. Health problems, difficulties in family life and problems with leisure time activities were found to be disadvantages of the three-shift system. The results showed that nurses experienced more mental and physical occupational stress than did the paper workers. The fixed system with longer leisure periods seemed to be more advantageous to health and quality of life. The female shiftworkers reported more psychosomatic symptoms and experienced their life situations outside work as much more stressful than did the men. All subjects used active physical coping styles and passive relaxation to recover from stress. It was reported that while the active coping strategy prevented stress, a passive somatizing style was connected with more symptoms.

Language(s) of text: English
Language(s) of summary: French

102

DAVIDSON, M   COOPER, CL
> STRESS AND THE WOMAN MANAGER
OXFORD, MARTIN ROBERTSON, 1983, ix, 230 p.

This is a comparative technical study on the sources of stress and its effects on female managers and their male counterparts. The data are drawn from sample surveys and detailed questionnaires addressed to a wide variety of industries and different levels of management groups in the United Kingdom. The study measures and evaluates the extent of stress among managers at different levels of the managerial hierarchy, and indicates that different types of stress affect women and men managers in varying degrees and that certain stress factors affect only women. The cost of stress is measured in terms of health and behavioural change. Stress is found on the whole to take a higher toll on the general health and work performance of women managers. Finally, the authors offer a package of recommendations aimed at minimizing the stress faced by women managers. The recommendations focus on organizational and policy changes as well as on training.

Language(s) of text: English
ISBN: 0-85520-623-3

103

FIRTH, J   SHAPIRO, DA
> "EVALUATION OF PSYCHOTHERAPY FOR JOB-RELATED DISTRESS"
in JOURNAL OF OCCUPATIONAL PSYCHOLOGY (London), 59, 1986, 111-119.

This article reports findings from a project to evaluate two forms of individual psychotherapy for managerial /professional men and women suffering from distress which they saw as related to their work. The purpose of the project was to compare and contrast the effects of "prescriptive" (cognitive/behavioural) therapy and "exploratory" (relationship-oriented/psychodynamic) therapy for various problems, including work-related problems.   All participants received both forms of therapy from the same therapist, which maximized sensitivity to technique effects. The results favoured prescriptive therapy for reduction of overall symptoms. However, no difference was shown between the therapies in terms of relief of job-related problems. This finding, contrary to the authors' expectations, did not throw light upon the paradox suggested by previous research that different psychotherapeutic techniques have very similar rates of effectiveness despite their different content. It is also argued that to treat individual cases of acknowledged distress is perhaps a better approach to stress management than the preventive group work for non-stressed subjects that is usually reported.

Language(s) of text: English
ISSN: 0305-8107

104

DINGERKUS, S
> "PSYCHOSOZIALE ARBEITSBELASTUNG UND BETRIEBLICHE FEHLZEITEN ORGANISATION-
SENTWICKLUNG PER PROJEKT"
(Psychosocial workload and occupational illness-related absences)
in HUMANE PRODUKTION - HUMANE ARBEITSPLÄTZE (Frankfurt), 11(2), 1989, 22-27.

In a spare parts stockroom of a car factory, the consequences of absenteeism caused by occupational illness were considered in connection with fluctuations in market demands provoking stress-induced physical and emotional disturbances. An empirical survey, carried out with a view to identifying psychosocial strain factors, revealed an interrelationship between subjectively appraised work strain and illness-related absences. The level of work satisfaction depended very much upon the occupational activity carried out by the worker. The article also reports on consequences emerging from limited in-company transfers. Commonly developed plans between superiors and workers for a smoothly functioning system of limited in-company transfers have positively enhanced cohesion among workers and their superiors.

Language(s) of text: German
ISSN: 0172-8334

105

LEVI, L
ILO
> STRESS IN INDUSTRY: CAUSES, EFFECTS AND PREVENTION
GENEVA, 1984, 70 p. (Occupational Safety and Health Series No. 51)

This monograph answers various questions on the subject of stress among industrial workers in simple, non-technical language. The author indicates that stress is caused by a mismatch between personal needs and capabilities and what the environment offers and demands, taking into account that vulnerability and endurance vary from one individual to another and even change in the same individual in different circumstances. Subjective, behavioural and physiological reactions to stress are described. The monograph also describes physical and psychosocial stressors in the work environment, and gives examples of work factors which can lead to stress, such as payment by results, automation and shift work. The particular vulnerability of specific groups of workers to stress (young, older, migrant, disabled and women) is emphasized, together with the importance of prevention, both at the individual and at the systems level. Finally, some principles and guidelines are proposed for the prevention of stress-related illness.

Language(s) of text: English
ISBN: 92-2-103539-5
ISSN: 0078-3129

This publication is available from ILO Publications, International Labour Office, CH-1211 Geneva 22, Switzerland. It is also available in French, German and Japanese.

106

LUNDBERG, U GRANQVIST, M HANSSON, T MAGNUSSON, M WALLIN, L
> "PSYCHOLOGICAL AND PHYSIOLOGICAL STRESS RESPONSES DURING REPETITIVE WORK AT AN ASSEMBLY LINE"
in WORK AND STRESS (London), 3(2), 1989, 143-153.

The authors present a study on the relationship between the perceived stress of male workers and their physiological responses to stress, in a work situation characterized by repetitive, monotonous, manual work at a Volvo plant in Sweden. Each worker was studied for a period in his normal job and a corresponding period off the job. The psychological and physiological data were obtained from self-reports assessing variables such as work demands, time pressure and mood, as well as from measurements of catecholamine and cortisol excretion, and of systolic and diastolic blood pressure and heart rate. The results showed that the workers perceived their work at the assembly line as monotonous and repetitive, with lack of control and low skill requirements characterizing the work situation. However, they reported relatively high social support. The results of the physiological measurements supported the assumption that the work situation was associated with mental and physical load. The results also showed that workers experienced work demands consistent with the level of physiological arousal induced by the work situation. The authors conclude that environmental stress at the assembly line is reflected in health-related physiological responses and that quantitative self-reports of regular workers on perceived stress are closely related to these physiological responses.

Language(s) of text: English
ISSN: 0267-8373

107

MARTIN, R WALL, TD
> "ATTENTIONAL DEMAND AND COST RESPONSIBILITY AS STRESSORS IN SHOPFLOOR JOBS"
in ACADEMY OF MANAGEMENT JOURNAL (Mississippi), 32(1), March 1989, 69-86.

This article examines the demands blue-collar work places on human attention and their interaction with responsibility to cause psychological strain. Two types of operators in shop-floor jobs were investigated in two separate but complementary studies: those using computer-based technology and those using other forms of manufacturing technology. The participants were given questionnaires containing measures of psychological strain as well as job satisfaction. The findings suggest that shop-floor work combining high attentional demand with high responsibility causes psychological strain. Employees working under such conditions reported greater job-related anxiety, more pressure and worse general mental health than their counterparts in jobs characterized by other combinations of these independent variables. Finally, the article discusses the implications for job design of new manufacturing technologies. It is suggested that where high responsibility is unavoidable, attentional demand should be limited either through the use of automatic monitoring devices or by designing jobs to limit the amount of monitoring required of individuals, and correspondingly, where attentional demand is high, cost responsibility should be reduced, either by job design choices or technology.

Language(s) of text: English
ISSN: 0001-4273

108

SIEGRIST, J   KLIEN, D
> "OCCUPATIONAL STRESS AND CARDIOVASCULAR REACTIVITY IN BLUE-COLLAR WORKERS"
in WORK AND STRESS (London), 4(4), 1990, 295-304.

The study described in this article analyses the influence of chronic occupational stress on heart rate and blood pressure during a standard mental stress test in a sample of male workers from steel and metal-processing plants. The authors based their research on the assumption that chronic occupational stress may reduce cardiovascular responsiveness to challenge. Three indicators to measure occupational stress were examined: cumulative workload, worsening of job conditions, and high demand and low job security. As expected, the results showed that the participants reacted to the mental stress test with reduced cardiovascular responsiveness. These effects persisted after adjustment for relevant factors that could have confounded the results, such as age, smoking and hypertensive status. Furthermore, the results were not affected by physiological baseline level, level of performance during test, or individual patterns of coping with challenge. The authors concluded that cardiovascular reactivity during experimental tasks should be considered to be not only a possible predictor of future cardiovascular risks, but also an outcome of an individual's exposure to chronic stress.

Language(s) of text: English
ISSN: 0267-8373

109

BRADLEY, G
> COMPUTERS AND THE PSYCHOSOCIAL WORK ENVIRONMENT
LONDON, TAYLOR AND FRANCIS, 1989, xiii, 254 p.

The book presents the findings of an intensive research project that was carried out between 1975 and 1985 in Sweden involving a state-owned corporation and an insurance company. Its purpose was to examine more closely how the psychosocial work environment is affected by the use of electronic data processing (EDP) technology. On the basis of a detailed analysis of the implications of computers at the state-owned corporation and the insurance company, the author concludes that computers cause stress. The specific sources of stress identified relate mainly to factors such as the removal of "stimulating" and "interesting" work, a feeling of insecurity, workpace and work irregularity, the risk of error, and physio-ergonomic problems. Overstimulation and understimulation stemming from volume of work and contact with other people are also perceived as stress factors. An analysis of the impact of psychosocial work environment on leisure, family and health suggests that work competes and conflicts with leisure and the family where the workpace is fast and the workload heavy, where the work is interesting and meaningful, and where repetitive and heavy physical work causes fatigue. The book proposes a package of measures that could be implemented at national, individual and corporate level.

Language(s) of text: English
ISBN: 0-85066-455-1

110

DY, FJF
ILO
> **VISUAL DISPLAY UNITS: JOB CONTENT AND STRESS IN OFFICE WORK**
GENEVA, 1985, ix, 138 p.

This book examines two data-entry jobs, keypunch and word processing, to see how they are influenced by the use of computers, and the potential for improving the quality of working life of users. It discusses the implications of computerization for work organization and working time, and the health, safety and ergonomic aspects of data-entry workplaces. It points out the need to improve several facets of data-entry jobs. Quantitative overload, qualitative underload, lack of control over one's job, lack of social support, working time arrangements, remuneration and incentive systems, and working environment factors are described as sources of stress for data-entry workers. The demographic, physiological and psychological characteristics likely to influence workers' susceptibility and response to occupational stress are analysed, together with the physiological, psychological and behavioural consequences of occupational stress which can lead to temporary or permanent maladaptive functioning or disability in the worker. The last chapter presents practical suggestions for redesigning jobs to make them more stimulating and rewarding without sacrificing organizational effectiveness. It covers the possible roles of governments, employers and workers and their organizations in job improvement.

Language(s) of text: English
ISBN: 92-2-105083-1

This publication is available from ILO Publications, International Labour Office, CH-1211 Geneva 22, Switzerland. It is also available in Japanese.

111

ELIAS, R
> **"CHARGE PSYCHIQUE, LE STRESS PSYCHOSOCIAL ET LA FATIGUE: LE ROLE DE L'INFORMATIQUE"**
(Mental workload, psychosocial stress and fatigue: The role of computer technology)
in CAHIERS DE NOTES DOCUMENTAIRES (Paris), (120), July-September 1985, 325-330.

This article discusses various concepts of fatigue in relation to mental workload and psychosocial stress induced by new technologies. The author comments on several surveys addressing the interrelationship between stress, fatigue and computer work, and stress effects that extend beyond the working day. Chronic fatigue is a first consequence of mental and somatic disturbances. It manifests itself in three major symptom groups: troubled nervous system, notably anxiety which affects relaxation and recovery phases; sleep disturbances; and psychosomatic disorders. The author stresses that an adequate research methodology is fundamental for the analysis of links pertaining to stress and fatigue. As regards characteristics and sources of psychosocial stress in computer technology, the article presents ergonomics as one important means to identify risk factors prevailing in the person-work environment. Advantages and disadvantages of computer technology at work are briefly enumerated, stressing that computer technology can create either a beneficial work environment or considerably hinder work satisfaction. The article concludes that an epidemiological approach aimed at detecting cause and effect of mental workload and fatigue is imperative with a view to preventing psychosocial stress and health impairment.

Language(s) of text: French
Language(s) of summary: English
ISSN: 0007-9952

112

ELIAS, R CAIL, F
> **"EFFETS DU STRESS PSYCHOSOCIAL EN INFORMATIQUE: RESULTATS ET MOYENS DE PREVENTION"**
(The effects of psychosocial stress in computer work: Results and preventive measures)
in CAHIERS DE NOTES DOCUMENTAIRES (Paris), (122), January-March 1986, 67-73.

The article presents two epidemiology-oriented surveys, involving two groups of data-entry operators, to illustrate specific working conditions which may create health hazards. The results of the first survey revealed that the major stress factors affecting the respondents were monotony, time pressure and poor contact with colleagues. The second survey showed monotony and insufficient means of control and error modification to be important causes of stress. The authors make statistical correlations between the main symptoms, work dissatisfaction and work design. The lack of compatibility between the operator's needs and job content appeared as the main stressor causing psychosomatic symptoms. The authors conclude by stressing how the right balance must be found in the computer/user interface by improving working conditions, eliminating monotonous and repetitive tasks, making certain jobs less tedious, improving access to information and facilitating human contacts. The need to prepare data-entry operators psychologically (e.g. by making them aware of the advantages, possibilities and weaknesses of job content) is also emphasized.

Language(s) of text: French
Language(s) of summary: English
ISSN: 0007-9952

113

JAPAN. MINISTRY OF LABOUR
> **SHOKUBA NI OKERU TECHNOSTRESS: GENJO TO TAISAKU**
(Technostress at work: Actual conditions and measures)
TOKYO, JAPAN INDUSTRIAL SAFETY AND HEALTH ASSOCIATION, 1990, 209 p.

This report contains the results of a study initiated by the Ministry of Labour to explore the changes taking place at work brought about by the introduction of microelectronic equipment, such as visual display units (VDUs). Software development engineers and VDU operators were chosen as the target groups for the study. The study shows that, although software development engineers are subject to stressful situations due to the nature of their job, they do not appear to suffer from stress more than other employees. For VDU operators, reduced autonomy and communication with colleagues makes their work monotonous. The workplace often is not arranged ergonomically and many operators are afraid of making mistakes. The report argues that the problem is not so much with VDU operations as such, but rather how to adjust VDU operations to workers. Based on the results of the study, the report proposes several principles for combating stress and fatigue of software engineers and VDU operators, such as providing more autonomy, on the one hand, and standardizing the work process, on the other.

Language(s) of text: Japanese
ISBN: 4-8059-0341-4

114

FRANKENHAEUSER, M   LUNDBERG, U   FREDRIKSON, M   MELIN, B   TUOMISTO, M
MYRSTEN, AL   HEDMAN, M   BERGMAN-LOSMAN, B   WALLIN, L
> "STRESS ON AND OFF THE JOB AS RELATED TO SEX AND OCCUPATIONAL STATUS IN
WHITE-COLLAR WORKERS"
in JOURNAL OF ORGANIZATIONAL BEHAVIOR (Chichester), 10, 1989, 321-346.

This article gives an overview of a research programme designed to study stress, health, work satisfaction and attitudes towards work among employees at the Volvo corporation in Sweden. The physiological stress reactions and stress experience of four groups of white-collar workers were examined (male and female middle managers and clerical workers). Each subject was studied both during and after a workday and during a work-free day at home. The results showed that the four groups had similar views about many aspects of stress and work, and predominantly positive attitudes to their jobs. Both managers and non-managers were under moderate, rather than heavy, pressure psychologically as well as physiologically. However, after work, interesting group differences emerged, particularly between the male and female middle managers, suggesting slower unwinding in female managers. The stress profile of the female managers was considered in terms of possible long-term health risks. The main common stress factors for managers were heavy workload, deadlines, responsibility for others, having to fire someone, and taking the job home. Lack of influence and too much routine appeared as stress factors for the subordinates.

Language(s) of text: English
ISSN: 0894-3796

115

McCLELLAN, K   MILLER, RE
> EAPs AND THE INFORMATION REVOLUTION: THE DARK SIDE OF MEGATRENDS
NEW YORK, HAWORTH PRESS, 1987, 106 p.

Our industrial society is changing into an information society due to computers, automation and robotics, which are altering the structure of the workplace, changing the balance of power in the world economy and creating new occupational trends. The text looks at the downside influences on worker health and well-being created by the information revolution and discusses how employee assistance programmes (EAPs) will need to adapt to help workers cope with the changes that are occurring. It refers to technostress and to the conditions in automated offices that produce a stress response and that are not the result of new technology. EAPs can help organizations to ameliorate or prevent the mental health problems resulting from office automation by providing a set of services, not only related to drug and alcohol problems, but also including participation of employees in the decision-making process; individual and group counselling; information and education of workers; and creation of working relationships through training courses.

Language(s) of text: English
ISBN: 0-86656-606-6

This publication also appeared as *Employee Assistance Quarterly*, Vol. 2, No. 2, Winter 1986.

116

SAINFORT, PA
> "JOB DESIGN PREDICTORS OF STRESS IN AUTOMATED OFFICES"
in BEHAVIOUR AND INFORMATION TECHNOLOGY (London), 9(1), January-February 1990, 3-16.

This study assesses how the perceptions of those who work on video display units (VDU) concerning job control, job content, job demands, and their careers and future influenced self-reported stress in automated offices. A model proposing that job control is a primary causal determinant of stress outcomes was developed to test how the above-mentioned job elements influenced stress in VDU users. The hypothesis put forward was that the effects of perceived job demands, job content and their careers and future influence stress outcomes only to the extent that they influence job control. A self-administered questionnaire was given to the participants, who were categorized into clerical, managers/supervisors and professionals. Contrary to expectations, it was found that job control was not an important contributor to stress outcomes. It was also found that the relationship between job control and stress outcomes was not influenced by the level of responsibility. A consistent finding was the critical role of their careers and future in influencing stress outcomes across job categories.

Language(s) of text: English
ISSN: 0144-028X

117

THEORELL, T AHLBERG-HULTEN, G SIGALA, F PERSKI, A SODERHOLM, M KALLNER, A ENEROTH, P
> "PSYCHOSOCIAL AND BIOMEDICAL COMPARISON BETWEEN MEN IN SIX CONTRASTING SERVICE OCCUPATIONS"
in WORK AND STRESS (London), 4(1), 1990, 51-63.

This article examines the cardiovascular risk factors related to job stress in various occupational groups: freight handlers, aircraft mechanics, air traffic controllers, physicians, waiters and symphony musicians. Blood pressure and blood chemistry, work environment and smoking habits, emotional state and sleep disturbance were measured approximately once every three months for a working year. A few clear patterns were visible in the biomedical data. Physicians and air traffic controllers showed relatively low blood pressure, whereas freight handlers and symphony musicians had relatively high levels. Waiters showed relatively low cortisol and testosterone levels, which could be interpreted as evidence of premature ageing. They also reported high psychological demands and poor social support, and more cigarette smoking compared to the other groups. In general, the findings supported results from other studies indicating that low decision latitude was associated with blood pressure elevation. While physicians, a group with high decision latitude, had low blood pressure, two groups with low decision latitude, freight handlers and symphony musicians, had high blood pressure.

Language(s) of text: English
ISSN: 0267-8373

118

YAMAZAKI, Y
> "WHITE-COLLAR? NI MITU HIRO STRESS NO ZOUDAI TO LIFESTYLE"
(Increasing stress and the lifestyle of white-collar workers)
in NIHON RODO KENKYU ZASSHI (Tokyo), 34(5), May 1992, 2-19.

Based on the author's recent research on male white-collar workers in the Tokyo metropolitan area, the article explores the links between the Japanese white-collar workers' work and lifestyle and their level of stress and fatigue. It is widely believed in Japan that white-collar workers have higher motivation and are less likely to be involved in industrial accidents than blue-collar workers. However, when it comes to stress problems from overwork, it is the metropolitan area white-collar workers who are primarily affected. As they are the "core" workers in the labour market, their work and lifestyle may in turn affect other workers. The article points out that excessive commitment to work is a central issue since it makes it difficult for workers to allocate time for family and community, and generally to live a healthy life. The author argues that while the traditional demarcation of gender role between husband and wife seems to have contributed to this excessive commitment, the white-collar workers' peculiar ways of coping with stress and fatigue, such as bar-hopping with colleagues, further exacerbates the situation. The article proposes to change the stress-prone work and lifestyle of white-collar workers.

Language(s) of text: Japanese
ISSN: 0916-3808

Case studies on dealing with stress at work

PART III

Case studies on dealing with stress at work

Introduction

Part of the work of the ILO on the problem of occupational stress is identifying examples of stress prevention and control at the workplace, so that guidelines and practical assistance can be developed based on successful approaches. To achieve this and to gain an international perspective on the problem, case studies were prepared from nine countries.

These 19 case studies on anti-stress programmes are intended to introduce the reader to a variety of situations tackled by such programmes and to the contribution the programmes make to solving stress-related problems. The programmes described cover a range of occupations, countries, types of intervention and methodological approaches. They have in common a special focus on stress prevention at the workplace, which, although expressed in different ways, clearly differentiates them from merely remedial and palliative types of interventions carried out when stress has already produced its damaging effects.

Even though limited in number and with no pretention of being broadly representative of anti-stress activities or comparable in approach, the cases provide insight into how to design and implement stress programmes. The experiences described also raise questions which are relevant to the general discussion of how to combat occupational stress effectively. Professor Robert Karasek analyses the cases in Part I of this *Digest*[1], providing not only a detailed map of the cases but also signalling trends and critically appraising factors that make an approach to combating stress successful.

For reasons of length, the case studies have not necessarily been reproduced in full.

The case studies are classified and presented in this part by type of intervention approach consistent with the classification by Professor Karasek.

Classification of case studies

   a.   **Large-scale work environment focus: Strategic**

1.   Managing stress in work settings at the national level in Sweden, by Professor L. Levi

   b.   **Large-scale work environment focus: Worker participatory processes**

2.   Union stress committees and stress reduction in blue- and white-collar workers, by P.A. Landsbergis, B. Silverman, C. Barrett and Dr. P.L. Schnall

3.   A participatory action research approach to reducing occupational stress in the United States, by Dr. B.A. Israel, S.J. Schurman, M.K. Hugentobler and J.S. House

4.   A union programme to reduce work and family stress factors in unskilled and semi-skilled workers on the east coast of the United States, by L. May

---

[1] R. Karasek: "Stress prevention through work reorganization: A summary of 19 international case studies", Part I, Section 2 of this *Digest*.

c. Large-scale work reorganization: Expert guided

5. A seven-point programme to reduce stress in air traffic controllers in Italy, by Professor G. Costa

6. Using research and practical interventions to prevent occupational stress in shiftworkers in Sweden, by Professor L. Levi and Professor T. Åkerstedt

7. Using ergonomic analysis and group discussion to identify and prevent stress in managers and assembly-line workers: A Mexican case study, by Dr. M. Matrajt

8. Computers and stress reduction in social service workers in New Jersey, by Dr. J. Cahill

9. A stress reduction intervention programme for meat processors emphasizing job design and work organization (United States), by M.J. Smith and D. Zehel

d. Task and work organization restructuring: Worker participatory processes

10. Using knowledge and discussion to decrease stress in Swedish public administration officials, by I. Eriksson, Dr. V. Moser, Dr. A.L. Undén and Dr. K. Orth-Gomér

11. Health circles for foremen at Volkswagen (Germany), by Dr. K. Kuhn

12. Job redesign and stress prevention for crane operators (Germany), by Dr. K. Kuhn

e. Task and work organization restructuring: Expert guided

13. Organizational approaches to reducing stress and health problems in an industrial setting in Sweden, by S. Kvarnström

14. Occupational stress in a Swedish high-tech telecommunication corporation: An integrated approach to an occupational health challenge, by Dr. B.B. Arnetz, M. Frånberg and C. Axling

15. A stress reduction programme for nurses at Osaka Medical College, by Dr. S. Chihara, Dr. H. Asaba, Dr. T. Sakai, Dr. J. Koh and M. Okawa

f. Person-based coping enhancement programmes: Expert guided

16. An individual-based counselling approach for combating stress in British Post Office employees, by Professor C.L. Cooper, T. Allison, P. Reynolds and G. Sadri

17. Reducing stress related to trauma in the workplace (United States), by Dr. M. Braverman

18. Individual-based training to reduce stress in managers and employees at a Canadian ministry, by N. Greco

19. Using training to prevent or reduce stress in a coalmining company in India, by Dr. G. Sastry

CASE STUDY NO. 1

Managing stress in work settings at the national level in Sweden

Professor Lennart Levi[2]

Context

Stress management has traditionally focused on individual approaches, usually by counselling individuals or small groups of employees on ways to adapt to, or cope with, various occupational stressors and/or their consequences. More recently, approaches have started to include encouraging employees to adjust their work environment to their abilities and needs, thereby improving the "person-environment fit", and advising management and supervisors to allow or even promote such adjustments.

Even more recently, the latter approach, usually combined with the other approaches, has been pursued not only on an individual or company level, but at the national level as well.

Targets for national action: Working conditions and workers' lifestyles

It is instructive to see how the Swedish Government has approached this task in a step-by-step manner. Following a decade of intensive interactions with the scientific community, in which available information on the inter-relationships between living conditions, lifestyles and health was reviewed, the Swedish Government presented its Public Health Service Act,[3] which states the following:

- "Our health is determined in large measure by our living conditions and lifestyle."

- "The health risks in contemporary society take the form of, for instance, work, traffic and living environments that are physically and socially deficient, unemployment, abuse of alcohol and narcotics, consumption of tobacco, unsuitable dietary habits, as well as psychological and social strains associated with our relationship - and lack of relationship - with our fellow beings."

- "These health risks ... are now a major determinant of our possibilities of living a healthy life. This is true of practically all the health risks which give rise to today's most common diseases, e.g. cardiovascular disorders, mental ill health, tumours and allergies, as well as accidents."

- "Care must start from a holistic approach. ... By a holistic approach we mean that people's symptoms and illnesses, their causes and consequences, are appraised in both a medical and a psychological and social perspective."

Three years later, the Swedish Government focused in on one of the key components of the "living conditions" mentioned in its Public Health Service Act, namely the work environment. It appointed and issued its terms of reference for a Swedish Commission on the Work Environment, against a background of the Government's concern about recent trends in work-related morbidity, long-term absence due to sickness and premature retirement.

---

[2] Director, Department of Stress Research, Karolinska Institute, Box 60210, S-104 01 Stockholm, Sweden.

[3] Public Health Service Act, Act No. 560, dated 21 March 1985 (*Svensk författningssamling*, No. 560, 1985).

In its instructions to the Commission, the Government called attention to the human suffering involved and the need to eliminate such phenomena from the labour market. However, the Government also called attention to the resulting public expenditures. In 1987 alone, these costs amounted to 37 billion Swedish kronor (approximately US$ 6 billion) and for the following few years were projected to increase to approximately 45 and 54 billion Swedish kronor respectively (approximately US$ 7.5 and 8.8 billion for a working population of 4.3 million). To these figures should be added the effects of decreased taxes to the central and local government, and the costs to enterprises and public authorities for standstills, operational disturbances, staff oversizing, recruiting substitutes for ill staff members and the like.

The Swedish Commission on the Work Environment presented its final report in June 1990. The report proposed amendments to the Work Environment Act[4] which would stipulate more clearly the following:

- working conditions are to be adapted to workers' physical and psychological abilities and needs;

- employees are to be given opportunities of participating in the arrangement of their own work situation, its transformation and development;

- technology, the organization of work and job content are to be designed so that employees are not exposed to physical or mental loads that may lead to ill-health or accidents;

- forms of remuneration and work schedules that involve an appreciable risk of ill health or accidents are not to be used;

- strictly controlled or tied work is to be avoided or restricted;

- work should afford opportunities for variety, social contacts, cooperation and connection between individual tasks; and

- working conditions should provide opportunities for personal and occupational development, as well as for self-determination and professional responsibility.

Based on these formulations, the resulting amended Work Environment Act now states the following concerning the characteristics of the work environment:

- Working conditions shall be adapted to people's differing physical and psychological circumstances.

- Employees shall be enabled to participate in the arrangement of their own job situations as well as in work on changes and developments that affect their jobs.

- Technology, work organization and job content shall be arranged so that the employee is not exposed to physical or mental loads that may cause ill health or accidents.

- The matters to be considered in this context shall include forms of remuneration and the scheduling of working hours.

- Rigorously controlled or tied work shall be avoided or restricted.

- It shall be the aim of work to afford opportunities for variety, social contacts and cooperation as well as continuity between individual tasks.

- It shall further be the aim for working conditions to afford opportunities for personal and occupational development as well as for self-determination and occupational responsibility.

---

[4] Work Environment Act, Act No. 1160, dated 19 December 1977 (*Svensk författningssamling*, No. 1160, 1977), as amended up to Act No. 677, dated 21 March 1991 (*Svensk författningssamling*, No. 677, 1991).

These objectives can be promoted using a stick -- liability to penalty -- but also a carrot -- financial incentives to management. Sweden has chosen to give priority to the latter approach.

Accordingly, to promote practical work along these lines, the Swedish Working Life Fund was set up by a decree of the Swedish Parliament. It is presently distributing a total of 15 billion Swedish kronor over a six-year period aimed at a radical renewal of Swedish working life. The amount is nearly US$ 3 billion for a total labour force of 4.3 million. The money has been collected from Swedish employers through a special charge. Through financial grants to the employers, the Fund is promoting a healthy work environment and work organization as well as active rehabilitation programmes in the workplace.

Theoretically, work-related disease may be prevented at any of several links of the pathogenetic chain. Thus, work environment stressors might be removed, modified or avoided by adjusting the work environment, organization and content. Preventive variables which interact might be increased (e.g. by improving social networks or expanding the workers' coping abilities). Physiological, behavioural and emotional pathogenic mechanisms might be interrupted (e.g. by blocking adrenergic beta-receptors, anti-smoking campaigns, psycho-therapeutic counselling, tranquilizers). Precursors of disease might be treated so that they do not progress to overt disease.

In order to safeguard individual rights, prevent the perpetuation of harmful or useless measures, limit losses to the community's purse and advance knowledge of the future, any of these, or other, actions must be evaluated when implemented. Such evaluation is the modern, humane substitute for nature's slow, cruel "survival of the fittest", and is a means of enabling people to adapt with minimal trauma to a rapidly changing work environment and to control this change.[5]

Criteria for action

Six criteria have been proposed which should be considered before setting specific goals for action against psychosocially-induced occupational and other health problems:[6]

---

[5] A.R. Kagan and L. Levi: "Health and environment: Psychosocial stimuli; A review", in L. Levi (editor): *Society, stress and disease*, Vol. 2: Childhood and adolescence (Oxford University Press, London, 1975), pp. 241-260; L. Levi: "Psychosocial factors in preventive medicine", in D.A. Hamburg, E. Nightingale and V. Kalmar (editors): *Healthy people: The Surgeon General's report on health promotion and disease prevention: Background papers* (US Government Printing Office, Washington, 1979), pp. 207-252.

[6] World Health Organization: *Report of the first WHO Interdisciplinary Workshop on Psychosocial Factors and Health* (WHO, Geneva, 1976).

(1) Public health significance of the problem, reflected in number of people affected, severity of its consequences and implications for other spheres of community life.

(2) Level of public awareness of the problem and priority assigned to it. A problem of demonstrable public health importance may not be perceived as such by the community and rank low in the order of priorities (and vice versa).

(3) Modifiability of the problem by the available means.

(4) Societal (and enterprise) cost of action (or of inaction), including not just economic costs but also social and ethical considerations, evaluated against projected costs of inaction.

(5) Possibility to identify target population for action. The group which manifests a psychosocially-induced disturbance may not necessarily be the group to which action should be directed to prevent the disturbance (supervisors or management may be the primary target population for preventing psychosocially-induced work-related disorders in workers, for example).

(6) Availability of an appropriate agent of change. In some instances, the agent would be personnel of the occupational health services, but in others there may be people who are better placed to reach and influence the target population (e.g. legislators, management, unions, supervisors).

After applying these criteria, occupational health services should function in the following two different ways: (a) by designing psychosocial remedial measures based on sound situational analysis (for example, making the occupational health service more responsive to the psychosocial needs of employees, strengthening health education and coping skills); (b) by working together with all three parties on the labour market to combat high risk situations, specifically on the structural level, as proposed in the amended Work Environment Act quoted above.

Whereas in each community the choice of a particular approach or strategy aimed at influencing psychosocial factors that affect health and health care will be determined by a range of situation-specific considerations, four general categories of approaches and strategies proposed by the National Institute for Occupational Safety and Health (NIOSH) in the United States can be applied in any community:

1. Improve job content and organization in accordance with, for example, the amended Work Environment Act or NIOSH's recommendations[7], which have yet to be implemented, for controlling psychosocial risk factors at work.

2. Monitor changes in work situations, workers' health and their inter-relationship.

3. Increase awareness, inform, train, educate.

4. Broaden goals and strategies of occupational health services.

Constraints to preventive action

Applying these strategies will sometimes be difficult owing to a large number of constraints.[8] First, there are constraints common to the health services in general: lack of manpower, funds, facilities, treatment and

---

[7] NIOSH: *Proposed national strategy for the prevention of psychological disorders*, Publication No. 89-137 (Cincinnati, 1988).

[8] Kagan and Levi, "Health and environment ...", op. cit.

prevention technology, and the wasteful use of such resources. Secondly, there are constraints particular to the field of mental health, including difficult ethical issues, ambiguities and vagueness of many of the concepts used, and the lack of operational content in many of the proposals made by experts. There is also the harmful separation of psychiatry from general medicine, and of the medical disciplines from psychological, social and economic fields of study. The medical profession as a whole has, in the past, shown a preference for the specialist approach rather than generalization, and has favoured disease treatment rather than health promotion. Furthermore, the medical profession has traditionally regarded health services as a goal rather than a tool to make life more satisfactory for the largest number of people. In order to counter-act the above-mentioned constraints, initiative is needed in several directions.

Monitoring

We need to monitor the physical and psychosocial conditions of work, and workers' health, well-being and performance. This will inform us of relevant trends and, most importantly, help elucidate the relationships between these sectors. We use the term monitoring for several purposes. The first and most important, although most difficult to achieve, is as an early warning system. In this capacity, monitoring can indicate impending trouble in the occupational ecosystem in terms of working conditions, health and quality of life at a time when something can still be done to prevent the problems. If the entire flow of events that translates this warning into a decision to act (or not act) functions optimally, the threatened trouble can be avoided through social action, particularly participation at tripartite level. But even when early warning can be given, in reality there is often little avoiding action to take. However, the warning may still be useful in that it gives time to prepare for the problems envisaged. Another equally important use of monitoring is to assess whether action to increase the quality of working life is effective or not.

Information that relates to many disciplines must be collected for monitoring. The collected information should be longitudinal and standardized, in order to make data comparable over time. Although not likely to be conclusive in any way, high and/or rapidly increasing rates for suicide, neuroses, cardiovascular disorders, substance abuse and/or distress, dissatisfaction and alienation would indicate a need for more detailed inquiry.

Monitoring environmental stimuli, level of living and quality of life serves as an excellent basis for epidemiological research and social action. If properly conducted and evaluated, the monitoring of these factors can be regarded as part of a national, or even international, experiment.

Tripartite decision-making, social action and research, therefore, should be closely integrated.[9]

Supporting activities

Besides applying existing information and acquiring new knowledge (i.e. research) to reduce the impact of negative psychosocial occupational factors on workers' health, a number of supporting activities are needed:

- to motivate and train occupational health workers and investigators for cooperation in planning, administration and evaluation of occupational health and/or social actions, and for testing key hypotheses;

- to develop terminology and methods;

- to coordinate activities and cooperate with international, regional and national organizations;

- to collect, store and retrieve information on published and on-going activities (documentation); and

- to formulate and disseminate information on occupational health/social actions in an appropriate manner.

---

[9] ibid.; Levi, "Psychosocial factors in preventive medicine", op. cit.

CASE STUDY NO. 2

Union stress committees and stress reduction in blue- and white-collar workers in the United States

Paul A. Landsbergis,[1] Beth Silverman,[2]
Charles Barrett[3] and Dr. Peter L. Schnall[4]

Context

In the United States, efforts to reduce occupational stress continue to focus primarily on the individual's ability to cope. Few workplace interventions have used an alternative approach of attempting to change sources of stress at the level of the organization[5] through employee participation, job redesign, labour-management committees or union programmes. One successful example of the alternative approach is an action research programme at a manufacturing plant in Michigan, jointly conducted by the union and company, and facilitated by university faculty.[6]

For organizational interventions initiated by management which focus on productivity and morale rather than stress (known as organization development, employee involvement, or quality of worklife), the literature suggests that programmes can fail because of lack of support by top management or supervisors, failure to delegate authority, a bureaucratic, authoritarian climate, and rigid job descriptions and personnel practices.[7] In addition, employees

[1] Hypertension Center, ST416, Cornell University Medical College, 525 East 68th Street, New York, New York 10021, United States; Lecturer, Harry Van Arsdale Jr. School of Labor Studies, Empire State College, State University of New York.

[2] School of Social Work, Columbia University, New York; Director, Human Services, District 65, United Auto Workers, New York.

[3] Health and Safety Coordinator, District 65, United Auto Workers, New York.

[4] Assistant Professor of Medicine, Cornell University Medical College, New York.

[5] J.M. Ivancevich et al.: "Worksite stress management interventions", in *American Psychologist*, Vol. 45, No. 2, pp. 252-261.

[6] B.A. Israel, S.J. Schurman and J.S. House: "Action research on occupational stress: Involving workers as researchers" in *International Journal of Health Services*, Vol. 19, No. 1, 1989, pp. 135-155.

[7] M.D. Hanlon: "Reducing hospital costs through employee involvement strategies", in *National Productivity Review*, Vol. 5, No. 1, 1986, pp. 22-31; R.E. Kopelman: "Job design and productivity: A review of the evidence", in *National Productivity Review*, Vol. 4, No. 3, 1985, pp. 237-255.

have been suspicious that such interventions will result in increased workload or "speed-up",[8] workforce reductions,[9] or be initiated as attempts to avoid unionization.[10]

Traditionally, unions have attempted to reduce their members' job stress through a variety of means,[11] including collective bargaining (for example, on job security, technological change, comparable worth), legislation [on computer monitoring, federal Occupational Safety and Health Administration (OSHA) law reform], and by organizing unorganized workers. A new development in the field of occupational stress intervention is the establishment of programmes by labour unions,[12] many of which are based on the model of a health and safety committee in operation. Such committees work to identify stressors as occupational health hazards, to mobilize the union's membership, and to bargain with management over workplace changes. An excellent example of this approach is an innovative programme by District 65 of the United Auto Workers (UAW). The programme was designed to educate the union's membership about stress and to establish permanent worksite stress committees.

District 65 is now affiliated with the United Automobile Workers International Union. However, its membership of 40,000, located primarily on the east coast of the United States in New York and New Jersey, consists of white-collar and blue-collar employees in more than 650 workplaces, ranging from small shops of five to ten employees to a major university with over 3,000 employees.

This paper will describe how the ideas for District 65's stress project first developed, discuss the impact of rising health care costs for the union, review the model used by the project, examine various activities of the union's stress committees, and discuss briefly some similar programmes developed by other unions in the United States.

Approach and issues

The stress project was initiated by the union's members' assistance programme (MAP), and is now jointly administered by the MAP and the union's education department. The MAP, made up of professionals and

---

[8] M.E. Gordon and R.E. Burt: "A history of industrial psychology's relationship with American unions: Lessons from the past and directions for the future", in *International Review of Applied Psychology*, Vol. 30, 1981, pp. 137-156; P.F. Buller and C.H. Bell, Jr.: "Effects of team building and goal setting on productivity: A field experiment", in *Academy of Management Journal*, Vol. 29, No. 2, 1986, pp. 305-328.

[9] Hanlon, "Reducing hospital costs through employee involvement strategies", op. cit.

[10] G.J. Grenier: "Twisting quality circles to bust unions", in *AFL-CIO News*, 14 May 1983, pp. 8-9 and 12; L.M. Jones, D.G. Bowers and S.M. Fuller: *Report of findings 1984: Task force on management and employee relationships* (Federal Aviation Administration, Washington, 7 November 1984).

[11] A.B. Shostak: "Union efforts to relieve blue-collar stress", in C.L. Cooper and M.J. Smith (editors): *Job stress and blue-collar work* (Wiley, New York, 1985), pp. 195-205.

[12] M. Lerner: *Occupational stress groups and the psychodynamics of the world of work* (Institute for Labor and Mental Health, Oakland, 1984); E.V. Martin: "Job stress -- labor and management issues", in B.G.F. Cohen (editor): *Human aspects in office automation* (Elsevier, New York, 1984), pp. 277-283; "Social stress and social welfare work", in *Women's Occupational Health Resource Center (WOHRC) News*, Vol. 8, No. 3, 1987, p. 9; J. Cahill and L.H. Feldman: *Planned introduction of microcomputers as a stress reduction strategy*, paper presented at the American Public Health Association Annual Meeting, November 1988, Boston, Massachusetts; N. Firestein, J. Carrese, C. Barrett and P.A. Landsbergis: *Reducing occupational stress through union worksite committees and worker education*, paper presented at the American Public Health Association Annual Meeting, October 1990, New York; L. May: *Work and family committees: A peer-based vehicle for prevention in the workplace*, paper presented at the APA/NIOSH Conference on Work and Well Being: An Agenda for the 90's, 17 November 1990, Washington, DC.

rank-and-file membership, builds on a long-standing tradition within the labour movement to address the "quality of life" concerns of working people both within the workplace and in the community at large. The MAP responds to members' needs, and is committed to educate, to advocate on behalf of, and to empower workers on the issues of rights, entitlements, and social policies and conditions (e.g. child care, dependent care, housing, legal, psychological, familial, or economic). Within the union, and more specifically within the MAP, staff, officials and activists regard workplace stressors as hazards which require a collective response. This is an important contrast to the traditional approach of managing stress by treating (and/or blaming) the victim.

District 65, which has had a self-insured health plan since the mid 1950's, has always had a staff person who could provide information and referral for "personal and/or social service" concerns. In the late 1970's the union expanded the use of professional social work staff, along with other staff and rank and file workers, to do outreach at the shop-floor level around a variety of human service concerns. In 1983, the MAP received a grant from the New York State Division of Alcohol Abuse and Alcoholism to further develop a labour-based approach to human services from a preventive health perspective. Education, training, counselling, and referral for a wide range of worker concerns were and are still central components of the MAP.

The members' assistance programme is part of a self-insured health and welfare fund which exists as a result of numerous multi-employer collective bargaining agreements. Social services are considered to be a necessary component of the larger health and welfare benefit package that working people require.

The health insurance coverage that is available to the union's membership has made a profound difference in the quality of life for thousands of working class men and women. The insurance coverage includes hospitalization, medical, disability, dental, optical, pharmacy, pension, death, and burial. The availability of such comprehensive insurance can even be considered a "stress reducer" for many members and their families. This health plan has been an important tool for organizing unorganized workers.

For many Americans, needing help for "personal" or family problems is seen as something to be ashamed of and not to be discussed openly. "Stress", however, is something almost everyone experiences and therefore is not stigmatized. One of District 65's local unions (made up of approximately 1,000 workers at a University) developed a family and worklife committee together with the assistance of the MAP. The development of this committee emphasized the need for interventions that would be helpful to individual union members, to the "shop" of workers, and ultimately to the union as a whole. To create awareness at the shop-floor level that group problem-solving and collective action are in the best interests of both the workers and the union is a difficult goal to achieve. It requires identifying and discussing the issues that can bring workers together. Stress was perceived by the MAP to be one of the issues that might help to increase cohesion and organization at the shop level.

Thus, the potential for helping members to identify multiple sources of stress, healthy and unhealthy ways of coping with stress, and available alternatives for altering their life circumstances was seen as a creative way to empower workers. One natural outcome of this educational approach was social support. From this it was hoped that members would develop strategies for alternative policies, procedures and/or benefits that would positively affect their work/family situation.

Target population

The primary targets of the stress project are female and Hispanic workers. (The membership of District 65 is over 40 per cent Hispanic and 50 per cent female.) As the service and clerical sector of the economy expands, unions will need to place greater priority on meeting the educational and social service needs of these groups. Initially the stress project was targeted at white-collar workplaces. However, more recently blue-collar worksites, and even unemployed members of the union, have been successfully included in the project as well. This has helped the union to increase the number of workers who can benefit from, and hopefully contribute to, the union's services.

Interventions

Since 1988, over 50 lunchtime workshops (in English and in Spanish) have been attended by over 800 UAW District 65 members in all five boroughs of New York City. The union was able to establish these workshops with the help of an occupational health and safety education grant from the New York State Department of Labor. The workshops include a 15-minute videotape entitled "Stress and Work" as well as bilingual written educational materials. The videotape focuses on the causes of stress in the workplace and provides a starting point for discussions on stress and workers blaming themselves for problems resulting from conditions at work, as well as ways to organize as a means to correct poor working conditions.

Eleven stress committees, facilitated by union staff and social work student interns, have been established at both blue-collar and white-collar worksites. Nine of these committees are currently operating. These committees, made up of eight to 12 members, provide social support, stress management information (such as relaxation training), identification and documentation of stressors, and forums for developing strategies for action. Such strategies might include group grievances, development of contract language, or meeting with and negotiating with management. These committees have provided an opportunity for workers to share experiences and feelings related to work in a structured setting. As a result, workers learn about similar experiences and feelings of stress in their co-workers. The committees begin with six weekly one-hour sessions, where they tackle specific stressors that workers identified at their own workplaces. After these first six sessions, the committees are encouraged to continue indefinitely. Additionally, two relaxation training sessions have recently been held and were well received -- one at a committee site, and one at the union's main office.

Improving the physical work environment. Currently, stress programme activities are being integrated with occupational health and safety education. This integration is based on the knowledge that workplace stress is a significant occupational health hazard, <u>and</u> that exposure to chemical and physical hazards at work is often a source of psychological stress. To facilitate this integration, a district-wide safety and health committee has been established which includes several stress committee leaders. Some of the common occupational hazards faced by District 65 members include poor indoor air quality and ventilation, work with video display terminals (VDTs), solvents, inadequate hazard communication training, ergonomic hazards, noise and asbestos.

In the union's blue-collar worksites, repetitive strain injuries (RSIs) are a major concern. (According to the US Bureau of Labor Statistics, over half of all reported occupational diseases in 1988 were RSIs). Conditions such as high workload demands, repetitive work, low skill and low control can cause or worsen existing repetitive strain injuries. These conditions also cause psychological stress and stress-related illness.

Various activities of the union's stress committees

- Between 1988-1989, members of the stress committee at a large private sector office conducted a survey. They identified the following as stressors: interpretation of vacation benefits, smoking policy, and VDTs, and used a newsletter to organize around these issues. The results of the committee's actions included demanding and successfully negotiating clearer contract language on vacation benefits, establishing non-smoking areas, and preparing contract language on VDT health and safety issues.

- At another office, meetings on stress-related issues and a health and safety committee walk-around inspection revealed nonadjustable VDT work stations, poor contrast and brightness controls on the VDTs, poor office lighting, crowded work conditions, fire hazards, a lack of an emergency fire exit, poor ventilation, and poor security. The committee convinced the employer to purchase better-designed computer monitors and to address the other environmental problems.

- A stress committee at a community organization identified various problems and stressors including: perceived racism, sexism, and "classism" between levels of the hierarchy; expectations from management that employees perform duties not included in their job description (which is being addressed through the grievance procedure); lack of a union "delegate" (one has since been elected); inadequate staffing, and inadequate numbers of Spanish-speaking staff, leading to increased workloads (and sleeping problems) among employees; and health and safety concerns such as poor ventilation and VDTs (an initial health and safety inspection has been conducted). One staff member states that, "The stress committee has helped me deal with group dynamics in the office more constructively."

• In a retail store (with a warehouse in the basement), a stress committee began its activities with periodic discussions on stress. The committee then became involved in a situation where high levels of employee anxiety arose over possible exposure to asbestos -- a known carcinogen. Two warehouse employees had noticed pipe insulation that was loose and creating dust, and therefore suspected asbestos exposure. The stress committee asked for assistance from the District-wide Health and Safety Committee. The two committees jointly organized worker training sessions on the health effects of asbestos and proper removal procedures. The union demanded that the employer test the material (it was determined to be asbestos), that proper protective equipment and work practices be used for removal, that the air be sampled after removal, and that all test results be shared with employees. In addition, a trained union member monitored the removal. The company agreed to all of the union's demands.

• A final noteworthy case involved a legal services office where two workers (both District 65 members) were shot and wounded by a disturbed client. The Stress Project was contacted by members at that office who were familiar with the Project. Representatives of the members' assistance programme and other union staff met with members at the worksite. The workers expressed their fears and anxieties in an emotional discussion. They feared that they, as lawyers, would be blamed for not adequately addressing the needs of a powerless client. One of the actions the group discussed as a way of coping with the stress and trauma of the shooting, was to write letters to the editors of local papers stating the need to increase public resources for poor clients in need of legal services. Private counseling was offered to the members. Additionally, MAP staff worked to ensure that the injured workers received necessary medical benefits and psychological support.

One of the concerns that members expressed was that increased security might disrupt the important relationship between workers and the community they serve. The members did not want the office to turn into a fortress. The Stress Project and other union staff developed and are distributing a survey about these concerns for members in other legal service offices, and are developing contract demands on workplace security and employee training on security procedures.

Directors of the legal services office met with MAP staff to identify and discuss the workers' job-related stress factors. One issue that was perceived to be a major stressor was that workers had to spend an inordinate amount of time identifying and linking their clients with a broad range of social services -- in addition to providing legal assistance. This task also required assessing the clients' needs (for example, mental health, substance abuse, developmental disabilities). The workers were neither trained to perform this task, nor did they have the time. During contract negotiations in one office, it was requested that a social worker be hired to carry out these functions. There has also been a request for training to develop basic interviewing and assessment skills for dealing with mentally ill or emotionally unstable clients. It became clear that in the legal services office, the job demands were great (high caseload), but the level of worker control was low. This was a result of too little time, inadequate training and a lack of resources.

In summary, a range of responses to a traumatic event was made possible. The workers as a group, both lawyers and support staff, were open to individual and collective problem-solving strategies that could lead to empowering activities.

Results

In summary, the District 65 programme has been able to change sources of stress in the workplace, and thereby help to prevent the feelings of helplessness and powerlessness that are often caused by occupational stress. These results have been achieved by combining traditional stress management with education, organization, and collective bargaining on stress as an occupational health hazard. Furthermore, utilizing an institution that has earned the trust of workers and using a collective strategy has proved instrumental in achieving the desired goals. This strategy is not dependent upon voluntary cooperation from management and it provides some protection against disciplinary action for employees who complain about stressful working conditions. At the same time, the strategy establishes an on-going mechanism that enables workers to tackle physical and psychological health hazards which they may face in the future. This programme is an example of "collective control",[13] which workers have traditionally used to resist deskilling, speed-up, work fragmentation, social isolation and arbitrary authority.

Other union stress programmes

Several other union programmes in the United States have utilized similar approaches for dealing with job-related stress. For example, in 1977, the Institute for Labor and Mental Health in Oakland, California, began occupational stress groups for unions and workers in that region. The programme was guided by the concept that among workers, self-blame for feelings of stress leads to a "surplus" sense of powerlessness.[14] These occupational stress groups, which were designed to validate workers' feelings, develop social support, and strategies for collective action to change stressors, provided a model for District 65 and other unions' stress programmes. Now reorganized as the Center for Working Life, the organization provides MAP-type services (counseling, stress workshops and education) for both employed and unemployed workers.

In 1979, the Graphic Arts International Union (GAIU) began a job stress project which held a series of workshops over the course of a month, in Detroit, Michigan, and Washington, DC.[15] The groups discussed a variety of approaches for dealing with stress (individual, support networks, collective action), and developed plans for correcting problems at their worksites. Stressors that were identified included: arbitrary and inflexible work rules, procedures that ignore the skill, commitment, and ideas of workers, coercive supervision, speed up, and physical hazards. Unfortunately, the loss of grant support from the National Institute of Mental Health severely limited this programme.

In the early 1980s, Local 1180 of the Communications Workers of America (CWA), representing supervisors at New York City's Income Maintenance Centers, became alarmed at stress symptoms among the membership. The Local's occupational health consultant, along with researchers from Montefiore Medical Center and Hunter College School of Health Sciences, conducted a study which documented high levels of burnout (emotional exhaustion, lack of personal accomplishment, depersonalization), and high rates of symptoms, such as insomnia, stomach problems and smoking.[16] Negotiations with the employer (the City of New York) eventually resulted in limits on the high caseloads of supervisors, and improved training for case workers. Previously, such areas had been considered "management prerogatives" and not subject to negotiation.

In the late 1980s, a CWA local union representing child welfare caseworkers in New Jersey helped establish a joint labour-management stress committee, and one "in-service" day per month for education on stress, or other group activities. One of the major achievements of the joint committee was the alteration of the outmoded computer system, which had been identified as a major source of stress.[17] The old system had involved an excessive amount of paperwork, limited access to data in the central computer, complicated coding, inappropriate feedback, rigid repetitive data-entry work, and poor ergonomic conditions. The intervention involved workers in defining their computer needs, and led to the development of a new microcomputer-based system which increased autonomy, skill, and decision latitude for the clerical staff. Besides creating a career ladder, the intervention also facilitated streamlined information flow, improved job satisfaction, and improved VDT health and safety.

---

[13] J.V. Johnson: "Collective control: Strategies for survival in the workplace", in *International Journal of Health Services*, Vol. 19, No. 3, 1989, pp. 469-480.

[14] Lerner, *Occupational stress groups and the psychodynamics of the world of work*, op. cit.

[15] Martin, "Job stress -- labor and management issues", op. cit.

[16] "Social stress and social welfare work", op. cit.

[17] Cahill and Feldman, *Planned introduction of microcomputers as a stress reduction strategy*, op. cit.

Finally, since 1987, the Oil, Chemical and Atomic Workers Union Local 8-149 in Rahway, New Jersey has been operating a successful work and family programme. Committees of union members meet on work time and negotiate with management on a regular basis. The goals of the programme are to change and improve employer policies that have a stressful effect on union members' personal lives.[18] Some of the policies which have been identified as causing stress have included: mandatory overtime, no advance notice of overtime, and no access to a telephone during worktime for assembly line workers. The committees also provide mutual aid to union members by assisting with information and referral to community organizations which can assist with personal and family problems. Some committees have helped prepare material for collective bargaining, which has helped members to win contract language on issues such as paid personal leave and parental leave.[19]

Conclusions

The effectiveness of the strategy of reducing occupational stress through union stress committees depends upon adequate financing and resources, and will be affected by the bargaining position of unions in their employment sector. Unfortunately this strategy has limited application in the United States since, at present, less than 20 per cent of the American labour force is organized into trade unions. On the other hand, growing awareness of the health impacts of job stress, combined with increasing stress due to job insecurity, deskilling and increased workload, could make stress and related health and safety issues increasingly important for union organizing.

Unfortunately, the economic difficulties now facing the United States -- an economic recession, federal and state budget deficits, and skyrocketing health care costs -- can be expected to negatively impact on efforts to reduce occupational stress, especially in the public sector. This impact may be felt in the following ways:

— Reduced federal and state budgets will result in less grant funding, which has been essential for the District 65 programme, as well as other occupational stress and occupational health programmes.

— Tightened federal and state budgets will result in reduced public agency staffing and increased workloads and job pressures for public workers. This in turn will increase job insecurity and lead to greater reluctance to complain about stressful working conditions.

— Increased unemployment regionally and nationally will lead to weakened bargaining power for unions, and greater efforts by employees to keep their jobs "at all costs".

— Federal and state budget cuts will reduce the ability to enforce occupational health regulations, including those related to occupational stress.

— The crisis of escalating health care costs has led to numerous strikes over proposed reductions in employee health benefits. Health care benefits were a prime factor in an estimated 78 per cent of strikes in 1989, compared to 18 per cent in 1986.[20] Rapidly rising health care costs have also financially hurt unions, such as UAW District 65, which provide comprehensive health care coverage for their membership.

---

[18] May, *Work and family committees ...*, op. cit.

[19] For an in-depth description and analysis of this intervention, see L. May: "A union programme to reduce work and family stress factors ...", Case Study No. 4 in this part of the *Digest*.

[20] Service Employees International Union: *Labor and management: On a collision course over health care* (Washington, 1990).

In the face of these obstacles, it is hoped that continued efforts, such as those described in this paper, and the active commitment of unions and others to occupational health and safety, a national health care programme, and economic reform will enable effective stress prevention programmes to grow. It is also hoped that such efforts and commitments will significantly increase the extent to which worklife is based upon security, adequate income, safety, health, skill development, social interaction, respect, and adequate time for family and community.

CASE STUDY NO. 3

A participatory action research approach to reducing occupational stress in the United States

Dr. Barbara A. Israel,[1] Susan J. Schurman,[2]
Margrit K. Hugentobler[3] and James S. House[4]

Context[5]

The present project began in the autumn of 1985 and was completed in the spring of 1992. It was implemented in an automobile components parts manufacturing plant located in south-central Michigan in the United States. The hourly workforce is represented by a major industrial union. In 1988, the facility was subdivided into two plants reporting to two different divisions with different management approaches, one using a more top-down autocratic management style and the other striving to introduce a more participatory approach to managing organizations.

At the beginning of the project, the plant employed approximately 1,050 people. Due to economic difficulties within the industry as a whole, about 250 employees were laid off in 1987. Following the subdivision of the plant into two factories in 1988, new jobs were created and, at the end of the project, the workforce was close to 1,100 employees. Throughout these fluctuations in total plant population, the following demographic characteristics remained about the same. Approximately 90 per cent of the employees are hourly workers (e.g. production, skilled trades), 95 per cent are male, 80 per cent white, and the average age is the mid-40s. Because this is primarily a machining and not an assembly facility, jobs are perceived as desirable. Consequently, the workforce is older and has higher seniority (over 20 years) than in an assembly plant.

Initially, the union and management leaders of this plant were contacted by two of the authors asking them to participate in the project. The authors had received a three-year grant from the National Institute on Alcohol Abuse and Alcoholism to conduct a participatory action research project for the purpose of reducing occupational stress. Following a period in which the criteria for site selection and the purposes of the project were discussed, the factory leadership agreed to be involved in and jointly support the project.

---

[1] Associate Professor, School of Public Health, University of Michigan, 1420 Washington Heights, Ann Arbor, Michigan 48109-2029, United States.

[2] Director, Labor Extension Programs, Institute of Management and Labor Relations, Rutgers - The State University of New Jersey.

[3] Assistant Research Scientist, School of Public Health, University of Michigan.

[4] Department of Sociology, Survey Research Center, University of Michigan.

[5] In that the background and conceptual framework of this project and the approach to participatory action research that is being used have not changed, portions of these sections are drawn directly from prior writing on the project. B.A. Israel, S.J. Schurman and J.S. House: "Action research on occupational stress: Involving workers as researchers", in *International Journal of Health Services*, Vol. 19, 1989, pp. 135-155; B.A. Israel and S.J. Schurman: "Social support, control, and the stress process", in K. Glanz, F. Lewis and B. Rimer (editors): *Health behavior and health education: Theory, research and practice* (Jossey-Bass, San Francisco, 1990); B.A. Israel, S.J. Schurman and M.K. Hugentobler: "Conducting action research: Relationships between organization members and researchers", in *Journal of Applied Behavioral Science*, in press.

Approach

This project is guided by a conceptual framework based on prior research and earlier models of social-environmental determinants of health,[6] and on a model of relationships among occupational stress, social support and health.[7] Figure 1 shows this conceptual framework of the stress process.

Figure 1: Conceptual framework of the stress process[8]

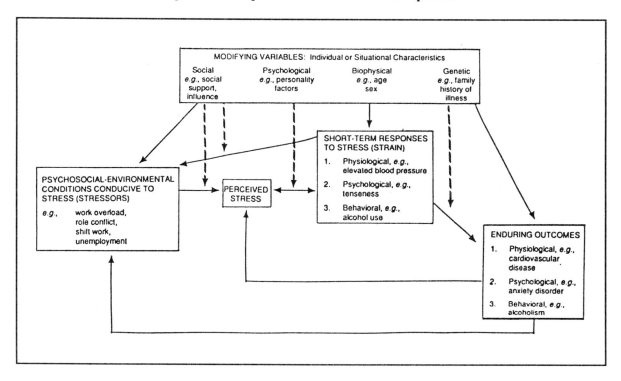

Note: Solid arrows between boxes indicate presumed causal relationships (direct effects) among variables. Broken arrows intersecting solid arrows indicate an interaction between the modifying variables and the variables in the box at the **beginning** of the solid arrow in predicting variables in the box at the **head** of the solid arrow.

This conceptual framework of the stress process suggests several broad guidelines for a more comprehensive approach to preventing the onset of occupational stress-related problems and illnesses. Such an approach focuses on multiple interventions aimed at both changing individual characteristics as well as characteristics of the social and physical environment. The guidelines that were followed in this project include:

---

[6] J.R.P. French and R.L. Kahn: "A programmatic approach to studying the industrial environment and mental health", in *Journal of Social Issues*, Vol. 18, 1962, pp. 1-47; D. Katz and R.L. Kahn: *The social psychology of organizations* (Wiley, New York, 1978); R. Lazarus: *Psychological stress and the coping process* (McGraw-Hill, New York, 1966); J. McGrath: *Social and psychological factors in stress* (Holt, Rinehart and Winston, New York, 1970); J.S. House: *Work stress and social support* (Addison-Wesley, Wesley, 1981).

[7] J.S. House: "Occupational stress and coronary heart disease: A review and theoretical integration", in *Journal of Health and Social Behavior*, Vol. 15, 1974, pp. 12-27; House, *Work stress and social support*, ibid.

[8] French and Kahn, op. cit.; Katz and Kahn, op. cit.; House, 1981, op. cit. This figure originally appeared in Israel, Schurman and House, 1989, op. cit. © Baywood Publishing Co., Inc., 1989.

— reducing sources of occupational stress (e.g. work overload, role conflict) through programmes which involve the persons experiencing these conditions;

— strengthening modifying variables, such as social support and control within the context of the organization;

— fostering collective action aimed at individual, organizational and social change in order to achieve lasting and significant change in health and quality of life;

— examining the effects of interventions on psychological, behavioural and physical well-being, rather than solely focusing on disease; and

— obtaining the participants' active involvement in and control over programme planning, implementation and evaluation.

Following the above framework and guidelines, a participatory action research (PAR) approach to stress was used in the company concerned. Participatory action research involves researchers and employees in a joint process aimed at meeting both research and intervention objectives.[9] The specific approach used in this project involved a cyclical problem-solving process of diagnosing, action planning, action taking, evaluating and specifying learning.[10] The approach includes the following key characteristics:

1. It is **participatory**, both in terms of employee involvement in most aspects of the research and action, and in that the issues addressed are generated by the employees themselves, not just by the theories of researchers.[11]

2. It is **cooperative** in that employees and researchers engage in a collaborative, joint process in which both contribute their expertise.[12]

---

[9] L.D. Brown and R. Tandon: "Ideology and political economy in inquiry: Action research and participatory research", in *Journal of Applied Behavioral Science*, Vol. 19, 1983, pp. 277-294; K. Lewin: "Action-research and minority problems", in *Journal of Social Issues*, Vol. 2, 1946, pp. 34-46; M. Peters and V. Robinson: "The origins and status of action research", in *Journal of Applied Behavioral Science*, Vol. 20, 1984, pp. 113-124; R. Sommer: "An experimental investigation of the action research approach", in *Journal of Applied Behavioral Science*, Vol. 23, 1987, pp. 185-199; G.I. Susman: "Action research: A sociotechnical systems perspective", in G. Morgan (editor): *Beyond method: Strategies for social research* (Sage, Beverly Hills, 1983); W.F. Whyte: *Participatory action research* (Sage, Newbury Park, 1991).

[10] G.F. Susman and R.D. Evered: "An assessment of the scientific merits of action research", in *Administrative Science Quarterly*, Vol. 23, 1978, pp. 582-603.

[11] L.D. Brown and R.E. Kaplan: "Participative research in a factory", in P. Reason and J. Rowan (editors): *Human inquiry* (John Wiley, Chichester, 1981); M. Elden: "Sharing the research work: Participative research and its role demands", in Reason and Rowan, *Human inquiry*, ibid.; M. Elden: "Sociotechnical systems ideas as public policy in Norway: Empowering participation through worker-managed change", in *Journal of Applied Behavioral Science*, Vol. 22, 1986, pp. 239-255; S. Kemmis: "Action research", in D.S. Anderson and C. Blakers (editors): *Youth, transition and social research* (Australian National University Press, Canberra, 1983); Susman and Evered, ibid.

[12] Kemmis, ibid.; Peters and Robinson, op. cit.; Susman and Evered, ibid.

3. It is a **co-learning process** in which researchers both insert their theories and knowledge and also recognize and build on employees' "local theory", and in which that understanding is used by employees to change the organization.[13]

4. It involves **system development** in which, through the action research process, a system (e.g. organization) develops the competencies to engage in the cyclical process of diagnosing and analyzing problems, and planning, implementing and evaluating interventions aimed at meeting identified needs, such as reducing work stress.[14]

5. It is an **empowering process** in which, through participation, employees gain increased influence and control over their own lives.[15]

6. It achieves a **balance between research and action** goals and objectives, in that researchers and organization members jointly determine and strive to maximize both increased knowledge and understanding of a given phenomenon, and take actions to change the situation.

Target population

The workplace stress reduction programme was targeted to the entire workforce of the manufacturing plant.

Intervention

This section will provide an overview of the key phases of project implementation. Several key intervention points have been selected to illustrate the development of the intervention process along with selected outcomes. The four broad phases identified are (1) participatory action research (PAR) group formation and development; (2) discrete solutions for discrete problems; (3) integrated problem identification and solutions for discrete units; and (4) systemic approaches to systemic-level problems.

Phase 1: Formation and development of the Stress and Wellness Committee. The approach to PAR employed in this project was put into operation by creating a representative group of employees to work in collaboration with the university team in designing, implementing and evaluating the various project activities. The formation and development of a PAR team is the first step of a PAR intervention. The successful completion of this task is central to project implementation. In this case, management and the union each selected an initial representative to work with the university team to constitute the project committee. This initial group jointly developed the selection criteria for the team, which included representativeness (different production areas, different shifts, and different demographic and occupational groups in the plant, such as women, minorities, hourly production, skilled trades and salaried/managerial employees), knowledge about the plant, having the trust and respect of peers, and having the ability to communicate well with others.

The committee formation process involved negotiations between the university team, which had concerns that the group contain key union and management decision-makers in order to provide the authority to act, and the labour and management representatives' strong feelings, based on their previous experience, that the committee not be "top-heavy" with union and management leaders. The representatives argued that the committee should include a substantial number of employees, both unionized and supervisory, who worked directly on the shop floor. They indicated that these employees were often left out of such efforts and that the leadership was often too busy to attend

---

[13] Elden, "Sharing the research work", op. cit.; Elden, "Sociotechnical systems ideas as public policy in Norway", op. cit.

[14] Kemmis, op. cit.; Susman and Evered, op. cit.

[15] Elden, "Sharing the research work", op. cit.

meetings or to follow through on projects. In the past, this had resulted in initial enthusiasm followed by inaction, culminating in disillusionment and project demise. They were determined that this project not perpetuate this pattern. The final composition of the "Stress and Wellness Committee" (SWC) (the name the committee chose for itself) thus included 26 members (considerably larger than originally envisaged by the authors), and was highly representative of the workforce. This process of forming the committee was the first step in establishing the principle of mutual control and ownership of the study's goals, methods and results.

Once the committee had been constituted, the next task was to lay the groundwork for the change process. The roles and relationships between and among researchers and organization members in PAR studies can be expected to have a significant effect on the design, implementation and results of the study. In particular, differences in values, interests, skills and knowledge, control, political realities, and rewards and costs can undermine the successful implementation of a PAR strategy if these issues are not anticipated and addressed.[16] During the first months of this project considerable attention was devoted to developing shared goals, norms and procedures, as well as to generating a commonly held "local theory" of the stress process and how it operated in this factory. The activities that took place during this group development phase were intended to create the common framework, knowledge, skill and shared influence that would be required for committee members (including the university team) to participate effectively in planning, implementing and evaluating interventions.[17]

During this initial phase, the university team had primary responsibility for agenda preparation, meeting facilitation and overall project coordination. Over time, these functions were transferred to other committee members, although the university team continued to play a major role in project administration and coordination.

The implementation of the project developed through a series of problem-solving phases that benefitted from the results of an ongoing evaluation process. This process guided the reassessment of the problems identified and the appropriateness of intervention strategies. It involved a change in problem-solving styles and strategies of the Stress and Wellness Committee members from a method of problem-solving characterized by discrete solutions for discrete problems, to a more integrated, systemic and multivariate understanding of problems and their solutions. The following discussion of the implementation phases presents how and why these transitions in problem-solving methodology occurred.

Phase 2: Discrete solutions for discrete problems. As a background for assessment of the situation, a first plant-wide survey was carried out, involving all workers on a voluntary basis. This survey was repeated two more times over the six-year study. Based on the data from the first plant-wide survey, the research team prepared a written report. The survey results identified a series of problem areas as sources of stress that were further illustrated with quotes from qualitative data. This report became the principle tool through which the SWC developed an understanding and interpretation of the meaning and implications of the survey data. In a two-day meeting, committee members and the research team discussed the findings and prioritized problems (stressors) according to such criteria as the prevalence of the problem, the magnitude of its effects on health, and the practical feasibility of influencing the problem. Four problem areas were selected as the initial targets for intervention: (1) lack of information, communication and feedback; (2) problems with supervisors; (3) lack of participation and influence over decision-making; and (4) conflicts experienced between producing quality versus quantity of product.

The SWC decided to form four subcommittees, each of which would address one of the targeted problem areas. A university team member was assigned to work with each group. The role of each subcommittee was to further define the problem and to prepare recommendations for solutions for the consideration and approval of the entire committee. Following approval by the SWC, the recommendations for each problem area would be presented to the plant management and union decision-makers. Importantly, the SWC's "charter" from union and management was to diagnose problems and develop recommended solutions; the power and authority to implement their recommendations belonged to the joint union and management leadership body, eventually termed the "business unit". This charter had major consequences as the project unfolded, factory leaders changed and the committee found itself, in many instances, without the power to take action on its recommendations.

---

[16] Israel, Schurman and Hugentobler, op. cit.

[17] ibid.

The initial problem-solving approach of the four subcommittees reflected the pattern typical for an organization with a history of searching for "quick fixes" and discrete solutions to what are considered discrete problems, rather than considering more integrated approaches to interdependent and complex problems. The following example from the information and communication subcommittee illustrates the first cycle of discrete interventions for discrete problems. Each of the other subcommittees also focused initially on single, rather specific solutions.

The problem of lack of information and communication, as defined by the information and communication subcommittee, appeared to be the most easily solved. The subcommittee reasoned that a daily newsletter containing information that people expressed an interest in might fill the information gap. After receiving approval from union and management leadership, the subcommittee began publication in February 1987 of a daily one-page newsletter containing information on a variety of employee and plant-related activities. When early informal feedback suggested limited enthusiasm among the plant workforce for the new media, the subcommittee concluded that the problem was one of appearance and visibility, and turned their attention to how to make the newsletter more attractive and more easily accessible. Therefore, the newsletter was redesigned and ten display cases were built and placed in strategic locations within the plant. These two strategies had an important effect: the committee experienced "success" early in the project by developing recommendations that were implemented.

Phase 3: Integrated problem identification and solutions for discrete units. After the initial cycle of discrete problem identification and solutions, the university team looked for ways to influence the committee toward a more systemic understanding of the complexity and inter-relatedness of the four problem areas they had identified. This was accomplished by encouraging the evaluation of initial action strategies and further in-depth problem analysis. For example, at the initiation of one of the university facilitators, the subcommittee addressing problems with supervisors developed a profile of an effective supervisor and then conducted a force-field analysis of the forces that support or hinder supervisors from behaving in accordance with this ideal profile. This activity led to a request from the subcommittee for additional analysis of survey data to see whether there were any differences in how different groups of employees evaluated their relations with their supervisor. The results surprised the subcommittee; the findings indicated that rather than being the source of the problem, shop-floor supervisors reported the highest levels of stress and the least amount of support from their supervisors in middle and upper management. In comparison, the hourly unionized workers were relatively satisfied with their relations with first-level supervisors. As a result of this new perspective, the subcommittee decided that improving relations between supervisors and those supervised, especially within management, was the key area to work on.

Union and management approval was obtained for the recommendations of this subcommittee. However, in providing supervisors with feedback on these data and the committee's recommendations, the supervisors indicated a high level of stress and frustration with the current performance evaluation system, which they stated was a major source of tension between first-level supervisors and their supervisors.

These feedback meetings increased the SWC's understanding of the inter-relatedness of the problems of lack of participation and influence and poor supervisory relations. Thus, the two subcommittees proposed that their recommendations be integrated into the pilot project proposal being developed by the "quality versus quantity" subcommittee. A pilot project intervention was proposed to management. It aimed at developing problem-solving teams in one department which would attempt to solve production problems. The SWC hoped to learn which aspects of the intervention could be developed into recommendations for broader diffusion of this approach throughout the plant. At the same time, a new performance appraisal system would be established involving a pilot group of managers and supervisors willing to experiment with a peer-based performance evaluation approach.

In late 1987, the pilot team problem-solving project was approved by union and management. In early 1988, a steering committee was formed to help coordinate and support the work of the pilot project problem-solving team. The steering committee included a union and management representative, the maintenance supervisor, the shop-floor supervisor as well as several members of the SWC. Committee members made presentations about the project to employees in the designated product area, and nine people from the second shift in one department volunteered to participate in a problem-solving team.

In April 1988, the university team and SWC members co-facilitated the first meeting of this problem-solving team in which the purposes of the project were discussed, operating norms were jointly developed, and baseline data were collected on the group's process and team members' expectations. After six months, an evaluation of the problem-solving team indicated that participants had acquired the skills to work together and had started to tackle the problem that they had selected to work on first. The evaluation data collected a year later indicated that the problem-solving team felt very positive about working together as a group, but had encountered barriers such as a perceived lack of information and communication, follow up and support from members of the steering committee. The group did not feel sufficiently able to use the skills it acquired, as problems identified were taken over by other people.

Based on the positive experiences as well as the difficulties the pilot project team had experienced, the SWC formulated a set of recommendations for the establishment of similar teams in other departments throughout the plant. Although these recommendations were verbally "approved" by top union and management, they were not actually adopted or implemented at this point in the project. Also during this period, the upper level manager responsible for redesigning the management appraisal system was transferred to another plant and the programme was never carried out. Thus, while during this phase the SWC took a more integrated approach to identifying and solving problems within a discrete unit of the plant, they also experienced difficulties and obstacles in trying to implement broader changes.

Phase 4: Systemic approaches to systemic-level problems. Through the learning process involved in problem diagnosis, planning interventions and evaluating outcomes, committee members began to develop a broader and more complex understanding of the inter-relationships of the major sources of stress that their action plans were targeted at, and the key organizational factors that had to be considered in the intervention process. The problem of whether and how to institutionalize the SWC's goals and methods in the organization emerged as a key agenda item for the committee. In particular, many committee members began to realize that solutions in the form of narrowly focused recommendations or very limited interventions (pilot project in one department or a newsletter, or a single training programme), even if successful in their narrower objectives, had little chance of influencing the larger plant organization.

As one example, the information and communication subcommittee had continued to try to improve the daily newsletter based on informal feedback from plant members and committee discussions of what information was useful. With a revised understanding of the problem and solutions needed, the committee proposed to suspend the daily newsletter and replace it with a four-pronged strategy: (1) opportunity for employees to ask questions about job or business-related matters from top management and union officials who would be available once or twice a month in a specially designated area; (2) quarterly business update meetings presenting information to all employees with time reserved for questions and answers; (3) regular meetings between supervisors and team leaders (hourly employees) at the department level; and (4) special information bulletins to all employees as needed.

This set of strategies represented a much more comprehensive approach that was intended to be implemented at the organizational level. Here again, top union and management "accepted" the SWC's recommendations, but no actions were taken except the introduction of a weekly newsletter to replace the previous daily newsletter.

During this period, the university team focused on helping the committee construct a theory of why "success wasn't taking",[18] that is, why the union and management appeared to be ignoring or resisting the committee's expert advice. Through analysis of their experience, the committee began to understand more clearly that achieving their goals of reducing stress and implementing a more comprehensive information and communication strategy required active management and union participation in implementing these strategies. Achieving their goals also required the modification of some of the standard ways in which "business was done" in the plant. The key question then became how to regain the active participation and involvement of top union and management. This process proved to be extremely difficult and was complicated by a variety of factors, the most important of which included the erosion of higher-level management representation on the SWC over time. This outcome was directly related to the fact that there were five different plant managers in the first five years of the project. This was also a result of the plant being reorganized into two factories - each assigned to a different corporate division. This meant that there were two separate management organizations within the plant, with different managerial philosophies, and differing commitment to the Stress and Wellness Project. Since the separation progress has

---

[18] R.E. Walton: "Diffusion of new work structures: Explaining why success didn't take", in *Organizational Dynamics*, Vol. 3, 1975, pp. 2-22.

occurred much faster in the factory attached to the original division than in the new one. The remainder of this section will focus on developments in this plant.

In April 1990, a new manager was assigned to the plant and expressed interest in the Committee's goals and recommendations, establishing further problem-solving teams and improving information and communication. However, a host of difficult production problems immediately diverted attention away from the project. No real progress was made in this period toward the goal of getting the involvement and commitment of union and management. Many committee members showed signs of becoming very frustrated and some were ready to give up in disgust. The university team concentrated on helping the committee develop a strategy for getting the leadership's attention. Since the end of the project was approaching, the SWC decided to propose an all-day planning meeting with several key managers and union leaders for the purpose of deciding the future direction of the Stress and Wellness Project.

The planning meeting took place in April 1991. Committee members made an initial briefing on the project's goals, methods, and an assessment of both accomplishments and barriers. The goals were described as (1) identifying sources of stress, (2) designing interventions, (3) evaluating results, and (4) designing additional interventions if necessary. One manager told the committee that it had left out an important goal and its omission was a key to the committee's difficulties in getting its recommendations implemented. This manager stated that the committee had been successful in the first goal of identifying problems, but in making recommendations had failed to create a real understanding of the project's goals and recommendations and, instead, had made managers and union leaders feel defensive.

This meeting crystallized a clear shift in the committee's overall analysis of its role and strategy in pursuing the project's goals. SWC members began to realize that it was the process of learning that had been important to them and had led them to an understanding of the systemic nature of problems. They began to theorize that unless the key union and management decision-makers themselves experienced the same kind of learning process they would continue to find it difficult to understand the committee's recommendations. At this point the committee focused on how to replicate learning processes rather than on how to communicate recommendations. One manager suggested that the committee's process and norms were similar to what was needed within the management staff as the basis for bringing about a more participative management style.[19] The plant manager proposed having an all-day meeting in which the committee would both share the results of the third and final survey with an expanded group of managers and union leaders, and engage them in open discussion of whether and how to incorporate the SWC's goals into the on-going efforts of the leadership to change the "way we do business".

This meeting took place in July 1991. The managers and union leaders noted that the problems identified by the committee as stress and health problems were the same problems that were causing quality and production problems. They noted too that the committee's recommended action steps conformed closely to solutions they had been discussing. Following this joint meeting, the management and union decided that the SWC goals were important to incorporate in the overall business strategy and leadership approach of the plant but that the responsibility for implementing the necessary action steps had to be located in the business unit rather than in a special committee. Management and union agreed to assume the leadership role in improving information and communication, improving relations between supervisors and supervisees, increasing opportunities to participate in decision-making, and removing the obstacles to producing a high-quality product. The SWC would no longer continue to function once the process of providing feedback from the results of the third survey was completed, but individual members of the committee would be called upon to serve on various tasks forces or projects aimed at meeting the newly incorporated Stress and Wellness Project's goals.

---

[19] At the first Stress and Wellness Committee meeting, the university team facilitated a process of generating norms to regulate the committee's process. These have been revised only slightly during the course of the project, and included: all ideas are important, full participation by all members, constructive communication, suspend personal biases, maintain confidentiality of information shared in meetings, consensus decision-making, no "paybacks" (punishment outside of meetings for things said in meetings), open discussion, agreement to disagree, joint union-management influence and considerate smoking.

As of January 1992, management and the union jointly had conducted meetings in all departments in which they shared information concerning the "state of the business" along with the results of the third survey. At the time the university team left the project site, the plant leadership was in the process of planning how to expand and restructure the existing employee participation efforts to include training on specific problem-solving methods linked to quality control. Part of laying the groundwork involves developing a more participatory culture among managers and supervisors in preparation for the more active involvement and influence of the hourly workforce.

Evaluation

Three waves of survey data allow for an examination of the causal priorities among the key variables in the stress model (e.g. social support, control, stress, job satisfaction, health). In addition, the survey data are being used to assess the extent to which there have been changes in any of the major variables (e.g. reduced stress) and whether such changes can be attributed to the interventions. In order to obtain employees' assessments of the interventions provided by the Stress and Wellness Committee, the plant-wide questionnaire also included specific items on, for example, the newsletter and the health screening programme.

The Stress and Wellness Committee's process and outcomes were evaluated both through fieldnotes of all meetings and major site contacts, and through an annual year-end questionnaire that included open and close-ended questions on such topics as the committee's problem-solving processes, the role of individuals and the university team, accomplishments and barriers. These data were analysed on an on-going basis. Periodically the university team would present the results to the committee as a way to examine their processes and make changes as needed. Entry and exit interviews were conducted with all members of the Stress and Wellness Committee, as well as with top union and management, to obtain their opinions of the project and the future strategies for meeting the project's goals. All members of the SWC who dropped out were also interviewed.

Although extensive conversations were held with top management on several occasions, due to subsequent management turnover, the university team and SWC were unable to gain access to business data that might have enabled an assessment of the project on some organizational performance indicators such as quality, scrap, sickness or occupational illness, and injury records. Furthermore, a successful programme to reduce absenteeism had been in existence in the plant prior to this project. This would have made it difficult, if not impossible, to attribute changes in absenteeism to any effects of the Stress and Wellness Project.

Selected results

Stress and Wellness Committee evaluation. Committee members completed the fourth annual evaluation questionnaire in December 1990, with similar questionnaires having been completed in 1986, 1988 and 1989. The 1990 results from both the open- and closed-ended questions suggested that over time committee members felt that they were very much a part of the group and had a sense of ownership over what the committee did. Furthermore, 85 per cent of the members stated there was a great deal of trust and openness between them and that the committee members' willingness to express their point of view increased since they joined the project. Most members stated they were very satisfied with the group's decision-making process, their own influence over the committee's decisions and the way the committee dealt with problems.

The majority of committee members indicated that this project was a good example of union and management working together, and that it had increased trust between hourly and salaried committee members. Committee members indicated that their influence differed in the two factories, with a far more positive assessment for the plant in which management had become actively involved. The major problems or barriers that committee members saw as having caused delays and interfered with reaching the committee's goals were lack of plant management support (particularly in one of the factories), the division of the plant into two factories, personnel turnover, as well as pending layoffs and market uncertainties. Even given these difficulties, more than two-thirds of the committee members described this project as one of the best compared to other programmes that they had participated in earlier, and more than 90 per cent said the SWC had provided personal growth for them.

These results suggest that many of the process objectives aimed at establishing a joint, co-equal, participatory problem-solving committee were met. The majority of the committee considered it somewhat or very true that good recommendations were developed by the committee, and that some progress had been made in the areas of information and communication and increased awareness about health matters. The SWC also noted that the barriers described above prevented more extensive implementation of the committee's suggestions -- at least up to the time of the 1990 committee survey. Given the increased management and union involvement over the final six months and the implementation of several of the committee's recommendations (e.g. departmental information meetings), there is potential for some of the desired changes to occur in the future.

Initial comparison of key variables in first and third plant-wide surveys. The major outcome objectives of the action components of this project were to reduce stress, strengthen social support and increase control over decision-making, and improve job satisfaction and health. Thorough analyses of the three plant-wide surveys to examine these possible effects have not yet been conducted. However, in a preliminary set of analyses, a comparison was made of all indices that measured the main variables in the project (approximately 60), and there were only eight indices where the mean score differed significantly ($p \leq .05$) between wave 1 and wave 3. There were indicators that co-worker support increased, as did overall negative feelings, problems with eyes and sleep-related problems. There was a reduction between the third and first survey in participation in decision-making, supervisor support and job security.

This relatively small number of changes between the two surveys indicates that, for the most part, employees' experience of different factors in the stress model have remained about the same. In the few areas where differences were found, things have gotten worse. This suggests that the committee has continued to identify the major problems within the factory that need to be addressed. Furthermore, the changes needed at the organizational level that would have an impact on the variables examined here have not yet occurred.

Survey assessment of Stress and Wellness Project activities. Questions were asked on the third survey to obtain employees' assessment of the value of the Stress and Wellness Project's activities. Concerning the weekly newsletter distributed in the plant, almost two-thirds of the survey respondents said it was "somewhat true" or "very true" that they read the newsletter every week; 42 per cent indicated that it was "somewhat true" or "very true" that the newsletter meets their needs for information; and half of the employees felt that the display centres located throughout the plant were a good way of sharing information.

Based on these results, the Committee felt somewhat positive about these interventions, but continued to recommend additional strategies to top union and management to improve communication in the plant. The "state of the business" meetings held throughout one of the plants towards the end of the project, and a commitment to continue such meetings on a regular basis, is one example of the union and management's adoption of a strategy strongly urged by the committee.

Key learnings

Throughout this paper, the strengths and rationale for using a participatory action research approach with its multiple research and intervention methods have been presented. However, this approach is not without its costs, and some of the specific issues and challenges that have been faced and the key learnings are listed below according to the research and action components of the project.[20]

Action component of the PAR approach

- Initially there was little trust between hourly and salaried members of the Stress and Wellness Committee. Hence it is important early in the process to establish jointly-held operating norms in order to develop a team characterized by mutual respect and trust, that uses cooperative problem-solving and consensus decision-making processes.

---

[20] Israel, Schurman and House, op. cit.; Israel, Schurman and Hugentobler, op. cit.

• Even though the project had the verbal commitment and support of top management and the union, many of the committee's main recommendations were not implemented until the plant leadership became directly involved in the committee itself. Their involvement in the PAR process, therefore, is necessary from the beginning.

• There were numerous changes in personnel, especially top management (e.g. five different plant managers in five years), and an effective mechanism needs to be established for informing and obtaining active support from new leadership.

• Over time the union leadership at the plant level became a major source of stability, continuity and support, especially as the committee learned how to communicate its needs and expectations of the union.

• The committee learned that it had to be very persistent, continue to ask questions, and follow up on requests and recommendations, hence better methods for helping people learn to "influence upward" are needed.

• It is difficult to introduce an organization-wide programme that involves an ongoing, long-term learning process without pre-specified, concrete objectives and strategies, into an organizational culture that is accustomed to highly specified, distinct, packaged programmes that emphasize "quick fix" approaches. Hence a mechanism needs to be created that involves key personnel in the process of learning the interconnectedness of the issues being addressed and the diverse strategies needed.

• The committee learned that it is not easy to transfer its experience and "success" in cooperative problem-solving processes to other organization members who have not participated in a similar process (e.g. in trying to diffuse recommendations for establishing additional problem-solving teams throughout the plant, some co-workers and managers were mistrustful and skeptical of what the committee was trying to accomplish).

• From the beginning, the university team recognized a major obstacle that was never fully overcome, which was that the project was not initiated by the organization. Because the organization did not invite the university team to participate (as would normally be the case in a PAR project), the project was not viewed as a structurally integrated part of the organization, but rather served in a more advisory capacity.

Research component of the PAR approach

• To conduct this type of intervention in research requires developing a multidisciplinary research team that has the diverse methodological as well as content and process skills, and that team members have an appreciation and respect for each other's contribution.

• The multidisciplinary character of the team can be enhanced by staying grounded in local theory, data and expertise, while also recognizing the research team's theoretical and practice base, in striving to reach a balance between meeting research and action goals.

• Effective implementation necessitates establishing relationships between the research team and the organization members that addresses the role-related tensions and differences that may develop.

• This approach requires a sustained effort in terms of financial and personal resources, given the time-consuming and labour-intensive aspects of this approach, that is often inconsistent with the shorter time-frame expectations of the corporate and academic world.

• The research team has to address the criticisms by some members of the academic community who suggest that PAR is not "scientific" (e.g. no control group, "bias" introduced by participation of organization members).

• This approach involves organizing and analysing an enormous amount of data, both quantitative and qualitative, that is further frustrated by the multiple objectives of using data and preparing documents for action as well as research purposes.

Concluding remarks

The experiences of this participatory action research approach to reducing occupational stress suggest that it is a promising methodology for efforts aimed at preventing work stress-related disorders as well as contributing to theory and basic research questions. Consistent with the conceptual framework of the stress process, this approach -- with its emphasis on process and outcome evaluation as an on-going integral component -- is a viable strategy for action and research at multiple levels of practice and analysis. The extensive data that have been collected and lessons learned from this project reinforce the value of the case study. The long time period needed to diagnose, implement and assess organizational change may suggest to some that this is not a feasible approach to addressing occupational stress. However, if our primary goal is to change work environments to reduce stress rather than to teach individuals how to manage stressful situations, then we need to continue with such efforts, and strive to shorten the "learning curve" as we work within new organizational contexts.

CASE STUDY NO. 4

A union programme to reduce work and family stress factors in unskilled and semi-skilled workers on the east coast of the United States

Lisa May[1]

Context

The Work and Family Program of the Oil, Chemical and Atomic Workers International Union (OCAW), Local 8-149, is a worker-based project with two main activities. Committees of union members meet and negotiate with management on a regular basis at the worksite to change and improve employer policies that have a stressful effect on union members' personal lives. The committees also provide mutual aid to members by assisting with information and referral to organizations in the community which can assist with personal and family problems.

The OCAW 8-149 represents close to 1,000 unskilled and semi-skilled pharmaceutical, heavy chemical, metals, plastics and public water authority workers in a geographic area from central New Jersey to Connecticut on the east coast of the United States.

The programme described here originated among pharmaceutical and plastics workers whose plants are approximately 45 per cent female and racially diverse. Major groups represented in the workplace are people of Italian, Irish, Polish and German descent born in the United States (44 per cent), African Americans (18 per cent), people of Latin American origin (19 per cent), and Haitians (15 per cent). While there is a wide range in age, the majority of people are between 30 and 50 years old. Most of those who are in this group are married or living with a partner and have children. There is also a particularly vulnerable 9 per cent who are single parents.

The environment of these workplaces often causes personal crises. Workers' behaviour is rigidly controlled. Individuals describe feeling as if they are in kindergarten or prison. In the machine operation and assembly-line jobs there is little opportunity for promotion, no control over how work is done, and the routine work provides no intellectual challenge. People experience anxiety about the danger of work errors or physical injury due to production speed and short-cuts. Upper management and supervisors rarely give workers acknowledgment for the tasks that are accomplished. The daily treatment employees receive from superiors is often degrading. These factors combined make the job itself a challenge to mental health and produce a high level of stress.

Issues

Since the mid-1970s an increasing number of male union members' female relatives and spouses have become full-time permanent workers. Once there might have been a mother or grandmother at home during the day to care for children and attend to other family activities. Gradually, this arrangement has all but disappeared due to the economic necessity of having two wage-earners in a family. While the social reality has changed, the social awareness of small employers has not.

Workers do not have the economic resources to pay for professional child care. The cost of quality licensed or registered child care can approach the take-home pay of a lower-paid industrial or clerical worker. Even when a family can afford such care, the services that do exist in the community are geared to the 9:00 to 5:00 daytime

---

[1] Work and Family Program of the Oil, Chemical and Atomic Workers International Union, Local 8-149, 90 Lewis Street, Rathway, New Jersey 07065, United States.

routines of professionals. Few programmes exist for night shiftworkers, people who work weekends, or industrial workers whose hours start earlier or run later than normal office hours. Informal arrangements are often made to fill the gap between parental care and school or child care. Inadequate and unstable before- and after-school care often causes parents to be late or forces them to leave work early. The basic need to take care of a sick child, an elderly relative or a disabled spouse can be a major source of stress when people have limited sick leave. This is especially difficult when use of sick time is restricted to the employee's own illness.

A common response to the dependent care dilemma is for spouses to work different shifts, allowing them to care for their children and elderly relatives themselves. This is another source of stress in the family. "I never see my husband", said one night shiftworker, "He leaves when I come home and I'm sleeping when he's home. On weekends we're too tired to do anything but stare at each other." Mandatory overtime or other schedule changes imposed by the job shatter such delicate arrangements. "When the boss tells me I have to work late it's a disaster. Either I get in trouble for refusing overtime, or my husband gets written up for being late. Both our jobs are put at risk."

The employers of OCAW members have expected workers to leave their personal and family lives behind when they come through the factory door. For eight to ten hours a day they have required that workers make the production task paramount, blocking out other aspects of life. The daily life experiences of executives are quite different from those who work below them. For example, their higher income allows a spouse to remain at home to care for dependents, or makes it possible to hire someone to come into their home to do child care, cleaning and cooking. Something as commonplace as personal use of a telephone available on a supervisor's desk is symbolic of the very different work-family environment that separates executives from the personal experience of lower-paid workers.

In the formal work structure, personal life has not been acknowledged. Occasionally, workers have broken this taboo by explaining that lateness or absences have been due to logistical problems with family responsibilities. The typical response from management has been, "That's of no concern to the company. We don't care what your problems are. We need people who will come to work on time. If you can't do it, you will be replaced".

By the mid-1980s, union representatives on the shop floor frequently were being faced with members' grievance and disciplinary problems that stemmed from conflicts between work and family responsibilities. The union representatives had no past experience with defending members' rights to challenge employer expectations when home and family issues were involved. They became angered by inhumane discipline, suspensions and terminations. They asked union leaders for solutions.

A one-day meeting between active unionists, their spouses and children, and academics in the fields of family studies and labour history was organized by the union. This "think-tank" with its unique mixture of contributors enabled unionists to put their individual work-family conflicts in a social and historical context. This helped them formulate a mandate for the union leadership. They pointed out that families wanted the union to continue to bargain for higher wages and support political legislation. However, they acknowledged that in the interim something had to be done to protect jobs and make the workplace more humane. These union members asked leaders to negotiate for contractual improvements that would decrease work-family stress and protect job security. They also recommended that the union work to develop new structures and strategies within the union to press for change on an on-going basis.

Child-care problems were initially identified as the main work-family stressor. As more people became involved in developing a strategy, the concerns broadened to encompass other problems caused by the demands of the workplace and the lack of social support to meet them. Identified family and social needs included care of children, elderly or ill family members; and medical, legal, financial and educational appointments that can be made only during working hours. Work policies that caused stress as people attempted to meet these family responsibilities included rigid time keeping (even being late by a few minutes led to discipline), inadequate sick leave (six days per year), and personal and medical leave, lack of telephone access, mandatory overtime, last-minute schedule changes, and lack of management sensitivity to workers' family responsibilities.

Target population

Nationwide the OCAW represents an even wider variety of workers and skill levels than those represented by Local 8-149. Since this intervention programme was initiated by Local 8-149, the workers it represents was the target population. Although not directly targeted by the programme initially, management also benefitted a great deal from this intervention.

Approach

In order to best grasp the scope of the problem and its possible solutions, the union wished to systematically evaluate work-family stress. It was felt that an evaluation by a respected external organization would have an impact in bargaining. A collaboration was formed between union leaders, activists, and Ellen Galinsky of Bank Street College of Education in New York, a researcher in family and work issues.

A survey developed by Galinsky was administered to union members by a team of activists. Galinsky's team also made in-depth individual and family interviews to explore the survey outcomes. It is noteworthy that the research found both younger and older children were aware of their parents' work-related tension because it spilled over into their parents' behaviour at home. Interestingly, the parents were unaware that they had communicated their frustrations about the lack of control over their jobs, or the stresses of difficult or demeaning interpersonal exchanges at work, to their children.

The results of the research prioritized needs involving (1) scheduling and time off work; (2) greater support from superiors for workers' needs to meet family responsibilities; (3) assistance in solving family and personal dilemmas that caused conflict in meeting work demands; and (4) improved communication with co-workers.

Once the survey results were available, the union officer in charge of member services began discussions with in-plant union representatives and members who were particularly interested in work-family stress. Possible goals and an organizational design to accomplish them were clarified from the results of the research combined with group discussions.

At work, people have the most time to locate help from co-workers for personal crises and transitions such as accidents, illness, death, divorce, marriage and child-rearing. When people are only recipients of help, self-esteem shrinks and resentment occurs. For many workers professional services seem distant and disconnected from the realities of the workplace. In contrast, the mutual aid that individuals can offer to each other increases self-esteem, reinforces identity and empowers. Since workers share the experience of job stress, they are in the best position to advocate for co-workers with management. Stimulated by their workplace experience of mutual aid and by labour traditions of self-determination, union activists designed peer assistance and referral activities as part of their solution.

Intervention

The largest plant in the union, a generic pharmaceutical producer with 150 union members, was picked as the place to begin working toward the desired changes. It was chosen due to its size and the fact that contract negotiations would be held there in 12 months. As a group prepares for bargaining, rank-and-file member involvement in union activities typically increases. The leaders anticipated that increased member participation would offer an opportunity to create a committee which would address these issues.

Eventually, the pharmaceutical group decided to form a committee with the following goals: (1) meeting regularly with management to consider ways of improving company policies in order to reduce stress on personal life; (2) providing co-workers with information about, and referral to, services in the community that can assist with personal matters; and (3) improving relationships between co-workers. The group chose to modify the existing health and safety committee structure, which had proven successful in the OCAW, creating a joint labour-management work and family committee.

Work and family committees that have formed subsequently in other factories have adopted the design developed by the initial committee. The committees rely on the membership to identify problems and recommend solutions. They work to sensitize the employers to responsibility for aspects of company operations which affect workers' family routines and well-being.

The following is a description of how a work and family committee is established and how it progresses to address the issues identified in a workplace. To start a committee in a new location, leaders poll the membership informally for their recommendations of co-workers who are able to protect confidentiality, understand union rights, are natural leaders, are concerned about personal and family needs, and may be interested in participating. The recommended individuals are informally invited to participate in building a committee. Elected positions are created in the committee's second year. Elections formalize the recognition of work and family representatives' roles both within the union and by management.

The committee gathers ideas from co-workers about workplace improvements that would reduce stress on personal life and types of community resource information that would be of interest to them. It also invites union stewards to express opinions based on the common discipline or grievance issues they have handled related to work/family conflict. From the workers' suggestions, the committee develops a simple questionnaire to determine the members' priorities for workplace change and community service information. The results of the survey determine its goals over one to two years.

In 1990, one committee's effort to change employer policy focused on pressing for temporary flexibility in the work schedules of members with dependent care needs for which there are no affordable social services. The committee invited guest speakers from social agencies to enlighten management about the issue and to describe available services and the eligibility requirements for those services. To further address needs of members for information about community services, it brought into the plant literature from community organizations on child rearing, child care and senior dependent services, debt and credit concerns, continuing education, and stress and health issues, including addiction.

The committee is advised by technical resource people. The officer responsible for member services provides members with education in social service knowledge, such as crisis, mental illness and warning signs of addiction. The officer helps them acquire communication and intervention skills, guides them to the range of community resources available, and provides technical advice on preventive education, referral methods and programme promotion. The president advises them on bargaining processes, grievance and arbitration options as well as development of contract demands.

There are significant differences between company-based employee assistance programmes (EAPs) and the work and family programme (WFP). The union-based WFP is active in workplace change. It looks to workers and their home lives as sources of problems that need to be fixed, as well as to the workplace as an originator of or contributor to problems at home. The WFP also looks at ways to improve the workplace. The programme is an attempt to recognize that many workers' problems are not rooted in individual illness, but rather are created by a clash between workplace demands and an absence of social support to meet them.

The WFP follows a community organizing model of advocacy and empowerment. While assisting individuals with personal difficulties it is important to recognize that problems may be rooted in the social, economic and political environment and are not necessarily the individual's responsibility. Committees consider how social support in and outside of work could be improved to build solutions where there are none on the job or in the neighborhood. They have supported campaigns for family leave and national health care.

Results

The work and family programme has led to a number of significant results.

Contract provisions. Elected union negotiating teams, consisting of in-plant representatives and the union president, have bargained with their companies for recognition of the union work and family committee and a formal joint relationship. Through bargaining, the right to use working time for committee activities has been won from employers who otherwise would not have agreed to support this cost. Adopted contract provisions have included the following language:

Contract A: Memorandum of agreement

It is the intent of this agreement to establish the basic procedures for a joint Work and Family Committee. The purpose of this Committee is to explore and recommend programs to help Employees more effectively deal with or prevent problems arising from the demands of the workplace and of the family.

The Work and Family Committee will consist of up to three representatives of the UNION and a like number from the COMPANY. The Committee will meet once each quarter for up to two hours.

Committee members from the UNION will be compensated at their straight-time hourly rate for actual time spent in committee business.

Contract B: Article 32 (Work and Family Committee)

The Company recognizes that its policies have an impact on the family lives of its employees and agrees with the goal of achieving a balance between work and family responsibilities.

There shall be established a joint labor/ management work and family life committee consisting of at least one Company representative and one Union representative from each shift. The representatives may meet for up to two (2) hours per month with no loss of regular pay with a representative from the Union Social Services program to review resources available in the community and problems for which members are requesting assistance. Labor/management committee meetings may be held quarterly for considering, recommending and reviewing conditions and practices affecting work and family life.

In addition to the monthly meetings referred to above, the Union representatives will be entitled to a reasonable amount of time during working hours to engage in work and family committee business.

When issues cannot be resolved at the joint committee level, groups prepare material for collective bargaining that has helped to win contractual change. For example, advance notification of overtime, restrictions on mandatory overtime and changes in work location, use of paid personal leave for the illness of any family member or for other personal needs, and parental leave have been won in bargaining. Precedents have been set on the amount of overtime that can be required.

From the contract clauses that mandated joint committees, detailed working policies specific to each worksite have been negotiated at the creation of each joint committee. Working policies include the following programme activities: quarterly joint labour-management meetings; monthly union committee meetings during working time; semi-annual presentations to co-workers during working hours in each area; periodic lunchroom literature displays; permanent literature racks in an accessible area; confidential information and referral during working hours; mediation between individuals and management.

Increased sensitivity in management. An increased level of sensitivity in management has been another significant outcome of this programme. This has been achieved by inviting speakers from outside agencies to address social and family needs at the joint labour-management meetings. Knowledge of the real limitations of community services has sparked employer interest in community child-care coalitions. On both an individual basis and with regard to overall policies, the result has been greater employer willingness to negotiate flexible arrangements when reacting to workers with family responsibilities.

For example, when a worker has temporarily required time off or needed accommodation in scheduling beyond the contractual allowance, special arrangements have been worked out; where assembly line workers were previously given no telephone access during working time (even in emergencies), the policy has been changed to allow in-coming and out-going calls; where arbitrary schedule changes previously created chaos in arrangements for child care and transportation, procedures now limit disruption of family responsibilities.

Links with community services. Additionally, the work and family committee's community service information and referral activities have created a source for prevention or intervention assistance for employees whose work is threatened by the stress of work and family responsibilities. For example, job problems related to lack of child care, responsibilities for ill or elderly relatives, addiction, and marital and family problems have been resolved through referral to support services in the community. Previously, because people didn't know where to turn for assistance, suspensions and terminations occurred regularly for such situations as lateness due to a child's delayed school bus and absence due to caring for a sick family member.

Training. The work and family committee's information and referral activities have led committee members to request additional training. They have wished to better understand aspects of mental health and chemical dependency that they have confronted in their work. Improving their skill in communicating with distressed people and with social services workers have also been priorities for training. A 20-hour training course has been developed and piloted with the participation of committee members. The union is seeking funding to develop a model of the work and family structure and the peer assistance training course that would be useful to other small labour organizations.

Social relationships. Professionals outside of the workplace lack the advantages held by workplace peers when attempting to reach or help workers. Co-workers are in a position to recognize a fellow worker's difficulty through the breakdown they may observe in a person's work performance or behaviour.

Workers' knowledge of the values, the influential management and union figures, the policies and the technical rights and procedures of the work environment place them in a key position to help other workers negotiate the system and to advocate on their behalf. Workers' familiarity with the demands of the job environment and its impact on personal and family life enable them to view co-workers' problems within a larger context so that solutions may be sought in both the individual and the job arena. Workers can identify systemic problems of job policy (such as overtime requirements resulting in child-care crisis) which lead to problems for many people. They can negotiate changes to reduce the difficulty or prevent further problems. By acknowledging and trusting the ability of co-workers to help one another, a programme like this can begin to counteract demeaning factors that workers often experience. The programme taps workers' unused skills, creates role models for help-seeking, and begins to destigmatize personal problems. Members' participation in the committee and use of the programme has had a positive impact on union cohesion. The committee has acted as an organizing mechanism.

Worksites with established joint committees have experienced an interesting change in the social relationship between management and work and family committee members. Previously in these workplaces, supervisors terminated or ignored people with problems because they didn't know what to do. For help with employees in difficulty, supervisors now go to packers and machine operators who are the union committee members knowledgeable in social service referral. This new work and family leadership group has gained the respect of management as well as co-workers, and has gained an increased level of self-respect in a routinely demeaning factory environment.

Challenges to programme success. The most significant barriers to the permanence of the committee's role have been the difficulty gaining agreements to use working time for planning, information, referral and the promotion of committee activities. Where this has been won, the committee is more accessible to the union members, and committee members experience less strain in their work.

There have been struggles over the confidentiality of communication between members and the committees. Some employers have been unwilling to approach employee assistance jointly or to involve peers in the outreach and support network. Where confidentiality and joint promotion cannot be assured, committees offer referral to community services exclusively as an internal worksite union programme. They hope that demonstrating the value of the programme over time may help in negotiating a joint programme that will suit their terms.

Ideally, as the committees mature and their workplace role becomes increasingly accepted by management, it may be easier to win additional time for committee activity during work. It may also become possible to negotiate funding for committee members to attend external education in social service skills in order to enhance their role and to learn about family-sensitive policies adopted by other labour-management groups.

Evaluation

A number of important variables contributed to the success of the work and family committee initiative. First, the OCAW 8-149 tradition of activism and ground-breaking initiatives made the union open to the creation of new structures and new leadership groups. The fact that the union leaders themselves had young children and employed spouses aided in their personal identification with the issues of work-family stress. Second, the social climate prepared employers to address work-family issues. They saw media attention given to the issues of drug use, the growth of employee assistance programmes in private and public employment, and child care problems. Third, with monetary gains hard to win in this slow economic time, the importance of non-economic bargaining demands had increased for both labour and management. This made the concept of a work and family committee easier to win in bargaining.

Every one to two years a membership-wide survey has been conducted asking members' priorities for workplace change and for topic priorities for community resource information. The survey results and a programme overview are evaluated through a review meeting. Review participants are union staff who work with the programme, in-plant union representatives and committee members.

The following elements are reviewed:

- Are stress-reducing goals being met? Are potential grievances being resolved in a timely manner? Has disciplinary action been avoided?

- Are structures and procedures stable?

- Is the programme visible/accessible?

When improvements are needed proposals are made and voted on in the meeting. New approaches are then carried out by the committee over the following year.

Follow-up

Continuing efforts. The committees plan to hold annual training sessions to attract new participants and replace those who may move on. An intensive seven-hour training course is being planned to familiarize shop-floor leaders with work and family issues and the role of the committee.

A priority has been placed on the right of committees to continue to meet and conduct business during working hours. In an increasingly difficult economic climate, there is pressure from management to reduce union activities during working time. However, elimination of this right would threaten the continuity of the programme by overburdening committee members' limited leisure time.

Committees plan to participate in all future contract preparations in order to insure that work and family issues are addressed as they evolve.

Committee training, member education and special services will be developed in response to members' needs. Growing concerns due to rising unemployment and the threat of job loss focus on debt and credit advice and retirement planning.

Future directions of the programme. Beyond the activities that they have been performing, work and family committees have given thought to future directions that would reduce co-worker conflict and increase social support. To address tensions between co-workers, committee members feel training in conflict resolution skills and prejudice reduction techniques would be valuable. They have shown interest in developing job stress committees using the approach and materials developed by District 65 of the United Auto Workers (UAW). Short-term stress groups using the District 65 video and workshop format were held in 1991 and 1992, and will continue in the future. As a long-term goal, they would like to influence job design to reduce the stress of monotony and lack of control -- issues that are often at the root of co-worker conflicts. The union plans to address job descriptions and work organization in contract bargaining. On a community level it would like to lobby social institutions, such as schools, to schedule office hours accessible to working people.

The committees have built support systems among union members to enable them to assist one another with work-family conflicts. The committees have fostered tolerance among management for the special temporary arrangements necessary to accommodate family needs. Work and family committee activists are committed to the principle that family and personal issues should be an on-going concern. As advocates for prevention of work-family stress they are developing a permanent presence in the internal life of the union and the workplace.

CASE STUDY NO. 5

A seven-point programme to reduce stress in air traffic controllers in Italy

Professor Giovanni Costa[1]

Context

The job of an air traffic controller (ATC) is generally considered one of the most stressful, due to the high levels of attention, vigilance and responsibility it requires.[2]

The basic task for an ATC is to convert a traffic demand into a traffic flow with the first objective being to guarantee safety, but also taking into account time and economic factors of flight management.

The job of an air traffic controller is essentially a planning task which requires the precise and effective application of rules and procedures. These procedures need continuous adjustments according to differing circumstances, often under time pressure.

The ATC's task requires high levels of technical knowledge, attention and vigilance, as well as the combined use of various instruments (radio, telephone, radar, computers, displays, etc.) and interaction with different people (pilots, assistants).

Therefore, the job deals with a complex set of activities which demand a very high level of expertise plus the practical application of specific skills pertaining to cognitive (e.g. spatial perception, information processing, logic reasoning, decision-making) and communicative aspects (e.g. technical language, English for non-native speakers) as well as to human relations.

According to Ammerman et al.,[3] the job of an ATC includes activities such as situation monitoring, resolving aircraft conflicts, managing air traffic sequences, routing or planning flights, assessing weather impact, and managing sector/position resources. Within these activities, 46 sub-activities and 348 distinct tasks have been identified.

The cognitive and operational processes of an ATC vary not only according to the number of aircraft under control, but also with the number and complexity of problems to be solved.[4] The ATC must constantly reorganize

---

[1] Istituto di Medicina del Lavoro (Institute of Occupational Medicine), Università degli Studi di Verona (University of Verona), Policlinico Borgo Roma, 37134 Verona, Italy.

[2] J.H. Crump: "Review of stress in air traffic control: Its measurement and effects", in *Aviation Space Environment Medicine*, Vol. 50, No. 3, 1979, pp. 243-248; R.B. Stammers: "Human factors in airfield air traffic control", in *Ergonomics*, Vol. 21, No. 6, 1978, pp. 483-488.

[3] H.L. Ammerman et al.: *FAA air traffic control operations concepts*, Vol. VI: *ARTCC/HOST en route controllers*, doc. No. DOT/FAA/AP/86-01 (Federal Aviation Administration, Washington, 1987).

[4] A. Bissert: "Analysis of mental processes involved in air traffic control", in *Ergonomics*, Vol. 14, 1971, pp. 565-570; S. Ratcliff and H. Gent: "The quantitative description of a traffic control process", in *Journal of Navigation*, Vol. 27, 1974, pp. 317-322.

his or her system of processing flight information by changing operating methods, in particular cognitive processes, conversation, coordination with assistants and anticipation, and solving problems as they arise.[5]

Issues

One of the most stressful factors of the job of an ATC is that it requires optimum use of all mental faculties at all hours of the day, irrespective of the workload. At the same time, it includes a high level of responsibility, not only with respect to the risk to human life, but also for the high economic costs of aeronautical activities. An air traffic controller's performance level can be impaired at certain hours of the day by an excessive workload. However, it can also be impaired during the night by lowered mental and physical efficiency, even with a lower workload. In fact, a lack of stimulation from a low workload can even further increase the normal drop in physical and mental efficiency during the night hours. This can be dangerous in an emergency situation.[6]

Shift work, in particular night work, is a further stress factor for the ATCs due to its negative effects on various aspects of their lives,[7] in particular:

(a) Disturbances of normal biological rhythms (especially disturbances to the circadian rhythms) beginning with the sleep/wake cycle.

(b) Effects on work caused by the changes in work performance and efficiency over the 24-hour period, with consequent errors and accidents as potential outcomes.[8] One aspect of this is the phenomenon known as "night shift paralysis", cases of which have been noted also among air traffic controllers.[9] This condition is characterized by immobility of the voluntary muscles while being awake: the subject can see and hear and is aware of the inability to move. Such attacks have an insidious and sudden onset, can last from a few seconds to a few minutes, show peaks around 5:00, and are directly related to both the number of successive night shifts worked and sleep deprivation.

(c) Medical effects characterized by the negative effects on health and well-being both from a subjective (discomforts, troubles) and objective (diseases) point of view. Commonly reported health effects include problems with the digestive system (disturbances of appetite, gastro-duodenitis, colitis, peptic ulcer) and the nervous system (sleep troubles, anxiety, depression).

(d) Social problems from difficulties in maintaining the usual relationships both at the family and social levels, with consequent negative influences on marital relations, children's education and social contacts.

---

[5] J.C. Sperandio: "The regulation of working methods as a function of work-load among air traffic controllers", in *Ergonomics*, Vol. 21, No. 3, 1978, pp. 195-202.

[6] S. Folkard and T. Monk: "Shiftwork and performance", in *Human Factors*, Vol. 21, 1990, pp. 483-492; G. Costa: "Shiftwork and circadian variations of vigilance and performance", in J.A. Wise, V.D. Hopkin and M.L. Smith (editors): *Automation and systems issues in air traffic control*, NATO ASI Series No. F73 (Springer, Berlin, 1991).

[7] G. Costa et al. (editors): *Shiftwork: Health, sleep and performance* (Peter Lang, Frankfurt, 1990); S. Folkard and T.H. Monk (editors): *Hours of work: Temporal factors in work scheduling* (John Wiley, Chichester, 1985).

[8] J. Rutenfranz and W.P. Colquhoun: "Circadian rhythms in human performance", in *Scandinavian Journal of Work, Environment and Health*, Vol. 5, 1979, pp. 167-177.

[9] S. Folkard and R. Condon: "Night shift paralysis in air traffic control officers", in *Ergonomics*, Vol. 30, No. 9, 1987, pp. 1353-1363.

These four aspects are very important to consider, particularly when consistently high performance levels are a must to ensure the public's health and safety.

Most research seems to indicate that physiological and biochemical responses are related to workload. The parameters used in researching this include the number of aircraft under control or expected to come under control, peak traffic counts, duration and type of radio communications, stress of time, and number and complexity of problems to be solved. However, there is a strong indication that these responses are largely influenced by subjective factors, such as personality traits, aptitude, skill, ability, motivation, experience and operating behaviour, which are often difficult to define and above all to quantify.[10]

Most of the studies show that in general the ATC's strain level does not differ greatly from that of a normal working population, although there may be great differences between different air traffic control centres.[11] There has been a tendency to measure stress and strain under high workload conditions, whereas in fact moderate or light activity is characteristic of many centres with low air traffic as are night hours for most high traffic centres. Research studies indicate that these demanding occupational activities may be risk factors for long-term stress-related illnesses, such as hypertension, coronary heart disease, diabetes, peptic ulcer and psychoneurotic disorders.[12]

Target population

The target group for this workplace stress-reduction programme was made up of air traffic controllers working for the Azienda Autonoma di Assistenza al Volo (AAAV). The AAAV is the Italian company in charge of all civil air traffic in Italian air space. There are 1,536 ATCs employed by the company. These ATCs are responsible for four flight information regions, which are controlled by four regional air control centres (Rome, Milan, Padova and Brindisi).

---

[10] V.D. Hopkin: "The measurement of the air traffic controller", in *Human Factors*, Vol. 22, No. 5, 1980, pp. 547-560; M.W. Hurst and R.M. Rose: "Objective workload and behavioural response in airport radar control rooms", in *Ergonomics*, Vol. 21, No. 7, 1978, pp. 559-565; J.W.H. Kalsbeek: *Some aspects of stress measurements in air traffic control officers at Schipol Airport*, working paper presented to the Symposium on Stresses of the Air Traffic Control Officers (University of Manchester, Department of Postgraduate Medical Studies, 1976), pp. 39-42, as cited in Crump, "Review of stress in air traffic control", op. cit.; S. Karson: "Some relations between personality factors and job performance rating in radar controllers", in *Aerospace Medicine*, Vol. 40, 1969, pp. 823-826; R.C. Smith: "Comparison of the job attitudes of personnel in three air traffic control specialties", in *Aerospace Medicine*, Vol. 44, 1973, pp. 918-927.

[11] Crump, "Review of stress in air traffic control", op. cit.; C.E. Melton, R.C. Smith and J.M. McKenzie: "Stress in air traffic personnel: Low density towers and flight service stations", in *Aviation, Space and Environmental Medicine*, Vol. 49, No. 10, 1978, pp. 724-728.

[12] Crump, "Review of stress in air traffic control", op. cit.; C.F. Booze: *The morbidity experience of air traffic control personnel*, Report No. FAA-AM-78-21 (Federal Aviation Administration, Washington, 1978); S. Cobb and R.M. Rose: "Hypertension, peptic ulcer and diabetes in air traffic controllers", in *Journal of the American Medical Association*, Vol. 224, 1973, pp. 489-492; J.D. Dougherty, D.K. Trites and J.R. Dille: "Self-reported stress-related symptoms among air traffic control specialists (ATCS) and non-ATCS personnel", in *Aerospace Medicine*, Vol. 36, 1965, pp. 956-960; M.G.P. Fisher: *Stress and illness in air traffic controllers*, report to the Committee on Regulation of Air Traffic Controllers' Hours (Civil Aviation Authority, London, 1989); R.M. Rose, C.D. Jenkins and M.W. Hurst: *Air traffic controller health change study*, Report No. FAA-AM-78-39 (Federal Aviation Administration, Washington, 1978); M. Singal et al.: *Hazard evaluation and technical assistance report: O'Hare International Airport*, Report No. TA 77-67 (National Institute for Occupational Safety and Health, Cincinnati, 1977).

Approach

It is clear that stress for air traffic controllers is mainly connected to work organization and conditions in the workplace.

Stress and strain depend on the inter-relationship between three factors: job demands; human resources, such as skill, knowledge, training, personality and coping; and work strategies, which involve organization, tools, environment and relations. Environmental factors and the characteristics of the workplace (microclimate, noise, lighting, space, instruments, tools, etc.) as well as organizational aspects (work planning, distribution of workload, composition of work groups, number of hours worked, rest pauses, shift schedules, human relations) can cause discomfort and stress and may therefore decrease performance, safety, well-being and job satisfaction. An effective strategy aimed at reducing stress should address all three aspects. The opportunities for intervention vary according to the existing situations, particularly with regard to technological and social factors.

The potential to make changes and improvements in job demands is determined mainly by technical factors related to the development of scientific knowledge with regard to air flight and control systems. Implementing new methods of automation in air traffic control activities[13] could profoundly change job demands and characteristics. One result of such changes could be a modification in conditions which are known to cause stress.

At the local level, a wide range of measures concerning the other two aspects have been implemented. In fact, specific arrangements of the work organization and careful attention to the psycho-physiological conditions of the ATCs are considered the main tools capable of reducing stress and improving the comfort and well-being of the operators.

Therefore, in order to reduce causes of stress and prevent negative effects on performance, health and well-being, both in the short and long term, AAAV and representatives of ATCs drew up several work agreements between 1982 and 1991 aimed at improving working conditions and organization. These work agreements were implemented after air traffic control was transferred from military to civil authority in 1982, and address the following factors: job planning and reliability of the work systems implemented in 1982; number of hours worked and arrangement of work teams and rest breaks (1985); arrangements of shift schedules (1985); environmental stressors (1986); ergonomics (1989); physical fitness and prevention of back pain (1991); and medical surveillance (redefined in 1982 and improved in 1989).

Intervention

Improving job planning and reliability of the work systems. An improvement in coordinating the flow of information between the Italian and European centres is now under way. This has been made possible by modernizing the telecommunication and radio assistance systems, and progressively automating the aeronautical information service, flight data processing and air traffic management.

These improvements allow for better planning of the air traffic and consequent workload among centres, sectors and single ATCs. These improvements subsequently also may reduce the possibility or the seriousness of many unforeseen situations by allowing for more reliable information and more time for making decisions, while eliminating many stressful and risky traffic peaks. At the same time, the way Italian air space is divided is being reconsidered in order to obtain a more balanced distribution of air traffic among the four regional air control centres, which would in turn allow for a more balanced workload among controllers.

Total radar coverage of Italian air space has been completed in the last four years. This permits the ATCs of the regional centres to operate under "multi-radar" assistance with an increase in levels of reliability and safety.

---

[13] J.A. Wise, V.D. Hopkin and M.L. Smith (editors): *Automation and systems issues in air traffic control*, NATO ASI Series No. F73 (Springer, Berlin, 1991).

Reducing working time and arrangement of working teams and rest pauses in relation to the workload. Because ATCs perform highly demanding tasks, agreement was reached to reduce the number of hours worked per week in an attempt to decrease the overall workload and stress. Thus, in the main centres the operative working week is 28 to 30 hours.

In addition, a rest break of 30 minutes has been scheduled for every two hours of work. The ATCs also have the possibility of varying the length and the frequency of the breaks according to the workload as well as the intensity and complexity of the air traffic. For example, during the morning shift at the Rome regional air control centre, there are normally seven floating ATCs whose sole task is to give the 51 ATCs working at 17 operative sectors the chance to rest. Moreover, some work sectors can be divided into subsectors during the busiest hours of morning and afternoon shifts in order to maintain a balance between the demands and the number of operators; conversely, they are grouped during most of the night hours.

Arranging shift schedules according to psycho-physiological and social criteria. Recent research has resulted in some recommendations for the design of shift work systems aimed at avoiding or reducing dangerous effects on the health, well-being and efficiency of shiftworkers.[14] The shift schedules of Italian ATCs follow these recommendations quite closely with a noticeable improvement in the ATCs' tolerance of shift and night work. The recommendations can be summarized in the following points:

(a) adopting a very rapidly rotating shift system at daily rotation (one afternoon, one morning, one night), so that there is less disturbance to the normal circadian rhythm of the body functions, including performance;

(b) one night shift followed by two days of rest to minimize sleep deficit and fatigue and allow an immediate recovery of lost sleep;

(c) adjusting the length of the shifts according to the workload: five to six hours on a morning shift, seven hours on an afternoon shift and 11 to 12 hours on a night shift;

(d) providing the possibility of a short nap during the night shift. During the night shift, all ATCs work together between 20:00 and 23:00 to 24:00, after which half of them rest in rooms next to the control room until 3:00. They then relieve their colleagues, who in turn have a rest period. The possibility of having a short sleep during the night has been found to have favourable effects on performance, physiological adjustment[15] and tolerance to night work;[16]

(e) delaying the start of the morning shift (at 7:00 or even 8:00 in many cases) to allow a normal sleep pattern;

(f) keeping the shift rotation as regular as possible in order to allow better organization of personal, family and social life;

(g) arranging a sufficiently long break (45 to 60 minutes) for a meal during the work shift, and providing hot meals;

---

[14] J. Rutenfranz: "Occupational health measures for night and shiftworkers", in *Journal of Human Ergology*, Vol. 11, Supplement, 1982, pp. 67-86.

[15] D.S. Minors and J.M. Waterhouse: "Anchor sleep as a synchronizer of rhythms on abnormal routines", in L.C. Johnson et al. (editors): *Biological rhythms, sleep and shift work. Advances in sleep research*, Vol. 7 (Spectrum, New York, 1981), pp. 399-414; K. Matsumoto et al.: "Effects of nighttime naps on sleep patterns of shiftworkers", in *Journal of Human Ergology*, Vol. 11, Supplement, 1982, pp. 279-289.

[16] K. Kogi: "Sleep problems in night and shift work", in *Journal of Human Ergology*, Vol. 11, Supplement, 1982, pp. 217-231.

(h) making agreements with hotels to ensure that ATCs who commute from long distances have comfortable bedrooms for the night between afternoon and morning shifts.

Reducing environmental stressors. More attention is being given to ensuring that the environmental conditions in the control centres are suitable and comfortable. In particular, microclimatic conditions are continuously monitored and maintained within the ideal range for thermal comfort. In addition, efforts have been made in the new centres to reduce noise inside the control rooms. Lighting differs between control towers (where there is the problem of attenuating the natural light by anti-reflex glass) and regional radar centres (where the lighting is regulated according to the displays used). In some centres where there are still old screens, ATCs work in dim lighting, while in modernized centres equipped with new radar screens, they can work comfortably at daylight levels in a less depressive environment and with lower visual fatigue.

Modifying and changing workplaces according to ergonomic criteria. For two years a programme has been in effect aimed at redesigning workplaces with full consideration given to ergonomic criteria. This has included the use of a new console designed for proper sitting posture, correct visual distances, proper input/output systems and better isolation between workstations to improve operating conditions.

ATCs have expressed high approval, particularly for the modern radar screens recently introduced in a regional centre. These modern screens allow better performance with greater comfort thanks to their greater width, more favourable visual contrast, higher reliability, greater possibility of storing and retrieving information, and a better control layout.

Improving physical fitness and preventing low-back pain due to fixed sitting postures. Besides the adoption of ergonomic chairs which give more comfortable support while working in a seated position, a programme for improving physical fitness has been planned. This programme aims at preventing low-back pain by providing gyms in the largest regional centres to be used by the ATCs during their relief periods. Technical guidance will be provided on the most appropriate exercises for an effective "postural pause".

Providing more appropriate medical surveillance. Because of the specific requirements of the task, it is necessary that operators have not only high intellectual and operative skills, but also be in good physical and mental health in order to guarantee the highest levels of vigilance and performance at all times.

Therefore, good medical surveillance is essential to ensure that operators are in good health and able to carry out their duties without unnecessary stress. In fact, the fear of losing their licence (and the accompanying economic benefits) because of health problems is often a further stress factor for the controllers.

Consequently the application of the precise norms and recommendations defined by the International Civil Aviation Organization (ICAO)[17] for the medical certificate of licence holders must be regarded as a target to be attained by preventive measures and not as a token fitness programme.

At present, controllers are submitted to a periodic checkup at least every two years for those under 40 and every year for those over 40. These checkups consist of a general medical examination supplemented by blood and urine analysis, electrocardiograms, visual and auditory tests, and, if necessary, further medical checks by specialists.

Furthermore, in order to have a better understanding of the interaction between occupational stress and well-being of the operators, an epidemiological study of all Italian air traffic controllers was started in 1990 consisting of medical checks and standardized questionnaires on living and working conditions, complaints, diseases, personality characteristics, stress factors and coping strategies, with the aim of defining possible stress-related disorders and diseases and suggesting further preventive measures.

---

[17] ICAO: *Manuel de médecine aéronautique civile* (Montreal, 1985).

Results

Although quantitative results for this particular intervention have not yet been collected, there are known results from other related investigations, which can help in understanding its possible impact.

Evaluation of acceptability of the workload, strain, performance and tolerance of night work

One study[18] examined three successive work shifts of a group of air traffic controllers from the Rome regional air control centre: afternoon (13:00-20:00), morning (7:00-13:00) and night (20:00-7:00). The number of aircraft under control per hour was recorded as an index of workload. Recordings involved subjective ratings (mood, physical fitness, fatigue) and objective measures [heart rate, vanillyl mandelic acid (VMA) excretion, reaction times, critical flicker fusion, oral temperature]. In addition, the subjects filled out questionnaires for personality traits (extroversion, neuroticism, anxiety) and behavioural characteristics (early morning energy level, rigidity of sleeping habits, vigour to overcome drowsiness).

The volume of air traffic varied greatly with peaks during the central hours of the day and low levels at night (see Figure 1). The subjective evaluation of the work strain was consequent with this trend (Figure 2) as was the cardiac response, which was slightly higher on average during afternoon shifts (87 bpm) in comparison with morning (83.3 bmp) and night (82.1 bpm) shifts. Occasional peaks (122-125 bpm) occurred during bursts of activity on the day shifts in connection to some stressful situations, such as temporary radar failure, misunderstandings with pilots or disputes with colleagues. During the night shift in particular, the subjects showed the same level of hormonal excretion (VMA) as during the day shifts, irrespective of the lower workload. This was probably the expression of the level of activation necessary to maintain alertness and vigilance in case of external understimulation. However, on the whole, both the ATCs' subjective ratings and the psycho-physiological responses indicated that the overall strain could be considered acceptable, both in terms of performance and adaptation to shift work. In fact, performance measures did not worsen significantly at the end of the three shifts and the normal circadian phase of body functions was not altered, as shown by the rhythm of the oral temperature (Figure 3). In particular, the night shift did not seem to represent a crucial stress factor. These positive results were due to the good organization of work, both in terms of shift schedules and the compensative measures adopted. The subjects did not show important interferences with their sleep behaviour, thanks to the possibility of having a short sleep during the night shift. Subjects generally took another short sleep on the morning after the night shift and recorded normal sleep hours (8:24 hours on average) on the successive night rest.

It became clear, however, that some psycho-physiological responses were affected by personal characteristics, in particular early morning energy level and ability to overcome drowsiness. These responses indicated the necessity of carefully taking into consideration differences between individuals.

---

[18] G. Costa et al.: "Stress and performance on air traffic controllers", in *Ergonomia*, Vol. 12, No. 1, 1989, pp. 93-100; G. Costa: "Strain evaluation in a group of air traffic controllers", in DLH Institute for Aerospace Medicine: *Proceedings of the CEC Workshop on Psychophysiological Measures in Transport Operations, 29 November-1 December 1990* (Cologne, 1990).

Figure 1: Intensity of air traffic in the Rome regional air centre

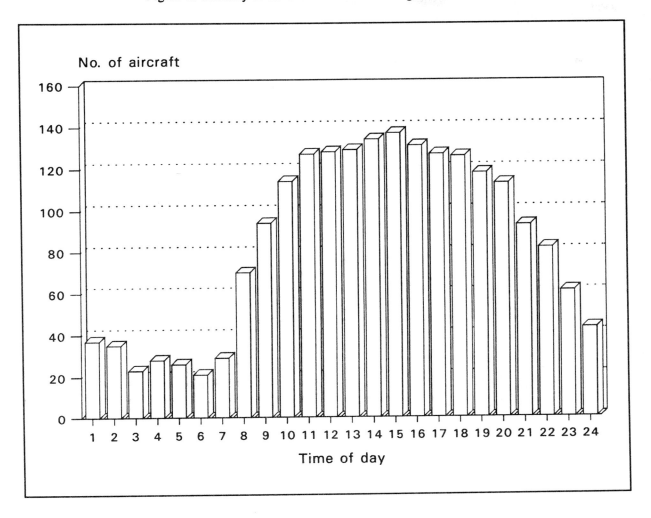

Figure 2: Workload and strain during three work shifts

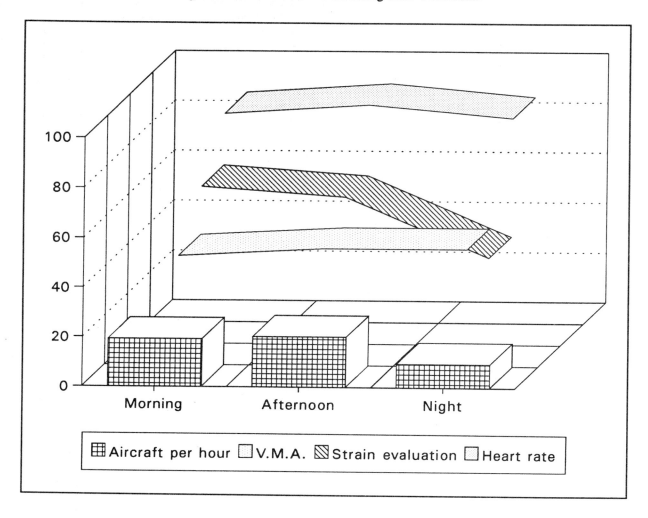

Figure 3: Oral temperature during work days and days off

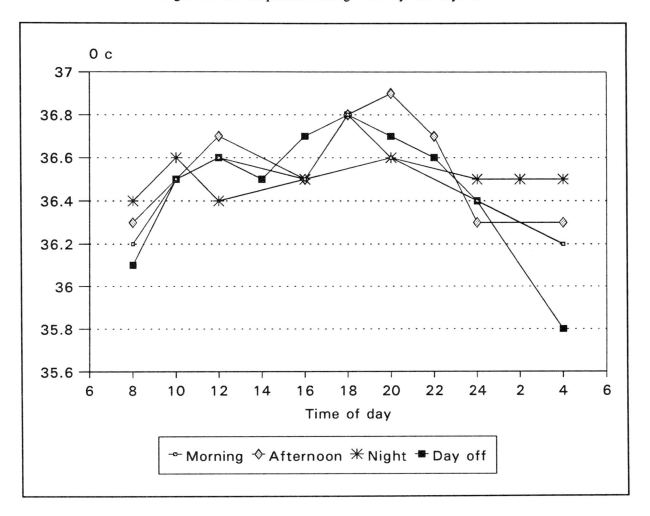

Evaluation of dismissals for health reasons

A retrospective inquiry into this subject[19] covering a seven-year period (May 1983-May 1990) showed that out of a general population of about 1,500 air traffic controllers, only 28 were found unfit for the job. Most cases concerned severe visual defects and only five people suffered from diseases which could be related to prolonged stress, such as peptic ulcer (two cases), ischaemic heart disease (one case) and psycho-neurotic disorders (two cases).

Analysis of the airmiss

The "airmiss" is when a situation of severe, possible or remote risk of collision occurs due to a lack of regard for the required distances between aircraft. An airmiss can be considered an indication of the level of safety, which can be influenced by several factors connected both with problems of traffic flow and control systems as well as

---

[19] G. Costa: "Protocolli in uso per il giudizio di idoneità al lavoro di controllore del traffico aereo", in *Atti 53 Congresso Nazionale Società Italiana Medicina del Lavoro e Igiene Industriale, Stresa, 10-13 Ottobre 1990*, Vol. I (Monduzzi, Bologna, 1990), pp. 861-867.

with human factors (alertness, vigilance, performance). An airmiss is obviously a condition of very high stress for the operators, who may suffer from psychic and/or somatic strain both in the long and short term.

The statistics reporting the annual incidence of airmisses from 1983 to 1990[20] (see Figure 4) showed a progressive decrease in number, despite the continuous increase in air traffic, which went up by more than 35 per cent in the period examined.

Figure 4: Annual incidence of airmisses

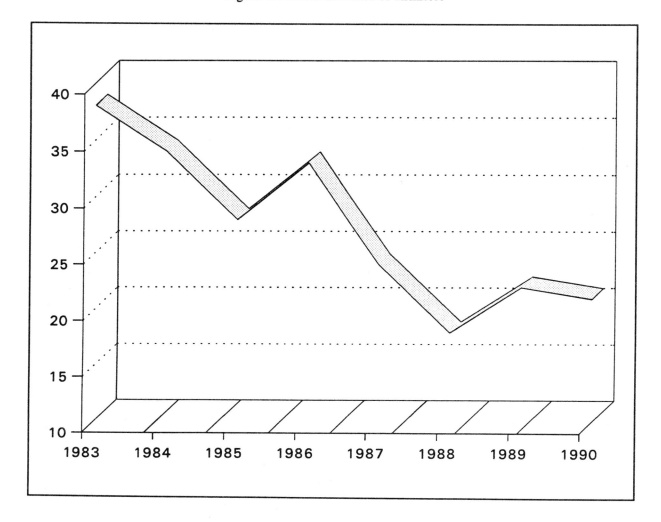

[20] Azienda Autonoma Assistenza al Volo: *L'assistenza al volo in Italia: Tecnologie e infrastrutture* (Rome, 1991).

Conclusions

The progressive decrease in the incidence of airmisses recorded in the last years, in spite of the high increase in air traffic, can certainly be seen as the positive consequence of the continuous adjustments carried out on the ATC system to increase capacity as well as safety. These adjustments dealt with improvements in traffic management and control systems as well as with more attention being paid to the working conditions and performance of the operators.

Moreover, the evaluation of the psycho-physiological responses of the ATCs in relation to traffic load and shift work indicates that proper arrangements of work organization and work hours can contribute significantly to making acceptable the strain connected with this demanding job.

This indication also seems to be confirmed by the very low incidence of cases of dismissals for health reasons, in particular for psychosomatic diseases.

CASE STUDY NO. 6

Using research and practical interventions to prevent occupational stress in shiftworkers in Sweden

Professor Lennart Levi and Professor Torbjörn Åkerstedt[1]

Context and issues

The temporal demands made on shiftworkers by their work schedules are well known. However, less is known about the ability of the individual to match these demands and the psycho-biological "costs" of such adaptation.

Between 1975 and 1986, some of these problems were studied at the Institutionen för stressforskning, Karolinska institutet (Department of Stress Research, Karolinska Institutet) and the Statens institut för psykosocial miljömedicin (IPM) (National Swedish Institute for Psychosocial Factors and Health) in a series of investigations utilizing interdisciplinary experimental as well as epidemiological approaches.

In a first series of studies, attempts were made to study circadian biological rhythms in the absence of the normal time cues. In order to study this, 100 healthy volunteers of both sexes were exposed to three days and three nights of continuous work.[2] In spite of strict standardization and equalization of environmental stimuli over the entire period, most circadian rhythms persisted throughout the experiment period. Results revealed pronounced decreases in the body's excretion of adrenaline and in body temperature. Also seen were shortfalls in performance and increases in fatigue ratings, as well as in melatonin excretion taking place in the small hours.[3]

A logical second step was to apply this information indicating persistent circadian rhythms to a real-life situation, where environmental demands conflicted with such rhythms. In the next study, physiological, psychological, chronobiological and social reactions were investigated when three weeks of night work were introduced to middle-aged male, Swedish track workers at Swedish Rail, who were normally on daytime schedules. The study found that although the endocrine system starts to adapt to the environmental demands induced by shift work (by "stepping on the gas" to keep awake at night and "slowing down" in the day to allow for some sleep), the usual one-week cycle is not enough to completely adapt to the transformation of night into day and vice versa. In fact, not even three weeks of night work are enough to cause an inversion of the circadian rhythms in most subjects. The original circadian rhythms either flatten out or persist. This results in fatigue, sleep disturbances

---

[1] Department of Stress Research, Karolinska Institute, Box 60210, S-104 01 Stockholm, Sweden.

[2] L. Levi: "Stress and distress in response to psychosocial stimuli", in *Acta Medica Scandinavica*, Vol. 191, Supplement 528, 1972.

[3] ibid.; J.E. Fröberg, C.G. Karlsson, L. Levi and L. Lidberg: "Circadian rhythms of catecholamine excretion, shooting range performance and self-ratings of fatigue during sleep deprivation", in *Biological Psychology*, Vol. 2, 1975, pp. 175-188; J.E. Fröberg, C.G. Karlsson, L. Levi and L. Lidberg: "Psycho-biological circadian rhythms during a 72-hour vigil", in *Försvarsmedicin*, No. 11, 1975, pp. 192-201; J.E. Fröberg: "Twenty-four hour patterns in human performance, subjective and physiological variables and differences between morning and evening active subjects", in *Biological Psychology*, No. 5, 1977, pp. 119-134; T. Åkerstedt and J.E. Fröberg: "Psychophysiological circadian rhythms in females during 75 hours of sleep deprivation with continuous activity", in *Waking and sleeping*, No. 4, 1977, pp. 387-394.

and indigestion. In addition, switching from habitual day work to three weeks of night work was accompanied by increases in physiological stress and social problems in both the workers and their families.[4]

To confirm these observations, the next step was to study the well-being of larger groups of shiftworkers. To this end, several hundred shiftworkers were studied using health questionnaires. In this study, self-selection into - or movement away from - shift work was minimal (i.e. no other jobs were available in the area of residence). The results showed higher frequencies of sleep, mood, digestive and social disturbances among the shiftworkers than among the day workers. The complaints about well-being reached their peak during the night shift.[5]

Briefly then, at least some types of shift work are likely to cause a variety of distress reactions, at least in shiftworkers who are vulnerable to such exposure.

Target population

Intervention was targeted to steel workers in a small community in central Sweden and police officers in Stockholm. Both groups work on shifts.

Approach

In the two cases under consideration, stress containment or abatement was achieved by (a) eliminating or reducing shift work, or (b) adapting shift schedules to workers' abilities and needs.

Intervention

Case I: Reducing shift work among steel workers

In the company under investigation, steel workers, before the change, worked according to one of the following schedules:

(1)   **Daywork**, with five work days a week, from 7:00 to 16:00. Saturdays and Sundays were both free.

(2)   **Two-shift work**, also with five work days per week with weekends free. The morning shift was from 04:45 to 13:00; the afternoon/evening shift from 13:00 to 21:15. Shifts alternated each week.

(3)   **Three-shift work**, which was the same as two-shift work with the addition of a night shift from 21:15 to 4:45.

(4)   **Four-shift work**, which was the same as three-shift work except that the shift rotation was faster (two or three days on each shift) and the schedule was continuous. As a consequence, free days were desynchronized with the natural week, which meant that only one in three or four weekends was free.

---

[4] T. Theorell and T. Åkerstedt: "Day and night work: Changes in cholesterol, uric acid, glucose and potassium in serum and in circadian patterns of urinary catecholamine excretion; A longitudinal cross-over study of railway workers", in *Acta Medica Scandinavica*, Vol. 200, pp. 47-53; T. Åkerstedt and T. Theorell: "Exposure to night work: Relations between serum gastrin reactions, psychosomatic complaints and personality variables", in *Journal of Psychosomatic Research*, Vol. 20, 1976, pp. 479-484.

[5] T. Åkerstedt and L. Torsvall: "Experimental changes in shift schedules: Their effects on well-being", in J. Rutenfranz et al. (editors): *Proceedings of the IVth Symposium on Night and Shift Work* (Dortmund, 1977); T. Åkerstedt and L. Torsvall: *Medical, psychological and social aspects of shift work at the Special Steel Mills in Söderfors*, Report No. 64 (Laboratory for Clinical Stress Research, Stockholm, 1977).

Because of the economic situation, the company in which the steel workers were operating decided to reduce working hours and shift work.

The reduction of shift work consisted in the following: (a) abolishing the night shift but retaining the other two shifts; (b) changing from shift work to day work; and (c) changing from four-shift work to three-shift work, i.e. from fast rotation and weekend work to slow rotation and free weekends.[6] Almost half of the three-shift and four-shift workers "moved down" one or more steps, yielding the following situations:

Changed	Number of workers affected
From three-/four-shift work to day work	21
From three-/four-shift work to two-shift work	69
From four-shift work to three-shift work	41

Unchanged	
Day work	18
Two-shift work	16
Three-shift work	73
Four-shift work	77

The existence of control groups (i.e. those with no change) allowed for the assessment of the effects of reducing shift work. Several months before this reduction, a questionnaire was issued to the steel workers.

A one-year follow-up showed that workers who had to change from three- or four-shift work to two-shift work (i.e. abolishing night work) showed a significant increase in well-being with respect to sleep/mood, gastro-intestinal functioning and social factors, along with an improvement in attitude toward their work schedules. Those who switched from shift to day work reported greatly increased social well-being, a shortening of sleep length during free days, considerably improved attitudes towards their work schedule and a reduction of absences due to sickness. Attitudes were mainly negative towards the change from fast rotation to a slow rotation of shift cycles in workers whose schedule was altered from four-shift to three-shift work.

It was concluded that abolishing night work results in a substantial improvement in mental, physical and social well-being. For obvious reasons, such an abolition may not be possible in those occupational settings where human activities need to be carried out round the clock. In such cases, various attempts to humanize shift work schedules may be a feasible alternative.

Case II: Adapting shift schedules among police officers

Change to clockwise rotation. The traditional duty rota for the police force in Stockholm involves a daily, counter-clockwise change in working hours. Based on the hypothesis that clockwise rotation would be preferable

---

[6] T. Åkerstedt and L. Torsvall: "Experimental changes in shift schedules: Their effects on well-being", in *Ergonomics*, Vol. 21, 1978, pp. 849-856.

because it should be more harmonious with human biology,[7] about 40 police officers were organized to spend four weeks on each of the two rotas.

Results of intervention involving change to clockwise rotation. The introduction of clockwise rotation was associated with improved sleep, less fatigue, lower systolic blood pressure and lower blood levels of triglycerides and glucose (i.e. positive effects on risk factors for ischemic heart disease). A further evaluation lasting six months with police officers in a non-metropolitan area also demonstrated decreased fatigue and less stress disorders, as well as improved sleep and health. However, the model had a social drawback in that it reduced opportunities for getting prolonged, unbroken leisure periods. The police officers therefore decided to go back to counter-clockwise rotation. After nine months on this system, they found, however, that the advantages of prolonged periods of leisure time were outweighed by the drawbacks which had been documented. Therefore, despite the disadvantages of reduced periods of unbroken leisure time, the police officers decided to return once more to clockwise rotation.

Repositioning of night shift. The main reason night work is usually associated with disturbances during sleeping and waking hours is that the shiftworker is required to work at night and sleep during the day. Both behaviours are clearly unphysiological.[8] This implies then that a series of work shifts should have less negative effects if the fatigue-inducing night shift is placed at the end of this series instead of at the beginning.

The intervention, targeted at 18 police officers,[9] investigated whether well-being would be affected by changing the position of the night shift from the beginning to the end of the shift cycle.

Originally, the police officers worked a compressed schedule of night shift, afternoon shift and morning shift. The new schedule reversed this (see Table 1).

Table 1: Old and new shift schedule

Day	Old schedule	New schedule
1	22:00-24:00	14:00-22:00
2	0:00-7:00 and 15:00-22:00	7:00-14:00 and 22:00-24:00
3	7:00-15:00	0:00-7:00
4	day off	day off
5	day off	day off

Results of intervention involving repositioning of night shift. Six months after the change the police officers completed a questionnaire about their reactions to the change. Table 2 presents the results of the questionnaire, indicating the responses in terms of "improvement" or "deterioration" in comparison with the situation before the intervention. Table 2 shows that the intervention, indeed, was accompanied by strongly reduced fatigue, improved subjective health and positive effects on the work situation. Non-significant trends were found regarding better mood, better sleep and positive effects on family life. The only negative effect was that the amount of leisure time was reported to have decreased (which, objectively, was not so).

---

[7] K. Orth-Gomér: "Intervention on coronary risk factors by adapting a shift work schedule to biologic rhythmicity", in *Psychosomatic Medicine*, Vol. 45, No. 5, 1983, pp. 407-415.

[8] T. Åkerstedt and M. Gillberg: "The circadian variation of experimentally displaced sleep", in *Sleep*, Vol. 4, 1981, pp. 159-169.

[9] K. Fredén, T. Åkerstedt, K. Olsson and K. Orth-Gomér: "Positive effects of displacing night work to the end of the shift cycle", in *Night and shift work: Long-term effects and their prevention; Proceedings of the VII International Symposium on Night and Shift Work, Igls, Austria, 1985* (Lang, Frankfurt, 1986), pp. 453-456.

Table 2: Effects of change in work schedule

Variable	Improvement (% change)	Deterioration (% change)	Statistical significance of change
Fatigue	less by 55	more by 18	.05
Workload	less by 55	more by 9	.01
Subjective health	better by 59	worse by 14	.05
Work situation	better by 55	worse by 23	.05
Sleep	better by 55	worse by 27	ns
Mood	better by 36	worse by 14	ns
Family life	better by 45	worse by 27	ns
Relations with superiors	better by 5	worse by 18	ns
Relations with colleagues	better by 9	worse by 5	ns
Amount of leisure time	more by 9	less by 68	.01

ns = not significant   NB. This questionnaire contains multiple answers.

The two studies illustrate the possibility of improving conditions in occupations where night work is unavoidable by arriving at a more natural arrangement of working hours.[10]

---

[10] T. Åkerstedt and A. Knutsson: *Oregelbundna och obekväma arbetstider som hälsorisk* (Irregular and inconvenient hours of work as a health risk), paper prepared for the Swedish Commission on the Work Environment, Appendix G (Allmänna förlaget, Stockholm, 1989).

CASE STUDY NO. 7

Using ergonomic analysis and group discussion to identify and prevent stress in managers and assembly-line workers: A Mexican case study

Dr. Miguel Matrajt[1]

Context

A number of high-level managers in a high technology multinational manufacturing company (Company Z) met the author of this paper in an occupational health meeting. Subsequent to the meeting, these managers invited the author (who is a specialist in work-related mental health) to a meeting in their company to seek advice about solving the company's human problems.

The author was able to meet with nine managers of the company (two vice-presidents and seven directors), who described the problems that they had identified: a general climate of deep-rooted discontent in practically all sectors of the enterprise; a decline in productivity, which was substantially greater at the managerial level; and an incidence of psychosomatic problems which clearly indicated the existence of stress. These problems had been identified over a period of two years. The enterprise had attempted to resolve them by using its own resources and acting on two principal fronts: redesigning work programmes and having the occupational psychology and public relations departments take actions (information, the organization of activities, etc.). Following the failure of these measures, the decision was taken to seek external advice.

The author proposed a three-day pilot study, as follows:

— the first day would be used to identify how the work was organized in general and the characteristics of the enterprise as an institution;

— the second day would consist of two group meetings (each two hours in length) and four individual interviews with managerial-level staff who would be randomly selected;

— the third day would be devoted to repeating the activities of the previous two days, but this time with assembly-line workers.

Further to this pilot activity, the author produced a written report containing preliminary remarks (the "provisional situation diagnosis") and a proposal for further work which set out objectives, time-periods and cost.

Issues

Company Z has two manufacturing plants located in two states in the Republic of Mexico, plus its company headquarters. The company has more than 4,000 employees. Company Z is organized in a similar way to its international headquarters and the other country branches. The corporate organizational structure is decided upon at the central level, with the participation of upper-level managers from each branch. The company has existed as such for decades and, in general, has been in constant expansion. A number of managers are rotated through

[1] Professor, Occupational Mental Health, Universidad Autónoma del Estado de Morelos, Providencia 1218, B-402, Col. del Valle, 03100 Mexico City, DF, Mexico.

various branches of the company and headquarters during their professional careers, and therefore possess an in-depth knowledge of the manner in which the company as a whole operates.

In relation to management methods, there are two channels of communication: the formal channel, which respects the organizational structure of the company, and the informal channel, which consists of rumour, gossip, news heard in bars, etc. However, the information received through these two channels is often contradictory, with greater weight being given to the informal channel. Similarly, there are two sets of standards and value systems which determine many decisions and cause stress. Personal problems in relations between managers were identified as contributing to problems in the work environment. For example, rivalry between managers is reflected in the actions of their respective personnel. This, in turn, produces a negative impact on the necessary levels of cooperation between departments. One significant result of decreased cooperation between departments is that more time is needed to carry out operations. This increases physical and mental burdens as well as family conflicts.

At the level of assembly-line workers, two particularly interesting issues emerged at the preliminary stage. The production programme was excessively rigid with rhythms that varied substantially for no apparent reason, and there was extreme ambivalence about relationships between colleagues, which clearly had its roots in the system of collective bonuses.

Target population

The target population for this stress prevention programme consisted of about 130 managers and 3,600 assembly-line workers at Company Z.

Approach and intervention

The objectives of the proposed action were the following:

(1) increase the understanding of the causes of the stress identified during the first phase and investigate other factors which require deeper analysis. This is termed the "situation diagnosis" (Phase A);

(2) seek, through the participation of specialists, managers and assembly-line workers, the removal and/or modification of the causes of stress. This is termed the "corrective phase" (Phase B).

These plans were organized in a first time-frame of 17 weeks. This period included three weeks for preparing Phase A; six weeks for implementing Phase A; four weeks for analysing the findings from Phase A and preparing Phase B; and four weeks for implementating Phase B.

A second period of 12 months included subsequent supervision, adjustment and follow-up of the results.

Four criteria were indicated for evaluating, on a cost-benefit basis, the advantages of undertaking the proposed programme.

(a) Since the company's overall productivity level was 7 per cent lower on average than that of other companies in the branch at national level (this was attributed to the impact of work-related stress), it would be sufficient to decrease this figure by one percentage point. A 1 per cent decrease would more than cover the investment made in the study and programme of action;

(b) Similarly, a 12 per cent decrease in psychosomatic problems among managers, even though their medical costs are covered by an insurance programme, would create savings in terms of lost work hours and the costs of training replacement managers. These savings would justify the investment in the study;

(c) Additionally, a decrease of 22 per cent in psychosomatic problems and unjustified absenteeism among assembly-line workers, who are also covered by social security for their medical care and sickness benefits, would recuperate the investment made in the study and programme of action.

(d)   In addition to these quantitative evaluation criteria, a qualitative benefit would result from the improvement in interpersonal relations and a decline in interpersonal problems.

Phase A: Situation diagnosis

Examination of the institution

Using institutional psychology methodology,[2] the characteristics of the company were examined, including leadership, explicit and implicit standards and values, formal and informal channels of communication, the sense of worker identification with the enterprise, the real level of receptivity to complaints and suggestions, the rigidity of the enterprise and/or its propensity to change, the origin and possibilities of change, etc. This information was collected by means of direct observations and interviews. This examination led to the following evidence:

(a)   The informal channel of communication (basically made up of rumour, gossip and news heard in the bar) was found to be an important cause of stress in the work environment. At the managerial level, the source and basic transmitters of this channel were the secretaries of the managers. The information that passed through this channel was impossible to verify, and it was impossible to refute false information. This informal channel of communication was therefore frequently used for the specific purpose of spreading false information about people.

(b)   Upper-level managers were convinced, as a result of information provided through the informal channel of communication, that the president of the branch would retire shortly, long before he was due to do so. They were also convinced that the replacement would be one of the branch managers. Both convictions were unfounded yet were still considered to be the absolute truth and were acted upon by those concerned. This may be termed the product of "institutional imagination".[3] On the basis of this product of institutional imagination, managerial-level staff threw themselves into under-cover competition, which was never discussed explicitly. This situation resulted in a compulsive desire to show capacity at work and of a loss of mutual collaboration and trust. This was another important cause of the stressful working environment.

(c)   Moreover, in Company Z there was a tradition of finding a scapegoat to blame for problems which occurred. The victimized individual would be obliged to leave the enterprise, even if the resolution of the problem involved an area broader than the area for which the supposedly guilty person was responsible. This was another important factor of stress, which gave everyone an incentive to show managerial capacity, even when it was not suitable to do so. The above problem produced the effect of exaggerating and providing an impulse for interpersonal conflicts, which were beginning to get out of control and which created a negative work environment.

(d)   These factors were responsible for the decrease in productivity. To compensate for this decrease and, against its own organizational values, the enterprise had extended the hours of work at the managerial level. This practice occurred without any formal agreement about the increase in hours. In the six months prior to the study, there had been an average of 58 hours a week of work in some sectors, in contrast with the 45 hours per week of the formal timetable. This situation increased the physical, mental and psychological burden of those involved. It also created a stressful environment during rest periods and meal breaks during working hours. The extension of working time had various consequences for the managers' relations with their families. The worst impact was on families which had been functioning well. Two groups emerged. One group consisted of managers whose families reacted negatively to the work situation, and a second group included those who had no family responsibilities. Managers in the second group were in a better position compared with the first group. Managers

---

[2] G. Baremblitt (editor): *El inconciente institucional* (Nuevomar, Mexico City, 1981); F. Guattari (editor): *La intervención institucional* (Folios Ediciones, Mexico City, 1981); R. Lourau: *Anàlisis institucional y socioanàlisis* (Editorial Nueva Imagen, Mexico City, 1977); O. Saidón and B. Kononnovich: *La escena institucional* (Lugar Editorial, Buenos Aires, 1991); E. Pichón Riviere: *Teoria del vinculo* (Nueva Visión, Buenos Aires, 1977).

[3] J. Volnovich (editor): *El espacio institucional* (Lugar Editorial, Buenos Aires, 1991).

who had had a good family situation were thus subject to an additional source of stress as a result of the longer working hours.

(e) The stressful environment at the managerial level was transmitted, by a chain reaction, to the workers for whom they were responsible. Nevertheless, not all sectors suffered equally from the increased requirements. There were even some for whom this provided an interesting incentive. The area where the changes gave rise to more stressful work requirements was the assembly line. The examination of the assembly line work programme showed that it was excessively strict in certain aspects. The work programmes were established centrally with the participation of upper-level managers from all branches. However, these had been influenced by the work culture of the company's headquarters.   For assembly-line workers, a degree of freedom was absolutely indispensable.

Ergonomic study

Using conventional ergonomic methods, the characteristics of the work were studied, including the organization of work, the tasks performed, the methods used for the selection of personnel, the specific training that personnel received, the specific characteristics of the work performed by each section, who planned the work, the extent to which workers participated in planning the work and/or changes that are made to the organization of work, hours of work, shifts, rest periods, the pace of work, the burden of work in physical, mental and psychological terms, and quality control. This study was carried out by means of direct observations, analysis of the organization of work in the company, interviews, etc.[4]

Finally, the data and standards that had been researched and tested at the international level and the data obtained in the factory were compared. The most outstanding of the findings was that the increased requirements on the assembly line pushed the physical, mental and psychological effort that was required beyond the recommended levels. This "over-requirement" resulted in more errors, an increase in the general stress level, and an exaggerated feeling of fatigue and widespread discontent. The authors believe that this was the most important factor behind the increase in unjustified absenteeism. In addition, certain aspects of the way in which the work was planned were unnecessarily strict for the performance of the task and for output. These included the manner in which individual breaks (for example, to go to the bathroom) as well as collective breaks were given, the time set aside for infrastructural work (such as the straightening up and cleaning of equipment), the rules governing the way in which a number of work-related tasks should be performed, and the authorization that was needed for dialogue and verbal exchanges.

Group study

A study was made of the work groups which were established (departments, sections, etc.), using group dynamic methodology. The study concentrated on roles, relationships, leadership, channels of communication, group image, etc. The study covered a total of 20 groups, based on two three-hour meetings with each group.[5]

---

[4] M. Freyssenet and H. Hirata: "Mudanças tecnológicas e partipação dos trabalhadores: Os circulos de controle de qualidade no Japâo", in *Revista de Adminiastraçâo de Empresas*, Vol. 25, No. 3, 1985; F. Guelaud et al.: *Para un anàlisis de las condiciones del trabajo obrero en la empresa* (INET, Mexico, and INDIA, Peru, 1981); C. Teiger: "Lo que pasa en las sesiones de formación de trabajadores", in *Plaisir et souffrance dans le travail* (AOCIP, Paris, 1988); C. Teiger: *Fatigue ou equilibre par le travail* (Entreprise Moderne d'Edition, Paris, 1980); B. Coriat: *El taller y el cronómetro: Ensayo sobre el Taylorismo, el Fordismo y la producción en masa* (Siglo XXI, Mexico City, 1985); C. Libouban: "Un aspecto nuevo de la carga de trabajo: La carga psíquica", in C. Dejours et al.: *Psychopathologie du travail* (Entreprise Moderne d'Edition, Paris, 1985).

[5] E. Pichón Riviere: *Del psicoanàlisis a la psicologia social* (Nueva Visión, Buenos Aires, 1977); G. Baremblitt: *Grupos, teoria y técnica* (IBRAPSI, Rio de Janeiro, 1982); A. Bauleo: *Contrainstitución y grupos* (Editorial Fundamentos, Madrid, 1977); F. Guattari: *Psicoanàlisis y transversalidad* (Siglo Veintiuno Editores, Mexico City, 1976).

Although the findings differed substantially between the managerial and assembly-line levels, in both cases highly stressful factors were found.

At the managerial level, the group dynamic was fundamentally determined by the personal leadership qualities of the heads of the groups. For example, if the heads of groups gave no importance to family relationships, they would set rigorous requirements for work and meetings outside working hours. In many cases, unconscious psychological pressure was exerted, since accepting or rejecting the chief's rules of the game was interpreted in terms of loyalty, solidarity, friendship, affection, etc., or as indifference, betrayal or plotting on behalf of a rival. Although in formal terms accepting additional hours and work was voluntary, the implicit standards of the institution endorsed the methods of work of the chief. For those who did not cooperate with the company's implicit standards, career opportunities were non-existent. Depending on their personal characteristics, some chiefs tended to relay to their inferiors the pressure which they received from their own superiors. This effectively would transfer their stress to others. However, other chiefs, whose tendencies were paternalistic, absorbed the whole impact of the stress and behaved as if they were protectors. Others made the success of their departments a fundamental factor for their own sense of well-being and self-esteem, which implied a requirement for perfectionism. Still others gave greater weight to collective responsibility and creativity. The group dynamic was also affected by two features which are very characteristic of a number of Latin American cultures, namely the importance of affective ties (for promotions and bonuses these were much more important than knowledge and/or work performance) and a form of communication in which silence, sub-text and untruths played a fundamental role. The interaction between all the above factors resulted in groups which varied broadly in their level of work-related stress.

For assembly-line workers, it was found that collective bonuses were the principal cause of stress. As is well known, in many companies the workers receive a basic wage and a series of bonuses which raise their real income substantially. These bonuses, which are paid to the whole section or shift, are the most significant proportion of the wage. In this way, each worker feels under much more pressure from their colleagues than from their immediate superior or the company. Psychologically, this establishes an extremely ambivalent relationship between colleagues. In other terms, synergy is established between the economic stimulus (it should be noted that the Mexican labour market is affected by chronic unemployment and low wages for unskilled work) and the psychological pressure of not wishing to appear guilty to peers and friends for the loss of the collective bonus.

Examination of individual cases

Through individual interviews and some figures from a test projection (TAT), a series of workers at both the managerial and assembly-line level, selected at random, were interviewed. This work covered 183 people. Each person was the subject of two one-hour or one-and-a-half hour meetings.[6]

This examination showed that the employees of Company Z have the specific characteristics of being very competitive, very individualistic, giving great importance to success and consumer goods, and to the modern cultural environment. All of these can be achieved, at least in part, as long as the employees remain in the company and make their careers there. Therefore, for all of the employees, regardless of their level in the hierarchy, belonging to and remaining in the company is given priority over many other objectives. In the case of some managers, this is given priority over any other objective.

Those employees who suffered from psychosomatic diseases were characterized by a greater tendency to deny interpersonal conflicts. In many of them, it was evident from their personal histories that their aggressive sides and their depressions produced greater unease than normal. They also demonstrated an inverted relationship between their potential for interpersonal expression and their manifestations of psychosomatic illness. In almost all cases, time pressure (having to complete a task in the short period set by others) was recognized as being highly stressful. Other stress factors which were expressed were (a) all love-hate relationships, even at the highest level

---

[6] M. Matrajt: *Salud mental y trabajo* (UAEM, Cuernavaca, 1986); M. Matrajt: "Industrializacón, proceso de trabajo y salud mental", in *Subjetividad y Cultura*, No. 1, 1991; M. Matrajt: *Estudios en salud mental ocupacional* (UAEM, forthcoming).

with loved ones; (b) the approval of the group (colleagues, family, etc.); (c) any situation which gave rise to guilt; and (d) situations of separation.

In total, this phase covered slightly over 400 persons (10 per cent of the total staff of the company). Once the provisional diagnosis of the situation was completed, it was decided that there was no need for medical examinations or neurological measurements. The work-related stress indicators contained in the evaluation were considered to be sufficiently firm. Although in the case of this company it would have been possible to propose laboratory tests in order to have medical information available, our intention was to test a model of action that was as cost-effective as possible and which could be applied widely in developing countries.

Phase B: Corrective phase

With all the information that had been accumulated and processed over four weeks, the team held a series of group meetings with large groups (between 30 and 100 persons) in their work areas. Two or three sessions were held with each group over a four-week period. Approximately 120 sessions of two to three hours each were held in order to make contact with all the employees in the company.

In all cases, the following procedure was used to try to reduce workplace stress:

- A brief description was given of the researchers' findings concerning the causes of stress in the section or working group.

- The workers were encouraged to discuss, amplify and reject the ideas put forward by the researchers, who continued to amplify the information that they had provided initially. For the team, the basic purpose was for the workers to confirm the hypotheses that had been advanced from their own experience, and to share with the team their thoughts and feelings concerning the work and its organization (including the causes of stress).

- At the first session, towards the end, the employees were invited to propose changes that would modify the causes of the stress. At that stage it was only important for them to put forward proposals so that everyone could discuss them at the following session. The role of the investigators responsible for coordinating each session was to promote the participation of all employees; to ensure that all ideas that were expressed were taken into account; to point out the psychological, group and institutional consequences of each proposal, and the need to take into account the productivity level of the company; to seek to ensure that the proposed modification was adopted as a collective proposal, which had to be fully understood by everyone; and to put forward the knowledge and experience of the researchers, including their findings in other sectors of the same company, so that the proposal would be as scientific as possible.

- In the following session (or sessions, as necessary), all the proposals were fully analysed. A plan was proposed for those which received the greatest consensus (leaving on the floor other proposals so that they could be re-examined if the most acceptable ones did not work), and a method of self-management organization was decided upon to implement the changes.

Further to these sessions, several initiatives and decisions were taken in order to modify the causes of stress.

Plan to modify causes of stress

- It was agreed that everybody would try to **not** believe any information that circulated through the informal channels of communication. They would furthermore try to change the formal channels of communication so that the latter could fulfill their function and be a credible source of information. At the managerial level, the employees undertook not to divulge classified information. Employees at the appropriate levels took the necessary initiative to impart the information needed to stop the imaginary institutional gossip, which had been a major source of stress.

- It was decided to analyse in depth the mechanism for attributing guilt to individuals for failures and problems which were, in fact, the result of decisions made by the company.

- Mechanisms were suggested to resolve interpersonal conflicts or, at least, to eliminate their impact on the work in question.

- It was decided to reform working hours in order to abolish the established practice of extending work hours and to prevent work hours from interfering with rest and meal breaks.

- It was decided to modify the criteria followed for changes in the speed of the assembly line so that the assembly line would not be considered the ultimate "solution" for the other productivity problems of the company as a whole.

- A detailed analysis was carried out of the requirements of the work programme. The analysis aimed at making changes which were in accordance with Mexican working traditions but which would not compromise productivity and efficiency. All employees, foremen and engineers participated in the analysis. With the participation of the above-mentioned groups, the physical and mental effort required to carry out the work was analysed in order to assess tolerance limits, and therefore to assess the real possibilities of overtime. Tentative parameters for each section would be established.

- At the managerial level, a detailed analysis was made of the different forms of group leadership with a view to maintaining personal styles as much as possible, while trying to eliminate features which caused stress for the rest of the team. For example, it was considered necessary to set aside time for regular reflection at the group level (every two or three months) in order to examine the organization of the work performed by the group as a whole.

- All the assembly-line workers participated in an analysis of the bonus systems. A series of changes were introduced (different changes for each sector of production) with a view to decreasing the ambivalence of the group relationships and the level of individual stress. For example, the procedures for the attribution of bonuses by section were replaced by a system of average overall performance (overall punctuality, overall assistance, etc.).

- Based on the findings of the individual and group studies, changes were suggested for the personnel selection and recruitment department. The suggested changes were to help prevent individuals with personality traits seen as risk factors from being placed in the sectors identified by the team as the most stressful. In addition, the team suggested that at all levels, but particularly at the managerial level, time should be formally set aside for group meetings and discussions concerning the organization of the enterprise and the relationships between peers, chiefs and their subordinates. These "meetings" should facilitate action and the search for alternatives, and should not become forums for confession, accusation or mere repetition of management's arguments. The team also suggested the voluntary organization of sports and social activities outside working hours.

Results and evaluation

Over the 12 months following the intervention, there was a decline in psychosomatic illness of 17 per cent at the managerial level and 15 per cent for assembly-line workers. The author believes that it is necessary to distinguish between the decline in absences (which is what concerns the company) from the decrease in the incidence of psychosomatic illness (which is what interests the team as occupational mental health specialists). Although the data were insufficient to establish a proportional curve, the general trend was for the progressive decrease of both indices.

A progressive increase in the company's productivity level was also reported, which was attributed to the decrease in stress-inducing situations. In the 12-month period following the study, the productivity differential from the average was reduced to 5.3 per cent with a general trend towards improvement. It was estimated that in the following 18 months the company would attain the general average. Unjustified absenteeism decreased and attained the average levels for the companies in the branch at the national level. The general human and work environment in the company improved substantially.

All four evaluation criteria which, according to our theoretical model, are indicators of changes in the work-related stress situation, showed a significant change in positive terms. In the final analysis, the examination and action undertaken had a double benefit: it corrected the effects of stress and prevented new ones.

CASE STUDY NO. 8

Computers and stress reduction in
social service workers in New Jersey

Dr. Janet Cahill[1]

Context

This project was implemented in the State of New Jersey child protective agency. This is the agency responsible for responding to allegations of child abuse and neglect across the state. The agency had approximately 4,000 employees distributed across 47 district offices and one central office. The major job categories were clerical, social workers, supervisors and managerial staff.

At the time of the intervention, this agency was experiencing a high degree of organizational strain. Caseloads were very high, often exceeding 100 cases per social worker. Agency staff were frequently exposed to hostile clients and complex case management issues. In addition, the types of cases being referred to the agency were increasingly severe, often involving sexual abuse and drugs and alcohol. Finally, the sheer scale of referrals, over 50,000 reported cases per year, created a tremendous backlog of work for all members of the staff. The paperwork generated by this large volume of cases presented a particular problem for clerical workers.

A 1988 study[2] concluded that staff members in this agency were reporting significantly higher levels of burnout and stress-related symptoms than national samples of social workers. The union representing the staff [Communication Workers of American (CWA)] brought the results of the 1988 survey to a legislative hearing where the overall performance and staff morale of the agency were examined. These hearings took place during a period of intense labour/management conflict. One concrete strategy to come out of the hearings was the formation of a labour-management stress committee. The committee was given the task of developing a programme to address the serious morale and burnout problems in the agency.

This joint labour-management approach was unusual for the State, in that both the top-level management of the agency and the union representing the social workers and clerical staff were actively involved. A second critical characteristic of the intervention programme was that it was designed to address both personal and structural sources of stress. In other words, strategies were designed to improve both the personal coping skills of the workers and to reduce the sources of stress in the work environment itself. Many studies have addressed the importance of recognizing stress caused by work environment factors.[3] This case study focuses on one of the structural intervention strategies to emerge from the committee: the microcomputer project.

Issues

A persistent source of stress that administrators, social workers and clerks in this agency reported was paperwork. An internal study found that social workers were spending approximately 60 per cent of their time on

---

[1] Department of Psychology, Rowen College of New Jersey, 452 East Third Street, Moorestown, New Jersey 08057, United States.

[2] J. Cahill and L.H. Feldman: *Evaluation of a stress management program in a child protection agency*, paper presented at the Eastern Psychological Association, Buffalo, New York, 1988.

[3] A. Minahan: "Burnout and organizational change", in *Social Work*, Vol. 25, 1980, p. 87.

paperwork. By alarming contrast, these same case workers reported spending only 14 per cent of their time in actual client contact.

The core of the agency's management information system was a mainframe computer located at the central office. Each of the 47 district offices of the agency was linked via terminal to the central computer. The intervention strategy was developed in part due to the problems presented by the computer system.

The existing computer system allowed for almost instant transmission of data from the local office to the central office. There was, however, no mechanism for the local office to capture or retain the information for its own use except as a screen image printed on local printers. In general, a summary of the initial intake form was sent back to the local office within 24 to 48 hours. However, frequent delays made this transmission uncertain. Inconsistent access to data has been identified as stressful in research studies.[4] An additional stress-producing factor was that the offices kept a redundant manual record-keeping system.

To successfully code the computer forms, case workers and clerical staff needed to master an extensive coding manual. Although these codes changed frequently, it was expected that the entire work force of the agency would learn and use the new codes. In practice, case workers did not keep up with the coding system unless their supervisors insisted or unless it was essential for their clients. This uneven compliance meant that in order to do their jobs, clerical staff either had to track down the information manually or take their best guess at the appropriate code.

In addition to the coding problems, the monthly reports that district offices received from the central data base were voluminous and difficult to interpret. The result was that the reports generally sat on the shelf from month to month, which indicated inefficient reporting procedures.[5]

Deskilling of clerical staff. Data entry for the centralized computer system consisted of rigid, repetitive work, usually with an extensive backlog of forms. Clerical staff working on terminals connected to the mainframe computer therefore had jobs that required little skill or flexibility, a high degree of repetition and little control over their work.

Health and safety. The existing computer workstations had several ergonomic problems. These included poorly designed equipment, lighting, monitors and work flow.

Prior to the intervention, the agency had made extensive efforts to address the paperwork problems it was experiencing. These efforts included purchasing stand-alone word processors, and setting up several committees. The perception at the local offices was, however, that these initiatives had been ineffective.

Target population

This intervention programme was developed to help eliminate stress factors that had been identified for case workers in the agency.

Approach

The stress committee decided to use a new microcomputer based information system to address some of the problems which were causing stress. The project had the following goals:

---

[4] G. Johansson and G. Aronsson: *Stress reactions in computerized administrative work* (University of Stockholm, Stockholm, 1980).

[5] C.A. Rapp and J. Poertner: "The design of data-based management reports", in *Administration in Social Work*, Vol. 10, 1986, pp. 53-64.

- Increasing the amount of local autonomy and decision-making latitude that the clerical staff had over the computer system.

- Increasing skill levels of clerical staff.

- Introducing the new system without increasing stress levels of staff.

- Implementing a career ladder.

- Improving health and safety factors, including installation of ergonomically correct equipment.

- Improving the job satisfaction of the clerical staff.

- Streamlining information flow between the local and central office.

- Providing health and safety training to the clerical staff around the use of microcomputers.

The goals and priorities of the project were determined by extensive discussions with office staff.

Intervention

A pilot office was set up to initiate the design of computer programmes to meet these goals. Initially, one computer was purchased and one clerk volunteered for the project. In addition, a professional computer programmer was hired as a consultant. It is important to note that the consultant reported to the stress committee and spent most of his time directly with the clerk and local district office manager. This local input was considered essential to meet the goal of local control and access of information. Additionally, the author "shadowed" a number of the clerical workers for several days, which meant observing or performing all of the work-related tasks that these employees performed. This technique allowed for a more concrete understanding of work flow, tasks, and the use of the existing technology.

The first achievement of the project was to enable local offices to get their own data sets quickly. Once that was accomplished, software programmes were developed with the general goals of the project in mind. These programmes were written by the computer consultant and were all menu driven.

Several of these computer applications were developed and field tested at the pilot office. Examples of these applications included: timekeeping system, operational plan programme, caseload trend analysis, litigation tracking system, mailing lists, inventory tracking system, service request programme, providers resource directory, and a critical indicators programme. The following is a brief description of one of the larger software packages, the clients programme.

Clients programme

The clients programme captured critical information at intake and carried relevant parts into many different forms and reports. The package was menu driven which significantly reduced training time. Each report could usually be generated with one or two keys strokes. This programme significantly reduced the amount of time that clerical and professional workers needed to manage paperwork for cases. The new programme also made it possible for new information to be entered only once, which reduced the amount of repetitive work performed. Once clients received a data set, it could automatically produce approximately 150 documents per case. While each of these documents individually may only represent a savings of 10-15 minutes per task, the cumulative effect has been quite striking. The agency has estimated that the clients programme was producing 1.5 million pieces of paper per year statewide. Before the clients package was installed, each of these documents had to be generated by hand.

Besides the increase in productivity and efficiency created by these computer applications, the project also changed the quality of work for the clerical staff working on the new computers. The programmes enabled the staff to have more variety in their tasks. Skill levels were increased since staff members had to learn a variety of programmes. In addition, they had much more control over the information that their office generated. As the project developed, they could output the information in increasingly flexible and sophisticated ways. Extensive efforts were made to insure that the new computers would continue to increase the skill level of these clerks. This effort established the foundation needed to create additions to the existing career ladders.

There were also two other change strategies that were pursued during the initial phase of the intervention. First, the committee researched and made recommendations for purchasing ergonomically correct computer equipment for the agency. Most of the committee's recommendations were followed during the next period of equipment purchases.

Second, a computer health and safety training programme was designed for the clerical staff. This training addressed problems such as eyestrain, musculoskeletal disorders, and fatigue. The committee also made several recommendations to reduce the likelihood of these problems developing. These recommendations were implemented throughout the agency.

After several successful applications had been developed, the agency decided to implement the programme statewide and made a commitment to purchase several hundred computers. This decision was supported by the union. An evaluation programme was designed to assess the impact of the new computer system on the clerical staff's work environment. The initial evaluation was targeted at clerical workers since they would be the group most affected by the initial change in technology.

Evaluation

In order to evaluate this intervention, a 56-item questionnaire was sent to all 624 clerical staff in the agency. The surveys were distributed before the intervention programme was implemented statewide and again approximately six months after the intervention process began. The first data set will be referred to as **Time 1** and the second as **Time 2**. Four hundred fifty-four responses were received at Time 1 -- a return rate of 72.9 per cent. At Time 2, 313 responses were received -- response rate of 50.3 per cent. These return rates were considered acceptable, particularly given that the usual compliance rates for the agency were quite low. Subjects were given an identification number to enable tracking individual scores from Time 1 to Time 2. However, both identification numbers were only available for 43 subjects. The remainder of the sample removed the identification number from the second questionnaire. The main reason that employees did not want to be personally identified appeared to be the deep distrust they felt toward the agency. There had been many major disciplines and grievances in the period prior to the study. Despite repeated promises of anonymity, most respondents removed the identification sheet from the questionnaire.

Later analysis indicated that there were no significant differences between the groups at Time 1 and Time 2. In addition, there was virtually no turnover in these offices during this period. However, the most valid way to interpret these results is as two independent snapshots of the work environment.

It should be noted that there was no control group in this study, which presented a methodological problem in objectively evaluating the intervention. It was not possible to arrange for a control group since an administrative decision was made to implement the programme statewide. This decision was largely influenced by the pilot office which received the project enthusiastically, and the requests of other offices to have the programme as soon as possible.

Questionnaire. The questionnaire was designed to assess the psychological and social structure of the work environment, and included the following scales:

(1)   Skill discretion -- perceived variety and level of skill needed to do the job.

(2)   Created skill -- perceived amount of skill development.

(3)   Decision latitude/decision authority -- perceived amount of control or autonomy over work.

(4)   Job satisfaction -- global level of satisfaction with the job.

(5)   Physical/psychological strain -- self-report of a variety of stress related symptoms.

(6)   Sleeping problems -- self-reported sleep disturbances.

(7)   Value of new skills -- perceived usefulness of computer skills.

(8)   Control over equipment -- perceived autonomy over the computer or other technology.

These scales were particularly focused on job control and job satisfaction, since these were the major factors targeted in the intervention.

Respondents were classified in three job categories according to the computer system on which they worked:

—   **Mainframe:** data entry into the centralized mainframe;

—   **Word processor:** this job involved working on a stand alone word processor. This machine did not have the capabilities of a microcomputer;

—   **Microcomputer:** this job category involved the use of the new microcomputer and applications. These machines were locally based in the district offices.

Given the goals of the intervention, it was anticipated that these job categories would show a different pattern of results from Time 1 to Time 2.

Results

The Time 1 data showed significant differences for skill discretion, created skill, decision latitude, and job dissatisfaction. Workers using the word processor reported significantly higher levels of skill discretion, created skill, decision latitude, and job satisfaction than workers using the mainframe system. These workers also reported significantly higher levels of decision authority than workers using the microcomputers. Thus, at Time 1 the results indicated that workers using the word processors perceived their work environments in the most favourable terms. No significant differences were found for the strain or technology measures.

It should be noted that at Time 1, the microcomputers had just been introduced into the offices and were primarily used to type reports.

A similar analysis was then performed on the Time 2 data. Significant differences were found for skill discretion, created skill, decision authority, value of new skills and control over equipment. The analyses indicated a significantly different pattern of results. Workers using the microcomputers now reported the highest levels of skill discretion, created skill, decision latitude, value of new skills and control over equipment, and job satisfaction. This pattern was the same for decision authority. No significant differences were found for strain or sleeping problems.

Overall, the results of the study indicate that the intervention had a positive impact on a number of key aspects of the work environment including: decision latitude, created skill, attitude toward technology, and job satisfaction. Clerical staff who actively use the new microcomputers and related applications appeared to have more control over their jobs, felt their jobs required more skill, had a better attitude toward technology, and were more satisfied. Anecdotally, the staff also felt that the computers greatly improved their efficiency, but this study did not use a direct measure of productivity.

Clerks who were assigned to input data into the centralized mainframe consistently reported the poorest perceptions of their work environments. These findings supported the conclusion that large, centrally managed computer systems were not as responsive to workers' need for autonomy as locally based technology. This on-going dissatisfaction with the mainframe system underscores the importance of including measures of both the work environment and productivity in any assessments of technological change.

Measures of strain did not show any change over time. This was considered a positive finding considering the short period of time between the two surveys. It was considered important that the changes did not **increase** levels of strain, given the extremely difficult organizational climate of the agency. If the skill discretion levels continued to increase for this workforce, it is reasonable to expect that measurable improvements in strain measures would also improve.[6]

Key elements to the change process

Most experts in the area of occupational stress would agree that real organizational change is difficult. This is particularly true in human service settings where overwhelmed staff are often resistant to change. The intervention process in this programme was designed with those realities in mind, and therefore put extensive resources into the change process itself. The most important of these factors are described below.

Preparatory staff work. This project paid a great deal of attention to the "human factor" of the intervention. Meetings were held in the offices before the computers arrived. The project was carefully explained and staff were encouraged to discuss their concerns. These meetings were extremely useful in allowing staff to voice their frustrations and suspicions about the change.

Marketing of initial programme. The first programme that was distributed to the offices was the timekeeping package. This programme was easy to use and was immediately appealing to the clerical staff because it saved them time and effort with a mandatory, often boring task. The programme was clearly explained to them and immediate support was available. This approach resulted in staff members telling others positive things about the programme and increased the level of acceptance from other offices.

Avoidance of using the technology as a staff reduction strategy. From a managerial point of view, it is tempting to justify the cost of the equipment and support by looking for ways to reduce staff at the same time. However, this approach was viewed as a counterproductive one in this agency for two reasons. One, there was a large backlog of paperwork. Time saved by the computer project was absorbed by other tasks that, while important, had simply been ignored before due to the work load. Second, obviously union and staff involvement would decline if the technology was viewed as a prelude to layoffs.

---

[6] R.A. Karasek et al.: "Job decision latitude, job demands, and cardiovascular disease: A prospective study of Swedish men", in *American Journal of Public Health*, Vol. 71, 1981, pp. 694-705.

Role of the union. The strong initial presence of the union was critical to making the change process a serious one. The union provided the initial political pressure to address the problems of the agency. They also kept up steady pressure to address structural sources of stress as opposed to solutions focused on the individual. Union representatives also encouraged front line staff members to participate in the programme. They advocated important follow-up changes created by the initial intervention. These included career ladders to reward the clerical staff for their increased computers skills, ergonomically correct equipment, appropriate training and broad dissemination of the project. Somewhat paradoxically, as the project gained acceptance, the union became less active. Toward the end of the intervention, this became almost exclusively a management project. The major reason for this was the realistic concern that the union had about its scarce resources. As the programme became institutionalized, the union felt it had to turn its attention to other, more pressing concerns. This illustrates the difficulty in sustaining proactive change when there are a variety of demands for union resources.

Role of management. Management also played an important role in the success of the project. It paid for the costs of the intervention. It bought the equipment, paid the consultation fees, and was willing to redirect a significant portion of the technology budget and personnel to the new programme. Management support was not uniform, however, and could be broken into two groups. One group was supportive from the beginning. A second group was much more resistant to the programme and at times even tried to sabotage it. This latter group largely came from the section of the agency that was responsible for information and technology, and seemed to feel threatened by the project. The author spent a great deal of time working with this group and sharing credit with them. This was a successful strategy and eventually several members of this group became the strongest proponents of the project.

Follow-up

This programme is now utilized by all offices of the agency. A new microcomputer unit was created and personnel assigned to it. There has also been a significant shift in budgetary resources to this intervention. These resources are being used to install networks and to move toward a "write it once" environment. Both the union and management advocated for and obtained additional career ladder steps for the clerical staff using the microcomputers. Thus, in terms of organizational acceptance, this initiative has redefined the use of technology in the agency.

The author repeated the "shadowing" of clerical staff in several offices. Substantial improvements in both productivity and skill levels were observed among the clerical staff using the microcomputers. At one point, the author observed a very junior clerk explaining one of the applications to a senior manager. This type of interaction supports the conclusion that the skills levels of the front line staff had significantly increased. Informal discussions indicated that the major problem the staff had with the new system was that it wanted even more computers.

Overall, this project demonstrated that structural organizational change involving complex technological issues is a goal which can be achieved. If there is a commitment to change, it is possible to find common ground on work environment issues, even in a hostile labour/management environment. This approach emphasizes the importance of including improvements in both productivity and the quality of working life as concurrent goals of technological change.

CASE STUDY NO. 9

A stress reduction intervention programme for meat processors emphasizing job design and work organization (United States)

Michael J. Smith and David Zehel[1]

Context

A psychological stress reduction intervention programme was implemented in a meat processing plant, together with an ergonomics improvement programme, to reduce upper extremity cumulative trauma disorders in meat processors. The meat processing plant has approximately 200 workers including meat cutters, meat processors, sanitation workers, maintenance workers, general labourers and warehouse order fillers. The plant is one component of a large retail grocery store chain. Beef carcasses (one-half of a cow) and pork loins are processed into various products, such as sirloin roasts, steaks, ground beef and pork chops, for shipment to the grocery stores which either sell the products as they are received or process them further. In 1989, the Occupational Safety and Health Administration (OSHA) inspected the meat processing plant and ordered management to institute an ergonomics improvement programme because of the high level of upper extremity cumulative trauma disorders in select occupations, such as meat cutters and meat processors.

The first author of this paper was hired by the meat processing plant to conduct a detailed ergonomic evaluation of operations and to suggest ergonomic improvements. During this activity, recommendations were made for redesigning some of the jobs in order to reduce psychological as well as physical stress. The management of the meat processing plant agreed to these recommendations and instituted them in 1990. The effectiveness of these recommendations in reducing physical and psychological trauma was assessed in 1991 and reassessed again in 1992.

It is important to understand the larger context in which this intervention was carried out. Meat cutting and meat processing jobs have traditionally been high paying, high status jobs in the United States. In the past, meat processing companies have been financially successful. Recently, however, meat processing industries have been undergoing severe economic hardship. One reason is that processed beef and pork imports have cut into their share of the market. Another factor is health consciousness, which means that American consumers are eating less red meat. As a result, profits have decreased, which has led to substantial lay-offs of meat cutters and meat processors. In addition, the meat processing companies have put pressure on the unions and workers to reduce workers' wages and benefits because of international and national competition to the companies. The unions and workers have had to agree to lower wages and benefits, which has in turn lowered the job status, making the jobs less desirable.

In the midst of this difficult economic environment, OSHA has increased inspection and enforcement of safety and health regulations in meat processing industries. Of particular interest are ergonomic hazards which produce upper extremity cumulative trauma disorders and lower back disorders. Meat processing companies have had difficulty responding to the OSHA demands because there are no federal regulations concerning these ergonomic issues. Recently, OSHA established general guidance to the meat processing companies[2] by issuing ergonomic guidelines for the red meat industry.

---

[1] Department of Industrial Engineering, University of Wisconsin-Madison, 1513 University Avenue, Madison, Wisconsin 53706, United States.

[2] OSHA: *Ergonomic program management guidelines for meatpacking plants*, OSHA doc. no. 3121 (US Department of Labor, Washington, 1990).

Over the last five years, OSHA has been very aggressive in inspecting and proposing financial penalties against meat processing companies. They have assessed penalties amounting to over $1 million dollars against several companies. In addition, engineering and administrative controls to improve ergonomics can cost up to several million dollars. The meat processing companies feel this financial pressure imposed by OSHA in addition to the competitive pressures they are experiencing. To add to the divisive environment, the unions have filed complaints with OSHA of unsafe working conditions. Such complaints require a federal inspection of the meat processing plant being accused of improper working conditions. These tensions make for "unfriendly" relations between the companies and OSHA, and between the companies and the unions. Such conditions make the climate very difficult for developing and implementing job redesign activities.

This programme was developed as a tripartite project, meaning the company, the union and the government were all involved. In addition, the university was involved through the faculty and students who conducted the analysis of the facility, job design and work organization, and recommended improvements. For this programme to be successful, it was essential that all parties be involved, participate fully and cooperate. However, several factors challenged this necessary cooperation. One important factor was that during the evaluation, the union and the management were in the process of collective bargaining over wages, fringe benefits and working conditions, which produced tension in their relationship. In addition, the company was not satisfied with OSHA representatives, who it felt lacked expertise in ergonomics. As a result of these tensions, the consultant had to spend a great deal of energy building rapport and developing cooperation among all of the parties involved. This was successfully accomplished mainly due to the consultant's long experience working with unions, companies and OSHA. The consultant was able to gain the trust of all three parties because they accepted him as a neutral participant and acknowledged him as an experienced expert. This provided an opportunity for cooperation to develop, which was essential for the programme.

Issues

The focus of the initial programme was to examine the job design and organizational factors that contributed to the high rate of upper extremity cumulative trauma disorders in meat cutters, meat wrappers and meat processors. By analyzing and examining the characteristics of the jobs, it became clear that these workers were also at risk for psychological distress. The analysis revealed that these particular jobs had characteristics known to produce job stress, such as machine pacing, short-cycle repetitive tasks with little variety and low content, a harsh physical working environment, the potential for job loss or lay-off, and strained relations with management. The jobs in this plant were typical of the meat processing industry, except the working conditions were better than average. Although the relationship between the management and union was strained due to the collective bargaining process, there was a cordial, cooperative interaction -- both parties recognized the need to cooperate to achieve the goals of the programme. The programme has been successful thus far primarily because management was responsive to both the consultants' recommendations and the needs of the workers throughout the analysis and intervention process.

Target population

The workers in the pork processing department of the plant were the target group for this job redesign and stress reduction intervention. The workers in this area included meat cutters, meat wrappers and meat processors.

Approach

The theoretical model that was applied to this programme is the "balance theory" for job design, aimed at stress reduction.[3] This model separates the workplace into five dimensions and examines the influences of each

[3] M.J. Smith and P. Carayon-Sainfort: "A balance theory of job design for stress reduction", in *International Journal of Industrial Ergonomics*, Vol. 4, 1989, pp. 67-79; C.L. Cooper and J. Marshall: "Occupational sources of stress: A review of the literature relating to coronary heart disease and mental ill health", in *Journal of*

dimension on job stress as well as the interaction among the different dimensions. These five dimensions consist of the person, the tasks, the work environment, the organizational structure, and technology. In order to redesign jobs to reduce stress, the consultant must first define the "good" and "poor" points in the work system. He or she can then redesign the system to improve its overall balance by improving individual or multiple dimensions. Whenever possible, dimensions with "poor" balance should be improved. When it is not possible to modify a "poor" balance point, sometimes the overall system balance can still be improved by modifying some other dimension. This is based on the concept that modifications in one aspect of the work system can influence other aspects in both positive and negative ways.

This theory provides a framework for evaluating jobs and determining where interventions can be useful. It can be used to show the relationships between job demands and job design factors. In this model, different elements of the work system interact to show how work is done and how effective the work is in achieving individual and organizational needs and goals. This is a systems concept, meaning any one element will have an influence on any other element(s). The four elements (not including the person) put demands on the individual. These demands can create loads which can be either healthy or harmful. Harmful loads lead to stress responses that can produce negative health effects. Each of the five elements in this model and some examples of the potential negative aspects are described below.

(1) **Environment.** A variety of aspects of the physical environment in the workplace have been shown to cause stress. Noise is the most well-known environmental stressor, which can cause an increase in blood pressure and negative psychological mood.[4] Environmental stress factors, such as cold and dampness, can affect employee motivation and the ability of the musculo-skeletal system to respond.

(2) **Task.** A wide variety of influences on job task has been studied, including content factors such as repetitiveness[5] and meaningfulness[6] as well as workload issues, such as overload and underload.[7] Machine-paced work tasks are more stressful than tasks not paced by machine.[8] Lack of participation[9] and lack of

---

Occupational Psychology, Vol. 49, 1976, pp. 11-28; R.A. Karasek: "Job demands, job decision latitude and mental strain: Implications for job redesign", in *Administrative Science Quarterly*, Vol. 4, 1979, pp. 285-308; J.R. Hackman et al.: "A new strategy for job enrichment", in *California Management Review*, Vol. 17, No. 4, 1975, pp. 57-71.

[4] D.C. Glass and J.E. Singer: *Urban stress: Experiments on noise and social stressors* (Academic Press, New York, 1972); S. Cohen and N. Weinstein: "Nonauditory effects of noise on behavior and health", in *Journal of Social Issues*, Vol. 37, 1981, pp. 36-70.

[5] T. Cox: "Repetitive work: Occupational stress and health", in C.L. Cooper and M.J. Smith (editors): *Job stress and blue collar work* (John Wiley, New York, 1985), pp. 85-112.

[6] J.R. Hackman et al., "A new strategy for job enrichment", op. cit.; R.D. Caplan et al.: *Job demands and worker health* (US Government Printing Office, Washington, 1975); B. Margolis, W.M. Kroes and R. Quinn: "Job stress: An unlisted occupational hazard", in *Journal of Occupational Medicine*, Vol. 16, 1974, pp. 654-661.

[7] M. Frankenhaeuser and B. Gardell: "Underload and overload in working life: Outline of a multi-disciplinary approach", in *Journal of Human Stress*, Vol. 2, 1976, pp. 355-346; D. Coburn: "Job alienation and well-being", in *International Journal of Health Services*, Vol. 9, No. 1, 1979, pp. 41-59.

[8] G. Salvendy and M.J. Smith: *Machine-pacing and occupational stress* (Taylor and Francis, London, 1981).

[9] J.R.P. French, Jr.: "The social environment and mental health", in *Journal of Social Issues*, Vol. 19, 1963, pp. 39-56; Caplan et al., *Job demands and worker health*, op. cit.

control[10] in task activities have been shown to cause emotional problems and even increase the risk of cardiovascular disease.

(3) **Technology.** The technology being used by workers often determines their ability to accomplish tasks and the extent of physiological and psychological load.[11] One of the main stress factors associated with the use of technology is related to workers' concerns as to whether or not they have adequate skills needed to use the technology.[12]

(4) **Organizational factors.** The organizational context in which work tasks are carried out often has factors associated with it that influence worker stress and health. Employee training and time to get used to a job or task have been related to stress and emotional disturbances.[13] Organizational factors, such as the ability to grow in a job and to be promoted (career development), can also be related to stress outcomes.[14] Other issues, such as work schedules (shift work) and overtime, have been shown to have negative mental and physical health consequences,[15] as well as role conflict and ambiguity, which can cause negative emotional consequences.[16]

(5) **Person.** A number of factors related to the person can result in the same physical and psychological effects that the first four elements of the model can produce. These factors include personality, physical health status, skills and abilities, physical conditioning, prior experiences and learning, motives, goals and needs.[17]

These five elements of the system work together so that individual and organizational goals can be achieved. We have described some of the potential negative outcomes of these elements in terms of job stress, but it should be noted that each element also has positive aspects which can counteract the negative influences. For instance, the negative influences of not having adequate skills to use new technology can be offset by worker training.

---

[10] Coburn, "Job alienation and well-being", op. cit.; R.A. Karasek et al.: "Job decision latitude, job demands, and cardiovascular disease", in Salvendy and Smith, *Machine-pacing and occupational stress*, op. cit., pp. 694-705; S. Fisher: "Control and blue-collar work", in Cooper and Smith, *Job stress and blue collar work*, op. cit., pp. 19-48.

[11] M.J. Smith, B.G. Cohen and L.W. Stammerjohn, Jr.: "An investigation of health complaints and job stress in video display operations", in *Human Factors*, Vol. 23, No. 4, 1981, pp. 387-400; G. Johansson and G. Aronsson: "Stress reactions in computerized administrative work", in *Journal of Occupational Behavior*, Vol. 5, 1984, pp. 159-181; O. Ostberg and C. Nilsson: "Emerging technology and stress", in Cooper and Smith, *Job stress and blue collar work*, op. cit., pp. 149-169.

[12] Ostberg and Nilsson, ibid.; M.J. Smith, P. Carayon and K. Miezio: "VDT technology: Psychosocial and stress concerns", in B. Knave and P.G. Wideback (editors): *Work with display units 86* (Elsevier, Amsterdam, 1987), pp. 695-712.

[13] Smith et al., ibid.

[14] Smith et al., "An investigation of health complaints and job stress in video display operations", op. cit.; R.J. Arthur and E.K. Gunderson: "Promotion and mental illness in the navy", in *Journal of Occupational Medicine*, Vol. 7, 1965, pp. 452-456.

[15] Margolis et al., "Job stress: An unlisted occupational hazard", op. cit.; T.H. Monk and D.I. Tepas: "Shift work", in Cooper and Smith, *Job stress and blue collar work*, op. cit., pp. 65-84; L. Breslow and P. Buell: "Mortality and coronary heart disease and physical activity on work in California", in *Journal of Chronic Disease*, Vol. 11, 1960, pp. 615-626.

[16] Caplan et al., *Job demands and worker health*, op. cit.

[17] L. Levi: *Stress and distress in response to psychosocial stimuli* (Pergamon Press, New York, 1972).

Similarly, the adverse influences of low job content can be balanced by a structure of supervision that encourages workers to be involved with and have control over their job tasks. The essence of this theory is to reduce both stress and the negative health consequences by "balancing" the various elements of the work system.

Situation before the intervention

Description of the workplace. The meat processing plant is located in a large city in the western United States. The plant is one building of a larger complex where products are prepared for sale in grocery stores. The building is one story high, approximately 3,000,000 cubic feet in volume, constructed of concrete blocks and fabricated steel panels, with concrete flooring. There are no windows in the plant processing area. The plant has good artificial lighting, is kept very clean due to federal food inspection regulations, is damp and wet because of extensive efforts to keep the floor, workstations and machinery clean, and is cold (approximately 40° F). There are several distinct work areas, including meat processing areas, a cooler for storing meat and a loading dock with several truck doors.

Description of the workforce. There are approximately 125-150 employees in the production area, depending on production requirements. This is an older, more experienced multi-racial workforce made up of both men and women. Most of the production workforce has been at this plant for more than ten years and most employees have gained additional experience in the meat processing industry at other meat plants. The average age of employees is approximately 50 years old, and the average age of the project participants was 45 years. All meat cutters must have the journeyman level of experience to be employed.

Management structure. The plant is part of a large chain of retail grocery stores that serves the entire western United States. This chain is a division of a larger national corporation of grocery stores that serve the entire United States. Decisions about financial matters, personnel actions, and health and safety matters are made at both the national and divisional levels and can affect the plant operations level. Before this project began, the plant had just undergone a reduction in management staffing and downgrading of management jobs due to financial cuts by the national corporation. Thus, the morale of the plant management was low at the beginning of the project.

There is a plant manager, a supervisor of the sanitation department (previously he was plant manager before the imposed changes), supervisors of each department and lead workers for each operation who supervise employees and schedule activities. The supervisor of sanitation had a unique role as he appeared to serve as the associate plant manager. He was also responsible for employee health and safety. About one year after the initiation of the project, the plant assigned one experienced worker to the new position of plant ergonomist to coordinate implementing the ergonomic recommendations. The plant ergonomist could instruct supervisors to take specific actions.

Psychological work environment. There is a striking similarity between the conditions of jobs that promote upper extremity cumulative trauma disorders and those that lead to job stress. This plant had a machine-paced conveyor belt operation for meat processing which required meat cutters to process a specified amount of meat per cycle. The pork room operations were also machine paced. Although the meat cutting jobs on these conveyor lines required the journeyman skill level and several different cutting actions, the content level of the cutting jobs was low. Other meat processing jobs did not require the same level of skill and also had low content. None of the jobs had much variety and workers had no control over the work speed. This case study will focus on the workers in the pork processing area. The following is a description of the pork processing department and of the various jobs and tasks involved.

Pork-processing department

There are three primary job categories in this area: meat cutters, meat wrappers and meat processors, and each has a number of simple tasks at each position. Thus, the pork processing department was a series of fragmented, simplified tasks on a conveyor line with each position adding to the finished product in the assembly-line tradition of Frederick Taylor[*].

Meat cutters. The pork processing begins at the saws where a whole pork loin is sectioned into five pork chops and one loin roast, which are then placed onto a conveyor for further processing. The saw operator processes approximately 340 15-pound pork loins per hour. This task is repetitive and simple, but requires great skill. The physical demands of the job are high -- the saw produces vibration, the pork loins are cold to touch (sometimes frozen) and the environment is cold (40° F.). The operator is self-paced, but is required to produce at very high rates to provide products for the rest of the line to process. There is no opportunity to socialize while working. Workers rate this position as the least desirable of the meat cutting tasks. Saw operators rotate daily between this position and other meat cutting tasks, such as pork loin trimmer.

The trimmer gets the pork loin roast from the saw operator and trims fat from about 340 pork loins each hour. After trimming is completed, the finished pork loin is placed onto a conveyor to the freezing tunnel. This job is repetitive and simple, but also requires skill as a meat cutter. The physical demands of this job are lower than those of the saw operator, but with the same environmental stressors. This task is self-paced and the production demand is much lower than that of the saw operator. The pork loin trimmers can talk with other meat cutters and meat processors while they work. This is a very desirable and easy meat cutting position which rotates on a daily basis.

Another meat cutting position is special cuts. This meat cutter takes pork loin roasts and country ribs from the conveyor and cuts off boneless chops and other special products. These are then prepared for packaging. This job is also quite simple with little content but, like the other meat cutting jobs, requires substantial skill. The physical demands are low but the environmental demands are high. The worker is self-paced and the workload is moderate. The special cuts meat cutter can socialize with other employees while working.

The final meat cutting position is the cleaver operator. This position takes frozen pork loin roasts and loads them into an automatic meat cleaver that cuts off pork chops. The job is machine-paced with a need to work fast to supply the pork chop trayers. The tasks are simple with little content and do not require specific skills. The environmental demands are high, especially the handling of frozen pork loins. In general, the meat cutting positions have the greatest prestige and are paid at the highest level in the plant.

Meat processors. The cuber takes pork chunks from a tray that is supplied to the workstation by another employee and places the meat into a cubing machine. The cuber catches the processed chunk and runs it through the cubing machine two more times, processing about 160 pork steaks per hour. Processed steaks are put onto styrofoam trays which are then put into a storage box. The skill level for this job is low. It is a simple job with little content, moderate workload and self-pacing. There is a chance for socializing while working.

---

[*] F.W. Taylor: *The principle of scientific management* (Norton, New York, 1967), first published in 1911.

> The chop trayer takes pork chops that are delivered to the workstation on a conveyor coming from the saws and cleaver. A set number (four to eight) of pork chops are placed onto a styrofoam tray and placed onto another conveyor. This job is machine paced with a high workload. The tasks are simple with little content and require low skill. The environmental stressors are high as the pork chops are very cold (sometimes frozen). There is an opportunity to socialize while working.
>
> The last meat processor position is the country rib processor. This position takes trays of country ribs from a conveyor and feeds them into a wrapping machine. When conveyor pacing permits, the processor removes the wrapped trays from a bin on the wrapping machine, checks the labels and places them into storage boxes on a dolly. The processor also takes roasts and tenderloins from the conveyor and places them into storage boxes on a dolly. This is a machine-paced, high workload position. There are multiple tasks so the variety is greater than for the other meat processor positions. The work is simple, lacks content and the skill requirements are low. There is no one close enough to socialize with while working.
>
> **Meat wrappers.** The wrapping machine operator on the front end takes the full trays of pork chops which come down the second conveyor from the trayers and loads them into a machine that wraps, seals and applies a price label to the trays. This is a machine-paced task that is very simple and has little content. There is little skill required and the workload is high. There is no opportunity to socialize due to machine noise.
>
> A second person on the back side of the machine takes the packaged pork chops and puts them into storage boxes, which are then loaded onto a dolly for removal to cold storage. This worker also inspects each package to ensure that the price label was properly placed. This is a machine-paced task that is very simple and has little content. There is little skill required and the workload is high. There is no opportunity to socialize due to machine noise.

Intervention

The intervention programme consisted of several phases, starting with an ergonomic assessment of all jobs in the plant to define risk factors for cumulative trauma disorders and to provide detailed job design information. The second phase was the development of engineering criteria by the experts to improve workstation and tool design, recommendations for improved work methods and worker training, and administrative controls such as job rotation. The third phase was a series of orientation and training seminars for first-line supervisors and workers. Next came the implementation of the expert recommendations. It was during this phase that the need for more comprehensive job redesign -- including considerations for psychological stress reduction -- was recognized. The rest of the case study will detail this effort to reduce psychological stress and the improvements made.

"Focus groups" were established within each department (1) to address the appropriateness of the recommendations, (2) to improve the recommendations, (3) to provide additional recommendations and (4) to help identify the best means for implementing the recommendations. The pork processing department spent a significant amount of focus group activity time recommending ways to improve the "quality of the work experience" to reduce both psychological and physical job stress.

The focus group in the pork processing department was made up of workers representing each job category and the plant ergonomic coordinator. The group met for one hour each week, concentrating on improvements that would increase the quality of working life and worker job satisfaction. Weekly meetings were held over a two-month period to suggest job design improvements and to discuss the suggestions with the other employees in the department.

At the end of the two-month period, the workers in the pork processing department approved a major job redesign recommendation which was to enlarge all of the positions by having all workers rotate among all positions. Thus, meat cutters would do meat processor activities and meat processors would do meat cutter activities. The rotations would take place every two hours each day or every other day, depending on the nature of the job tasks, the logistics of rotation and the production needs of the department. The rotation schedule would be worked out between the workers and the first-line supervisor.

The plant ergonomic coordinator presented this recommendation to the plant manager and other supervisors. There was much discussion and the expert consultants were invited to evaluate the proposal. The experts were highly supportive of the proposal, which convinced management to test it. The job rotation system was implemented in the pork processing department about four months later. The rotation programme was expected to increase task variety; to increase skill development and use; to provide every worker with an opportunity to work at a position some of the workday or workweek where social interaction on the job was possible; to provide all workers with alternate periods of work at lighter demand and heavier demand positions; and to give all workers the chance to work at higher prestige meat cutter positions. Job rotation was not expected to improve exposures to machine-paced work, heavy workload or the environmental stressors of these jobs.

Evaluation

Two methods were used to determine the effectiveness of the job enlargement on reducing stress and improving the quality of working life. The first was a checklist survey of health status and working conditions which workers filled out. The checklist contained 15 statements about health status or feelings about working conditions. The checklist included a scale ranging from "never" to "always" to define how often the worker experienced an item in the past week (see Appendix 1). Workers filled out these forms during the project and again approximately one year after the job enlargement programme was implemented.

The second assessment method included unstructured interviews and conversations with employees and supervisors conducted by the ergonomic coordinator and one of the expert consultants. Initial interviews and conversations were conducted during the course of the ergonomic evaluation by the consultant, with more conducted by the plant ergonomic coordinator and the consultant over several months after the job enlargement was implemented. The focus of the interviews and conversations was to define positive and negative aspects of the job enlargement and the physical ergonomic improvements. The results of the checklist, interviews and conversations are discussed in the next section.

Results

The results of the checklist showed small differences in the workers' responses between the first measures and those one year later. Meat wrappers indicated a clear improvement in musculo-skeletal complaints related to six factors (finger/hand pain, wrist/hand pain, night hand pain, arm pain or numbness and neck/shoulder pain), while only a slight improvement was reported in the musculo-skeletal complaints of the meat cutters and a slight worsening for the meat processors.

Meat cutters indicated improvement in two psychological indicators (nervous/irritable and tired), while for the other psychological indicator (chest pains) there was no improvement. There was improvement in one psychosocial factor (work pressure) and a worsening in two psychosocial factors (job satisfaction and job control). For the meat processors, there was improvement in one psychological indicator (nervous or irritable) and a worsening in one psychological indicator (tired). There was no improvement in any psychosocial factor and worsening in two psychosocial factors (job control and work pressure). For the meat wrappers there was improvement in two psychological indicators (tired and chest pains) and worsening in one psychological indicator (nervous or irritable). There was improvement in one psychosocial factor (work pressure), a worsening in one psychosocial factor (job control) and no change in one psychosocial factor (job satisfaction). Overall, there seems to be some improvement in psychological indicators for meat cutters and for meat wrappers, but not for meat processors. For psychosocial factors there appears to be an overall worsening effect for meat cutters and meat processors.

Interviews and conversations showed that meat processors and meat wrappers had very positive feelings about the job enlargement programme. The programme gave them more variety, a chance to do more challenging tasks that were only done by the meat cutters previously, it created opportunities for more skill use and skill development, and it provided for social interaction and reduced isolation for certain workers. On the negative side, new skills, particularly those of meat cutting, were sometimes hard to master, the job demands in terms of workload were still very high, and most of the tasks were still machine-paced. Overall, meat processors and meat wrappers felt there were more benefits than liabilities with the new, enlarged jobs. They reported that their overall job satisfaction was greatly increased, even though this was not reflected in their responses on the checklist survey results.

A different pattern emerged from the responses of the meat cutters. While they were generally happy with the increased rotation away from the physical demands of cutting meat, most were unhappy with the lower job content level and skill requirements of the tasks performed at meat processing and meat wrapping positions. They felt that self-esteem and peer esteem were reduced when they were required to perform these "lower level" tasks. For the meat cutters, the increased variety was not positive as there was less skill use. As with the meat processors and meat wrappers, the meat cutters felt that there were still the stressors of high workload and machine-paced tasks. The overall job satisfaction of the meat cutters was somewhat lower after the job enlargement programme. This was supported by their responses on the checklist survey.

In terms of the workers' perceptions of the amount of job stress, the meat cutters, meat wrappers and the meat processors felt that there was less job stress with the new job enlargement programme. Even though the meat cutters were less satisfied due to lower skill use, they felt that the overall job environment in the pork processing department had improved which led to less tension and more positive employee interaction.

Supervisors expressed great satisfaction with the job enlargement programme. It provided them with greater flexibility in assigning workers to different positions when key workers were out sick since all workers were cross-trained in all positions and could fill in as needed. The supervisors also felt that the pork processing department was more productive under the new system of enlarged jobs. Additionally, supervisors felt that the new job design programme had produced substantial improvement in terms of job stress and workplace tensions.

Discussion

Certain factors stand out as problematic with regard to this effort to reduce job stress. First and foremost, several serious job stressors were not improved with this job enlargement programme. There was still a high production demand with accompanying high workload and work pressure. The process was still machine paced and provided little or no opportunity to exercise control or decision latitude. While the variety of tasks increased for all jobs, the skill use and content for some jobs was reduced. Although there were basic improvements for all of the jobs, these improvements could have been overpowered by the lack of improvements in these other factors mentioned above that were not improved.

Due to the nature of the plant technology, the plant layout, the materials handling system and production demands, it was not possible to obtain acceptance from the plant management to modify many of the major job stress factors mentioned above, for example, the machine pacing of the work. In addition, the effort to reduce stress had to be tied to other ergonomic activities that were aimed at reducing cumulative trauma injuries. Thus, we were severely limited in the nature of the stress reduction interventions that could be proposed. The balance theory[18] indicates that several elements in the work system must be considered simultaneously when making job design improvements to reduce job stress. Unfortunately, this could not be accomplished in this case study. The balance theory also states that modifications in one aspect of the work system can influence other aspects in both positive and negative ways. Thus, the changes in job design imposed by job enlargement produced a positive "balancing effect" for some jobs, but did little to improve others and may even have produced a "negative balancing" in some jobs. For instance, the job enlargement resulted in greater variety and improved skill use for the meat wrappers, but this same increase in variety produced less skill use and lowered job satisfaction for the meat cutters. Job design approaches that take a "systems" perspective have a greater potential to produce positive results, while the effects of "piecemeal" approaches are harder to predict and can be positive or negative. Based on our experience in this case study, we propose that job design approaches for stress reduction should be systematic and comprehensive in order to obtain the best results.

---

[18] Smith and Carayon-Sainfort, "A balance theory of job design for stress reduction", op. cit.

Appendix 1

Current health questionnaire

Please answer the questions listed below regarding your health. We want to know how you have felt this past **week** including today. Do **not** put your name on this questionnaire, but be sure to indicate your job title and department at the bottom. No one will know how you answered the questions. This information will help us to improve your working conditions. Thank you.

Please circle the number that indicates how often you have experienced each of the following during the last **week**.

	Never	Sometimes	Often	Always
1. You had headaches	1	2	3	4
2. Your hands or fingers got numb	1	2	3	4
3. You had a cold or sore throat	1	2	3	4
4. You had back pain	1	2	3	4
5. Your wrists or hands hurt	1	2	3	4
6. You woke up at night with hand pain	1	2	3	4
7. You felt nervous or irritable	1	2	3	4
8. Either arm hurt or felt numb	1	2	3	4
9. You felt very tired at work	1	2	3	4
10. You had pain in your neck or shoulder	1	2	3	4
11. You felt pressured to work fast	1	2	3	4
12. You felt you were in control of your job	1	2	3	4
13. You had chest pains	1	2	3	4
14. You liked your job	1	2	3	4
15. Your legs hurt	1	2	3	4

Please fill in your job title and department below. Thank you for your help.

Job title _____   Department _____

CASE STUDY NO. 10

Using knowledge and discussion to decrease stress in Swedish public administration officials

Ingeborg Eriksson, Dr. Vanja Moser,
Dr. Anna-Lena Undén and Dr. Kristina Orth-Gomér[1]

Context

In the late 1970s and early 1980s, worksite interventions in Sweden focused on the psychosocial problems in the work environment. The Swedish Work Environment Act[2] was complemented by regulations concerning the psychosocial work environment. The Act states that working conditions must be tailored to the physical and mental needs of individuals. During that period, different agreements were developed in order to regulate psychosocial factors in the work environment.

Programmes aimed at the prevention of negative work-related effects, such as accidents, effects of toxic substances, non-ergonomic design, etc., had already been developed and implemented for many years. Regardless of improvements made in the physical work environment, a magnitude of occupational health and safety problems remained. The concept of stress was used and accepted as a key to what were, in many cases, sensitive psychosocial problems. A study of Swedish civil servants found that stress was the topic that had the highest priority among the work environment problems. Stress-related problems had also been observed by physicians as having increased in frequency, manifesting in various complaints which seemed to be related to increased stress in the workplace. There was also an increased demand for stress management programmes. As a result of these problems and demands, it became clear that methods needed to be developed to reduce occupational stress in Swedish civil servants.

Target population

Subjects were obtained through the occupational health care centres which serve all Swedish civil servants, which number approximately 400,000 men and women and make up 9.3 per cent of the Swedish workforce. Each centre serves about 3,000 civil servants.

Five workplaces, situated in three different areas of Sweden, were chosen to participate in the project. The basis for selection was an expressed need for professional help from the health care centres resulting from a stressful work situation.

Four intervention groups (a total of 94 subjects: 68 women and 26 men, average age 44 years) and one control group (35 subjects: 29 women and six men, average age 42 years) participated in the study. The control group did not receive any intervention during the project period.

The groups were all small work units within larger central government offices. The participants worked mainly in administration, all were clerical workers, and the majority worked with computers. All personnel in these

---

[1] National Institute for Psychosocial Factors and Health, Karolinska Institute, Box 60210, 104 01 Stockholm, Sweden.

[2] Work Environment Act, Act No. 1160, dated 19 December 1977 (*Svensk författningssamling*, No. 1160, 1977), as amended up to Act No. 677, dated 21 March 1991 (*Svensk författningssamling*, No. 677, 1991).

workplaces, including supervisors, participated in the project. The main characteristics of these groups are given below.

Intervention groups (Total: 26 men, 69 women; average age: 45 years)

Tax authority: 16
National telephone company: 35
Health insurance office: 18
Municipal court: 25

Control group (Total: 5 men, 30 women; average age: 42 years)

Tax authority: 35

Ten people chose not to participate in the project from the start. Another four subjects dropped out at the first measurement, and four at the second measurement. Fifteen subjects did not participate in the last measurement after the intervention was implemented. Ten of those 15 dropped out of the study because they had left their jobs by that time.

Approach

Before the intervention is initiated, the organization is scrutinized by the intervention leaders (usually one psychologist and one physiotherapist) so that they may get acquainted with the organization and evaluate whether the timing and preparation of the intervention are appropriate and adequate. This initial survey is done by interviewing key people, observing the worksite and analyzing work environment questionnaires, if available.

Since the stress management programme triggers expectations of stress reduction and other changes at the worksite, it has been most important to involve leaders and supervisors in the intervention process (at the planning stage, during implementation and at follow-up). Educational activities should result not only in increased knowledge, but also in a restructuring process where it is essential that decision-makers are involved.

This motivating process cannot be stimulated within the confines of a fixed model, therefore the model has to be adapted to the needs of each worksite. It is critical that the intervention leader have in-depth knowledge of the organization. It is also vital to sort out responsibilities and expectations between those who carry out the intervention programme and the target group. Responsibility for any changes is always in the hands of management, whereas the programme leaders act primarily as advisors. It is our experience that the participants' expectations of the intervention are often high and unrealistic. Thus, before the intervention is implemented, it is important to establish a realistic level of change that can be achieved.

It should be noted that there are also situations where it is advisable not to intervene. Examples of some situations where the intervention is less likely to succeed are if the organization is in the middle of a major restructuring process; if leadership/management is in conflict; if top management is not functioning well; if there is lack of support from supervisors.

Intervention

The stress management programme began as an educational programme focusing on psychosocial stressors. However, it was soon observed that this information stimulated expectations and increased motivation to deal with job stress in the group. Therefore, a structured model for stress management in organizations was developed.

The programme now consists of two parts. The first part is educational, designed to increase knowledge about psychosocial stress factors in the work environment and to facilitate stress management in the organization and in the group involved. This programme also deals with individual stress management issues, such as health habits, life-style factors, relaxation techniques, etc.

The second part of the programme is more practical, involving group discussions about stressors, relaxation training, individual stress testing and development of an action plan to reduce stress at the worksite. Each participant also makes his or her own action plan for stress management.

It has proved important, and successful, during the educational part of the programme to combine general information on how stress affects people, including physiological explanations for mental and physical stress symptoms, with examples of stressful situations from the participants' work situations. It is also essential to increase participants' knowledge and understanding of the different kinds of work pressure put on employees in different work groups and on employees at different levels in the organization. The objective of this awareness-raising is to avoid the "scape-goat syndrome" where one person or group is seen as responsible for all problems. The important link between stress and its impact on workplace efficiency is also explained and demonstrated.

The educational part of the programme is presented in a "popular" form, where lecturing is mixed with pictures that depict stressful situations and stress reactions in a humorous way.

The participants are also trained in different techniques to help them cope with stress individually. It is preferable if one of the intervention leaders is a medically trained professional (physiotherapist, nurse or physician) who can inform the participants about health-related aspects and, in addition, teach relaxation techniques. Relaxation training consists of two types: one, which is more time consuming, is relaxation in a supine position, preferably practiced at home or during breaks. There is also a shorter relaxation technique, done in a sitting position that can easily be practiced during working hours.

Group discussions concern workplace stressors and different measures to deal with them. Ideally, the groups should be composed of employees from different levels in the organization and the intervention leaders should try to create a relaxed atmosphere where everybody feels free to speak.

The group discussion should result in an action plan. Prior to making their action plan, the groups are encouraged to check some important factors in their work environment known to have an influence on stress. These factors are work organization, work demands, control over work, working hours, work methods and routines, information systems, physical environment and equipment facilitating work and cooperation, staff development and ways to improve social support.

The action plan thus includes a list of problems (stressors), proposed actions to solve the problems, a notion of who is responsible for the action, the period of time when necessary actions should be made and time for follow-up.

Evaluation and results

Measurements were taken before, during and after the intervention and included medical examinations and questionnaires.

Social support at work was assessed through the use of questionnaires. Four different support functions were assessed: appraisal support (feedback from supervisors), belonging support (support from the work group), instrumental support (support and help with problems), and supportive working atmosphere.

Strain at work was measured according to the theory that the combination of high job demands and small decision latitude constitutes a work situation which can lead to stress symptoms.

The medical examination was performed by the occupational health centres and included assessments of smoking, exercise and dietary habits, height, weight, resting blood pressure and heart rate. Blood samples were drawn for standard laboratory blood testing, which included, among other things, measurement of cholesterol levels.

Among improvements that could be observed were a more open social atmosphere at the workplace; improved work organization and planning procedures; more effective systems for information exchange; discussions of the managerial function; management training; and improved physical work environment.

The most important quantitative changes that took place in the total intervention group were the perceptions that work was more stimulating and increased feedback from supervisors. The rating of workload also was reported as having decreased, though in a more limited way, despite the fact that no "actual" decrease in workload took place during the project time (Figure 1).

Figure 1: Changes in psychosocial work characteristics

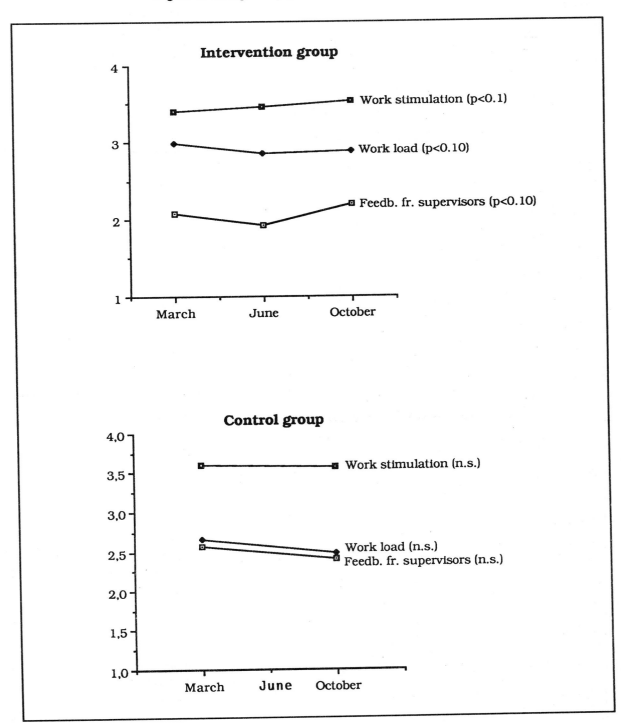

During the first phase of the intervention programme, several of the ratings for psychosocial factors showed an impairment, particularly social support at the worksite. This might indicate that the intervention triggered conflicts among the participants. However, by the end of the intervention, the ratings were back to baseline values, indicating that any conflicts that had developed were short-lived.

The most consistent and positive physiological change that was found was a significant increase of the "good" cholesterol HDL (high-density lipoprotein). At the same time, there was a decrease in the "bad" cholesterol LDL (low-density lipoprotein) and a sharp decrease in triglyceride levels in response to the intervention process. Blood analyses also indicated that the intervention had an impact on lipoproteins, which implicates a decreased risk for cardiovascular disease (see Figure 3). This decrease could not be explained by changes in dietary, exercise and smoking habits, since these variables remained stable during the intervention process.

Figure 2: Changes in serum lipids

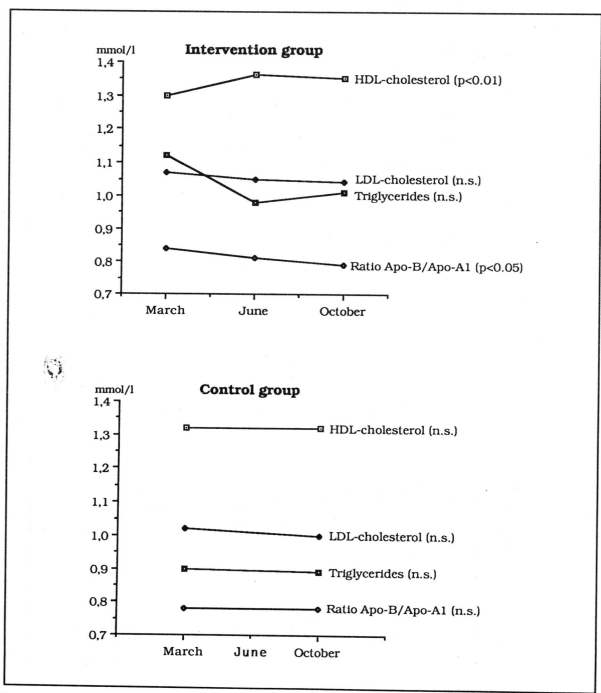

A majority of subjects had regular eating and exercise habits which did not change during the intervention. The average number of cigarettes smoked per day was 14.9 before and 15.0 after the intervention. The average weight was 66.9 kilos before and 67.6 kilos after the intervention.

In the control group, few psychosocial or physiological changes could be observed.

Discussion and follow-up

The experience with this intervention programme shows that the structure of the organization, management and style of leadership, as well as company culture are important factors in determining the outcome of an intervention. In other words, positive changes occur more often in organizations where employees have a higher degree of decision latitude. Even more positive results can be achieved when superiors/leaders take an active part in changing the environmental conditions of a workplace.

Based on this knowledge and experience, it is of utmost importance that an intervention programme be strongly supported from the beginning at different management levels, especially at top management levels, as well as by union representatives.

Although the subgroups in this study were too small to be analyzed separately, observations indicate that the stress management programme was most effective in groups that had a high degree of autonomy, high decision latitude and high initiative skills. The participants who managed the most consistent and best organized intervention programme showed a significant decrease in their ratings of "workload" and a significant increase in "feedback from supervisors". This group worked actively and independently with their action plan and their supervisors also took a very active part in the programme.

Another group, which worked in a more bureaucratic organization, showed impairment in several psychosocial work environment variables, i.e. "social atmosphere" and "workload". The analysis showed that this group, in spite of great interest and involvement, had organizational problems in executing the stress-reducing actions they had planned.

It is believed that with more time, more positive results could be reached in the subgroups that had problems executing their action plans due to low leader support and a tradition of not taking initiatives or making decisions.

In general, follow-up over a period of several years is recommended. Of course, over a longer time period it would be impossible to determine what effects are due to the intervention and what effects are caused by other factors. In this specific programme, follow-up has been problematic due to drastic political and economic changes in the society, which have resulted in major job layoffs and restructuring in the public sector.

Whatever the mechanisms causing these important physiological changes may be, the intervention programme is considered to be a complement to conventional treatments aimed at lowering blood lipid levels. Both changes in diet and pharmacological treatment are time-consuming and expensive. The magnitude of the change in blood levels which resulted from this intervention programme is comparable with the level of change that can be achieved through dietary and sometimes pharmacological treatment.

If corroborated in further studies, these results may provide a tool for preventing adverse psychosocial and physiological health effects from conditions in the workplace.

CASE STUDY NO. 11

Health circles for foremen at Volkswagen (Germany)

Dr. Karl Kuhn[1]

Issues and approach

In an attempt to combat problems associated with work-related stress factors, the health department of Volkswagen AG tested a new concept -- the health circle. The objective of the health circle concept is to enable the worker to accurately perceive and express stress loads and to actively participate in reducing those loads.

In industrial health circles, workers are encouraged to actively participate in stating and discussing any health-related problems they may have and any work-related stresses they may perceive. Intrinsic to the health circle concept is the recognition that because of the special relationship between an individual and his/her work situation, outside experts cannot easily understand the factors which may cause an individual stress. Therefore the workers who are affected by workplace stress factors must actively participate as experts in discussing the problems related to their own jobs. In this way, workplace stress factors can be analysed and relevant strategies can be developed to reduce or eliminate them.

Health circle activities not only can have noticeable positive effects on the participants' health, but depending on the extent to which they are put to use by the company, also on shop-floor production. Therefore the results can be positive for both the workers **and** the company.

However, for workers to participate in this process, they should be able to accurately perceive their job-related stressors and to express and discuss them. Therefore, it is necessary to help workers recognize and reduce fears of failure, attitudes of resignation, defense mechanisms, etc. In this way, it will be possible to establish a basis for health-promoting behaviours. From the workers' discussions of stressors on the shop floor it will also be possible to trigger processes which can lead to reducing or eliminating stressors.

Target population

This intervention was targeted at shop-floor foremen and assistant foremen at two enterprises of Volkswagen. From each of these two enterprises, 15 foremen and assistant foremen from different branches of the company participated.

Intervention

At Volkswagen AG, the health circle was used to enable workers to achieve four objectives which complement and support each other:

- To expand their knowledge and understanding of stress development;
- To improve personal stress management by adopting sound health-promoting behaviours;
- To create a work environment which is beneficial to health;
- To recognize and modify work conditions which lead to stress.

---

[1] Director, Gesundheitsschutz und Arbeitsbedingungen, Statistik, Bundesanstalt für Arbeitsschutz (Federal Institute for Occupational Safety and Health), Vogelpothsweg 50-52, 4600 Dortmund 1, Germany.

In order to make this achievement possible, the health circle intervention is supported as follows:

- **Information sessions** are held to inform both the potential circle participants (the target group) and all company superiors about the health circle concept and to enlist their support.

- **Discussions with experts** are organized by the circle moderators with company superiors, personnel department representatives, works council representatives and company doctors.

- **Interviews** take place with the circle participants in order to gain a better understanding of the job situation from the participants' point of view.

- **Workplace visits** are organized in order to give the health circle moderators a general idea of the existing job situation.

- **Medical examinations** of circle participants are made by the company doctor. One of the objectives of the medical examination is to identify possible risk factors. The examination is supplemented by detailed advice throughout the duration of the circle activities.

- **Continuous flow of information** on the issues generated by the circle activities is guaranteed. This flow of information should occur between the circle participants and other people in the plant who are not participating in the circle. The objective is to satisfy the need for information for people both inside and outside the circle.

- A **contact committee** is created to stimulate open discussion at plant level about problems on the shop floor which the circle participants have mentioned. The committee includes representatives of the circle participants, their direct superiors, representatives of the personnel department and works council, a company doctor and the circle moderators.

- **Introductory seminars** are organized, which are of two types and which have different target groups:

  — A two-day introductory seminar for circle participants brings workers into contact with the subconscious areas of their physical, mental and social sources of accomplishment. Participants receive factual information about the subject of stress, learn about relaxation techniques, and exchange views on experiencing stress. Also participants' thought and behaviour patterns are observed.

  — A one-day introductory seminar for the members of the contact committee is intended to familiarize them with the important function they will have as a member of this committee.

- The health circle usually comprises an **orientation stage**, primarily designed to have participants develop and test new health-promoting behaviours, and a **project stage**, during which the health circle participants initiate small personal projects and discuss their experiences with the projects. The result of these stages is the gradual compilation of a catalogue of in-plant work conditions which, according to the circle participants, repeatedly lead to stress.

- **Expert groups** are formed when the necessity arises. Their purpose is to deal with problems and address participants' ideas for solutions which may exceed the technical competence of the contact committee or which may require more technical clarification. The membership of the expert groups depends on the types of problems which need to be addressed.

- A **status analysis** takes place at a predetermined time at the end of the project period. The purpose of the status analysis is to clarify to what extent the health circle has achieved its objectives. It should also determine whether or not the circle should continue its activities.

Results

At Volkswagen, the concept of the health circle was aimed at facilitating workers' perceptions and/or expressions of loads and stressors. Through the implementation of this intervention programme, significant changes in perception were observed. Of particular significance was the fact that the circle participants changed their way of communicating -- previously characterized by self-defense -- into a more genuine open form of communication.

At Volkswagen AG, many of the circle participants became conscious for the first time of the events which cause them stress. This new awareness is also regarded as a significant result of the intervention.

Equally important were the sessions with the contact committee, during which the activities of the health circle were presented to the workers in the plant. When preparing for the initial sessions with the contact committee, the participants had to cope with a great deal of anxiety. However, after working in the health circles, the anxiety was acknowledged and participants were able to deal with it. As a result of these meetings the participants generally showed an increased will and commitment to their work.

The health circles, together with the meetings of the contact committee, yielded a number of significant results.

- Many of the circle participants started to introduce modifications at their workplaces on their own initiative. These modifications helped the participants to break the pattern of certain "vicious circles" which had been causing stress.

- Participants created a "problem catalogue" listing conditions on the shop floor which from their point of view repeatedly cause stress. Short-term solutions were found for some of the problems, while medium- to long-term solutions are needed for the others. Certain organizational problems on the shop floor were solved by defusing particular stressors. However, a number of problems appeared to be difficult to solve. Some of the circle participants were disappointed by this fact.

- The level of understanding in management about factors which cause stress to foremen has increased. New regulations have been created which aim to reduce loads and stressors.

- The foremen themselves reformulated their loads and stressors in a new and distinct way, which also effectively reduced stress factors. In addition, the circle participants committed themselves to find solutions to problems which were known to repeatedly cause stress for the foremen.

- The relationships between work and health have become clearer for almost all of the participants. Most important this includes the fact that behaviours which may impair health (such as excessive demands that one may make on oneself) are now more likely to be recognized as undesirable and are more likely to be changed (for example by adopting behaviours in the workplace which are more compatible with health). For the majority of the participants there has been an immediate improvement in their state of health.

Evaluation

This project was scientifically supported by interviews, questionnaires and analysis parameters. In particular, qualitative (narrative) interviews were carried out before and after the intervention phase. The interviews indicated a resultant improvement in health conditions among many of the participants. It also became clear that health circles, used as an instrument of change, can help employees to reduce their stress level, improve their personal coping mechanisms, as well as enable them to participate actively in creating healthy working conditions.

Follow-up

A follow-up phase is in progress. In the meantime, Volkswagen has introduced, on a continuous basis, a number of improvements containing some elements of the concepts described in this case study.

CASE STUDY NO. 12

Job redesign and stress prevention for crane operators (Germany)

Dr. Karl Kuhn[1]

Context

Starting in 1985, a steelworks company introduced and developed 16 health circles for workers in various job areas, including operators of hot rolling mills and cold-roll stands, crane operators, finishing department workers and maintenance workers. These circles met for a total of 200 sessions, during which all types of work-related stress (psychological stress and muscular loads, environmental influences, accident hazards) were discussed by the workers concerned. The focus of the sessions was also to examine work-related stressors with a view to introducing improvements. The course and results of the sessions are illustrated using crane operators as the example. Due to its success, health circles are now carried out on a permanent basis in the company.

Issues

Control operations mainly occur during mechanized processes and handling tasks. These operations often require both the coordination of motor and sensory tasks and the conversion of information into action. The operation of overhead travelling cranes, which are used mainly in the iron and steel industry and in non-ferrous metal smelting plants, are a good example of control operations.

Analyses of crane operators' job tasks showed that the job demands a high level of mental and motor skills. These skills are most needed in performing crane operation and control tasks. The same skills are also required for work organization in terms of the "time-related decision margin". Other demands which the analysis revealed are those related to the "accuracy of information pick-up" and to all work environment factors, including being able to identify types of hazards. On the other hand, the analysis revealed that the job tasks of crane operators are not very demanding physically or in terms of posture.

Target population

The target group for this workplace stress prevention programme was made up of crane operators at a steelworks company in Germany.

Approach

The "health circle" approach to preventing occupational stress was developed by employees of the Thyssen steelworks in cooperation with an external team of experts. As a means of preventing stress-related health problems, the health circle method helps to clarify questions through the use of group discussions.

This method is based on the concept of actively engaging workers in occupational safety and health (OSH). The experience that workers have with loads and stressors is valuable for OSH on the shop floor. The health circle

[1] Director, Gesundheitsschutz und Arbeitsbedingungen, Statistik, Bundesanstalt für Arbeitsschutz (Federal Institute for Occupational Safety and Health), Vogelpothsweg 50-52, 4600 Dortmund 1, Germany.

discussions utilize workers' knowledge and experience to propose modifications in job design. Through this process, workers become experts on their own behalf. Health circles help workers and management to systematically process information about the loads and stressors that workers experience at work.

Each circle is made up of several workers; for example, two crane operators and a pit worker. Also involved in the health circle are the occupational health doctor and other OSH experts, such as an ergonomist or safety officer, and the foreman responsible for the work area concerned as well as a shop steward. The works manager is free to join the sessions at any time. Members of the external research team act as session moderators. This combination facilitates bringing together the workers' experience and knowledge of possible job design modifications with the knowledge and experience of the other participants. The mix of expertise also helps to ensure that the participants' contributions are examined by all circle members and that a high level of information is maintained. Furthermore, this group composition increases the likelihood that the two social partners will accept the proposals.

The objectives of the health circles are to find answers to two questions:

1. What work situations are related to physical and nervous ailments in the workers of a job group, such as crane operators? It is known that ailments are an indicator of work-related impairments and can be used as an early warning system for chronic health problems. The health circle method therefore fulfills a screening function by helping to indicate the connection between work-related loads and ailments, i.e. those which are characteristic of a job group.

2. The second goal of the circles is to develop proposals for improving the design of jobs as a means of eliminating workers' health problems and improving the overall health of the workforce.

Intervention

Each circle met at intervals of every three to four weeks for a total of 12 one-hour sessions, generally at the end of a work shift. The session hours were paid for by the company as normal work hours.

The circles were conducted as part of an established programme with the following stages:

Stage 1. During this stage, job characteristics which were perceived by the workers as stressful were compiled. Job characteristics which had been designated as stressful by several workers were given particular attention. In some cases, more than 100 job characteristics were evaluated as being stressful or problematic. Both muscular and psychological as well as environmental and accident hazards were discussed.

For example, the repair and maintenance workers were unanimous in designating as very stressful the search for faults and elimination of them during machinery and plant breakdowns. They reported that in addition to the stress from correctly analysing and successfully eliminating the fault, the time pressure, the numerous questions asked by their superiors during the fault diagnosis, the work interruptions due to other short-term intermediate tasks, and incomplete or not up-to-date plant drawings were also perceived as major stressors.

The crane operators frequently mentioned the problem of being fully responsible for injuries to persons and damage to equipment, while the time pressure created by the ground team often caused them to be in conflict with the safety provisions. Moreover, they reported that the ground team disregarded traffic rules.

It was interesting to note that the workers hardly ever considered production requirements as being problematic. Rather, they complained about certain aggravating conditions of their work which they considered to be avoidable.

Stage 2. Adverse health effects experienced by workers during or after certain job situations were determined during the second stage. All workers belonging to a specific job group were given a questionnaire to complete about the relation between workloads and negative health effects. Thereafter, the stressful situations frequently related to certain ailments in the workers were screened out. This was done to facilitate making the connection between the work-related loads of a specific job group and their physical and nervous disorders. For example, crane operators repeatedly stated the following complaints in connection with "concentration demands" and/or "time and output pressure": head congestion, headache, irritability, nervousness and neck pain. In several cases they related "having trouble with colleagues or superiors" with stomach-aches, irritability and nervousness. When the results were evaluated, the connections made between stress and ailments which had been repeatedly mentioned by the workers of the group were screened out. The frequently occurring work-related ailments were interpreted as indicators of potential long-term health hazards.

Stage 3. The results of the inquiry in Stage 2 were summarized and presented to the health circles for the purpose of an in-depth discussion. Due to the confidential nature of the health-related information, only the workers, works doctor and moderator participated in the evaluation discussions. The next step was to search for possible modifications in designing jobs that would meet health requirements.

About 20 to 60 proposals for change were made in each circle. These covered technical and organizational solutions as well as proposals relating to behaviour.

For the crane operators, many proposals for change were concerned with high mental demand and the stressful responsibility for accident-free crane operation. A number of proposals were aimed at improving the field of vision by a better design of the crane cab; by fitting it with mirrors to suppress blind areas; by installing a camera/monitor system to exert better control on the teeming ladle; or by fitting swivel screens, anti-glare film, etc. The purpose of the proposed measures was to eliminate avoidable strains and anxieties, whereas the responsibility for safety was not considered as problematic. Proposals to reduce problems related to cooperation included more frequent safety instructions, installation of intercom systems to reduce misunderstandings, and allowing ground workers to ride on the cranes occasionally as a way to increase their understanding of the job in total.

Stage 4. In a final stage, proposals were elaborated in writing and passed on to the works departments for implementation in so far as they were feasible financially, organizationally and technically.

Potential barriers to success

One potential barrier to clear communication in health circles is that the "language" used by the different hierarchic levels and/or disciplines may not always be clear to the others in the group. This can be particularly problematic for the workers in the group, who are generally inexperienced at describing their loads and stressors in large groups. Therefore, it is the moderator's job to ensure that all group members understand what is being expressed with regard to potential modifications. A new type of comprehension - one which must be learned - is required for a democratic discussion of work, workloads and potential job modifications.

The health circle sometimes requires that the participants step outside of their usual role in the workplace. For example, the normal role of safety officers and occupational health doctors involves the interpretation and application of existing regulations and occupational health and safety standards. Their tasks are essentially confined to the prevention of occupational diseases and accidents. This area is covered by a dense network of regulations. However, many non-specific illnesses, such as cardiac/circulatory or gastro-intestinal diseases, are often at least in part due to conditions of work. Such health problems present new challenges to both safety officers and workplace physicians since these diseases are recognized as being caused by a number of factors, not just one. Preventing non-specific health problems requires adopting a holistic view of the workplace. A further challenge to these experts results from the fact that there may be no laws or standards set to regulate the multiple workplace factors which can cause, directly or indirectly, non-specific diseases.

Health circle activities can challenge the usual roles of middle management superiors as well. These managers, i.e. foremen and shop stewards, may feel that their competencies and functions are threatened as a result of the workers' participation in job design. Such feelings were revealed during discussions of inadequacies at work which caused stress to workers. When workers complained about the way their tasks were organized, it gave the foremen the impression that they were being criticized for their jobs. As a result, the managers' initial reactions were defensive. Additional talks, however, with these foremen revealed that they were overloaded with new tasks that had been added to their usual functions. Because of their own burden, the superiors had lost sight of the workers' actual work situation. When this subject was discussed by the team, greater understanding about this project was demonstrated by the foremen. They also showed a willingness to use the circle activities to solve their own workload problems along with those of the workers.

Results

The results of this circle approach can be summarized as follows:

- The circles created an atmosphere of trust. Thanks to this atmosphere, it was possible for workers to speak out about health problems which result from working conditions. It was also possible to obtain recommendations for new ways of designing jobs.

- The method uncovered major occupational health problems. Furthermore, numerous minor problems arising in the course of a routine workday were mentioned which also had some importance for the workers in terms of adverse health effects. In this regard, the question was raised as to why many such problems had existed for years without any action having been taken, particularly since these shortcomings jeopardized production in certain cases. In reality, the issue was primarily one of shop organization. No one person felt responsible for such aspects of work and no recognized procedure existed for solving these problems. The foremen were generally overloaded with production and personnel tasks. Management perceived its tasks to be in a different dimension. The occupational health doctor and safety officer were either uninformed about the problems, or did not give priority to certain questions. In many cases they felt that it was too much trouble to deal with issues for which they received little or no support from management and for areas not governed by standards and regulations.

- As was determined in the health circles, stressful and health-impairing job characteristics are partly a result of technical or organizational shortcomings. Therefore, many proposals for improvement have two goals: diminishing certain loads and stressors and, at the same time, streamlining job organization.

- Six to 18 months after the end of the circle activities, detailed evaluation talks were held with the people who had participated in the circles. On the whole, all groups supported the way the circles had been composed and the method that had been used. All participants were in favour of continuing the circle activities.

Health circles prove advantageous for all parties concerned. For the **workers and shop stewards**, the circles are useful for addressing job problems which otherwise would go unnoticed during the routine workday, or which would not be noted in reports. In addition, the mixed composition of the circle, involving various levels of the workplace hierarchy, is a useful factor in exerting pressure to take action and introduce improvements.

For the **occupational safety and health experts**, new information can be gathered about loads, stressors and risks that was previously unknown. Thus, additional factual arguments are generated, which are particularly useful when applications for improvements are filed with the relevant company bodies.

The superiors appreciate the enhanced communication with workers. They consider that the circles are helpful in uncovering weak spots, in increasing worker motivation, in improving conditions of work and in reconsidering long-standing routines.

Evaluation

After implementing the health circles, the morbidity rate within the department was reduced by 50 per cent. As a result of this evaluation, a psychologist was appointed to monitor the health circles.

CASE STUDY NO. 13

Organizational approaches to reducing stress and health problems in an industrial setting in Sweden

Sven Kvarnström[1]

Context

Over a number of years, a high rate of absence due to sickness has been a major problem in Swedish industry. Absence rates due to illness have been higher than in most other comparable countries. From the viewpoint of enterprises, this has contributed to decreasing productivity and increasing production costs.

For the employees, the high sick leave rates have reflected unsatisfactory conditions of work and human suffering, but also a threat of plant shut down, with the temptation for management to relocate to other countries with lower sick leave rates, higher continuity in production flow and fewer production problems.

ASEA Brown Bovery (ABB) is a group of companies with approximately 215,000 employees in 140 countries. In Sweden, ABB has 30,000 employees in 150 companies. Through structural adjustments, it is reasonably easy for the group to relocate production from one country to another. Employee awareness of this fact creates a high level of crisis consciousness.

This is the story of a department facing such a crisis and in which a very high level of sick leave absence reflected stress at work.

Issues

The department in question was producing a relatively simple product, not requiring advanced technology, but with a relatively large variety. The labour force was comprised of approximately 20 female workers, all of whom had a low level of education. The work process was very easy to learn, but also monotonous and routine, with little decision-making responsibility given to the workers. The department was part of an enterprise in the ABB group with a total of 1,500 employees.

The sick leave absence rates for blue-collar workers in this enterprise were overall very high throughout the 1980s and considerably greater in this department than in the other sections. In 1988, sick leave in this department amounted to no less than 35 per cent (expressed in per cent of available working time). This means that more than every third working day was lost to sick leave.

No statistical data are available on the distribution of diagnoses for this specific group. However, long-term sick leave was the dominating type of absenteeism, with 55 per cent of such cases characterized by various musculo-skeletal disorders, mostly without objective signs and with rather vague symptoms.

This high sick leave rate was accompanied by low productivity. A major index of productivity and quality is that the merchandise can be delivered on schedule. Initially, only 10 per cent of what this department produced was delivered on time. Another measure is personnel turnover, again very high, at 39 per cent annually.

---

[1] Medical Director, ASEA Brown Bovery (ABB), 721 83 Västerås, Sweden.

It was calculated that the costs of recruiting and training new employees were 55,000 Swedish kronor (approximately US$ 10,000), and the costs for one day of sick leave were estimated to be 700 Swedish kronor (approximately US$ 130).

In an attempt to clarify the natural history of this situation, all workers who were employed in this department five years earlier were reviewed. It turned out that 14 of these 18 employees had reported to the occupational health service of the enterprise for musculo-skeletal disorders in the neck and shoulder region. Eight of these workers had been granted premature retirement for what was considered to be an occupational disease.

This situation could have served as an impetus for closing the department and moving the production abroad. Instead, ABB chose to improve conditions of work as a means to solving these problems.

Target population

The target group for this intervention programme was 20 female blue-collar workers, whose work was known to be monotonous and routine.

Intervention

As already indicated, the musculo-skeletal aches and pains reported by many of the employees were difficult to objectify. Partly for this reason, they were met with distrust from some members of the management. This caused strong resentment on the part of the employees because their complaints were not taken seriously. Although such an attitude on the part of management was, in fact, not typical, the employees were inclined to generalize from occasional negative experiences that this was the typical attitude. All told, this distrust represented a very potent stressor which also became an obstacle in our attempts to rehabilitate the employees in question.

Therefore, a logical first step by the occupational health service was to convince management that the causes for sick leave and the reported complaints were real and should be taken seriously, and not be seen as reflections of low motivation to work.

One way to achieve this was to conduct electro-myographic analyses of the aching and corresponding non-aching muscles when the complaints were unilateral. A complementary approach was to inform management about the availability of microscopic analyses of muscle fibres from the aching parts of the body. These analyses were made at the University of Linköping.

We considered it likely that at least part of the symptomatology was due either to short cycle, strongly repetitive work operations, or tasks characterized by static muscular tension. Our first attempt was to identify and eliminate such ergonomic problems, but also to increase variety at work by introducing job rotation. The actual work sites and work processes were video recorded. In addition, workloads were registered, supports were tested out, and all concerned received education and training in ergonomics. Although the analysis was based on a rather holistic model (Figure 1), the emphasis was primarily on the physical ergonomic issues, and less on psychosocial factors (the lower right part of the model).

Figure 1. Hypothetical model for associations between different factors relevant
to occupational cervico-brachial disorders and static loading

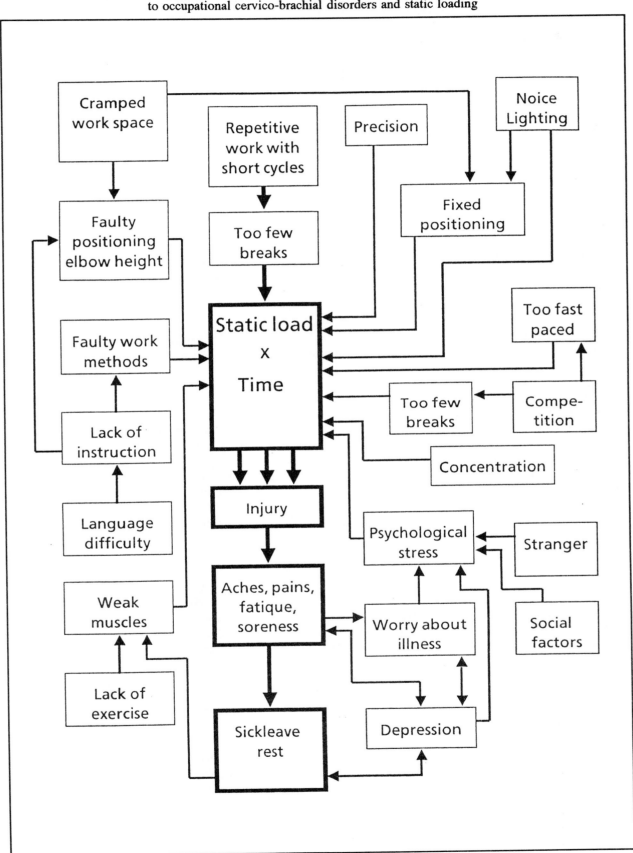

Progressively, it became clear that the key to the problem was less in inconvenient physical work positions, and more in the characteristics of the psychosocial work environment. Therefore, in 1988, more attention was subsequently devoted to the organization of work: introducing more variety and increasing workers' decision-making latitude and individual control of their own work situation. We also found that the work tasks did not provide enough stimulation and challenge. On the other hand, the interpersonal relations between the workers and their supervisors were not found to be problematic.

It was decided that the intervention should aim at increasing variety, increasing understanding of the various links of the production chain, as well as job enlargement and job enrichment.

This was achieved by a step-by-step increase of workers' competence through education and training, enabling the workers to rotate among various assembly and operation tasks in the automation group. When this had been achieved, workers were further trained to be in charge of product control and packaging.

These three steps in employee development were compulsory for all employees of the department. They were followed by three additional steps aimed at job enrichment, namely planning of materials, securing quality and coordinating production. These latter two tasks had been formerly entrusted to salaried employees.

Most of the employees attained a developmental level beyond the three first mandatory steps, but not all considered themselves sufficiently competent to take responsibility of overall planning and coordination of the work for the entire group. This latter task was allowed to rotate among the members of the group who had achieved the highest level in this competence staircase.

This training process was not conducted in the traditional way, which usually consists of trainees passively attending formal lectures. Instead, the trainees accompanied a trained worker or salaried employee to "learn by doing".

No professional lecturers were used in this training programme. Instead, skilled workers and salaried employees were encouraged to take on one apprentice each and to train her for the new tasks. Care was taken not to place new work demands upon an employee who had not yet received adequate training. By harmonizing job demands and corresponding competence through step-by-step education and training, employees were able to succeed in their new roles, with positive effects on their self-esteem resulting. It was of great importance to provide adequate time for this process, and not to underestimate the difficulties of assimilating sufficient knowledge. The workers had only primary school education and needed time to develop their competence. If the pace of this process had been accelerated, there would have been a risk of failure, followed by a reduction in self-esteem, subsequent difficulties in assimilating new knowledge, new failure, etc., potentially creating a vicious circle.

One aspect of the improvement of working conditions and work content was the relation between the group of workers and the supervisor. As already indicated, we aimed for an increase in the decision-making latitude of the workers, in addition to job expansion, and job enrichment, leading to a group takeover of many, but not all, tasks previously belonging to the supervisor. The intention was not to create self-governing groups. Thus, the role of the supervisor changed considerably, from initially providing instruction and exercising control to that of a moderator, integrator and delegator. This was not an easy transition, particularly because the employees needed to be taught to take initiatives on their own instead of expecting and following instructions from above.

In addition, the group members were in various stages of development, such that the supervisor had to take on several rather different roles simultaneously. Again, such a transition required time. In hindsight, it is clear that the group and its supervisor should have been given a longer period for this complicated transition in order to achieve an outcome even better than the one described below.

A final component in this programme was to designate a special production officer to implement the day-to-day improvements in working life proposed by members of the group. In this way, workers suggesting improvements were allowed to implement their own proposals and to see the results with very rapid feedback. Thus, new ideas were promoted much more efficiently than with the old system which required expert review of each proposal, economic rewards and resulted in late implementation.

Results

Although the intervention had some difficulties, some of which are discussed in more detail below, the outcomes were highly encouraging overall.

As previously mentioned, the intention of the programme was to reduce sick leave rates and personnel turnover rates by 50 per cent.

It turned out that personnel turnover decreased very rapidly from 39 per cent annually to 0 per cent. This dramatic change took place before the present period of business depression, and is therefore best explained by the improvement of the psychosocial work environment.

The change in sick leave absence rates is a more complex question, best evaluated with respect to two separate groups of employees.

The first group was made up of workers with chronic musculo-skeletal disorders and complaints. All had been on long-term sick leave, most for more than one year. Attempts to rehabilitate them had resulted in some of them returning to work, which exacerbated their symptoms. We did not succeed in appreciably reducing the sick leave of this group. However, because the continued sick leave eventually led to premature retirement for many of them, they are not listed as being on sick leave and are no longer employed by the enterprise.

The other group, without manifest occupational disease, had a sick leave rate of 14 per cent at the beginning of the project. This rate decreased rapidly to 4 to 5 per cent, and for the third trimester of 1991 the figure had fallen to 2 per cent. This was a level far below what was expected or considered feasible by the occupational health officers.

This outcome coincided with the introduction of personnel economic accounting in the ABB group. This meant that the boards of directors reported annually not only the economic outcome, but also changes in sick leave and staff turnover.

Productivity also improved dramatically at the beginning of the intervention period. It should be recalled that prior to the implementation of these measures, the rate of on-time delivery was only 10 per cent. At the end of the intervention period, this rate increased to 98 per cent! This remarkable result is most likely due to the following:

—   The product line included several varieties of the same basic product. Attempts were made to have small stocks of each of these. To match stocks to the customers' requests for rapid deliveries, production had to be closely geared to variation in demand.

—   With the new organization, all workers knew the demands and their day-to-day fluctuations, as well as what was available in stock. The worker in charge of each day's planning knew the potential of each worker to fulfill these requirements and organized the group accordingly. If demands were high, the group decided to work overtime. When demands decreased, members of the group could take a day off.

However, the picture would not be complete without a report of some difficulties which occurred.

Some 18 months after the start of the project, an entirely new generation of products was introduced with a subsequent rapid increase in demand. To match this, it was considered necessary to include more workers who were brought in from other departments. Accordingly, workers not trained for this type of organization were introduced into the work group.

At the same time, the supervisor came under increased workload and had to devote more efforts to solve purely technical problems, leaving less time for interaction with the members of the group.

The original group had consisted of workers who knew each other well and who formed a tightly-knit network. With the introduction of new workers, this was no longer the case. In addition, the number of interpersonal interactions within the group increased dramatically.

This increase in interactions led to several intra-group conflicts. Although the original training and competence developments were intended to include education in conflict and crisis management as well as group dynamics, communication skills and leadership, priority was in reality to technical education, training and development.

These interpersonal components were subsequently also introduced, and problems in this area gradually disappeared.

Evaluation and follow-up

This case study examines the implementation of such an intervention programme with the principles described above in the manufacturing of a relatively simple and rapidly producible "low-tech" product. Other enterprises in the ABB group manufacture huge power generating stations and power transmission, or construct nuclear power plants on other continents.

Needless to say, the experiences described in this case study cannot, without considerable modification, be applied mechanically to these other product areas or to other cultures.

Most of the positive outcomes thus far come from the shop floor. Attempts to apply these to offices have been less successful.

Whatever the setting, technical development is so rapid and competition so fierce, that it is mandatory to make use of the total potential of all collaborators. This can only be achieved by delegating the tasks to groups with defined objectives. These groups are not self-governed in the sense introduced some years ago. Instead, if a large amount of responsibility is delegated to individual workers, a new type of effective leader is needed more than ever. Such leaders must be able to instruct, convince, collaborate and delegate as needed, depending on the ever-changing and increasingly challenging tasks, as well as on the specific composition of the group.

The experiences described above have since been utilized throughout the ABB group. Twenty-five similar groups have been created in this specific enterprise, based on competence development and increases in each worker's responsibility. Management has increasingly come to understand the enormous potential inherent in each worker on the shop floor.

The idea has spread from this to other enterprises within the ABB group, encouraging each enterprise to review the experiences and to find its own solutions, always based on competence development and delegation, and an increase in workers' responsibilities. As of July 1992, 540 groups within the ABB group in Sweden were working along these lines.

Rapid technical development, combined with the constant change of products and changes in the composition of each group, make this programme a never-ending process.

CASE STUDY NO. 14

Occupational stress in a Swedish high-tech telecommunication corporation: An integrated approach to an occupational health challenge

Dr. Bengt B. Arnetz,[1]
Mats Frånberg and Carl Axling[2]

Issues and approach

A growing number of employees at a multinational telecommunication company complained about symptoms characteristic of "hypersensitivity to electricity and video display units". The problems were severe enough that day-to day activities were adversely affected. The senior management decided to create a specific task force whose goal was to work with this new occupational health problem. The committee, consisting of engineers, project managers and health representatives, decided to work with a variety of factors. One member dealt with the electromagnetic environment. Others addressed the psychosocial and individual environment.

Generally, when a company is confronted with a new environmental issue, the approach is to ask the authorities for information and guidelines. When there is no information available, the work environment law still puts the responsibility on the company. One way to take that responsibility is to gain knowledge.

A project was therefore launched to gain knowledge in this area where it was close to non-existent. The project was put into operation in the form of an action programme in order to help staff members who were already hypersensitive and to prevent others from developing the same problems. It was carried out in agreement with the safety committee and the trade union representatives. The objectives of the project were:

— to help improve the health of those who already were "hypersensitive to electricity and video display units";

— to address the conditions of the working environment of employees with early symptoms to prevent them from developing a full-blown condition;

— to apply general measures to prevent the condition from developing in the first place.

— to provide employees with honest, objective information.

The project was based on the hypothesis that a combination of factors (electromagnetic fields, climate, organization of tasks, individual characteristics, visual ergonomics, light and sound) was at the origin of the employees' complaints.

It was also determined that a number of factors were necessary for the success of the project, which included the following: support from upper-level management; active interest from the company occupational health physician; a progressive attitude and a driving force; respect for the rules of society; and consideration of the total working environment. An extensive network of Swedish and international researchers, suppliers, consultants,

---

[1] National Institute for Psychosocial Factors and Health, Work Environment and Health Section, Stockholm; and Department of Stress Research, Karolinska Institute, Box 60,205, 104 01 Stockholm, Sweden.

[2] Ellemtel Telecommunication Systems Laboratory, Älvsjö, Sweden.

institutions, and companies was established. These groups, together with the corporation, made it possible to gather knowledge.

Target population

This project was targeted at video display unit workers in a high-tech Swedish telecommunications company. The programme was implemented from the fall of 1989 to 1992. Following the initial trial period, the programme became an integrated part of line-management responsibilities. Based on the results of the research, the intervention programme subsequently involved management, members of the company's occupational health service, and representatives from other departments as diverse as personnel and the electronics department. Their skills and cooperation were essential to the programme's success.

Intervention

A detailed occupational environment survey

The specific purpose of this survey was to assess the role of the VDU, the psychosocial work environment, and individually-based factors in the development of "hypersensitivity to electricity".

A standardized questionnaire was distributed to a total of some 340 employees. These included all subjects who were known to constantly suffer from "hypersensitivity to electricity" as well as those who suffered from it predominantly at work. Also included were employees with no symptoms. Answers were received from over 71 per cent. The questionnaire covered the following areas: socio-economics, marital status, occupational title, job function, work time including work at home, use of VDU at work and at home, job content, job satisfaction, psychosocial work environment in general, education, skill development, work strain, control over the work processes, physical and mental symptoms, past medical history, smoking and alcohol habits, exercise patterns, social support, general well-being, psychosomatic index, index over skin problems, somatic ache index, sleep-quality index, VDU-ergonomic index, a mental worry index, sensory-respiratory index, a satisfaction and dissatisfaction index, and personality type.

Subjects were classified into three main groups; those that stated that they (i) were "never hypersensitive to electricity"; (ii) were "sometimes (predominantly at work) hypersensitive"; or (iii) were "always hypersensitive to electricity". In addition, since skin symptoms are the major and consistent complaint among subjects suffering from "hypersensitivity to electricity", we created an index of skin symptoms. The index was based on responses to the following questions: redness, burning, pain, perspiration, sensitivity to light, swelling, itching, dry skin, pimples, superficial vessels, symptoms from the hair, and eczema. These are the symptoms that have been studied in the area of VDU-related skin problems and also reported in the case studies of "hypersensitivity to electricity".

Results of the surveys

Of the entire sample, 82 per cent were males. There was no significant difference found with regard to the sex distribution in the groups that experience hypersensitivity.

We found that of the three groups, the subjects constantly suffering from "hypersensitivity to electricity" were most likely to spend at least 75 per cent of their work day in front of the VDU.

The results indicated a dose-response association between "hypersensitivity to electricity" and time without symptoms. Thus, among those "always hypersensitive", 75 per cent could only work one hour or less at the VDU before having significant problems. Among those with no "hypersensitivity to electricity", 22 per cent were able to work with the VDU for a period longer than three hours without symptoms, and 40 per cent for an extended period of time without any problems whatsoever. Thus a work interval of three hours or more without a break will result in almost uniform problems among patients with "hypersensitivity to electricity" and among 40 per cent of patients without "hypersensitivity to electricity".

People in the "always" and "sometimes hypersensitive" group had a significantly higher rate of absenteeism than the other two groups. The "always hypersensitive" group expressed a desire to have more work than the other groups. Members of the "always" group developed new skills in their jobs more than members of the other groups, and believed more often that more advanced jobs were available to them. This same group was found to use analgesics and selenium and take vitamins more than the others. Another significant difference was that more than half of the "always" group had removed their dental fillings containing mercury and replaced them with plastics. Finally, overall health was rated significantly worse among the "always" group compared to the other two groups.

When asked where they perceived "hypersensitivity to electricity", 73 per cent of the "sometimes hypersensitive" group perceive it only at work, while another 26.7 per cent had problems at work as well as at home. For the "always hypersensitive" group, the equivalent proportions were 14.3 per cent and 85.7 per cent respectively.

There were no significant differences between the groups with regard to the functioning and reliability of the computer or system with which they worked. However, subjects in the "always hypersensitive" group were found to be more dependent on their computer and have less opportunity to substitute with non-VDU work in the case of a VDU malfunction. There was no significant difference with regard to the number of years subjects had worked with the computer as there were no significant differences with all other points contained in the questionnaire.

Discussion of main results from survey

Based on assessments, no statistically significant differences were found in a number of background variables, such as sex, age, VDU experience, personality trait, moodiness, general mental well-being and prior medical history. Only factors related to the work organization and work content differed as did the potential for psychosomatic reactivity. These findings indicate that employees with "hypersensitivity to electricity" basically are no different from those who do not suffer from this condition. The only differences are that those with hypersensitivity appear to be better educated, more devoted, harder working and perceive a frustration between their own professional goals and those that the organization and the software are able to satisfy.

Our survey suggests that there is a need to look more closely at the psychosocial and organizational work environment in order to understand the various factors contributing to "hypersensitivity to electricity". In addition, stress management and active coping skills should be taught to people at risk. Low emitting VDU and electromagnetic sanitation of the workplace is very costly and such actions alone have not proven to be sufficient. Rather, management and employees need to look at the "total picture" and work at improving the high technology VDU environment from a software ergonomics and psychosocial point of view as well.

The introduction of the VDU in the office has resulted in major changes in both work content and work organization. The individual worker carries a much higher degree of responsibility and control over the work product. Subjects need training in order to better cope with this increased responsibility. There is also a need to assist people in setting reasonable goals with their VDU work, as well as ensuring that subjects are better able to recognize mental and physical symptoms indicative of work-related stress.

Based on the results of this survey, as well as frequent contacts with management, employee representatives, the occupational health survey and employees themselves, we instituted a broad-based intervention programme.

Action programme

The company action programme is based on respect, rapidity and broadness.

Respect means that the company's managers and industrial health service listen to employees and take their problems seriously. Respect means that the employee's professional identity is supported when it is threatened by hypersensitivity. The goal is to ensure that the hypersensitive employee can continue to work, even if this requires providing a different type of work environment. Respect also means that the employee must tell the manager and the doctor about hypersensitivity in order for action to be taken.

Rapidity means that the action programme is tested and works smoothly. The company physician sees the employee within a few days. Managers know that the employee must stop working in the environment that the employee considers to cause the hypersensitivity.

Broadness means that the action programme has a broad spectrum of measures in both the physical and psychosocial environment.

With the aim of prevention in mind, all new workstations have been equipped according to ergonomic recommendations. Old workstations have been rebuilt. An electromagnetic map of the whole premises has been developed, floor by floor. Additionally, a power transformer has been shielded that produced magnetic field in the offices above it.

An in-house all-day seminar was held with the most prominent Swedish researchers in this area. Representatives from various scientific disciplines were invited and employees were able to hear first hand about recent developments in the field.

Employees are now provided with information about stress, how the work is organized and ergonomics. It is important to know how one's surroundings affect both the body and soul, and to be aware that individual characteristics and attitudes can also influence the physical and mental condition.

Hypersensitivity: The first encounter. A routine procedure begins as soon as someone reports that he or she is hypersensitive. Almost immediately, the individual gets to see the company physician, the safety engineer and the physiotherapist. Individuals who find their situation difficult to deal with get the support of a psychologist.

In addition, there are resources in the form of the company's own personnel in the electronics departments, the building and general services sections, and the personnel department. If that isn't enough, contacts are used with an international network of researchers in medicine, psychology and technology.

Mildly hypersensitive individuals. In collaboration with researchers and suppliers of computer equipment, display screens with the weakest possible fields were developed. When electrical equipment is placed in workrooms and laboratories, both the magnetic and electric fields are intensified. The company's knowledge of electronics is used to lower these levels, for example, by moving electrical equipment a little further away, by equipping desk lamps with grounded, shielded cables, by grounding desk legs in metal and by eliminating snarls of cable.

While the company attempts to rectify the electromagnetic environment, they also try to influence the psychosocial environment. For example, when the company cannot change a display screen and lighting, co-workers, managers, the people who service the computers, and the industrial health service are involved to a degree quite out of the ordinary. This kind of attention is beneficial. The social climate is improved by the discussions concerning work organization, working methods and tools. Taking part in the planning of the work and the development of the organization is stimulating and increases the motivation of the employees.

Of course, the importance of the parameters related to climate, electric and magnetic fields, and the psychosocial environment is not limited to the workplace. These factors must even be reckoned with in one's own home.

Acutely hypersensitive individuals. A whole workroom has been shielded against electric and magnetic fields using transformer sheet steel and all-welded aluminum sheet steel. At the same time, the patterns of movement demanded by different tasks are examined in the room. The results will later provide the basis for redesigning both the physical and psychological working environment.

One of the suggestions that has been made is to visit co-workers in person instead of sending them messages electronically. Besides providing a natural opportunity for exercise, it also contributes to good human relations. Also, instead of display screens with cathode ray tubes, liquid crystal displays or projections by means of wide-screen television are used.

It is important to review display characteristics, image quality, resolution, stability, colour, luminance and lighting as well as indoor climate. Work station design and layout also play an important role in the outcome of symptoms from the musculo-skeletal system.

As part of the programme, the following questions are now reviewed for individual employees:

Employee review

— Does a clear and focused job description exist for the employee?

— Are regular progress reviews planned with the employee?

— Is there a good balance between freedom, control and possibilities for career developments?

— Do personal career goals and job content match with real possibilities and limitations of the job?

— Have regular break periods and relaxation opportunities been scheduled?

— In what way has the introduction of new techniques influenced the job content?

— Is the individual given sufficient opportunity to influence work processes and content?

— Has the reliability of the information system been optimized?

— Does the total work load force the employee to perform too much overtime over an extended period of time?

— What organizational, personal and other changes occurred at the time symptoms of hypersensitivity to electricity and video display terminals first appeared?

Results and evaluation of the intervention programme

The integrated programme was successful in slowing down the occurrence of new cases with "hypersensitivity to electricity and video display units". All subjects with hypersensitivity were able to return to work or further deterioration was prevented. Individuals with symptoms of hypersensitivity continue to work for the company. Most of them perform their regular duties, sometimes according to other working methods, or within other departments, or with the help of other tools.

Although the general approach used in this case will most likely be of value for other telecommunications and high technology corporations with similar problems, we wish to emphasize the fact that the work of the project is valid only within the company with the company's conditions.

Also, we do not know how the various parameters relate to or interact with each other, nor do we know if the parameters have a different effect when the condition is new versus when it has already been established.

The company has applied a number of alterations in the area of electromagnetic environments. The company has achieved effects of such quality that individuals have stated that their conditions are considerably improved. Nevertheless, no conclusions can be drawn with regard to the underlying cause of hypersensitivity, and whether electromagnetic fields play any role whatsoever; it could just as well have been factors of a psychosocial nature that resulted in improved well-being among the employees.

Neither can we determine if these factors interact or if only one factor is at work. We do, however, consider it plausible that there is a complex interaction between various factors. It is clear that the psychosocial factor has some effect.

We do not see any connection between the air-quality on the company's premises and hypersensitivity. The ventilation system has been inspected and found in good working order. A general recommendation for increased comfort is to lower the temperature in the workrooms.

Equipment and furnishings constantly give off chemical emissions of, for example, solvents, brominated phenyls and formaldehyde. We do not know if there is a connection between chemical emission and hypersensitivity. This must be researched further. "Multiple chemical sensitivity" is a growing problem in the United States but so far rather uncommon in Sweden.

Many of the hypersensitive employees have had their amalgam fillings removed, and have reported that they are less hypersensitive after having done so. However, we cannot see any unequivocal connection here.

It has been speculated that the flickering light from display screens and fluorescent lamps can cause a variety of symptoms. There are similar theories for infrasound, noise and ultrasound. We feel that these areas need more research.

Following the corrective measures work performance was improved. Technical developments and the use of new video screens improved the person-machine interaction. Management was very supportive and created an atmosphere where hypersensitivity was taken seriously. In some cases adaptation of an employee's home was done at the expense of the company. Stress management programmes have been launched. In addition, applied research programmes have been implemented to help people become more resistant to stress and improve their ability to set realistic goals with regard to workload and other demands.

The company has developed an open communication strategy. Information is given to all employees concerning various theories behind the symptoms. In addition, management's idea of how to cope with the challenge is presented in a candid atmosphere.

"Hypersensitivity to electricity" is a relatively new problem. It is a result of the recent introduction of new information technology. With the on-going demand for "mean and lean organization", high technology will be developed to support relatively fewer workers to do more sophisticated and demanding tasks. If poorly implemented, we will see large numbers of workers developing a syndrome we call "techno-stress". This is a new form of stress where qualitative and quantitative overload is combined in an environment with high control and good opportunities for personal growth.

Follow-up

Following the implementation of the programme, the number of new cases of "hypersensitivity to electricity and vidual display units" decreased considerably. During the first year of the programme, approximately 15 new subjects became ill. In contrast, during the last part of the programme, only two or three new cases have been identified. Furthermore, subjects out on sick leave have been able to return to productive work following physical and psycho-social modifications in the work environment and a more open atmosphere for discussing work-related concerns. Project planning and scheduling, shortness of time and the need for overtime are all issues that have been addressed. The programme has been successfully implemented also in other office environments.

The company has also introduced psycho-physiological assessments as a means to evaluate supposedly improved physical and psychosocial work environments along with more traditional methods, such as management perception, productivity, and labour turnover and absenteeism.

Conditions of Work Digest, Vol. 11, 2/1992

CASE STUDY NO. 15

A stress reduction programme for nurses at Osaka Medical College[1]

Dr. Seishiro Chihara,[2] Dr. Hiroyuki Asaba,[3]
Dr. Toshiaki Sakai,[4] Dr. Jun Koh[5] and Makiko Okawa[6]

Context

There are 80 medical schools in Japan. Each school has one or more affiliated hospitals to facilitate clinical training of students in the various fields of medicine. Medical school hospitals have the greatest variety of functions, including education and research, as well as providing specialized treatment and diagnostic techniques for local people. In addition, medical school hospitals usually are affiliated with nursing schools. Many nursing schools, in fact, are incorporated in the hospitals to meet the need for nurses. Senior nursing staff members also serve as teachers in their wards.

Osaka Medical College Hospital is a general hospital with 983 beds, annexed to the medical college. The hospital provides clinical training for student, state-registered nurses.

There are 56 beds on the psychiatric ward, with about 90 per cent of these beds constantly occupied. At the time of investigation, there were ten patients suffering from schizophrenia, nine with neuroses, five with manic depressive psychosis, four with dementia, two with mental retardation, one with epilepsy, one with toxic psychosis and 17 patients with diverse mental disorders. Of these patients, two were also suffering from severe somatic diseases, such as terminal cancer.

The nursing staff was made up of 16 state-registered nurses (five males and 11 females) and four assistant nurses with prefectural registration (three males and one female). The average age of the male state-registered nurses was 33.6 years and 26.2 for the female; 30.5 for male assistant nurses and 25.0 for the female. The nurses worked in three shifts: 08:00-16:00, 16:00-23:00 and 23:00-08:00 hours. The hours of work were 40 per week with six days of leave every four weeks, making 150 to 200 days per year depending upon night and extra duties.

---

[1] We are deeply indebted to the nursing staff of the neuropsychiatric ward in Osaka Medical College who participated in the study and gave us frank opinions. We are most grateful to Dr. Kuroda, Dr. Toyoda, Dr. Sonn, Dr. Okamura and Dr. Emura, who helped us in organizing and conducting the intervention programme. We especially appreciated the good understanding and kind support given by Ms. Segawa, Director of Nursing at Osaka Medical College. We are also grateful to Dr. Kobayashi, Mr. Yasuhara and Mr. Misawa in Kohnan Hospital for their invaluable advice.

[2] Professor, Department of Psychology, Osaka Medical College, 2-7 Daigakumachi, Takatsuki City, Osaka, Japan.

[3] Director, Kohnan Hospital; guest-lecturer at the Department of Neuropsychiatry, Osaka Medical College.

[4] Chairman, Department of Neuropsychiatry, Osaka Medical College.

[5] Department of Neuropsychiatry, Osaka Medical College.

[6] Head Nurse on the neuropsychiatric ward at Osaka Medical College.

During the daytime shift, state-registered nurses took turns in assuming responsibility for general administration of the ward, as well as for medication or somatic care of the patients. Every patient was assigned a nurse. Twenty-three physicians were assigned to the ward: 12 senior physicians (one professor, four lecturers and seven assistant lecturers) and 11 junior physicians. The junior physicians assumed primary clinical responsibilities under the supervision of the senior physicians.

A group of eight student nurses was stationed on the ward and rotated every two weeks. The nursing staff was responsible for teaching these student nurses, a job which required considerable time and effort. In addition to their clinical duties and teaching nursing students, the state-registered nurses had to cope with junior ward physicians who had limited clinical experience. This placed an extra burden on the nurses.

Issues

In order to provide a broad field of clinical training for physicians and nurses, patients with a variety of disorders requiring special attention and treatment are admitted to the neuropsychiatric ward. Psychiatric patients who also have somatic diseases are cared for on the neuropsychiatric ward, but are cared for by non-psychiatric doctors as well. As a result of the different patients and the range of care they require, the nurses have to provide a variety of somatic care of a specialized nature. They feel, however, that providing specialized somatic care is not their primary task and express a feeling of inadequacy in carrying out these duties.

Thus, the nurses play many roles on the ward and some areas of their work are not clearly defined. They have a heavy workload with high demand, but they have limited control over the work. Wages are one of the most important factors not to be overlooked. Both the amount of the wage and the status it implies are important. When the distribution of wages is perceived to be unfair, interpersonal conflicts and resentment increase. Nurses' salaries at medical school hospitals are less than those at non-teaching hospitals.

Psychiatric nursing is not popular among young nurses. There is still a certain amount of prejudice towards psychiatric patients, often considered to be violent and dangerous. According to a report of the Japanese Association of Psychiatric Hospitals, 11 nurses and six physicians died due to injuries inflicted by patients at work between July 1961 and July 1991; there were some 200 incidents of injuries inflicted upon the staff of public psychiatric hospitals between 1980 and 1989. Another reason that psychiatric nursing is avoided by young nurses is that the effects of treatment are usually not as obvious as in cases of surgery or medicine. Recruiting young nurses is not an easy task and their rate of turnover is high. In a society where an employee tends to stay with one employer until retirement, the high turnover rate of nurses deserves a comment. Some degree of turnover in a teaching hospital is to be expected. Ambitious young nurses come to work at a medical school hospital to learn and broaden their clinical experience. When they have accomplished this, they move on to make room for younger colleagues. To keep a medical school hospital as an active and stimulating place of higher learning, a certain rate of turnover is necessary. Fortunately, there is a shortage neither of nurses nor qualified applicants for the psychiatric ward of Osaka Medical College, but all of these job-related factors combined were found to produce a great deal of stress in the nursing staff.

Target population

This study, and its subsequent stress-reduction intervention programme, was targeted at all nurses on the psychiatric ward at Osaka Medical College. The staff consisted of 20 nurses, all of whom participated in this study.

Approach

A questionnaire containing a checklist (Annex 1) of relevant issues was used to scan the problems. Each nurse evaluated the problem issues on the checklist and assigned a value to each one indicating its degree of importance. Nurses also added their own problems if they were not listed on the checklist. Nineteen out of 20 nurses responded to the questionnaire, and one partially answered the questions.

Eleven nurses considered "increased workplace complaints" as a significant or important problem. "Interpersonal conflicts", "increased turnover", "production not meeting expectation" and "lowered work performance" were also considered as major problem areas for the nurses. Five nurses stated there were no problems.

The relative importance of the different issues as indicated in the checklist was confirmed by the responses given by the nurses in the unstructured part of the questionnaire, which indicated three major problem areas.

— **Problems concerning the work.** "Our work is not effective"; "I cannot feel satisfaction in the work"; "The work is complicated and heavy"; "One has to deal with non-psychiatric problems, such as surgical and gynecological"; "Lack of information"; "Lack of working initiative"; "Lack of responsibility of each individual on the ward"; and "No way out other than resigning". These problems were related to the multiple roles the nurses had to play and also indicated low working morale due to a lack of opportunity to participate in decision-making.

— **Interpersonal problems.** "Arrogant behaviour of the senior staff"; "Lack of leadership"; "No clear policy"; "Poor interpersonal communication"; "No trust between co-workers"; "No chance to complain"; "Many complaints in the workplace"; and "Senior staff are obedient to their superiors and strict towards subordinates". These comments indicated a lack of trust in the administrative staff of the ward. Nurses' comments also indicated that relationships among co-workers were not based on trust.

— **Complaints against the physicians.** "Nurses are carrying out tasks which should be performed by doctors"; "Doctors are not cooperative"; "Doctors' orders are not clear"; and "The training of junior physicians is not satisfactory and the nurses are having to train junior physicians". Junior physicians with limited clinical experience were creating problems by having to take the major clinical responsibilities on the ward which should have been covered by the senior physicians.

The results of the questionnaire were discussed with the nursing staff and ward physicians. Problem issues that could be addressed within the time limit of the study were selected as well as one intervention method.

Intervention

In order to address occupational stress factors which are related to the way a large teaching hospital functions, an intervention programme aimed at organizational and structural change is needed. However, it was not feasible to tackle major organizational change within the time limit of this project. We could only attempt a small-scale intervention targeted at problems on the ward.

For this stress reduction intervention programme, we selected those problem issues which had been identified by the majority of nurses as "significant" or "important" workplace obstacles: increased workplace complaints and interpersonal conflicts. We believed that if the nurses could solve these problems by their own efforts, then they would regain confidence in themselves and be motivated to work on other problems in the future.

Two intervention methods were considered particularly suitable, namely improving cohesion among co-workers and establishing better channels of information and communication. Both methods had the potential to solve some of the workplace complaints. However, the existing interpersonal conflicts would impede efforts to improve cohesion among co-workers. Therefore trying to help establish better channels of information and communication was selected as the best intervention technique.

It was expected that the nursing staff's role confusion and workplace complaints would diminish once they were provided with precise and sufficient information. Improving communication would decrease both interpersonal conflicts and some workplace complaints related to interpersonal problems.

Three senior physicians were chosen to act as key people for implementing the intervention and helped to improve the channels of interpersonal communication between the nurses. The physicians were neutral concerning the interpersonal conflicts of the nurses and could provide moral support to the staff. All the ward physicians cooperated with the study.

As background, it is necessary to explain some aspects of Japanese group behaviour, which may differ somewhat from that of Europeans. We firmly believe, however, that individual Japanese are basically no different from people of any other cultural background.

Most Japanese rarely reveal their inner thoughts openly, but only confide in the people with whom they have informal and close relationships. A Japanese individual is afraid of his or her opinion being openly rejected by others and would always try to avoid such a situation. Thus, an informal relationship is an important factor in understanding group mentality based on a delicate mutual dependence. Individuals should always be seen as an integral part of their group, with which they share their destiny.

Those intending to implement a new project involving an entire group should avoid an open debate. First, they should make an effort to gain informal agreement for the project from many members of the group, particularly influential and vocal ones. Only after the informal agreement has been obtained should they present the project and seek formal acceptance. Keeping order in a workplace is of primary importance. Open debate is avoided because it can disturb the harmony of the group.

It was once considered to be a virtue to bear the unbearable in life, and in work in particular. Older generations of Japanese were taught to consider life as a mountain to be climbed with a heavy load on one's back. If one accepts constant hardship and suffering as a part of living, one has no reason to complain. As individuals, Japanese workers may resent hardship in their work; however, workers do their best to perform their functions as part of their workteam, because the workteam constitutes a system of mutual support. Although the workteam does not always provide sufficient support, workers need to be an integral part of the system and therefore do their best for the group.

Stability is another important factor. A typical Japanese person is basically against any major changes and will accept drastic change only when forced to by circumstances. Evolution is preferred to revolution; one continuously adapts to the constantly changing milieu, only to avoid a sudden and drastic change.

Before this study began, the chain of command on the psychiatric ward was good and the staff functioned as a highly qualified nursing team. However, the atmosphere on the ward was tense. Everyone was aware of the situation, but no one wanted to upset the status quo.

In an attempt to improve channels of informal communication, the intervention was introduced. The intervention period was 1 September to 31 October 1991.

The programme was implemented by first organizing a number of small social gatherings -- initiated by the physicians -- where the nurses could express their thoughts and opinions freely. On 17 October, we arranged a party for the nursing staff and ward physicians in a local restaurant where everyone participated and socialized, except the staff on night duty. Nurses and physicians communicated on an equal basis in a relaxed and friendly atmosphere. This was the only meeting involving the majority of the staff, but similar meetings in smaller groups were organized after work where nurses exchanged their opinions and views.

Results

As a result of these informal gatherings and the opinions and views exchanged, ward physicians made special efforts to talk to nurses more frequently on the ward, listen to their suggestions, be precise in their instructions to nurses, explain the rationale behind their instructions, provide relevant information, give nurses opportunities to ask questions and discuss their problems, and pay more attention to non-verbal communication.

Other positive outcomes were that the senior physicians spent more time helping junior physicians. The junior physicians were then able to be more specific in their instructions to the nurses and were better able to explain the reasons behind their orders.

The final questionnaire (Annex 2) showed that the number of nurses who considered "workplace complaints" as important or significant decreased from 11 to eight. Those who considered it of limited importance changed from six to eight; and those who considered it of no importance changed from two to four. For "interpersonal conflict", the number of nurses who considered it important or significant decreased from nine to seven; and those who considered it of no importance increased from two to five. The number who felt interpersonal conflicts were of limited importance did not change. Overall, the number of nurses who considered the problems to be important or significant decreased. The nurses who considered there were no problems increased. The number of nurses who considered the problems limited was unchanged. Therefore there was a general tendency to feel that the problems decreased.

Evaluation

The tangible effect of the intervention was weak, but there was a definite improvement in the atmosphere of the ward. The favourable effect may be attributed to the fact that the nurses were given opportunities to express their resentment by participating in the study and that attention was paid to their well-being. The nurses regained hope of improving the frustrating situation in the workplace by actively taking part in the process of improvement. This was reflected in one nurse's remark: "I thought there were few concrete effects. But the atmosphere of the workplace has improved. Now I work more pleasantly than before. I realize now the importance of our own attitude to work stress". We reconfirmed the importance of effective communication channels.

Follow-up

During the intervention, the physicians took the initiative and the nurses played rather passive roles. However, our ultimate goal is that the nurses should develop their own stress prevention programmes and support systems. We are planning to have regular meetings to inform nurses, to enable them to identify workplace stress and prevent their problems. We also would like to extend this stress reduction programme to other workplaces.

Checklist for the evaluation of stress prevention programmes

A. Problem issues recollection

To investigate the grade of problems, please check each issue nil, limited, significant or important.

- absence from work and postponement of duties
- lowered work performance (both qualitative and quantitative)
- increased number of accidents
- increased psychosomatic disorders
- increased workplace complaints
- interpersonal conflicts
- risk-taking behaviour
- increased turnover
- lower motivation and morale
- production not meeting expectation
- overall

B. Please describe your own problems concretely.

_____

_____

_____

_____

_____

_____

Annex 2

Checklist for the evaluation of stress prevention programmes

A. Problem issues recollection

To investigate the effects of the intervention, please check each problem issue nil, limited, significant or important.

- workplace complaints

- interpersonal conflicts

- overall

B. What do you think about the effects of this programme?

_____
_____
_____
_____
_____
_____

CASE STUDY NO. 16

An individual-based counselling approach for combating stress in British Post Office employees

Professor Cary L. Cooper,
Tricia Allison, Peter Reynolds and Golnaz Sadri[1]

Context

The cost of employee stress to organizations, whether work-related or from personal causes, is both well-known and well-documented.[2] The costs can come in the form of inefficiency, high accident rates, absence due to illness, early retirement on medical grounds and even premature death. Increasingly, employers in the United States are being held legally liable for their employees' physical and mental problems when these result from exposure to job stress. Similar cases are beginning to appear in Europe.[3] The trend towards in-company counselling or employee assistance services is also on the increase.[4] The British Post Office is one organization which has gone further than most in this regard. During the autumn of 1986, the Post Office hired full-time stress counsellors for its occupational health services in two large regions.

Issues and approach

The idea of a specialist counselling facility within the Post Office was formulated by the Chief Medical Officer at that time. Stress had been identified as an organizational problem in the 1970s, when stress factors were found to be the second highest reason for medical retirement after musculo-skeletal illnesses. In 1984, a working group was established to identify the need for counselling on stress among Post Office staff. Members of the working group were selected to provide an appropriate balance between the business functions and the line managers. At the same time, representation was ensured from each of the three administrative levels of the business. The group included a range of opinion and experience in both the counselling and health education fields, as well as in the operation and resources of the Post Office as a whole. Evidence -- both written and oral -- was taken from a number of specialists well known in their fields.

A report was presented by the group the following year, acknowledging that the Post Office already offered basic counselling support to employees through their nursing and welfare officers. It was, however, recommended that the role of the specialist be to deal with more complex and deep-seated psychological problems, of the kind which previously may have been referred to an agency outside the Post Office. It was also assumed that, unlike external specialists, in-house stress counsellors would have the benefit of a broad knowledge of the postal business and methods used. They would, therefore, be better able to understand and directly help employees, particularly

[1] School of Management, University of Manchester Institute of Science and Technology, P.O. Box 88, Manchester M60 1QD, United Kingdom.

[2] V.J. Sutherland and C.L. Cooper: *Understanding stress: A psychological perspective for health professionals* (Chapman and Hall, London, 1990).

[3] J. Earnshaw and C.L. Cooper: "Employer liability for stress on the job", in *Employee Counselling Today*, Vol. 3, No. 2, 1991, pp. 3-5.

[4] L.R. Murphy: "Workplace interventions for stress reduction and prevention", in C.L. Cooper and R. Payne (editors): *Causes, coping and consequences of stress at work* (John Wiley, New York, 1988).

where the problem was work-related. Furthermore, it was felt that the external agencies knew less than in-house counsellors about the organizational factors of workplace stress.

The report further pointed out that the stress counsellors also might be able to identify whether any Post Office structures, policies or practices were causing psychological problems for employees. With this information, they could brief senior management about aspects of the business operations which were causing psychological difficulties, without identifying individuals or breaching confidentiality. Furthermore, in the future, the counsellors could help to ensure that business practices would be formulated in a way that would minimize the impact of stress on staff.

Yet another advantage of in-house stress specialists was that they could provide training to management, to increase sensitivity about their own and subordinates' problems, as well as helping them become more competent in handling interpersonal issues. These, then, are the potential advantages of providing in-house counselling services, as opposed to using more conventional and external employee assistance programmes.

Target population

The target group for this intervention was all employees of the British Post Office in the north-east and the north-west of England. Counselling was made available for all workers in these regions. However, it was envisaged that management could also benefit from the programme by receiving training from the counsellors.

Intervention

In the model used for this programme, tension arises when an individual perceives that he or she lacks the resources to cope adequately with certain events which have developed in his or her psycho-social environment. This tension may have a number of outcomes, both in the individual's personal and work lives, involving reduced physical and mental well-being and reduced performance. The tension may lead to maladaptive behaviours, such as drinking, smoking, withdrawal from family or work (or over-involvement in these areas), and search behaviours which may lead to seeking help from others. In creating a counselling resource, the Post Office has attempted to provide a service whereby the clients can be guided to discover or create within themselves the capacity to cope more effectively with their present problems and, ideally, with future problems.

The counsellors may intervene in three primary areas: they help individuals to deal with particular personal or work-related problems; they attempt to increase the employees' capacity to withstand perceived stressors; they attempt to reduce the number of stressors likely to be experienced by members of the organization.

In trying to achieve the above objectives, the counsellors tended to use primarily a client-centred counselling approach. This approach enabled the employees to highlight their own problems, look at alternative solutions, assess the costs and benefits of different courses of action, and prepare and implement a plan of action to deal with the problem(s).

In this project, the following four main areas of activity were designated for the counsellors: to set up a confidential counselling service for employees; to help or advise other Post Office functions; to provide feedback to the Post Office on the need for counselling; and to provide feedback on morale or job satisfaction.

The counsellors' first month of service was spent gaining knowledge and an understanding of the organization. In an organization with the size and complexity of the Post Office, this period was quite necessary and created an important foundation for what was to follow.

Locating the counsellors within the Post Office's occupational health service implied certain organizational consequences. First, many people perceive a health clinic as a doctor's office which you visit when you are sick. For these people, the concept of occupational health may shift from advice to treatment. Second, location within the occupational health service implied certain professional ethics governing conduct and confidentiality. For example, liaison with management is, for many people, an issue closely linked with confidentiality, since, within an organization, some level of feedback to management is essential. However, it is important that in practice, the ethics be in the client's best interest. This means, for one thing, that a counsellor must have a client's permission before making indications about a client in feedback to management. All branches of the organization aim to care for employees, but may not be trusted equally by individual employees. If a client denies permission for a counsellor to discuss an issue with management, then the counsellor must find a way to deal with the frustration without breaching confidentiality. This is potentially difficult, but the track record suggests that where trust in the counsellor has been established and the content has been discussed, refusal is rare.

From the outset, the Post Office counselling service was intended to be an "open access" service. As a result, referrals have been received from all quarters. Obviously, because counselling was located in occupational health, a large number of referrals came from this service. However, on-going publicity (letters to employees, articles in the house magazine and presentations to management groups) was used to promote other means of referrals. During the first two years of the programme, 40 per cent of the referrals to counselling came from occupational health, 31.5 per cent were self-referrals, 19 per cent were referred from welfare, and the remaining 9.5 per cent came from areas such as management, personnel and trade unions.

At the beginning of the project, the counsellors expected that it would take six to nine months to gain a foothold in the organization and establish credibility among the various interest groups. However, these assumptions proved incorrect. Aside from the first month, which was spent in induction, the caseload for the first several months was over two hundred. Furthermore, this was spread across the entire organization, including cleaners, mail carriers, postal officers and executives, technical engineers and senior staff. This shows that problems do not respect organizational position or boundaries.

It is perhaps worth mentioning something about the quality of referrals. First, it is remarkable how few have been inappropriate. Where this has been the case, it has been the result of self-referral. Second, the complexity of many of the cases has been striking. The implication from this is that the level of professional knowledge and skill required for counselling work in an industrial or commercial setting must be extremely wide-ranging. Many external agencies specialize in particular problem areas, or have teams of workers containing specialists, who together create a whole. In contrast, it is likely that a counsellor within an organization will have to deal with all kinds of problems alone.

During the first two years of the counselling programme, 46 per cent of the caseload was in mental health and stress issues. In general, these clients suffered from anxiety and/or depression. Of the remaining 54 per cent of referrals, 24 per cent sought help for "relationship" problems, with the majority focusing upon marital difficulties. Other areas included alcoholism and addictions, bereavement, assault, physical illness or disability, social problems and panic attacks.

Evaluation and results

A major component of the British Post Office stress counselling programme was systematic evaluation. This section of the paper will highlight the evaluation of the impact of in-house stress counselling in the British Post Office.

The evaluation part of the stress counselling project was conducted in two regions of the Post Office, and subsequently extended to a third.

To assess the effectiveness of stress counselling within the Post Office, before and after data were collected on absence due to sickness, job satisfaction, mental health, self-esteem, organizational commitment and changes in health behaviours.

To determine whether the scores of the self-report measures for the client group changed after counselling, the data was statistically analysed, and is displayed below in graph form in Figures 1 to 6.

Pre- and post-scores on questionnaire measures for client and control groups

Figure 1: Anxiety

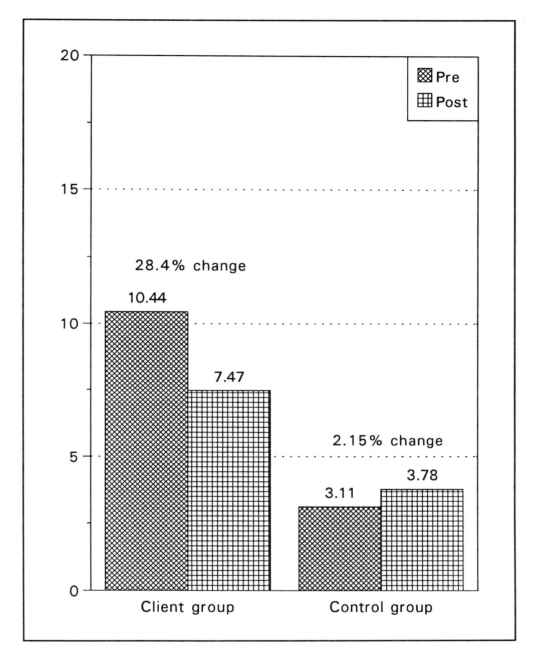

Figure 2: Depression

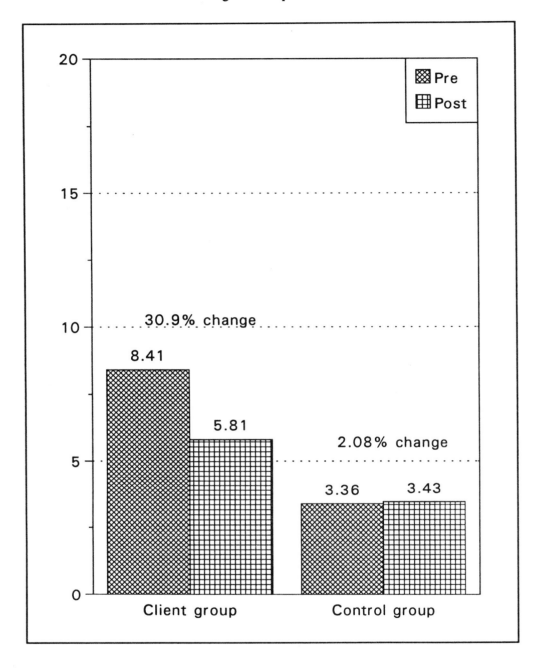

Figure 3: Psychosomatic symptoms of stress

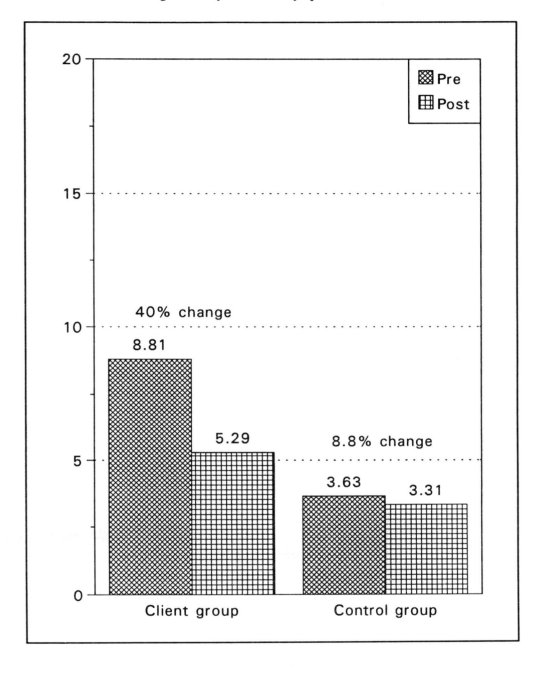

Figure 4: Self-esteem

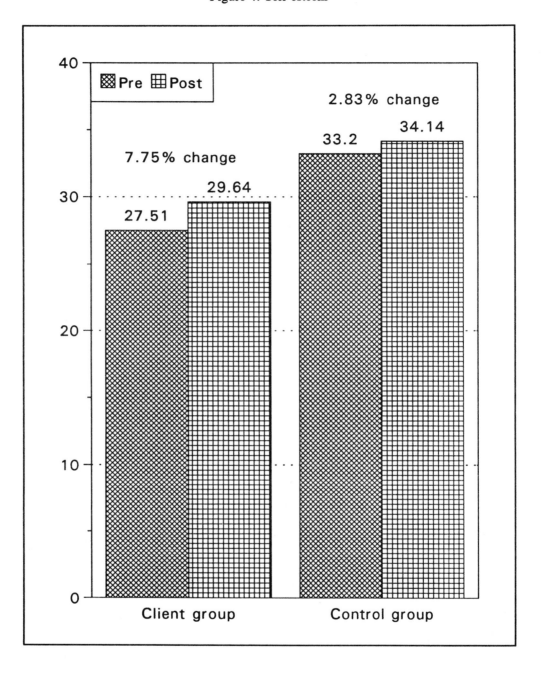

Figure 5: Job satisfaction

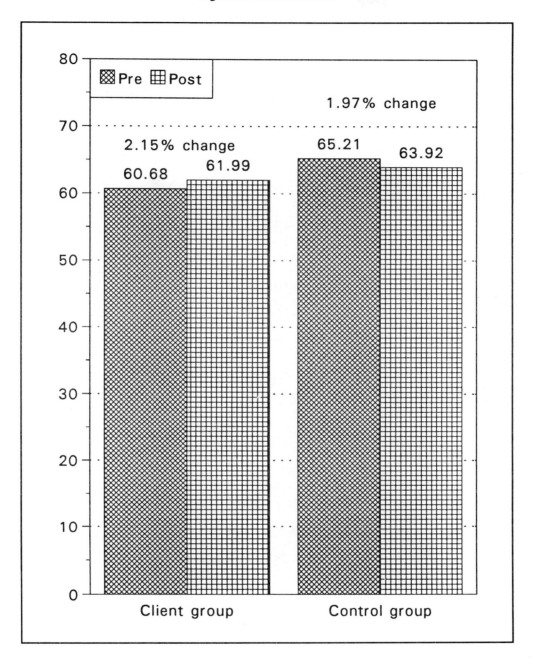

Figure 6: Organizational commitment

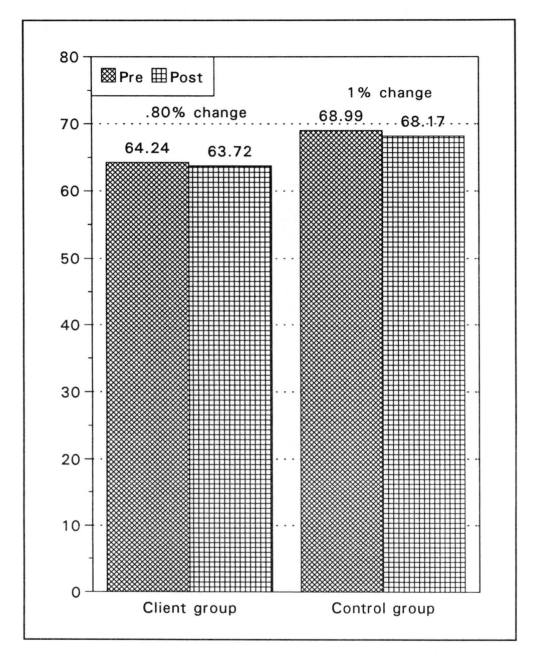

Results presented in the figures indicate that clients' psychological well-being improves at the completion of counselling. Statistically, clients are significantly less anxious, less depressed, suffer from fewer psychosomatic symptoms of stress and have a higher level of self-esteem. Clients also show significant changes on a number of behavioural items. After counselling, the following behaviours decrease in the client group: consumption of coffee and cola soft drinks, food, tobacco, or alcohol as ways of coping with events. Respondents also indicate that they feel less guilty about drinking. On the other hand, they use more of the following measures to relax at work: relaxation techniques (e.g. meditation or yoga); informal relaxation techniques (e.g. deep breathing or imagining pleasant scenes); exercise, leaving the work area and going somewhere (e.g. lunching away from the organization, taking time out); and use of humour. Clients also find more time to relax and "wind down" after work. No significant differences were found between pre- and post-questionnaire scores for the control groups.

It can also be seen in Figures 5 and 6 that, although counselling had an impact on the mental well-being of those receiving counselling, it had little effect on the level of job satisfaction or commitment to the organization.

Figure 7 represents in graph form changes in the level of absence due to sickness in the six months following counselling, compared to the six months immediately preceding counselling.

Figure 7: Levels of absence due to sickness

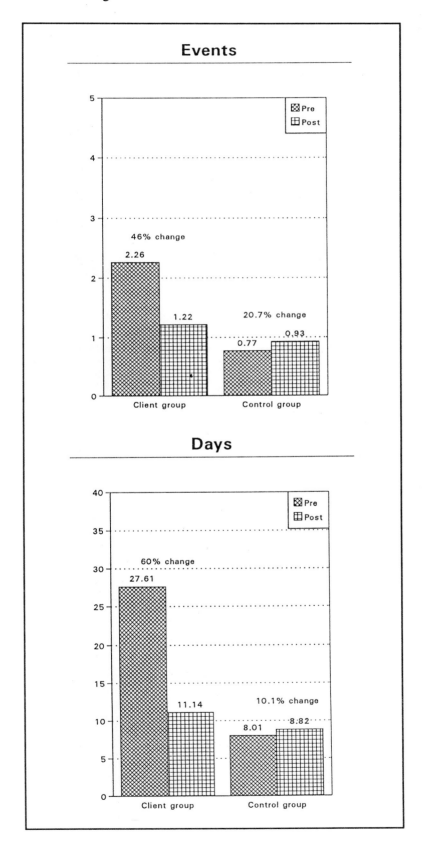

This figure shows that there is a significant decrease in the number of absences due to sickness and days lost (and in warnings given) in the six months immediately following counselling. Pre- and post-scores for the controls of postal employees showed no significant differences.

This project involved an empirical evaluation of an in-house stress counselling service provided for postal employees in the United Kingdom. Results of the measures used showed a number of significant changes in experimental pre- and post-scores, particularly a decline in absences due to sickness. Pre- and post-counselling data for absences due to sickness were presented for 188 experimental subjects and 100 random sample controls. No significant differences in absence rates were observed for the control group during a comparable pre- and post-period.

One important indicator of the mental ill health of this group is the finding that 25 per cent of the sample had had some level of suicidal thoughts. The effectiveness of the counselling service is shown by the changes between pre- and post-scores obtained by this group. Anxiety, somatic anxiety and depression all fall significantly and self-esteem rises significantly.

One criticism of the control group used in the study is that to make the two groups comparable, it is necessary to have pre-scores set at the same levels and then to observe subsequent changes. Due to the fact that records of absences due to sickness within the Post Office are not kept on a computerized system, it was not possible to sample a sufficient number of records to identify employees with high absence levels who did not visit the counselling service. Furthermore, employees with high levels of absence are subject to an internal disciplinary procedure. Therefore, employees involved in the procedure could not have been viewed as a control group but rather as a second treatment group.

Counsellors can help to create greater awareness of potentially problematic lifestyles and indicate ways in which individuals can change to help themselves, largely through the use of stress management techniques. The results of this study indicate that the counsellors may have served such a function because some lifestyle changes or health behaviours are indicated.

The analysis of the experimental group showed an improvement in level of anxiety, somatic anxiety, depression and self-esteem. However, work attitudes (i.e. job satisfaction and commitment to the organization) showed much less of an improvement. This might be explained by the fact that counselling is an intervention targeted at the individual and has its greatest impact at this level. It is, perhaps, somewhat ambitious to increase a person's coping capabilities and expect this to act as a panacea for all organizational problems. At times it may be necessary to effect changes at work (i.e. job redesign, organizational change, etc.) to achieve more favourable attitudes towards the organization. The present findings warrant further research on the effect of implementing workplace stress interventions targeted at the individual as a way to work on work-related attitudes. It may be of value to note that while work attitudes may not change after counselling, work behaviour is likely to change, not only in terms of reduced absence (evidence of which is found in the present study), but also in terms of improved productivity and better relationships with superiors and subordinates.

CASE STUDY NO. 17

Reducing stress related to trauma
in the workplace (United States)

Dr. Mark Braverman[1]

Issues and approach

It is only recently that companies have begun to pay attention to the effect of traumatic events in the workplace. Such events arise from many sources. Some jobs carry higher than normal risks of exposure to crime or injury. Sudden death or injury, violence or the threat of violence, can strike any workforce, having a profound effect on the way both groups and individuals function. Other less violent threats to security also affect a workforce, such as the possibility of job losses brought on by downsizings, restructuring or relocation. Many companies have developed "disaster plans" for responding to crisis situations. Such plans may include procedures for evacuations, policies for public relations, procedures to protect the company from legal action, and policies for death benefits.[2] What is often overlooked in any crisis response plan is the profound effect of the event on actual survivors and witnesses -- the employees themselves. Despite the concern of individual managers or supervisors, few companies have developed comprehensive "crisis readiness" plans to directly confront the acute and long-term effects of traumatic events on the health and morale of employees. The key elements of a crisis response plan provide the necessary structure in a workplace which help ensure that a successful resolution of the traumatic event can occur. Together these elements are designed to address three main areas of concern.

(1) **Communication**. Traumatic events in the workplace inevitably disrupt established networks of communication, both formal and informal. When employees cannot talk about what has happened or cannot have their questions answered and fears addressed, their ability to carry out usual job functions suffers, both on a team and individual basis.

(2) **Support for management**. Traumatic crises present an enormously stressful situation for management. During a crisis the people in positions of responsibility and leadership may feel an acute lack of control over operations and the well-being of their employees. As a result, their ability to manage may suffer. They may feel unsure about how to respond effectively when they are struggling with their own feelings of shock, grief and confusion. However, during a crisis employees will look to management to restore the sense of control, safety and normalcy which has been shattered.

(3) **Prevention of traumatic stress**. Some individual employees will be at risk for post-traumatic stress reactions as described earlier. Post-traumatic stress problems in individuals will affect general workplace morale and the ability of the group to return to normal functioning and productivity within a reasonable period of time.

---

[1] Crisis Management Group, Inc., Echo Bridge Office Park, 377 Elliot Street, Newton Upper Falls, Massachusetts 02164, United States.

[2] R.H. Truitt and S.K. Kelley: "Battling a crisis in advance", in *Public Relations Quarterly*, Vol. 34, No. 1, 1989, pp. 6-8.

Intervention

Before the event

International Computer Corporation (the name is fictitious) designs and manufactures mainframe and minicomputers for business applications. A company with over 60,000 employees in the United States and Europe, International has a reputation for progressive human resource policies. This had included a management philosophy that emphasizes independent effort, a strong health promotion programme and a well- established employee assistance programme(EAP). Early in the 1980s, the human resources department, in collaboration with the manager of corporate health, requested that the EAP develop a plan for responding to traumatic events affecting International employees in the workplace. A "traumatic incidents protocol" was developed with a consulting firm specializing in workplace trauma. The plan included criteria for the identification of traumatic incidents, designation of human resources representatives responsible for initiating trauma interventions, designation of external providers to provide consultation and employee services, and guidelines for matching the level of response to the type and severity of the traumatic incident. A protocol document was distributed widely throughout the organization's operational and support services management. Training and orientation in the protocol was integrated into existing training structures.

The event

On a Monday in early 1985, an employee in the chemical storage area of International's manufacturing facility was injured when he inhaled highly toxic fumes from an improperly-sealed container. An investigation showed that the safety procedures designed to protect workers from such exposure had not been properly implemented. The injured worker was discovered by co-workers working in the area. Emergency medical personnel and nurses from the facility health clinic responded to the scene. The employee was taken to the hospital where he died the next day. Representatives from site management and corporate health and safety were on the scene and at the hospital.

Initial consultation

The next day, a committee of managers including manufacturing, facilities, health and safety, personnel, employee assistance and health services, and representatives from corporate, including environmental health and safety, public relations, legal and health services, assembled at the facility to discuss and plan a response to the incident. A consultant joined this group in order to plan and coordinate a crisis management intervention for employees of the facility.

The decision to initiate an intervention is typically reached within 12 hours following an event. Management and the consultant then identify a crisis response team (CRT), with the following tasks:

CRT tasks

- Determining the circle of impact. Who are the groups affected, and what are the natural groupings? It is important to extend the "circle of impact" as far as necessary and to not discount or underestimate the impact of an event on groups who may not be seen as directly affected.

- Determining procedures for communication. There must be a coordinated process for deciding the method of communication. This can be via electronic or written means, or through face-to-face meetings. This is also the time for establishing what the facts are, what, if any, constraints there may be on information that can be shared, including legal issues, issues of confidentiality, and, if necessary, dealing with the media.

- Confronting representatives of the media can be stressful for employees as well. Reporters will often approach employees as they enter or leave the workplace or try to reach them over the telephone. Managers can use the initial communication to remind employees of their right not to talk to reporters. Employees should be informed of the appropriate corporate channels where they can direct reporters.

Implementing the intervention

It was decided to focus intervention efforts on the manufacturing side of the facility where the accident took place.

Week 1: With manufacturing employees. At the Tuesday meeting, the immediate need was to establish communication with night-shift employees already on site and with workers arriving for second and third shifts. It was arranged that those employees would meet by work group at the beginning of their shifts. Prior to those meetings, managers and supervisors met with personnel, top management, EAP staff and the consultant for briefings at which time they were brought up to date on details of the incident and on the format of the group meetings. At the conclusion of each meeting employees were asked to return a brief, confidential questionnaire.

During the first week of the intervention, 375 feedback sheets were collected from employees. The following is a summary of concerns that were directed to management.

- Safety concerns: 239 (64 per cent).
- Communication problems: 136 (36 per cent).
- Fear of working at the facility: 112 (30 per cent).
- Need for new procedures, training: 55 (15 per cent).
- Distrust of management: lack of concern for employee welfare: 59 (16 per cent).
- Expressing anger at management: 39 (10 per cent).
- Expressing support for management: 21 (6 per cent).

By Friday, every organization within manufacturing had met in these meetings. The number of employees at each meeting ranged from 15 to 80, depending on the size of the organization. In general, 50 to 100 per cent of each organization attended the group meetings. For groups which could be more impacted by the event, such as health and safety and health services, smaller groups of less than 20 were established to ensure the opportunity for sharing and more intensive emotional debriefing.

In the first week, 24 group meetings were held. In all, approximately 1,300 employees attended at least one group session. During the first few days, in the peak of intervention activity, a team of ten counsellors from the consultants and EAP combined were on site meeting with groups and individuals.

Week 2: Follow-up with engineering employees. During the second week, follow-up meetings were arranged with individuals and groups from the first week, as well as meetings with the major engineering organizations. Although this level of intervention had not been originally planned for engineering, a groundswell of feeling arose from some of the nearly 700 engineers and clerical support staff who felt ignored and slighted. This prompted the CRT to extend the intervention program to them. These employees were experiencing levels of fear and distress equal to those in the manufacturing side of the facility. Each of these meetings was chaired by the organization's manager. In addition, each meeting was attended by the personnel manager supporting the group as well as by the international facilities manager, who was on hand to provide technical information and to answer questions about the accident and about safety procedures. Nine group meetings took place during the second week.

The table below presents the outline for a typical group meeting. These meetings combine an informational, educational and emotion-sharing approach. Running the meeting is **not** delegated to the crisis consultants: it must remain very much the managers' meeting. The first order of business is information. For people in crisis, information is essential, particularly relating to safety. Furthermore, by taking responsibility for providing information, management establishes itself both as being in control and as caretaker. Throughout a crisis, information conveys both a sense of control and comfort. It is important that the managers directing the meeting be connected with the work organization. However, in the case of events involving violence or safety issues it is often important that senior management or managers with special information or relevant expertise also be present.

Post-trauma employee meeting

I.   **Introduction, framing** (management)

—   Identification of the event, sharing of feelings
—   Introduction of consultants, others, purpose of meeting

II. **Information** (management)

—   Update, assurance of continuing information
—   Questions and answers

III. **Trauma education** (consultant)

—   Theory of post-traumatic stress
—   Normalization of signs and symptoms
—   Coping strategies

IV. **Group sharing** (employees, management, consultant)

—   Ground rules, agreements for safety
—   Voluntary sharing of reactions, thoughts, concerns

V.   **Wrap-up** (management, consultant, EAP)

—   Review and reinforcing of group themes and issues
—   Information about counselling services

At the conclusion of the meeting, employees are offered a variety of ways to access a counsellor, taking into account the importance of privacy.

Eighty-five engineering employees were seen by counsellors in individual sessions in a two-week period. Several employees, particularly those closest to the event, experienced sleeplessness and anxiety. These reactions subsided within a week. There were also people who felt they may have been responsible for what had happened and worried about how they would be perceived by fellow employees. Ten employees were referred for further counselling or medical care because of issues that required longer term care. The majority of individual cases seen by counsellors or medical care providers involved fears of returning to work in areas with potential hazards or doing work requiring the use of a breathing apparatus. In all cases, these issues were resolved through the use of counselling and, in some cases, with counsellors initiating talks with line managers and personnel consultants.

Conclusions and results. The trauma in this case was seen at several levels: first, as the intervention progressed, it became clear that the tragedy had a serious effect on some individual employees whose reactions indicated that they felt safety in the plant was inadequate. Reactions further indicated a lack of confidence in the company as well as individuals feeling that their own safety was at risk. Second, the incident affected specific work organizations within the site. Some of the reactions were expected, such as the feelings of the facilities staff who had responsibility for carrying out safety procedures. These groups experienced feelings ranging from guilt to anger. Others were less predictable, such as the engineers who expressed frustration at being kept in the dark about safety and design issues: "Why are we never consulted about these things? We have something to contribute here!". Thus, some of the issues and concerns that surfaced were reactions to the immediate crisis while some reactions indicated issues that had existed prior to the tragedy but which surfaced with greater force and urgency as a result of the death. This may have been due to accidents and incidents which had occurred in the recent past as well as the particulars of this case, i.e. the failure of safety equipment.

Based on the data reported above, the consultant made the following recommendations to company management:

Recommendations

- Conduct a thorough evaluation of employee attitudes and concerns about safety procedures and the effectiveness and adequacy of safety training. Establish programmes emphasizing employee accountability in safety, and the development of management policies to actively elicit and support employee participation.

- Conduct supportive, team-building activities for staff (e.g. off-site retreat). Create programmes to enhance ongoing accountability and feedback about safety issues.

- Training and education about the procedures involving safety in the manufacturing areas should be extended to engineering and support staff, especially non-technical personnel.

- Every effort should be made to adequately disclose to all employees the process and findings of the investigation into the death. Following that, and perhaps even more importantly, site management must convey the sense that a thorough re-evaluation of safety procedures will follow this incident. This should include a disaster plan, which will include thorough disaster and emergency training to all employees.

- There is a need for programmes to allow engineers to participate in safety evaluation and planning. There was a strong sense that they had expertise and ideas that they would like to offer.

CASE STUDY NO. 18

Individual-based training to reduce stress in managers and employees at a Canadian ministry

Nicolas Greco[1]

Context

The Ministry of Manpower, Income Security and Vocational Training is one of the most important ministries in the Government of Quebec. It employs approximately 4,800 staff, of whom 2,500 are in direct and continuous contact with roughly 650,000 clients.

The Ministry assists people who are underprivileged in terms of their means of employment. It provides the clientele with assistance programmes to facilitate their reintegration into the world of work. The Ministry has an annual budget of CAN$ 2 billion for income security cash allowances.

In accordance with Government policy in Quebec, the Ministry has been supporting a programme of assistance for its own staff since 1986. The assistance programme was developed when the Ministry considered that between 15 and 30 per cent of its employees were handicapped by emotional problems at some stage of their careers, and that 10 per cent of them had personal problems which affected their work.

Managing an employee with chronic problems is a heavy burden for the team in which he or she works. Aware of this fact, the Ministry has given priority since 1987 to a preventive approach intended to assist employees whose personal problems may affect their work. The Ministry enlisted the help of the Société internationale du Programme de Diminution des Tensions (SIPDT) (International Society for the Stress Reduction Program) to provide managers additional management and prevention tools to be used in implementing the employee assistance programme. At the same time, the Ministry made efforts to establish a management philosophy based on people, services and results. It took steps to help mobilize human resources, developed means to encourage the management of change, planned activities which would prevent violence in the Ministry, and promoted dialogue in order to improve relations between employer and union.

For this purpose, in 1988 the SIPDT formulated the training programme "Management of employees with operational problems - specific methods, a preventive approach" targeted at managers and team leaders in the Ministry.

Following their training, the majority of managers (90.3 per cent) recommended that the preventive approach also be extended to employees, since their work caused a high level of stress. Thus, since 1989, the Ministry has been offering the SIPDT training programme to its employees as well as to managers.

Issues

The Ministry has been experiencing a number of important changes that may cause an increase in the level of stress and tension among employees, thereby increasing the number of dysfunctional employees. These include, inter alia, an increase in the number of clients; budget cuts in public service (followed by a period of strikes); the abolition of jobs and the reassignment of the work; the announcement of a computerization project for all the work of the Ministry; and an increase in the number of files to be processed.

---

[1] Société internationale du Programme de Diminution des Tensions (International Society for the Stress Reduction Programme), 810 rue Normandie, Longueuil, Quebec J4K 3P8, Canada.

Furthermore, absenteeism and staff turnover are increasing significantly. This creates added stress on the rest of the team who has to divide the work among themselves in order to ensure continuity of service to the clients.

A survey of 229 employees in the Ministry during the period 1989-1990, supplemented by individual and group interviews with managers, showed that the dysfunctional problems of employees were related more to psychological than to material needs: the need to be valued and appreciated both by management and clients; the need for more human contact with managers and clients; and the need to lessen existing tensions were among the most mentioned needs. Failure to address the needs of employees within the existing organizational structures led to a constant climate of stress. This, in turn, generated demotivation, a decreased willingness to take responsibility, conflict-ridden relations between colleagues or with management, feelings of insecurity related to the reactions of clients, increased fatigue, psychosomatic disorders, and deep apprehension of burnout.

Target population

The target group consisted of managers, team leaders and employees in the Quebec Ministry of Manpower, Income Security and Vocational Training.

Approach

The training programme utilized a preventive health approach, based on the knowledge that a balanced individual projects a state of well-being to interpersonal relations and behaviour. The approach is based upon the following axiom: well-being is the prerequisite for responsible behaviour.

To this end, it is necessary to provide skills to individuals which enable them to minimize the harmful health effects of stressful situations. Similarly, individuals can adopt skills and learn ways to behave in an environment in which the tension cannot always be regulated. The advantage of this approach is that it can be adopted easily by any individual, regardless of personal values or social or cultural background. Because of this flexibility, it was possible to apply the approach to the various contexts and situations causing stress within the Ministry.

In the first phase of the programme, the Ministry and the SIPDT designed a training programme for managerial staff (managers and team leaders).

The training for managers was aimed at the prevention of health and behavioural problems related to stress on both the personal and interpersonal levels; the management of the quality of communication within a team; and the development of specific management methods for employees with functional problems.

Once this first stage was completed, the SIPDT's preventive approach was extended to employees in other centres of the Ministry, throughout the different administrative regions. The training for employees had the following objectives: to prevent health problems and functional difficulties related to the stress in daily work; develop resistance to intense stress; improve interpersonal relations and the general working environment; and improve output and motivation.

Managers in the Ministry supported a stress reduction training session for employees because they believed the benefits would be increased effectiveness of their administrative units, an improved climate at work, and increased quality of service to clients.

After training, evaluation reports on the training of managers and employees were published and disseminated.

Training for managers

The training programme for managers focuses on two main issues: managing employees with functional problems, and preventing stress and dysfunctional problems at work.

Managing employees with functional problems. Training in this area aims at clarifying the role of the various types of managers in the Ministry in relation to employees with functional problems. In particular, the responsibility of management to assist employees is emphasized.

The training is geared at developing the manager's ability to identify behaviour that is inappropriate for work. The manager, however, is trained to act only on symptoms that affect work (such as decreased output, lateness or absenteeism) and not on the values or attitudes of the employees. When the manager notices that an employee's behaviour is different from what is expected by management, the two parties will discuss the situation together and try to solve the problem. In order to maintain an open exchange, managers are trained to take into account the feelings of the employee.

The manager's goal is to encourage individuals to try to resolve their own problems. To this end, the manager and the employee work together to develop a timetable and follow-up plan for resolving the problem. It is expected that once the problem is resolved, the employee will regain his or her proper level of output at work.

Because managers have constant interaction with both individual and groups of employees, it is important that they be able to adapt to all types of stressful situations whether routine or in a crisis.

Preventing stress and dysfunctional problems at work. This stage of the training, which is entirely devoted to the prevention of stress, is centred upon the manager as an individual. The prerequisite for managing others is controlling oneself.

The training provides managers with effective methods of controlling themselves, decreasing the intensity of emotional stress, and preventing health problems and fatigue. Managers are encouraged to analyse each stressful situation as objectively as possible. Based on their analysis, they should act -- not react -- to neutralize a situation of emotional intensity.

With these skills, the manager plays a key role in creating an environment where employees can openly discuss work-related stress factors.

Training for employees

This training has three stages: (1) intra-personal communication; (2) interpersonal communication; and (3) the individual's responsibility in the group.

Intra-personal communication. This stage begins by making a distinction between two sources of stress: internal and external.

The mechanisms of intra-personal communication are based on discussions and consist of:

— identifying the psycho-physiological mechanisms that individuals have in common, regardless of their social and cultural background, their values or their psycho-physiological state;

— identifying physical symptoms that may be associated with stress;

— based on the participants' feelings and experiences, identifying the impact of stress on their health and behaviour;

— recognizing the defence mechanisms that individuals use to combat stress.

Participants learn in the training that, although they may not be able to eliminate the sources of stress, they can control the degree to which stress affects them. For example, techniques such as controlled breathing and relaxation can be used to reduce tension at will. Learning and using these stress-reduction techniques helps participants develop the ability to adapt to stressful situations at work and prevent psychosomatic disorders.

Controlled breathing helps the individual to confront sources of stress while maintaining self-control by decreasing the emotional impact of a stressor. This method acts at the mechanical, chemical and nervous levels. It helps the muscles to relax, which results in an immediate reduction of stress and of emotional and mental tension. Controlled breathing can be used preventively, as well as during a stressful situation to help regain self-control.

Relaxation is a technique which is complementary to controlled breathing. Relaxation allows the individual to discharge emotional tension that has built up in the body. This technique helps one to recover quickly from accumulated psychological and physiological fatigue. In time, this individual develops a capacity not only to cope with, but also to resist, stress.

Interpersonal communication. The individual's physical and psychological condition has a direct impact on his or her relations with others. Based on this knowledge, the second part of the training focuses on interpersonal relations.

Employees learn that any communication can have a physical impact on the communicator when there is tension carried in the message. However, more important than words, a person's psycho-physiological state is the first message that is conveyed in an exchange. Individuals therefore become aware that, while other people affect the amount of stress that they experience, they also are a source of stress for other people. Calmness is just as contagious.

Through exercises and role playing, the participants then develop methods for regaining calmness within themselves. They also learn communication techniques which help to establish positive relations with others.

These methods may be used with colleagues, managers and clients in the workplace.

The individual's responsibility in the group. The last part of the training enables employees to understand their interactions with the other members of the group. The verbal language or body language of an individual can cause an increase or decrease in the stress level of the whole group. Understanding how an individual can affect the group helps to develop the employee's sense of responsibility for establishing and maintaining a positive work atmosphere.

Another important outcome of the training is that individuals develop a sense of solidarity with and responsibility to their team out of their awareness that everyone in a group responds to stressors in similar ways, regardless of social and cultural differences.

Evaluation

An evaluation of the impact of the programme was based on the following methods:

A preliminary evaluation.

— An analysis of the reports and surveys conducted by the Ministry;

— interviews with persons in charge of the human resources department at the Ministry;

— a survey conducted by the SIPDT of a sample of 229 employees from various administrative regions in the Ministry. The pre-test questionnaire used in this survey was written in collaboration with the Ministry and was based on four main points: (a) the level of general satisfaction at work; (b) the individual's health; (c) the quality of the individual's interpersonal relations; and (d) the suggestions that can be made to improve the individual's situation at work;

— individual and group interviews with managers from various centres of the Ministry.

Evaluation of the training. At the end of the training session, the participants are asked to fill out an evaluation questionnaire regarding the content, the procedure, the general organization and the implementation of the acquired methods. They are also asked to give recommendations regarding the programme's approach.

Evaluation of the impact of the programme. The evaluation of the programme takes place eight weeks following the training during the follow-up session. It is based on the answers given in the follow-up questionnaires, which are filled out by all participants in the training programme. The questionnaire requires that participants evaluate the impact of the implementation of the methods acquired in training. The questions address the participant's health, interpersonal relations and the general climate at work.

The evaluation is supplemented with summaries of verbal exchanges made by the participants as well as with comments from the management teams.

Results

For managers and team leaders. A total of 377 managers and team leaders were trained between January 1988 and May 1990.

After two years, the managers noted that the number of new active files on employees with functional problems had fallen by one-half. The Ministry assessed the impact of the programme during the follow-up to the training. As a result of the programme, it found that managers were better equipped to deal with difficult situations, having an improved capacity for action, and better able to control their stress level.

According to the findings of the evaluation report, the majority of managers who were questioned had observed an improvement in their state of health and in the quality of their communication. They were also more aware of the impact of stress and reported the following: a decrease in fatigue and greater effectiveness at work; a decrease in psychosomatic problems (insomnia, migraines, backache, ulcers, etc.); a decrease in stress caused by apprehension; a calmer atmosphere in the work team; and an increase in self-confidence.

The majority of the managers questioned also stated that the training enabled them to improve their management style by learning to make a more objective analysis of a stressful situation; to be better prepared for meetings with employees; and to clarify the roles of the various levels of managers in the Ministry for providing assistance to employees with functional problems. Furthermore, the majority of managers questioned observed positive behavioural changes at work by employees with functional problems.

Several managers noticed a change in their working relations and in their family relations.

For employees. Since September 1989, 1,020 employees, mainly from the six administrative regions of the network of the Ministry (representing 80 per cent of the employees in these regions), attended training courses.

According to the evaluation report made by the Ministry, the majority of employees who were trained stated that the training had enabled them to understand their own psycho-physiological mechanisms that operated in stressful situations. The majority also noted that the training had made it possible for them to prevent stressful situations in their work environment and in their families. More than half of the employees who received training also reported the following results: they used the new techniques to manage stress; the relations and atmosphere in the team were improved; and eight weeks after the training they observed an improvement in their health.

Follow-up

Follow-up sessions are conducted both with managers and employees. Follow-up consists of half-day meetings, which are divided into three stages:

- **Auto-evaluation.** The managers fill out a questionnaire in order to determine the impact of training on a personal level and to study the results of the suggested approach concerning the management of employees with functional problems.

- **Exchange and discussion**. Participants share the results obtained and the problems encountered, and fine-tune and find solutions through sharing of individual experiences, including those of the trainer.

- **Practicing techniques**. The stress-reduction techniques are put into practice.

Three sessions are conducted in separate stages.

Initial meeting with the manager. The objective is to inform the manager of the procedure to be followed in the meeting with the employees.

Meetings with the employees. These half-day meetings are conducted in groups of 12 employees. Management teams are not included unless they are invited by the employees. The meetings involve an auto-evaluation of the employees through a written questionnaire, discussion of the results obtained, determination of adjustments to be made taking into account the difficulties encountered, and discussion of ways for implementing information-sharing projects at the office.

The participants are especially encouraged to write their observations on the follow-up questionnaire and to suggest improvements that can be brought to the approach. These comments are fully transcribed in the evaluation report and distributed at all management levels in the Ministry (local, regional and central).

Meeting with the management team. This meeting includes the manager and the team leaders and is to present a summary of the evaluations and verbal exchanges made by the employees; to consider how skills can be implemented at the office; and to review, if necessary, the problems discussed by the employees and to work out possible solutions.

Employees are encouraged to work together with the management team to find solutions to problems. They are also encouraged to develop a practical stress prevention project designed to address their specific needs. The follow-up sessions make it easier for employees to express themselves freely and to state their needs. Emphasis is placed on the potential for taking action, bearing in mind the possibilities and constraints of the organization. Employees are encouraged to take responsibility for implementing solutions.

The following solutions were given special emphasis in the follow-up sessions:

— improve communication between managers and employees;
— create methods to improve the dissemination of information;
— create a social support mechanism which facilitates discussions between individual employees and between management teams and employees;
— re-evaluate the organization of work at the practical level and arrange for a space for relaxation and leisure at the workplace.

As a result of these activities, several regional directorates have approached the Ministry with requests for their employees to receive similar training. The Ministry is continuing to invest in the prevention of stress as a means of preserving its primary source -- the human being.

CASE STUDY NO. 19

Using training to prevent or reduce stress in a coalmining company in India

Dr. Ganesh Sastry[1]

Context

Western Coalfields Limited, a subsidiary of CoalIndia Limited, was established in November 1975. The mining operations of the company are spread over the states of Maharashtra and Madhya Pradesh in central India. Western Coalfields Limited is spread over seven areas with operations in 66 mines that are organized into sub-areas. More than 85 per cent of the total manpower (over 80,000) is deployed in underground mines and more than 12 per cent in open-cast mines. The rest of the manpower is deployed in area services, area offices and company headquarters.

The company has a welfare base that includes the provision of amenities, such as housing, water supply, medical facilities, education and cooperatives, for the entire workforce and their dependents. In the areas and sub-areas, there are recreational facilities, including stadiums, playgrounds and coal clubs.

While meeting the existing and increasing demand for coal, the company has been maintaining productivity. At the same time it has been mechanizing and modernizing the mines and the equipment. The technology of Longwall with power support was introduced in 1982 in underground mines. Modernization has been undertaken in the coal-transport system. The capacity and utilization of equipment, such as draglines, shovels, dumpers, dozers and drills, is being upgraded regularly. The coal reserves are being exploited both through existing mines and from the planning of new mines. The company has to meet the demand for coal from the power, steel, cement and rail sectors. Hence, the targeted production level planned and achieved by the company is always increasing.

Issues

In January 1988, the company saw that stress prevention was a crucial part of its human resources development. The reasons included the fact that the harsh work environment in coalmines requires specific coping strategies, and the capacity of employees for coping with the stressful occupation needed reassessment.

Approach

A prevention programme was envisaged, based on a definite perspective about stress as the principal factor affecting quality of life. It was felt that this perspective would be a key factor in helping individuals to take an objective view of the risk factors for producing stress on the job and in helping them to become aware of their own susceptibility to stress.

The company, through its human resource development (HRD) strategies, would help the individual integrate this awareness into an effective coping strategy aimed at improving efficiency and productivity. The company would benefit in terms of increased output, improved industrial relations, and a qualitatively improved presence in the company. These benefits to both the individual and the company would be achieved within a set time-frame. The programme would be reviewed every six months to evaluate its impact and whether or not it achieved the objectives.

---

[1] The Resource Training Consultants, Muralidhar Apartments, Khare Town, Nagpur 440 010, India.

The job functions selected for the programme would be based upon similarity in factors that could produce stress and in levels of experience among the workers. The selection of individuals to participate in the programmes would be based on similarity in socio-economic support systems.

Target population

The target group for this stress reduction intervention consisted of senior managers, middle-level managers and junior executives, all at company headquarters. Later, the programme was extended to supervisors, foremen, maintenance staff, loaders and operators. Workers' representatives and other opinion leaders were targeted for their input toward the programme's development.

Annex I shows the distribution of the programme participants by job category.

Intervention

The anti-stress programme started in January 1988 and was developed at three levels.

Level I. This level involved senior managers and middle-level managers. The training programme module designed for this target group focused on the manager's role in creating and maintaining a supportive workplace environment.

Level II. The programme at this level involved the operators and loaders. The training programme module designed for this target group dealt with improving the trainees' capacities to adapt to stress through lifestyle modifications and promoting a positive collective coping approach.

Level III. Six months after the programme was initiated, another training was launched, designed for the supervisors, foremen and maintenance staff. The training for this target group emphasizes its role as opinion leaders and counsellors at work and outside on issues related to the coping strategies of co-workers. The programme also focused on the target group's responsibility to provide feedback on the various stressors that might exist.

Finally, in order to encourage a useful approach to coping with workplace stress from the outset of the programme, a training module was designed and introduced for junior executive trainees.

Programmes at all levels were aimed at assessing individuals' susceptibility to stress; reassessing job stress in terms of qualitative content (i.e. participation in decision-making, interpersonal relationships, role ambiguity, responsibility for persons and situations) and workload (production target, deadlines, time management); and developing a proactive approach to initiating workplace stress-reduction techniques aimed at improving health.

The progress of the programmes was coordinated for all the levels and for the various target groups. The resulting information constituted the basis for reviewing the impact of the programme.

These training programmes are described below.

Level I: Senior and middle-level managers

Duration of training programme: Three days. Eleven training programmes were conducted between January 1988 and February 1991 at headquarters and in different area offices.

Needs assessment: The participants answered a questionnaire to assess six categories of stressors: individual, job, family, lifestyle, environment and health status.

Training methods: The methodology used in the Level I training programme included questionnaires and tests, role playing, and lectures. Individual counselling was also within the scope of the programme.

Training topics -- Level I

- Stress as an integrated human response (involving both the body and the mind);

- Assessment of individual susceptibility to stress;

- Identification of stressors related to (i) job-qualitative content (participation in decision-making; interpersonal relations at work; role ambiguity; responsibility for persons and situations); and (ii) job workload (production targets; deadlines; time management);

- Study of Type A behavioural patterns and their correlation with job functions and coping strategies;

- Comprehensive lifestyle review, including habits for coping, regularity of sleep and meal schedules;

- Assessment of risk for coronary heart disease (CHD) after considering all factors, such as environment, personal habits and lifestyle;

- Assessment of health status (especially insomnia, irritability and somatic complaints) related to ability to cope with stress;

- Development of positive ways of channeling stress, such as hobbies and creative diversions;

- Relaxation training in yoga and imagery.

Level II: Operators and loaders

Duration of training programme: Three days. Eight training programmes were carried out between August 1988 and February 1991.

Needs assessment: Participants were identified after discussion with the workers' representatives. The needs for the group were listed during these discussions. These contained the details pertaining to lifestyle, physical work environment, socio-economic factors and related influences on coping, such as habits, living conditions and health status.

Training methods: The methodology used in the Level II training programme included lectures, brainstorming, buzz groups, role playing, questionnaires and tests, and individual counselling.

Medical personnel were used during the Level II training programmes to provide information about stress as a possible factor which causes disease, directly or indirectly, through poor coping methods. The results of the training programmes were correlated with the data available from the medical personnel.

Training topics -- Level II

- Stress and its relevance to health and efficiency at work;

- Assessment of susceptibility to stress;

- Identification of stressors relating to excessive workload, equipment operations and maintenance, work organization, job/family imbalance, physical work environment, personal habits at work, shift work and its impact on health, and other related socio-economic factors;

- Comprehensive lifestyle review with particular emphasis on personal habits;

- Assessment of risk for CHD related to habits such as smoking and other forms of tobacco consumption;

- Assessment of health status with particular attention given to proneness to backache, insomnia, work-related physical fatigue, and irritability in relation to ability or inability to cope with stress;

- Developing and sustaining a positive approach for both individuals and groups to channel stress. A special emphasis is put on developing creative diversions;

- Time scheduling with regard to shift work in order to safeguard the regularity of sleep and meal schedules;

- Relaxation training in yoga and imagery with suggested scheduling for shift work.

Level III: Supervisors, foremen and maintenance staff

Duration of training programme: One day.

Needs assessment: The job profile of supervisors, foremen and maintenance staff was studied in detail. The needs of the group were listed after discussions with the target group.

Training methods: The methodology used in the Level III training programme included buzz groups, brainstorming and lectures.

> ### Training topics -- Level III
>
> - Understanding individual and group methods for coping with job stress;
>
> - Identifying stressors in the physical work environment;
>
> - Counselling as a skill to help promote individual and collective coping strategies, as well as improved scheduling;
>
> - Relaxation training in imagery to improve the efficiency of responses in emergency and safety-related situations;
>
> - Increasing awareness about Type A behavioural patterns, related to personal habits and the importance of feedback regarding the impact on workers from targets and performance demands.

The training programme used for junior executive trainees were identical to those in the training programmes for senior and middle-level managers. The inputs however, were organized into a one-day module and conducted in English (instead of Hindi), with an emphasis on the trainees' role in facilitating a positive coping and supportive environment. Also emphasized was the importance of keeping channels of communication open with regard to information on stressors, their impact and coping trends.

Results

Level I. During the training programme, a significant number of managers indicated the qualitative content of the job as stressful. Only a small percentage of senior managers (11 per cent) and middle-level managers (7 per cent) considered that the amount of workload was **not** stressful. This information has been given to the company. It has been suggested that the existing channels of communication in the company have to be examined. During the first feedback period, 39 per cent of the senior managers and 28 per cent of the middle-level managers indicated improved responses to the qualitative content of the job. They related this improvement directly to the programme.

Eighteen senior managers and 41 middle-level managers indicated that workload -- including production targets, deadlines and time management -- were stressful for them. At the first feedback session, two senior managers and three middle-level managers indicated improved responses to stress from the workload.

Due to the demanding physical environment in the coal sector, it was determined important to assess the participants for Type A behavioural patterns. The results indicated a clear predominance of Type A behavioural patterns in the managers. Additionally, a range of stress-related health complaints, including insomnia and irritability, were identified in a significant number of the managers. At the first feedback session, 47 per cent of the senior managers and 39 per cent of middle-level managers indicated a reduction in their stress-related health complaints. They directly attributed the improvements to the better scheduling of the work day as well as their use of relaxation techniques.

A significant number of managers reported using tobacco as a way of coping with stress. At the first feedback session, 53 per cent of senior managers and 29 per cent of middle-level managers reported a reduction in tobacco consumption. A number of these managers related the reduction directly to the training programme. Consumption of caffeine (more than four cups of tea or coffee per day was considered excessive) was also assessed as a coping mechanism. A significant number of the managers reported excessive use of caffeine. However, at the first feedback session, 32 per cent of senior and 35 per cent of middle-level managers reported a reduction in consumption of tea or coffee to a moderate level. All of these participants attributed the reduction to the training programme.

Level II. During the training programme, 104 operators (out of 162) and 112 loaders (out of 242) indicated that the workload of the job caused stress.

Using methodologies including brainstorming and group discussions, specific strategies were decided upon to help the trainees cope positively with identified areas of job stress.

The physical work environment (dust, noise, climate and work postures) was found stressful by 40 operators and 72 loaders. At the first feedback session, more than half of the operators and 26 per cent of the loaders indicated improved responses to the stressors in the physical work environment. However, many of the operators and loaders did not consider the physical work environment stressful. This indicated a certain capacity to adapt to the stressors.

More than half of the operators and loaders complained of health problems, such as backache and physical fatigue, due to the work postures and the physical work environment. Corrective work postures were demonstrated and buzz group sessions were used to discuss corrective measures. Some of the loaders and operators related significant relief from their health complaints to the training programmes.

The demands of the work schedule (mainly the shift duties) were indicated as stressful by 42 operators and 60 loaders. Therefore, new day schedules with realistic scheduling of sleep, meals and exercise routines to safeguard the body's rhythms were arranged. At the first feedback session, more than half of the operators and loaders reported an improvement in their ability to cope with shift duties. Trainees attributed the improvement to the new day schedules that were decided upon in the programme.

A significant number of the operators and loaders also reported monotony and boredom from repetitive work, smoking and other forms of tobacco consumption, and a lack of creative activities during non-working hours. The training programmes helped to reduce monotony and boredom, as well as help participants decide upon and incorporate into their lives creative leisure activities. Also important was the result that 34 per cent of the operators and 54 per cent of the loaders reduced their use of tobacco. They attributed this to the CHD risk education and lifestyle review they received in the training.

Although as many as 120 operators and 210 loaders reported a lack of creative diversions, only 28 per cent of the operators and 27 per cent of the loaders reported beginning a creative activity. The analysis of this finding, compared with the improved responses for monotony and boredom, indicates the possibility that other factors, in addition to creative diversions, need to be identified and incorporated into the topics for the training programme.

Level III. At this level, no final assessment has yet been produced.

Overall, the programme has led to the following outcomes:

- Among a cross-section of job functions, there is now an increased awareness of job stressors and their impact.

- Due to the programme's emphasis on developing strategies for coping positively with stress, a number of trainees are applying these strategies to stressful job situations.

- The existing recreational and health care support systems are now seen as more meaningful and useful.

- The anti-stress programme has led to improved job-family balance among all job functions. This is vital in coal mines where the job and the place of residence are located near each other.

- Strategies aimed at helping individuals and groups to develop active creative diversions for leisure time indirectly have had a favourable impact on job performance and efficiency.

- Feedback sessions have revealed improved health status, directly correlated with the programme in many cases.

- During the period when the programme was implemented, there was a reduction in absenteeism among the Level II participants.

- The participatory methodologies used in training have led to better acceptance of the coping strategies decided upon during the programme.

- The emphasis in the training on supportive approaches for managers, on positive coping strategies for operators and loaders, and on counselling both on and off the job for supervisors, foremen and maintenance staff has had a positive impact on industrial relations in general.

Follow-up

The following proposals for follow-up are made:

- The scope of the stress prevention programme as a human resources development intervention has to be broadened in the future.

- The topics covered and methodologies in the training programmes have to focus more on the issue of social support systems.

- The stress prevention programme should contain training programme modules exclusively designed for medical personnel. These could be used to lead to the development of a health-care system which gives importance to stress, in terms of etiology and diagnosis.

- The stress prevention programme should include training modules for women -- housewives as well as working women -- that focus on their role in creating a positive coping environment within the family.

- The training programmes should be implemented just prior to the periods when production pressures are likely to increase. This timing would increase the relevance of the programme.

- As noted in the analysis, middle level managers need modules especially designed for them. The training material should be job-specific.

The stress prevention programme at Western Coalfields as an intervention at various levels has increased awareness of the potential for stress from the work and physical environment in the coal sector. The programme also brought into the open the various coping trends particular to the coal sector, and the strategies that can be developed toward coping positively with stress.

Since the stress prevention programme is on-going and likely to become broader-based in terms of target groups and content, new approaches can be studied and incorporated into the programme.

In view of its established relevance and acceptance by the target group, the stress prevention programme at Western Coalfields can be used as a model for developing and implementing other similar interventions.

Annex 1

Distribution of participants by job category

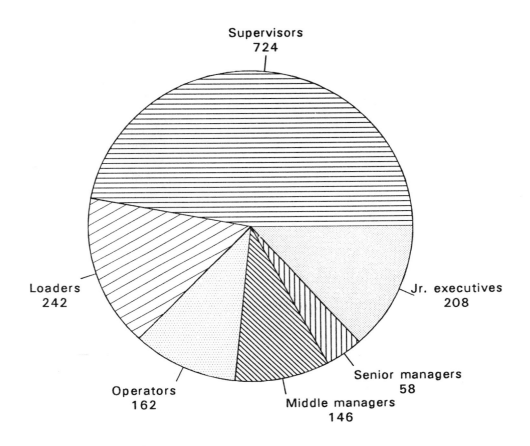